PORT OF TWO BROTHERS

Lawrence Jr. Thanks for
wanting to read this book
God bless
    Paul L Schliene
        Phil 1:6
        10/1/2000

PORT OF TWO BROTHERS

THE AMAZING STORY OF TWO MISSIONARY BROTHERS
AND THEIR WORK ON THE AMAZON

PAUL L. SCHLENER

P.O. BOX 167
AUMSVILLE, OR 97325

Association of Baptists for World Evangelism
P.O. Box 8585
Harrisburg, PA 17105-8585
(717) 774-7000
abwe@abwe.org

ABWE Canada
160 Adelaide St. South, Suite 205
London, Ontario N5Z 3L1
(519) 690-1009
abwecanada@compuserve.com

 PUBLISHING®

PORT OF TWO BROTHERS
Copyright © 2000 by ABWE Publishing
Harrisburg, Pennsylvania 17105

Library of Congress Cataloging-in-Publication Data

Schlener, Paul L., 1926–
  Port of Two Brothers
  Autobiographical, Non-fiction
  ISBN 1-888796-21-9 (Trade Paper)

Printed in the United States of America.

TABLE OF CONTENTS

DEDICATION

I dedicate this book to my wife, Jessie, the fairest lady of the land, who was always there with me and for me; and to the four greatest kids on earth: Timothy James Schlener, Leanne Kay Pearson, Cynthia Lou Bollback, and Rena Marie Hopson, who sacrificed so their mom and dad could stay on the job.

Paul L. Schlener

ACKNOWLEDGMENTS

By God's providence and grace, my brother, John, and his wife, Fran, led Jessie and me to a saving knowledge of the Lord Jesus Christ while we were in our late teens. For this we shall be eternally grateful.

My mother, who all but worshipped her children, saved most of the personal letters I wrote to her and dad. These old letters were great reminders of past events.

A tap on my shoulder after Easter morning services in 1990 got my attention. Mrs. Rose Reynoldson said, "Mr. Schlener, excuse me, but I think the stories about your missionary experiences should be in writing." She dug in her purse for a business card that described her position at Seattle Pacific University. A year later, while struggling to build our house, I put together a few paragraphs and sent them to her. For six years, draft after draft returned littered with corrections and words of encouragement. Thanks a million, Rose, for all your time, work, and great inspiration.

When I learned that my 886-page manuscript would have to be reduced, I was rescued by Helen K. Hosier, distinguished Christian author of more than 50 books. She went through the manuscript four times to trim some 300 pages.

My faithful wife, Jessie, suffered "static from the attic" as I buzzed her often from my attic office for help. Daughter Cindi Bollback enhanced many paragraphs with good critique. Tim, Leanne, and Rena kept me accurate on events that occurred when they were still living at home. Phone calls to John and Fran jogged my memory.

I wish to thank Jeannie Lockerbie Stephenson and Kristen Stagg of ABWE Publishing for their patience with me as a first-time author, and for the countless hours Kristen spent wading through the sometimes muddy waters of my manuscript.

A special thank you to ABWE, and to all the churches and individuals who kept the Schleners in the "Green Hell" for all those years.

Paul Schlener
Moses Lake, Washington
March 2000

FOREWORD

It is a great honor to write the foreword for this most unusual and interesting account of two missionary families as they followed God's leading for their lives.

I have been in the fortunate position to observe their spiritual progress from the day they accepted the Lord as their Savior until their retirement.

Truly, they have run with patience the race set before them to the honor of God, bringing the salvation message to thousands of souls through their own efforts and the efforts of other young people they trained and sent out to follow their example.

The Schleners exemplify what can be accomplished by a child of God totally under His direction, no matter the location or the difficulty of the task.

Paul's relaxed and humorous writing style will hold your attention from start to finish. You will live, work, and travel with them from the first day they arrived in Brazil until their return to the United States.

Is God sufficient to supply all our needs through Christ Jesus? The Schleners' lives and experiences give off a resounding yes—whether facing anaconda snakes, raging rivers, violent storms, medical emergencies, humidity, or boredom.

One lingering thought that will follow you as you read is, "I can do all things through Christ who strengtheneth me" (Philippians 4:13).

Paul R. Goodman

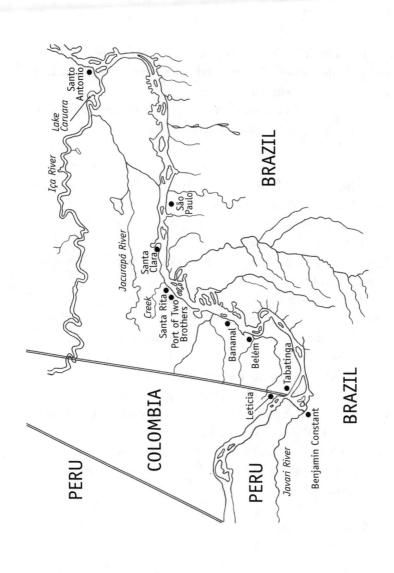

PROLOGUE

For a traveler to get a hint of the vastness of the Amazon River, he needs to fly over it and cut through its muddy water for hundreds of miles in every kind of vessel in all kinds of weather. To get a real feel for its size, a person has to live on its banks for years.

Think of a landmark 200 miles from wherever you are at the moment. That's how wide the mouth of the Amazon River is as it empties into the Atlantic Ocean. It takes one hour and fifteen minutes to fly across its mouth—from Belem to Macapa—in a two-engine airplane. And 200 miles is also the distance it shoves its fresh water and sediment into the ocean.

If the Mississippi River is the "Father of Waters," the Amazon should be called the "Granddaddy of Fresh Water Streams." Not all scientists agree that Africa's Nile River is a few feet longer than the Amazon River; and the Amazon drains a region of more than 2.3 million square miles (one-third of the country of Brazil), more than twice the area drained by the Nile.

This huge drainage ditch discharges between 9 and 32 million cubic feet of water per second into the Atlantic Ocean, and deposits a daily average of three million tons of sediment near its mouth. That's enough water to cover the entire state of Texas to a depth of more than one inch. The Amazon River has more than 200 navigable tributaries, although the total number of tributaries remains unknown. Ocean steamers can travel 2,300 miles upriver, even during the dry season.

It is easy to understand why the people who live on the shores of this gigantic river call it the *Rio Mar* [ocean river]. Their lives depend on it. It's the main highway; it fertilizes great areas of jungle, providing dozens of varieties of fruit. Annual flooding deposits rich topsoil on lowlands, which makes for quick-growing, healthy plantations. At the same time, flooding restocks lakes with hundreds of varieties of fish. And fishing lasts year-round, with no licenses to purchase and no limits on daily catches.

If you can hold in your mind a picture of the immensity of the amazing Amazon River, you will be able to understand better the following experiences I am about to share with you.

PART ONE

FROM PHILADELPHIA TO THE AMAZON RIVER

(1951)

CHAPTER ONE

WITH ONE-WAY TICKETS, it wouldn't be easy to turn back. Our salary was small, and all we had was in our suitcases. My wife, Jessie, and I were on our way as young missionaries to what geographers call "The Green Hell," the jungles of Brazil bordering the mighty Amazon River.

Where would we sleep the first night? What kitchen and bathroom facilities would we find, if any? When would our scanty equipment arrive, if ever? Would we wake up in the night with the cool body of an anaconda snuggled up to us? What about piranhas?

Jessie and I were in our mid-twenties before we were suspended above the earth higher than any Ferris wheel could lift us. My brother, John, had lots of flying experience as a bombardier/navigator during WWII, while his wife, Fran, had flown hither and yon trying to keep up with him. Here we were—two brothers with our wives—bound for the greatest adventure of our lives.

Jessie and I were so uninformed about flying that we didn't know enough to be scared. Our calm during the short hop from Philadelphia to New York in a C-47, en route to Brazil in August of 1951, reveals our naiveté. Looking back, after flying to and from Brazil dozens of times in 40 years, we remember that short run and tremble. We were tossed, twisted, bounced, and fishtailed through thunder and lightning.

Across the aisle sat John and his family. The WWII veteran of 13 missions over Germany had his head bowed and eyes closed in white-knuckled prayer that God would use His angels, the pilot, and any other means necessary to see us through the turbulence to safety.

John and Fran had two boys, John Jr., seven, and David, a year-and-a-half. A glance at my wife, Jessie, holding four-month-old Leanne in the aisle seat, renewed my admiration for her. Young, effervescent, and beautiful, she was willing to confront the unknown with a baby and little boy. Our son, Timothy James (Tim Jim), was two.

It took more courage and motivation than I realized for Fran and Jessie to take their children to live in the Amazon jungle. Our destination was 2,000 miles inland from the mouth of the great river. We were comforted knowing a small group of established missionaries awaited us. Orville and Helen Floden, full of the expertise required to live and work in the Amazon, had lived for several years in the frontier town of Leticia, Colombia. Texans Jack and Joyce Looney, with their two sons, Roy Neal and Terry Nick, had spent a year across the border in Benjamin Constant, Brazil. The Flodens and Looneys encouraged us with letters that offered suggestions regarding equipment we should bring, and expressed great pleasure at the prospect of the two Schlener families devoting themselves to pioneer missionary work downriver from them in Brazil.

In Miami, we Schleners were to meet missionaries Blake and Mary Rogers, returning to Leticia from furlough. We first met the Rogerses during missionary candidate classes in October 1950. Blake was consumed with optimism about the country of Brazil and its people. In less than a year after candidate classes, John and I traveled tens of thousands of miles in a Studebaker Champion, looking for churches to sponsor us. We scarcely met the financial requirements for our mission agency, the Association of Baptists for World Evangelism (ABWE).

We met the Rogers family at Miami International airport so we could travel together to the Amazon. How great it was for us "greenhorns" that our travel plans coincided. The Rogerses gave us a sense of security and optimism; they already had been over the trail. They and the Flodens were honest about enduring the difficulties of life: the climate, and lack of supermarkets and hospitals. They had survived the poisonous snakes, piranhas, tarantulas, scorpions, and other creeping things with a minimum of complaints; now we looked forward to giving it a try.

Instead of squawking about how I expected her to keep our four-month-old girl alive during the trip, Jessie went to the store and purchased 32 eight-ounce glass baby bottles. After the bottles and their nipples were sterilized, she filled each one with boiled water and tightened the tops with the nipples inverted into the water. With these she packed a supply of canned evaporated milk. From Philadelphia to New York, Guiana, Belem, Manaus, and all the way upriver to Benjamin Constant, the milk and water were fine.

The sweltering, steamy heat of the jungle air took the spunk right out of us. Within minutes our cotton seersucker suits were soaked with perspiration. All those baby bottles full of water and the cans of milk were more than enough to lug, but we also had a portable car bed—with Leanne inside—and a scientifically packed diaper bag. Brazilian customs authorities and baggage inspectors looked as though they were prepared to eat foreign tourists alive. Our huge stack of stuff didn't lighten their gloom.

The restaurant in the non-air-conditioned Grande Hotel in Belém required male patrons to wear shirts, coats, and ties. The management had coats and ties hanging in the foyer to loan sloppy American tourists. We couldn't read their dress code signs, but they made us understand, so John and I donned the sweaty coats and twisted ties before proceeding to dinner. So much for the brief relief from our seersucker suits.

Spacious tables were beautifully spread with linen tablecloths and napkins, candles and flowers. Waiters, serious as judges, wore white starched shirts with black bow ties and black coats, reminding us of penguins. With the agility of magicians, our waiters turned our drinking glasses right-side-up and filled them with crystal clear ice water. We were desperate for a drink, but didn't dare touch it. We had been thoroughly warned, fairly threatened, not to drink any water unless we were sure it had been boiled for at least 20 minutes. The famous Brazilian soft drink called *guaraná* (gwah-rah-NAH), supposedly safe for human consumption, spared us from dying of thirst. The drink comes in tall brown bottles with pretty labels. Soon our table looked like a forest of beer bottles as we downed bottles of *guaraná*.

Although the restaurant was deluxe, we were leery of the food. Blake didn't share our wariness. He grabbed a knife and a fork and pitched in. I concluded his only fear was that the waiters might clear the table before he finished.

Our thoughts were interrupted from worries about contaminated food and drink by a funny fiddler. He was short, bald, and fat, and I guessed him to be close to 60. His starched shirt was stretched nearly to popping. The slipknot on his tie was cinched so tight that the points of his collar stuck straight out. The tourniquet effect turned his jolly face the color of a ripe apple. The kids especially thought he was great as he shuffled by our table, sawing out a samba on his battered violin. He looked so friendly that we felt he was welcoming us to his country.

In the 1950's U.S. citizens enjoyed prestige in South America, more welcome than in the 1990's. At Federal Police headquarters, the officials were friendly and accommodating. The chief asked in fairly good English, "Where will you live in Brazil?"

"We'll be staying in Benjamin Constant for a few months before moving downriver to open a new area for the mission," John said.

The chief's eyebrows drew together, deepening the wrinkle between his eyebrows, as though he was about to throw a fit. The scowl remained while he took a long drag on his cigarette. Smoke billowed generously from his mouth and nose while he softy exclaimed, "Noooo," drawing out the syllable in disbelief. He sat down and wagged his head, looking at Tim and Leanne,

John Jr., and David. He finally lifted his gaze to each of us parents like we were supposed to know better than to take our families into that area.

"My friends, you can't be thinking about taking your families there!" He spoke slowly, emphatically. "That area is populated with every kind of outlaw from murderers, smugglers, border hoppers, and dope traffickers to fugitives."

We looked at each other, trying to think of something intelligent to say. Finally, John said, "No one has warned us about those dangers, but we'll check it out." The chief continued to puff on his cigarette and wag his head, probably wondering how long we would last. If that officer were still alive today, it would be a pleasure to share with him how, by God's grace, we stayed just shy of 40 years and had a wonderful, fulfilling life with some of the finest people on earth.

. . .

After three muggy days and even muggier nights in Belém, we still had two more legs, of 1,000 miles each, before reaching Leticia. We had our permanent resident identification papers with our photos, signatures, and columns of Brazilian regulations. In those old photos, Jessie looked like a teenager and, although I had lots of hair, I didn't look old enough to shave.

An airline employee in Belém took our tickets at the terminal and pointed to the tarmac. We walked across the cracked blacktop, our shoulders sagging with all the baggage we carried. Already sweating in our seersucker suits, we climbed the ladder and boarded a DC-3 for the 1,000-mile flight to Manaus, capital of Amazonas, Brazil's largest state.

I wondered how many emergency landing sites existed for a plane with wheels on the upcoming journey over the Amazon River. And I didn't like the streaks of oil leaking from the cowling.

"John," I grumbled, "this rig has an oil leak."

"No problem. That's normal for radial engines," he said. I
didn't believe him. Why would oil be coming out of an engine
if there wasn't a leak?

DC-3's sit on their haunches like dogs, so we trudged uphill
to our seats, stowed our stuff, and strapped ourselves in. In a few
minutes, after one whale of a backfire from the jiggly engine on
my side, an enormous cloud of smoke issued forth. I just knew a
piston had cracked.

Down the runway we roared, taking off up into the sky and
the relieving coolness of 10,000-foot altitude. We were awestruck
to see the vastness of the jungle spread out below like a green
ocean. The jungle was a huge, uninhabited garden with thousands of square miles where human feet have never stepped. We
were given a moving picture out the windows as small villages
with plantation clearings swept by. All human habitation, scarce
as it was, lived close to water.

There were no emergency landing fields. I was reminded of
this when I noticed the little stream of oil from under the cowling increasing to a flood. But our engines hummed nicely and
we were already preparing to land in Manaus.

The man who met us at the airport had a smile that covered
every nook and cranny of his face. How he knew we were arriving was a mystery; we had never met him before. He was Willard
Stull, a veteran missionary with another mission agency. He had
no obligation to raw recruits just passing through the city, but
there he was.

He was a whiz at getting our suitcases away from the stone-
faced baggage inspectors. When Willard stepped into the baggage
claim area, he had a transforming effect on the employees. We
didn't understand any of the gibberish exchanged between Willard and the baggage handlers, nor did he slip the fellows any
legal tender. But we were waved on, which was like being
released from captivity.

The Rogers family piled into a rickety taxi that had long

outlived its life expectancy. The two Schlener families stashed their stuff in Willard's station wagon, which surely taxed the machine to its limit. While the airport was miserably hot and muggy, the station wagon was a veritable oven in those days before air-conditioned cars.

Weaving through traffic at a good clip, we scattered chickens, pigs, and emaciated dogs and Willard tested the agility of fool-hardy pedestrians who crossed the street in front of us. In vain I tried to slam on the brakes from the back seat. I was taking my typical deep breaths to prevent nausea when the left rear tire blew. We wobbled and swayed until Willard regained control and brought the car to a thudding stop. I remembered the statistics that claim air travel is the safest method of transportation. Maybe they were right. Still in our seersucker suits, John and I helped Willard, mostly by prayer and supplication, while he changed the tire that had blown to shreds.

Mrs. Stull couldn't have been a quarter-inch over five feet. Her given name was Grace, which matched her character to a T. She welcomed us cheerfully into her home, a gang of 13 thirsty, hungry, sweaty people, loaded with luggage of every description, including dirty diapers. The first thing Grace did was place a jug of cold water on the counter. She knew what we wanted without asking.

The Stulls simply accepted the fact that they couldn't change the weather, and were determined to enjoy life in spite of the discomforts. They had a higher calling than going to Brazil for a life of ease. In time, we reached that same conclusion.

That Willard and Grace loved the Brazilians was evident by their attitude toward the monumental task they had undertaken. Years later we realized that in meeting us at the airport, seeing us through customs, and putting us up in their home, the Stulls had made a sacrifice. But they made us feel as if we had done them a favor.

The Stulls were up at 4 a.m. to fix our breakfast and help us load ourselves and our baggage into the station wagon and taxi. It was still dark when we unloaded at the airport at 5 a.m. The only light in the terminal was from the dim flicker of kerosene lamps.

At 5:30 the dawn was gray, but bright enough to load the plane for the 1,000-mile flight to Benjamin Constant, on Brazil's frontier with Peru.

. . .

Our passenger plane for this final stretch was a converted PBY Catalina Navy patrol bomber, built shortly after the Pilgrims landed at Plymouth Rock, but an impressive-looking flying machine nonetheless. The single wing, perched high above the fuselage, looked as big as a volleyball court. Two radial engines were mounted on the massive wing. The fuselage was simply an enclosed aluminum boat with an extended tail. Over the years we learned to respect this plane as the safest for flying over jungle and water.

By the 6 a.m. departure time, the weather was still cool and comfortable as we strapped ourselves into the wicker seats. Things started buzzing, whining, groaning, and squeaking. One engine roared. The second required a few more revolutions before it popped, thundered, then smoothed out to synchronize with the first. The whole plane began rocking when the pilot accelerated both engines to a scream at the end of the runway. Then down the bumpy asphalt we rattled and vibrated until we lifted off the ground.

Everything was calm for a full minute—almost enough time to relax—when two solid blows to the fuselage jarred the entire aircraft. I looked around but the few other passengers didn't seem to be alarmed. John grinned; Blake was red-faced with laughter. It was good to be with someone who had been through this before and knew about landing gears thumping into place.

Tefé (Teh-FEH), a town two hours from Manaus, on the

shores of a beautiful lake by the same name, was our first stop. The landing was perfect, although I had forgotten about the landing gear popping out, and suffered more moments of terror when they snapped into place.

A *senhorita* led us to a spacious dining hall which had been recently painted. Two long tables with clean, bright-checkered tablecloths, heavily loaded with food, got our attention. But tempting as the sights and smells were, we were afraid to eat, preferring to arrive in Benjamin Constant in good health and hungry, rather than risk amoebic dysentery.

Months later my brother, John, and I traveled to Manaus to clear our equipment through customs and have it shipped upriver. When we stopped in Tefé on the return trip, we were the first ones to that same luxuriously spread table, and the last to leave when passengers were called to board the plane.

The vastness of the never-ending jungle continued to fascinate us. Thatch-covered houses with tiny clearings for plantations were the only breaks in the green ocean of foliage and water. We wondered if the tiny plantations were the Indians' only source of livelihood. We survived four water landings and take-offs before reaching our destination. The flight lasted an entire workday. The kids were tired; we all felt a little nauseated. It was encouraging to hear the only words we could understand from the crackling intercom: "Benjamin Constant, next landing." This was the town the Federal Police warned us to stay away from, located where the Javari River empties into the Amazon, marking the border between Brazil and Peru.

We clumsily stepped out of the plane into a dugout. Laden as we were, we welcomed the strong hands that steadied us until we got our balance in the round-bottomed craft. Two lithe, sure-footed fellows in coveralls slowly pushed the canoe away and gently dipped their paddles into the water. One blow from those broad paddles would have lopped us all over like dominoes, for we were standing with nothing to hold on to.

From 50 yards we could easily spot the pale missionaries standing in the midst of a sizeable group of people with healthy suntans. Our leather-soled shoes were hazardous on the clay riverbank. John and I were top-heavy, carrying the youngest children along with our baggage, leaving no free hand to catch ourselves should we fall. But we arrived upright on dry ground to meet our fellow Americans. Jack and Joyce Looney greeted us with broad smiles and Texas drawls. Joyce's melodic voice remarked how encouraging it was to double the size of the field council to eight members.

Orville and Helen Floden, with their bouncy year-and-a-half-old, curly-haired daughter Elizabeth, had traveled 12 miles from Leticia, Colombia, to meet us. Helen, tall and slim, welcomed us with a bright smile. Orville's smile couldn't be classified as bright or dazzling. Each corner of his mouth might have moved an eighth-inch from center, barely enough to classify as a smile. But while he wasn't much of a smiler, his laugh was unusual. When something struck him as funny, he went into a spasm of silent laughter. His mouth stretched, his stomach bounced, and his eyes watered until he had to gasp for breath.

After refreshments at the Looneys' home, we formed a procession for the three-quarter-mile hike to the house that had been prepared for us. Men grabbed our suitcases and carried them on their heads while Jessie and I toted Tim and Leanne.

A group of friendly ladies and kids joined us, checking us out and giggling at our funny speech. As we gawked at all the huts and shacks along the way, I whispered to Jessie, "I wonder what kind of a shanty is waiting for us?" She just raised her eyebrows, the only way to gesture with her hands full.

CHAPTER TWO

OUR HOUSE WAS MADE from boards that had never been painted; the tin roof was badly rusted. Narrow, steep steps rose five feet from the ground to the front door at the angle of a stepladder. It was fun trying to manipulate those narrow rungs with no hands. The floor was high above the ground to allow room for floodwaters, which fluctuate an average of 30 feet each year. The house was divided down the middle with a board partition about seven feet high, making an 8 x 16-foot room for each Schlener family.

John recalls, "I was the first one up the steps to check both sides of the partition. I noticed the right side had only a large single bed, while the left side had a double. So I dropped my baggage on the left to occupy the roomier territory."

The place had been scrubbed clean. Bedding consisted of pillows, sheets, and a thin cotton blanket for each bed. We wondered about the mosquito nets. What would it be like to sleep under one? This Hilton Hideaway had no bathroom, not even an outhouse. There was no kitchen, therefore, no sink, range, refrigerator, or dishwasher. And no washing machine. Two pots for each family served as our bathroom, but without much privacy.

The outside wall on our side of the partition was so close to our Brazilian neighbors that Jessie could reach out the window and touch their house. John and Fran had a wide open view of the Javari River and no neighbors for at least 30 yards. It would take a hurricane for Jessie and me to feel a breeze through our two unscreened windows, which almost always had to be closed for privacy. John certainly had a knack for pickin' and choosin'.

Bathing at the river's edge, partly clothed, was refreshing. We doused ourselves with water, using mixing bowls or pans the way our neighbors used gourds. Our closest neighbors extended their bath time to scrutinize us while we bathed, until they were convinced that we were white all over.

Nobody sleeps without a mosquito net in an unscreened house near the water or jungle. Mosquitoes and various species of bats are always hungry. Before retiring to our narrow nest, Jessie and I made sure our kids were isolated from these pests by tucking the thin cloth under their mattresses all the way around their beds while trying to avoid tearing the flimsy fabric. Jessie and I bumped heads and elbowed each other, working up a sweat in our hurry to get the kids tucked in.

When our turn came, we learned that we should have tucked in the mosquito net *before* we climbed in bed. With a small section of the net untucked we could slip in easily and quickly. We brought a flock of those pesky bloodsuckers into the net with us. They had us trapped. Sitting side by side, Jessie zeroed in on the intruders with a flashlight while I smashed them between my hands with enough violent force to stun a large animal. We heard John and Fran clapping away on their side of the partition, too. Later, the Indians taught us how to outsmart mosquitoes. "Big hand, big wind, blow *carapana* [mosquito] away. One finger, no wind. Wait till land. One tap, dead."

Around 1 a.m. we were startled by rain on the tin roof. With no ceiling between floor and roof, nothing absorbed the roar. Strong wind brought heavy rain in driving torrents. Thunder cracked and boomed. A loose piece of tin flapped, keeping time with the howling wind. Lightning flashes brightened our room through cracks in the walls. But not a hint of breeze entered our net. God's blessing for us during storms was the slight temperature drop in our tiny cloth shelters.

On the other side of the partition, strange activity was taking place. Bare heels thudded on the board floor, and a scraping sound of something heavy being dragged made us wonder what was happening.

"Hey, John," I hollered above the noise, "what's going on over there?"

"Oh, this blasted roof leaks like a sieve and we're trying to find a dry spot the size of this bed," he shouted back.

"We're in great shape over here; a little crowded but no leaks in the roof. See you in the morning!"

. . .

Every morning for a week, two huge alligators slipped out of the water to sun themselves on the opposite riverbank, their cavernous mouths yawning. I couldn't take my eyes from those giants until they finally slid back into the water, which they did without a sound.

The seventh evening of the alligators' sunbathing, I asked, "Jack, do you have a rifle I could borrow? Mine is in our equipment, hopefully on its way to Manaus. I'm itching to have the hide of one of those monster alligators."

"Sure," said Jack. "I have an old .22 bolt action that you can use."

I was wishing for a .30-06 or a .30-30, but a well-placed .22 slug would do the trick. I hardly slept that night thinking about how I would skin one of the reptiles and stretch his hide out to dry. There was film in the Argus C-3 so Jessie could take a picture of me holding the rifle with one foot placed on the alligator's head.

Jessie would have a fancy alligator purse, with a belt and shoes to match. And I could show up back home at Kootenai Valley Days Rodeo in Bonners Ferry, Idaho, with a pair of alligator boots, a belt, and a hatband from the beast I killed on the muddy bank of the Javari River. Our sponsoring churches would see my photo in our newsletter, recognize how courageous we were, and increase their contributions. Material to build our home downriver was practically in the bag.

Next morning, wide awake before daylight, I waited until it was light enough to see my game. I opened the shutter to view my trophy, but neither of the brutes appeared. I wolfed down my breakfast and looked again. Nothing. For several mornings I scanned the riverbank, but the alligators never returned. So much for my big plans!

While scanning the opposite riverbank, still hoping to see the alligators, I spotted a heavy flat-bottomed boat coming our way. It looked overloaded, asking far too much from the feeble 10-hp motor. It was the Flodens' boat, the *Mensajeiro* [Messenger]. Today was to be our first field council meeting. Getting acquainted before the meeting was fun. The chairman welcomed the Schleners as official members of the Central Amazon Field Council. We were full of questions, and our associates were full of answers and counsel, especially in regard to language study. They strongly urged us to spend every minute we could in language study.

Worship services in the Looneys' home held little meaning for Jessie and me since we didn't understand Portuguese. Evening services were most burdensome. The town generator across the street didn't have a muffler, and its exhaust port was aimed straight at the Looneys' house. We cheered when it broke down or ran out of fuel, preferring the dim light from hissing gasoline lanterns to the deafening generator.

Jack found a man who was willing to help us learn Portuguese. Felizberto was the best clarinetist in town, continually in demand for all-night carousals. His speech was rapid, and he usually reeked of sugarcane rum which kept him high-spirited while squeaking out sambas all night.

In an attempt to hide his liquor-induced halitosis, Felizberto invariably arrived at study sessions nibbling on a clove. To keep the clove in place under his tongue while teaching, he had to speak from one side of his mouth. And he was missing one front tooth, which threw his pronunciation off enough to confuse us. We were on the verge of developing facial twitches, trying to build a workable vocabulary under his tutelage. But Felizberto was a happy fellow, as his name would suggest (Feliz means happy, Berto is Bert; so, Happy Bert).

In an attempt to reach people outside town, Jack and Joyce conducted Sunday school downriver a few minutes from Benjamin Constant in the little settlement of Santo Antonio. "How about coming with me to Santo Antonio next Sunday afternoon, Paul?" Jack asked one Thursday. "I'll let you lead in prayer. It'll be good experience for you."

I stared at Jack in disbelief before answering. "How can you do this to me, Jack? You know bloomin' well I wouldn't be understood. They'll think I'm using the Lord's name in vain, or that I'm casting a spell on them . . . or something."

"Naw, these folks know you just arrived. They don't expect you to speak well. We've only been here a year ourselves and have a long way to go before we will be speaking well," Jack said. "The people will respect you for trying. You'll be glad you tried."

What it will do is give me cardiac arrest, I thought. But I went to work with the language book and dictionary.

Lord, teach me to pray in Portuguese, and without error that would bring reproach to You. If ever I could use the gift of tongues, Lord, it's now. But it looks as if this Portuguese language will have to come the hard way. This was my prayer almost word for word before I wrote on an index card the petitions to God I planned to make on behalf of the little Sunday school.

I slept intermittently Saturday night. On Sunday morning, only my body was in church with my family. "Jessie," I whispered during the service, "I'm going to tell Jack I can't make it to his meeting this afternoon. Shouldn't I help take care of the kids?"

"Sissy!" she hissed in my ear. Her diagnosis was correct.

The five-minute trip to Santo Antonio seemed like 30 seconds. Before I realized it, we were shaking hands with a room full of friendly people and Sunday school was in progress. Jack held forth while I glued my eyes on him. Muhammad Ali could have belted me in the midriff and it wouldn't have fazed me, I was so tense. My hearing was tuned for Jack's remark that included the two words "Paul" and "prayer."

When they finally came, I knew for sure because Jack nodded as our eyes met. I pulled the index card from my pocket and folded my arms across my chest, partly to keep my heart from jumping out. With the card in my right hand, I knew from practice at home that I could read the prayer with my head bowed. I made it all the way through, hoping to finish without disaster. Jack was right. I felt good afterwards. It was good to start using the language for something other than buying food.

"Aren't those kids afraid of piranhas?" Jessie asked as we watched the naked neighbor kids slide down the slippery riverbank on their bare bottoms. They had worn a groove in the clay to keep them on track. I shuddered to think of the possibility of a pointed, hardwood root popping out of the clay. We stood on an immense raft of logs, dousing ourselves with water during the hottest time of the day.

"The water is so riled up where those kids hit that even piranhas might be afraid to enter the area," I said. But the laughing hilarity from the kids affected us.

"Let's give it a try. We've been dangling our feet in the water for an hour and we still have our toes," Jessie reasoned.

"Okay, but this might be the worst way to lose weight fast," I warned. Our swimming was the closest a human being can come to diving in and coming back out without getting wet.

CHAPTER THREE

MONTHS BEFORE THE SCHLENER TEAM arrived in Brazil, Orville Floden and Jack Looney traveled on an antiquated Brazilian steamboat several hundred miles downriver from the borders of Peru and Colombia into the vast unevangelized area of Brazil. The riverboat pulled into muddy riverbanks to trade for raw rubber, dried fish, or cordwood. Jack and Orville were able to glimpse towns along their way and talk briefly with some of the local citizens.

They reported on their trip at our first field council meeting. They listed the names of towns and villages they visited, guessing at populations and distances from one another. The field council suggested we Schleners look for a location not too far from Benjamin Constant and Leticia, where mail and supplies were available. The lack of medical attention bothered us. That stretched our faith because of our children. "There's a doctor here now," Jack said, grinning. "He's not bad, if he's sober when you need him."

"We can do better than that in Leticia," Orville assured us. "We have a fine doctor, but no hospital. And we have a dentist with an alcohol flame to sterilize needles, and a treadle machine for drilling."

We laughed, but it wasn't so funny a few years later when we found ourselves slumped in the dentist's cowhide chair. I could tell by the hide that the cow was a Guernsey.

All 10 field council members agreed that the Schleners should settle 50 to 100 miles downriver from the frontier—a good first step toward penetrating the vast unevangelized area. The sparse population consisted of Indians, Brazilians, and mixed breeds known as *caboclos*. Poverty, illiteracy, superstition, and disease plagued the inhabitants. Insects, crawling vertebrates, intestinal parasites, and intense humidity would do their best to hinder us from reaching the people with the message of salvation. Thrilling reports of great numbers of converts to our sponsoring constituency would be as few and far between as were the villages.

Hearing the reports from the survey trip didn't give us the feeling of being promoted, nor would we get a boost in salary for serving in a hazardous area. Jessie was ready to pack our suitcases and head back to the United States to continue life in an apartment. "You and I could give it a go," she said to me, "but is it right to subject our kids to this?" We remembered the hymn written by J. B. Bounds:

> Anywhere with Jesus over land and sea, telling souls in darkness of salvation free, ready as He summons me to go or stay, anywhere with Jesus when He points the way . . . Anywhere with Jesus I can safely go.

We recalled the Sunday evening service at Tabernacle Baptist Church in Seattle when Jessie and I, at 19 and 20 years of age, turned our lives over to the Lord. We asked Him to use us according to His will, however or wherever that might be. The Lord challenged us through the words of Charles E. Prior's hymn,

> I'll go where you want me to go, dear Lord, O'er mountain or plain or sea; I'll say what you want me to say, dear Lord, I'll be what you want me to be.

Jessie and I found ourselves in a foreign country sooner than we expected. John had graduated from the Bible Institute of Los Angeles in 1949 and I graduated in 1950. That same year ABWE accepted us as missionary candidates and appointed us to the Amazon River country in Brazil.

While still in the United States, I had imagined the worst

with regard to jungle survival. I figured we would be dumped off at the edge of the river with a few basic hand tools, hack out a clearing, and make lean-to shelters until we could build permanent homes. And that was pretty close to what happened.

• • •

I had qualms about entering the jungle on foot, which is the only way it could be entered, except by canoe through the swamps. North Idaho's Kaniksu National Forest, lush as it is, is sparse compared to Brazil's tropical rainforest.

No fewer than two at a time should even think of stepping into that tangle, I reasoned to myself. While breaking trail, a person should have one eye on the trees looking for pythons, and the other focused on the ground for anacondas and bushmasters, the largest of all poisonous vipers. A .22 rifle seemed puny, and I wished for a pair of .44 magnums.

One afternoon Jack Looney said, "I think we should take a quick trip about 50 miles downriver to the village of Belém [which means Bethlehem, the same name as the large city at the mouth of the Amazon]. We had better zero in on a location soon, because by the time we find a place and wait for lumber to be sawed in Colombia, you will be tired of living out of suitcases." We were already tired of it. Jack continued, "I mention Belém because the owner of the trading post there was so friendly when Orville and I visited him."

"Sounds good. When do we start?" John asked.

"Let's go tomorrow," Jack said.

It was barely light enough to see when we stepped into Jack's little 12-foot aluminum boat with a 10-hp outboard engine. As we headed downriver I wished for at least a 20-foot cabin cruiser with bunks, commode, and refrigerator. Instead, our equipment consisted of a change of clothing, towels, mosquito nets, hammocks, canned goods, and a .22 rifle; I can't remember if we were smart enough to take a first-aid kit.

Motels and restaurants were unknown back then. Communication with our families was impossible after we waved good-
bye and slipped around the far side of Benjamin Constant. Jack
had gotten the little boat and motor shortly before this trip and
used it for the 12-mile trips between Benjamin Constant and
Leticia, never traveling far from home in the small craft.

Skimming along in the tiny craft I found myself forgetting
about the lack of conveniences and becoming totally absorbed in
scenery. Schools of porpoise swam so close they startled us. "Jack,
did you ever get one of those lunkers on a hook?" I shouted
above the motor. He shook his head. I broke out in goose bumps
just imagining one of those biggies on my line in all that open
water.

It was August and the river was low, so Jack had to keep an
eye out for sandbars. When the prop touched one, we were
jerked forward until he pulled us into deeper water. The prop
was well polished by the time we arrived back home.

"Here comes a flock of ducks," John shouted. We wondered
what kind they were this far south. In a few seconds we could see
that, if they were ducks, they had suffered head-on collisions with
a concrete wall. It turned out they were large green parrots with
wing motions exactly like a duck's.

"What's the word for parrot in Portuguese?" I bellowed to
Jack.

He leaned toward me, eyes fixed on the river ahead, and
slowly enunciated, "Pah-pah-GUY-oh."

I tried to pronounced it and finally concluded, "Man, what a
lot of trouble to say 'parrot'."

A quartet of brightly colored macaws crossed our path. They
flew lower and slower than the green *papagaios*. Their raspy
squawks sounded loud above the whining motor.

A few minutes before the village of Belém came into view,
Jack pointed toward the riverbank at a disturbance in the trees

and vines. Monkeys tore through the jungle to get out of sight, frightened by the howl of the little 10-hp motor.

"What's the word for monkey, Jack?"

He leaned toward me again and drawled, Texas style, "mah-CAH-coo." I began to wonder if it might be easier to teach the Brazilian people English than for me to learn Portuguese.

. . .

Jack spotted the village first. On the plane into Manaus, John and I had seen the mixing of the Rio Negro's black water and the coffee-with-cream color of the Amazon; this was a small version of the same scene.

People living near the trading post had heard our outboard motorboat, a rarity in 1951. All activities at the trading post came to a halt as soon as we rounded the bend and pulled into shore.

"That's the trader, Senhor Antonio Roberto, leaning on the porch rail," Jack said quietly. "We'll walk right up to the foot of those high steps that lead to the verandah and pause at ground level until he invites us to come up—if he does," Jack said in an aside. "Just smile and say *bom dia* when he shakes your hand."

Antonio Roberto was, for many years, the main trader and proprietor of vast sections of land in the county of São Paulo de Olivença. As he stood watching our approach, he was the picture of friendliness. His white, wavy hair and the natural smile on his handsome face set him apart from the average village citizen.

"Gentlemen, good morning! Please come up and rest awhile," Antonio invited us. John and I followed Jack. Antonio took our hands in both of his, giving us a greeting that was far more than "good morning." From gestures that accompanied his friendly words, we understood he wanted us to sit down. Our humble "good mornings" seemed inadequate after such a flowery speech. I'm not sure Jack understood Antonio's entire spiel since he asked Antonio to repeat himself.

Gloria, Antonio's neatly dressed wife, greeted us before excusing herself to the kitchen where it was obviously her habit to sample her preparations.

Antonio proudly introduced his sons and daughters. Each child approached in turn and reached up with an open hand saying, as a question, "Blessing?" Our only response was, *"Bom dia,"* which the children thought a stupid answer.

An Indian girl served us *guaraná* immediately after the introductions. We knew enough to say thank you, but she never made eye contact. Everything about us was so different, from boots to windburned faces and stammering speech, that she had a hard time keeping a straight face. She set the empty tray on a table and disappeared into the kitchen where we heard giggling.

Jack talked business as best he could with his limited vocabulary. Antonio did not want to sell any land. He offered excuses, but also made a suggestion. "At this very moment, a man called Roberto Backsman is at my other trading post in the next village called Palmares, eight miles downstream. He owns land next to the village of Santa Rita, 40 miles further downriver. Being a German, he's had a rough time since WWII and might want to sell some of his land."

"Sounds good," Jack answered, thanking Antonio for his hospitality.

• • •

Backsman, a man in his mid-fifties, arrived in Brazil in the early 1900's with many other Germans during the rubber boom, when the automobile industry gained momentum in the United States and Europe. The Germans' plan was to get rich quickly by extracting latex from rubber trees for export. The immigrants all died materially poor and none of them, as far as we know, ever professed to be Christians. These young Germans married Brazilian women, full-blooded Indians, or *caboclos,* raising large families.

Roberto Backsman, rather than getting into the rubber business, traveled to the headwaters of the Amazon tributaries and extracted logs to be floated down to sawmills. He prospered until WWII, when Brazil became suspicious of Germans, and his activity was restricted.

Backsman had more book-learning than most of his compatriots. He could read English well, but was seriously limited in speaking. A throaty, high-pitched voice made him hard to understand. But he taught his own children at home and urged them to study.

We were encouraged to discover that Backsman was willing to sell some land and would accompany us to the village of Santa Rita. Because the extra weight strained our boat's tiny engine, the trip took longer and consumed more fuel than we expected. I sat next to Mr. Backsman, who looked at the floor or his feet the entire time, never uttering a word. As we approached Santa Rita, Mr. Backsman lifted his head slightly and pointed. I looked back at Jack to see if he had seen the casual gesture. He smiled, nodded, and aimed the boat at Backsman's port.

When we touched the riverbank, I grabbed the bowline and stepped out to tie up to a short stake. What looked like hard clay was mud the consistency of butterscotch pudding. This made the day for Jack and John as they guffawed, watching me pull my feet out of the mud. Mr. Backsman may have been smiling inside but he remained stone sober as I scraped and splashed water to get rid of the fluffy mud.

Women and children dressed in soiled work clothes, their heads wrapped in cloth, watched our every step as we trudged up the riverbank. We smiled, nodded, and followed Mr. Backsman in single file. He greeted his children, handed his seven-year-old son a small bag of candy, then showed us to our room. I felt sorry for Backsman's daughters, wondering if Jorge would share the candy.

Backsman's storehouse consisted of a hand-hewn hardwood plank counter, with cobweb-covered shelves in back. They might have held a good stock of merchandise in times past, but now were nearly empty. The old scales were rusty. Shutters hung askew. Badly torn screens sagged. Rat droppings littered the floor. Light showed through the tin roof.

Mrs. Backsman, seeing her husband in the boat with strange people, deduced she would have overnight guests, and sent a sweeper to give our room a quick once-over. The girl couldn't reach the highest spider webs with her broom. Heavy with dust, the webs looked like safety nets for bats. Lizards darted around the walls, somehow escaping the spider webs. Contamination from bats, rats, and mold made for foul odor. We opened the large shutters to let in fresh air.

All three of us understood our hosts' plight, recognized their unselfish hospitality, and thanked God for a place to spend the night. A wobbly bench, a worn hammock, and an ancient chair offered us relaxation while we perused our surroundings and waited for the next move.

A small corner table held a large china basin and pitcher that might have come from Germany years ago. Next to the set was a small spouted enameled pot sitting on an aluminum tray. On the same tray was a cloth bag the size of the foot section of a man's sock with two sticks, the size of drumsticks, fastened to the open end. It was blue with mold, and looked poisonous to me.

"Jack, what on earth is that setup on the table?" I hadn't even finished the question when someone knocked on the door and little Jorge darted inside. He snatched up the tray with the pot and the moldy bag, and flew back out of the room.

Jorge's complexion and wavy hair were dark like his Indian mother's, but his little hooked nose and thin lips were duplicates of his father. We noticed Jorge's stiff neck when we first saw him. We learned he had suffered from arthritis since infancy.

Upon arrival at Backsman's home we smelled the luscious aroma of roasting coffee. Most women in rural areas of Amazonas place dried coffee beans in a shallow clay basin over the fire and stir the beans with a wooden spoon or a stick until they turn brown and snap. Sugar sprinkled over the toasting beans melts as the stirring continues until every bean is coated with burned sugar. Set aside to cool, the beans become dry and crisp, ready to be ground in a hand-operated coffee grinder or crushed with a mortar and pestle. The coffee is then ready to brew into a rich, sweet beverage that only a small portion of mankind has been privileged to taste.

Another knock on the door announced the reappearance of Jorge, carrying the same tray that had undergone a thorough restoration. The pot had been transformed to like-new shininess. A tiny sugar bowl filled with tan-colored sugar sat next to three demitasses with saucers.

As the door slammed behind Jorge, we all looked at each other, then made a beeline to the table. We groaned as we inhaled the fragrant coffee bean nectar. The little pot held a one demitasse serving for each of us. We tipped the miniature cups to get every drop. Sweat beaded on our foreheads and trickled down our backs after the hot coffee. We stood in the windows to catch any breeze.

The next move was a frantic disturbance among the chickens outside our window. We watched the comical show. Women and children who had greeted our arrival and prepared coffee now chased chickens, one of my favorite childhood sports. We were surprised at how fleet-footed the pursuers were. As spectators, we tripped over one another, and bumped heads getting from one window to the next to keep up with the action. The agility and endurance of the ladies impressed us. One middle-aged chaser slipped on a muddy spot, hit hard on her tailbone, and bounced back up as though she were on a trampoline. They finally singled out a victim for the kill, slowing the squawking chicken to a limp with a blow from a thrown stick before pouncing. Everybody was out of breath but staggered with laughter as they discussed the chase. We didn't realize all that fuss was for us until we were called to the kitchen an hour later.

As we stepped into the kitchen, the main cook booted two pigs and sent them oinking out of doors. Our Brazilian friends say, "The best seasoning for food is hunger," and hungry we were. It wasn't long before we were clicking away with our spoons, smacking our lips, and accepting seconds. The food was so flavorful, thoughts of amoeba and hepatitis escaped our minds. If one or two little intestinal parasites sneaked into our food, they were paralyzed by another demitasse of strong, sweet coffee that topped off our meal.

Mr. Backsman called to Jorge. "Joca [nickname for Jorge], come here. The men have finished eating, so lead them down the trail to the creek and through the village. Take this new machete."

John and I had wondered what it would be like to walk into the vast Amazonian jungle, which geography books called "The Green Hell." I wondered if the Lord would let one of us be bitten by a bushmaster this soon in our missionary career. A pair of hip boots would be the safest prevention, I thought. But snakes can drop from trees, too.

"Jack, did you bring any anti-venom serum along?" I asked.

"Nope. Didn't think we would be setting foot in the jungle."

As we followed Jorge, I kept looking back to see how long it would take to lose sight of Backsman's house. Jack Looney was no "Jungle Jim," and none of us had ever committed ourselves to the guidance and protection of a seven-year-old. Because the trail was seldom used, Jorge had to swing the big knife to nip off vegetation that had grown over the trail. The machete looked as long as Jorge was tall, and too heavy for him to wield. I doubted that the boy and machete combo would pose much of a threat to a jaguar. The swish of Jorge's knife and our soft footsteps were the only sounds. I was ready for a viper to nail me in the calf. Had someone touched me from behind, I would have been the first man in space.

Towering trees reached for the sun, letting only a few strag-
gling rays touch the jungle floor. We were shaded most of the
way to the creek, only about four city blocks from the river's
edge. Dry season was at its peak, so the creek trickled silently in
its bed of hard gray clay, over and under old stumps and snags.

The same trail took us back to Backsman's where we turned
left onto a wider path that led to the little village of Santa Rita,
about two city blocks from Backsman's property line. John and I
were glad Jessie and Fran did not accompany us, for here was a
picture of real dilapidation. *This* could not be the place God
expected us to spend our lives endeavoring to reach people with
the message of salvation.

Where were the people? The only signs of life were a few
chickens scratching around in mud under the kitchen of the first
house, while two skinny pigs shoved their snouts around in the
same filth. The debris under the second house hadn't been dis-
turbed by the rooting crew, so we took a closer look and saw that
the swill teemed with worms and gave off a foul odor.

"Where are the people, Jack?" I asked. "I can't blame them if
they moved away."

"I think they are working in their plantations," Jack answered,
"either across the river in the flood lands, or deeper in the jungle
behind the village. Someone might be at home in this house,
watching us through the cracks."

Depressed as I was from the combination of sights and smells,
I couldn't avoid smiling as we stopped in front of the crookedest
house I had ever seen. It leaned so far to one side I couldn't tell
what kept it from toppling over.

Mr. Backsman was willing to sell the piece of land between
his fence and the village: 175 yards of river frontage that reached
about a mile into the jungle. What John felt, I didn't know. But I
wasn't in any mood to celebrate over Backsman's offer.

CHAPTER FOUR

THE 10-MEMBER ABWE FIELD COUNCIL gathered in Leticia for a special meeting, mainly to hear the report of our adventuresome trip. That evening, after all the kids were asleep, we united in a lengthy time of prayer. It didn't take long to unanimously agree that the Backsman property should be purchased, and the two Schlener families should establish residence there as soon as possible.

Neither Jessie nor Fran had seen the place, which seemed all for the best. Or was it? They were concerned enough about the 100-mile distance from town, where there was a doctor at least some of the time. The fastest we could get there from the new location was 18 hours, *if* we had gasoline on hand, and *if* we could keep the small outboard motor humming. Jessie and I reminded ourselves that when we turned our lives over to the Lord, we did so unconditionally. John and Fran made the same commitment, and maintained the same convictions.

The Lord kept calling our attention to His promises: "My grace is sufficient for thee; for my strength is made perfect in weakness" (2 Corinthians 12:9). "Faithful is he that calleth you, who also will do it" (1 Thessalonians 5:4). "My God shall supply all your need according to his riches in glory by Christ Jesus" (Philippians 4:19). Along with His promises, we had the gentle counsel of our heavenly Father: "Rejoice evermore. Pray without ceasing. In everything give thanks; for this is the will of God in Christ Jesus concerning you" (1 Thessalonians 5:16-18).

Those pertinent verses of Scripture gave us confidence until we couldn't wait to finalize purchase of the Backsman property. Jack gladly loaned John and me his boat. The little outboard

motor pushed us into Backsman's port after seven hours. Mr.
Backsman walked soberly down to the port, looking at the
ground. A file folder, tied with string, was squeezed between his
bicep and chest. The folder contained the moldy, yellowed title to
the land we wanted to purchase. Inside he had to have been rejoic-
ing at the prospect of receiving a few hundred bucks. He stepped
on board and we continued 30 more miles to the county seat.

In the 1950's foreigners were rare in the town of São Paulo
de Olivença. The few German settlers from Santa Rita seldom
went there, since they were not held in high esteem. Some of the
more well-read Brazilians knew about WWII. John and I were a
different breed, although Schlener is a German name. As we
stepped into the auditor's office, all activity halted as the office
crew gave us a once-over.

Everything about John and me screamed "foreign." Our
clothing was noticeably different. Our noses competed with Mr.
Backsman's for length, and when we attempted to speak, the
employees fought to suppress their laughter.

John was pegged as a war hero after his one-man dramatic
presentation. The little finger of his right hand was missing, as was
part of his wrist bone. For lack of sufficient vocabulary, John
turned into a human airplane with gestures and sound effects to
explain the reason for his maimed hand. His head bowed toward
the floor, as though peering into a bombsight, causing several of
his spellbound listeners to follow suit. He explained with great
difficulty that the Germans didn't like being bombed, so they
shot back and nailed him on his thirteenth mission.

We were amazed that the auditor required us to name our
property. Since it was privately owned, a name was necessary for
identification purposes. Excusing ourselves, John and I went outside to talk. We chuckled to ourselves, wondering why a name
was needed for this collection of trees, vines, thorns, and animals.
Who else would want the place?

"How does 'Tarantula Tangle' sound?" I asked John.

"Maybe 'Jaguar Junction' would work," John suggested.

Crocodile Corner and Alligator Acres were offered and rejected as ridiculous.

"Hey, I remember seeing an aeronautical map with a village called Port of Three Brothers," John blurted. "What about calling the place Port of Two Brothers?"

When the auditor heard the name we had chosen, he thundered, "That's fine." He lit a fresh cigarette from the butt of a used one, took his pen, dipped it in the ink bottle, and started to write. For a chain-smoker, the auditor's hand was steady as his nicotine-stained fingers pushed the pen across the official document. Various sizes and colors of official stamps were pasted on the papers, signatures written across the surfaces, and the transaction was finished. We had already paid Mr. Backsman U.S. $350 in Brazilian money for his land. The Port of Two Brothers, approximately 90 acres of Amazon jungle, was now the property of the Association of Baptists for World Evangelism. Quite a sizeable chunk of God's earth for the price.

Mr. Backsman offered John and his family the abandoned storage building to live in while building their house. Orville Floden, a former draftsman for the John Deere Company, drew up plans using the same dimensions as those of the Rogerses' house: three bedrooms and an exterior bath, and a laundry room with overhead cement water tanks. Orville figured the room sizes to conform to standard three- and four-meter lumber available at a military sawmill upriver from Leticia.

"Sounds better than an A-frame covered with banana leaves," I said to Jessie. "But where will the money come from?"

John cabled the United States from Leticia, managing to borrow $2,000 dollars from Dad Schlener and Fran's dad, Martin Read. John's retirement from the military as a disabled veteran would facilitate repayment of these loans. But poor Paul and Jessie were still praying and waiting. All I got from the military was scared, seasick, and $300 dollars mustering-out pay.

Our dad used to call me a worrywart when I was kid. I think I inherited the weakness from him. He went broke during the Great Depression, and started over again out West. He was normally soft-spoken and slow to speak. His pressure release valve was to pace back and forth in the backyard, chewing one-inch pieces of cheap cigars while he talked to himself. This changed dramatically when he became a Christian at the age of 55.

Jessie might have had some concern about our future housing, but she just shrugged the problem off whenever it was mentioned.

"Jessie, can we build a house with our $50-a-month rent allowance?" I asked one day, feeling depressed.

"Well, Mr. 'Soldier of the Cross,' do you believe the Lord brought us here to serve Him?" she asked.

"Yup, sure do," I answered confidently.

"Oh?" she said, stretching the little word up the scale a few notes while raising her eyebrows. "You really believe that?"

I affirmed, "We would never have made it this far without God's provision."

"And you don't think we can exist very long in this climate with these two little kids without a decent place to live?" she continued.

"That's exactly what I think. Our bodies have never completely dried since we arrived in this steam bath. We have never scratched so much in our 25 years of existence. Tim and Leanne already have heat rash, chigger bites, and who knows how many intestinal parasites," I griped.

Jessie was ready for the fatal blow. "Well, we both agree that God provided what we needed to come to this place. And we both realize our health won't hold up without at least fair living conditions. So why can't we believe that where the Lord leads, He provides? And that He will provide the right house for us, at the right time?"

What an answer! Jessie could have qualified for a job at a psychiatric clinic. I felt like a little boy in Sunday school, learning the fundamentals on how to trust God. Then I thought how great it was to have a lady like Jessie by my side; a professional might have socked me 100 bucks for that counsel. The Lord did provide the right amount of money at exactly the right time, but that time hadn't come yet.

· · ·

While we Schleners were occupied with our first field council meeting and river trips to purchase property, two great things happened: our equipment arrived from the United States at customs in Manaus, 1,000 miles downriver; and a lean-to kitchen and privy were added to our temporary dwelling, thanks to Jack and Joyce Looney.

Our new kitchen, the outhouse, and the 40-foot wobbly walkway connecting the two were constructed with poles and split palm trees still juicy from the jungle. Under this elevated walkway we saw—for the first time—frogs being swallowed by snakes. The poor victims did their best to escape by kicking their feet, still protruding from the snakes' jaws.

Some crosspieces of the walkway weren't nailed down before quitting time. After dark that night, John stepped outside. Everything was fine until he stepped too close to the edge, whereupon the opposite end flipped up, dumping poor John into the bog below.

The second day after the completion of this welcome project, a snake held a certain fellow hostage inside the privy. This fellow was afraid to move, holler, or even breathe until the snake—mere inches from his shoulder—decided to return to the swamp for a smaller toad. After this experience, we always made careful inspections before stepping inside our outhouse.

We looked forward to doing our own cooking after our equipment arrived. Under the thick thatched roof, the kitchen would be much cooler than under rusty tin, but the place was not bat-, rat-, snake-, or mosquito-proof. Evenings during rainstorms were a little spooky. Bats swooped low as their radar picked up sound waves from us and our gas lanterns.

Our new addition was barely finished when John and Fran accepted Orville's offer to load what stuff they had and move down to Backsman's. I spent a couple of days helping them set up and scrub the entire place with caustic soda. While Jessie and I missed the fellowship, we had more space in the house, and we got to take over the double bed.

Willard Stull telegraphed from Manaus that our equipment had been released from customs at a cost of $73 per family. He loaded our stuff on a boat that would arrive at the Port of Two Brothers any day (or week, or month). John and Fran would take responsibility for the stuff and store it in a large tent.

Jessie and I were determined to remain in Benjamin Constant to concentrate on language study. We were eager to gain Portuguese-speaking ability before going to live among the people with whom we'd be working. So we continued our studies with Happy Bert.

Not many weeks later, we heard an outboard motor whine to a stop in front of the house. John stepped out of a dugout, grimacing as he straightened his aching back that had been bent for 18 hours. He grabbed his satchel and climbed up the riverbank, his body shaped like the letter Z.

"How are you river rats surviving at Piranha Paradise?" I hollered from the window.

"We ain't been et yet, but we've eaten some of them, and are they ever tasty," John said, referring to fried piranha. "How are you vacationers doing here at the resort?" he asked.

"Vacationers, my foot!" Jessie and I threw back in unison. "These treks for our meals and lugging the kids is making us lean and mean. And this heat is getting to us."

John dropped onto the hard bench with a groan and said, "It won't be long and you'll be smelling this place up with burned toast and fried fish, so stop your bellyaching!"

"What do you mean?" Jessie asked.

"The reason I'm here now," John continued while he reached around as far as he could to rub his back, "is not only to buy food and pick up mail, but to let you know our equipment arrived the day before yesterday."

Jessie screeched loud enough that ladies doing laundry at the river's edge pivoted in our direction. So eager were we to receive enough of our equipment to take care of ourselves while studying the language, the following evening at 11 p.m.—not considering the perils of night travel—Jack, John, and I started downriver in a dugout, towing Jack's little boat. With nary a breeze to raise a ripple, the big river was glassy smooth, a deceptive promise of good weather. Cruising along at about eight miles an hour with John's 5-hp motor created a cooling breeze. A full moon illuminated the whole countryside, laying a perfect path on the water for us to follow. Hot cups of coffee refreshed us in the coolness of the tropical night, and our conversation was light.

How great it will be to have a kerosene refrigerator and a kerosene range in the kitchen, I said to myself.

After several hours of blissful cruising, the clear sky grew smaller and the breeze stiffer. Ripples began to tap lightly against Jack's aluminum boat. Distant lightning illuminating the sky reminded me of the aurora borealis we used to see in northern Idaho.

Each of us had a gut feeling we might be in trouble. Minutes passed without conversation. Three major typhoons on board the baby flattop U.S.S. *Cape Esperance* during the Philippine Liberation Campaign had made me afraid of turbulent water. During the second typhoon, three destroyers sank in the storm. That traumatic experience left me with a built-in respect for wind and water.

"Jack, she's kickin' up a little breeze. What do you think?"
I asked.

"These storms sometimes go by. We've still got a lot of
moonlight. A little wind won't hurt us," Jack answered, in an
attempt either to reassure us or establish himself as expert.

The harmless bursts of light we had seen in the distance
turned into jagged streaks that stabbed the earth. Only seconds
passed between lightning flashes and thunder rumbles; thick
clouds hid the moon.

"Jack, I'm sure you noticed that the man in the moon
sprouted legs and took himself behind the protection of the
clouds," I said.

"We still have plenty of light," Jack repeated.

Jack was a good guy, or he would have told me to shut up.
But he wasn't a talk-aholic. Later, Jack built and captained a 30-
foot riverboat, and could have written a book on the region's
weather patterns. John didn't say much.

The wind became more than brisk, creating waves. I wondered what we could do. If Jack and John had a perfect plan, they
didn't share it with me. If we had pulled over to the riverbank
where immense chunks of earth were breaking off, we could
have been sent to the bottom of the river. Had we pulled over to
stop, waves would have beat us against the shore.

It was dark now. The tops of the trees were indistinguishable
from the sky without starlight. This was the first time I realized
how much light stars give, even without the moon. Nobody
spoke. Not even a dim flicker from a tiny kerosene lamp shone
from the shoreline.

I remembered how God compares physical darkness to spiritual darkness in the Bible. In either case we are totally helpless
until, out of the darkness, a light shines—which is what we were
praying for that night.

His neck stretched to the limit and his eyes bugged out trying to see, John gripped the throttle. He slowed the little engine,

steering while the current pushed us along. Our flashlights grew dim and still we couldn't see. We were afraid to pull over to shore and afraid not to. Then we saw a tiny, flickering light ahead. It's amazing how even a little light can bring a ray of hope.

Like the chairman of a board, John said, "All those in favor of meeting the people who are keeping that flame burning, regardless of race, creed, or color, raise your right hand." It was too dark to count the votes but the little 5-hp, throttle wide open again, pushed us straight for the light, thumping logs and catching weeds on the propeller, until our prow touched the blessed clay bank.

A man, silhouetted against the flickering light, walked down the round-rung ladder toward us. We didn't know whether he would say hello, good-bye, or take some whacks at us with his machete. The family in this little wooden shack might have been frightened when we pulled into their port during the wee hours of the morning. Fortunately, the man was a friendly Indian, whose Portuguese vocabulary was even more limited than ours.

The young mother held her baby in a sling, and four other children huddled in a corner next to their mom. All six of them stared at us in wonder. With a half-dozen words our host explained, "Hang hammock here. Family sleep other place." The air was not fresh with three of us under the same mosquito net, nor was our resting place soft. But we were grateful to God that we made it safely to shore. Outside, the wind howled and rain pounded on the thatch. A faint chorus of croaking frogs completed the music that allowed us to sleep for a couple of hours.

At gray dawn, our gracious host accepted a few cruzeiros in appreciation for his hospitality. He fondled the Brazilian money like a curious child, then handed it to his wife. The decision not to eat hotcakes, ham, and eggs for breakfast was easy. We cinched our belts one notch and pointed the dugout downstream, hoping Fran would have a kettle full of something edible when we arrived. And she did. After a hearty breakfast, Jack returned home in the little aluminum boat. Jessie and Joyce were glad for his blow-by-blow report of the trip when Jack reached Benjamin Constant.

Overloaded with equipment, our slippery, round-bottomed dugout had barely enough room for us to stand. John and I stacked things too high, so our load was top-heavy. If another storm threatened on the way from the Port of Two Brothers to Benjamin Constant, pulling over to shore wouldn't suffice. The stuff would have to be offloaded onto the riverbank.

Whirlpools rocked us enough to let water into the dugout, keeping one of us busy bailing with a stainless steel mixing bowl. By God's grace, the weather was made-to-order perfect. The trip took 20 monotonous hours, but setting up the equipment once we arrived in Benjamin Constant gave Jessie and me a new lease on life. I stumbled over stuff, and jumped from one item to the other with hammer and crowbar. The gleaming white kerosene refrigerator looked out of place against rough, hand-sawed, unpainted wall boards. Jessie and I took turns sticking our heads inside. I touched a match to the wick, and within two hours we guzzled limeade with ice cubes tinkling in our tumblers.

I leaped from the fridge to the crate containing our flimsy three-burner kerosene range. Jessie thought I was mad the way I ripped the crate apart and sniffed at the pine. The stove's finish was that old-fashioned, white-speckled dark blue enamel. I filled the gallon jug with green Colombian kerosene, tipped it upside-down, and listened to the fuel gurgle into the tubes. We lit all three burners and held our hands over them, then stood back and watched the blue and yellow flames through the little windows.

My favorite culinary tool was next. It was the tin portable stovetop oven with two spiral, nickel-plated steel handles, a small glass window, and a temperature gauge. "Put it up there, Paul. Let's see if the temperature gauge works," Jessie commanded. I had it in place before she'd finished speaking. It fit perfectly over two burners, and the gauge shot right up to 400. "Now," I said with one hand on her shoulder, "it's your turn. I want to see and smell a batch of beans with chunks of pig bubbling in a kettle over that one burner, while a johnnycake bakes in the oven."

Soon we used Portuguese words to buy everything we could see that was edible, and some which didn't look so edible—like the wormy, buggy flour. I became more fluent in Portuguese words having to do with food than on any other subject.

Jessie soon inundated the little thatched kitchen with luscious odors. Bread baked in the oven, fresh fish with bananas sizzled in the skillet, and coffee glugged away in the percolator. Tough, stringy beef from critters butchered at the water's edge, manioc root, and green bananas spiked with onions, garlic, and cilantro made for a stew fit for a king. Tapir meat was usually more tender than beef. But months passed when none was available, so we came close to worshipping the top section of that Servel fridge, which kept meat frozen.

Tim was a big boy now with a real pith helmet, engineer's boots, and a popgun: ready to go hunting. Leanne, now six months old, squealed over her new highchair. That chair was a blessing for Jessie, too. She could place a couple of ice cubes on Leanne's highchair tray, where the baby pushed them around. Leanne was never able to get hold of one, but slapped them with both hands, splashing the ice water on herself.

Ice cubes weren't so bad, but one morning after breakfast while Jessie was straightening the bedroom, I called her to come see what was on Leanne's tray. "What are those miserable things?" Jessie shrieked, jerking Leanne out of the highchair. "Why didn't you take her out of the chair?"

Leanne was pushing two pink baby rats around her tray with her index finger, watching them squirm as she touched them. They had fallen from the thatch.

Not many days later, we found Leanne munching when we hadn't given her anything to eat.

"What are you chewing? Come on, spit it out," Jessie pleaded.

Reluctantly, Leanne pushed onto her juicy chin a dry, crispy cockroach that had also fallen from the thatch.

"Mr. Paul L. Schlener, this . . . is . . . too . . . much!" Jessie proclaimed. She had my attention. The middle initial of my name wasn't really necessary for me to understand to whom she was speaking. But it did convince me that she was in earnest about the "too much."

"While we are trying to study, along with washing diapers by hand, cooking food that comes in the rough, boiling our drinking water, swabbing these rough floor boards with disinfectant every few days, washing our own clothing and mosquito nets by hand, trying to keep the kids from being consumed by animals and parasites . . . *we need a hired girl, soon!*"

This expository message from the queen of the house had been in preparation for several days. But the baby rat episode was the last straw that triggered the release of Jessie's lively discourse.

Joyce Looney hired a girl named Ermelinda for us. She was a few years older than we, just under five feet tall. Her dark, wavy hair glistened with brilliantine. She was a great help, and a pleasure to have around the house. Not only were we more relaxed with Ermelinda helping us, it was good to practice our Portuguese on her, even though her dentures occasionally came loose while speaking. She was excellent with Leanne and Tim Jim. We could spend more time on our "Hooked on Portuguese" study books and pay closer attention to Felizberto.

PART TWO

FROM BENJAMIN CONSTANT TO
THE PORT OF TWO BROTHERS

(1952)

CHAPTER FIVE

FOR 10 MONTHS JESSIE AND I remained in Benjamin Constant. Our kindergarten course in Foreign Missions was now complete and we were ready to move downriver to the Port of Two Brothers. It was a challenge learning local customs. But we were now expert at walking lightfooted—in a crouch—through slippery mud puddles, and scratching heat rash and chigger bites. The abrupt change of diet triggered dreams of tossed salads and apple pie, but we learned to enjoy beans, rice, bananas, and fish, and agreed with the Brazilians that hunger is the best seasoning for food.

Felizberto, despite his clove-chewing habit, had successfully dragged us along in the Portuguese language to the point where we were able to converse with our neighbors about everyday matters. Stretching my language efficiency to the limit, I delved into theology and homiletics enough to prepare a three-minute salvation message. I was convinced that if I were given the opportunity, I could explode for that long with the eloquence and fervor of Martin Luther, and bring sinners to their knees in repentance. When I finally had the opportunity, eloquence and fervor were markedly lacking and, within a short time, most of my listeners were close to sleep.

Weeks before leaving Benjamin Constant, Jessie and I saw the reality and ugliness of death in this remote location. A few minutes after midnight one night, Jessie awoke mumbling, "What sort of people would be doing carpentry this time of night?"

"I don't hear anything," I said, sitting up to listen. Then the noise started again: rip, zip; rip, zip; the sounds of a handsaw. After a brief pause we heard tap, tap, tap, tap, thump; like a nail being pounded.

"Maybe someone has a leaking roof," I groaned.

"Why wouldn't they do their repairs in the daytime?" Jessie grumbled.

Joyce Looney appeared at our door right after breakfast the next morning. "Hi folks, what's happening around here?" she greeted us. "Nuthin' but the three S's I bet: sweatin', studyin', and scratchin', right?"

"You're right, Joyce. Sit down and have a refreshing glass of cloudy, lukewarm river water," Jessie offered. "We were aroused at frequent intervals last night," she complained. "It sounded like hollow pounding."

"What kept you awake last night is the reason I'm here," Joyce said gravely.

Jessie and I glanced at each other, wondering what she meant.

"You heard friends and relatives building a coffin for a man who died," Joyce explained. "They don't usually start until around midnight." Joyce had our full attention as she continued. "An elderly gentleman from our church passed away yesterday and will have to be buried before dark today." Then she offered an invitation. "It would help cheer the family if you would come with me to sing. Would you do that? I know it would mean a lot to the family and the other Christian friends who will be there."

"Sing at a funeral?" Jessie gasped. "Joyce, I have never even attended a funeral."

"You haven't?" Joyce was surprised. "This is one you won't forget. Things like this are rough down here," she forewarned us.

Jessie hesitated before agreeing. "Well, we might as well start getting accustomed to what goes on down here, both life and death. What do you think, Paul?"

"I think we should go. Just don't ask me to speak," I begged.

It was late in the afternoon when Joyce returned so we could walk together to the home where we would sing before the body was taken to the cemetery. Jessie and I were stunned when we saw the corpse lying on the table from the doorway of the tiny home. His hands folded across his chest held a burning candle forced upright between stiff fingers. Other candles burned on the table at his side. Wilted flowers arranged around the body made a feeble bid to brighten the scene. People sat on benches against the four walls, leaving barely enough room to walk between them and the table.

Joyce was highly esteemed by everybody in town, especially by the church folk. When she stepped inside, there was a surge of the customary weeping and wailing by most of the mourners. This subsided as quickly as it started. We paused to look at the corpse while those around us shifted to make room for us on a bench.

The moment we entered the house we were overwhelmed by the odor. The zinc roof was so low and the day so stifling hot that decomposition of the body was accelerated. The air in the little room had become so foul that those with handkerchiefs or cloths of any kind held them over their noses. A man walked around the room burning tar on a clay basin, giving off smoke to help alleviate the situation.

We joined in singing hymns, which drew a crowd outside. People couldn't believe we were singing, "We will live, we will live in that land that Jesus is preparing for us. We will live joyfully without anguish, sadness, and pain!" Most of the crowd was accustomed to hearing sobs, groans, and dismal chants.

Jack had gone to Manaus to purchase an engine for his boat, but Joyce handled the situation well. She prayed before the lid was placed on the cloth-covered box Jessie and I had heard being constructed the night before, and four men carried the simple coffin to the cemetery. There was more singing at the graveyard.

On the way back to our house at the edge of the river, I thought aloud to Jessie, "What a great difference in the way dead

people are laid away! Back in Bonners Ferry, at the first funeral I
ever saw, a person is embalmed, stuffed, and painted to look
alive. This fellow was decaying before our very eyes with cotton
stuffed in his nostrils to keep the worms inside and a cloth tied
around his chin to keep his mouth closed."

"That is enough. Please!" Jessie begged. "Let's try to forget
these things for now!" She looked a little ill. But I couldn't forget so quickly. Sizing up my two funeral experiences, I decided I
would rather have been in the poor man's shoes when he died—
crude coffin and all. From what we could determine, the man we
had just seen laid out on the table had put his trust in the Lord
Jesus Christ. Now he was absent from his wasted flesh and in the
presence of the Lord who died for him.

That first funeral was still fresh in our minds several weeks
later when Joyce appeared at our door again. "You might not be
so glad I came," Joyce said. Another man had died. "The wife of
the Christian brother wants you to sing at the graveside before
he is buried."

Staring out the window at the blue sky, Jessie heaved a sigh
and said, "Paul, believe it or not, I have some encouraging news
for a change. The Flodens and Rogerses surprised us a couple
days ago for a quick visit to let us know our order of lumber will
be ready soon, and money came from the mission to pay for it."

. . .

The word "soon" in South America means only that the
foretellers, such as those who promised our lumber, had tongues
in working order. And I learned "tomorrow" never meant "the
following day." Jack was constructing a 35-foot riverboat to be
used for evangelism along the Amazon and Javari tributaries. He
smiled when we said our lumber would be ready soon. But he
offered to take Jessie and me and our equipment to the Port of
Two Brothers when we were ready. "It'll be a slow trip. I doubt

if we'll make it in daylight," Jack warned us as we loaded the launch the day before departure. "And we'll have to rig a Rube Goldberg transom on the back end of the hull so we can use your outboard motor for power."

Our lumber was finally ready in October, four months after we had first been told "soon." We would share the Backsman bungalow with John and Fran and their children, John Read, eight, and David, two-and-a-half. We hoped this would work out until we could finish boarding up the workshop, make and hang a door, and build an outhouse.

The downriver trip, Jessie's first long trip on the river, was enjoyable. Amazon skies are beautiful beyond description. There is no pollution, so the sky is a brilliant azure and the billowy clouds are dazzling. The sky is so cerulean that its reflection occasionally makes even the muddy Amazon look blue.

A hundred yards from shore we saw John racing down the makeshift steps, two at a time, to the water's edge. We looked like secondhand dealers coming home from an auction as we pulled up to the muddy bank of the Port of Two Brothers. Our assortment of beds, highchair, kerosene stove, refrigerator, homemade table and chairs, suitcases, footlockers, steel drums, barrels of gasoline, and cans of oil made the load impossible to arrange neatly.

Holding little David, Fran looked down at us from the precipitous edge of the riverbank where great chunks of clay had broken off. In July the river is near its lowest level, making the climb from the boat to the top of the riverbank about 50 feet.

John had men clearing the jungle with axes and machetes, and a tent had been pitched to store our equipment until our houses were built. After hugs and handshakes all around, Fran took Jessie for a walk through the adjacent village while Jack, John, and I unloaded the hodgepodge of equipment before darkness and mosquitoes engulfed us.

We didn't make it. Less than 15 minutes of twilight remained after the sun set, then the mosquitoes descended on us. Insect repellent didn't faze the critters. So for half an hour we men ran up and down the riverbank as the little bloodsuckers nailed us all over.

When the last item was finally flung into the tent, the three of us did a 100-yard dash to the Backsman bungalow, trying to get inside as quickly as we could.

"Don't let any mosquitoes in," Fran shouted.

Jessie, Fran, and the kids were being eaten up by the mosquitoes because shutters had been left open at the wrong time. Evening meals should be eaten by 5:30 p.m. in unscreened houses. This allows time to wash dishes before the mosquito onslaught, which usually subsides at seven. That first evening we ate under a mosquito net draped over us and the table so we could eat in peace.

In a few days the 12 x 16-foot workshop and outhouse were finished enough to be inhabited. We moved in simultaneously with rats, bats, termites, cockroaches, and ants. Our little thatched-roof dwelling became their nocturnal haven. We learned to appreciate our mosquito nets even more than in Benjamin Constant, because we slept in the attic, just inches from the thatch. Our mosquito nets were fastened near the roof's peak, which was about six feet off the floor. The beds were positioned down the middle so we could get all the way around them to tuck in the kids' nets.

After climbing the ladder with the kids, tucking them in, then doing the same for ourselves, rustling noises in the thatch and swishing sounds from bats flying around didn't bother us . . . *much*. Mosquito nets, thin and flimsy as they are, became sanctuaries of protection. After we were all stretched out, relaxed, and starting to dry off from the intense humidity, the sound of a child's voice, "Mommy, I have to go potty!" was bad news. We learned to limit suppertime drinks.

The workshop construction was not an example of good engineering. I respected my bother's opinions on how the construction should be done, since he was nine years older than I and more experienced. Not only had he been a peacetime Marine and a bombardier in WWII who received a Purple Heart, he was also a grease monkey, and had driven a one-wheel truck in the Civilian Conservation Corps. Then he became a painter. My civil engineering experience was limited to a couple of small table lamps and a medicine cabinet I built in high school shop class. It was good to have an older brother to blame for our blunders.

"For crying out loud, how did this happen?" I roared one morning, splashing my way to the kerosene stove to put on the coffee. Heavy rainfall the previous evening made for a cool night's rest, but now mud and water covered one-third of the cement floor.

The workshop was located on land that sloped downward from the front end. So John and I dug down several feet until we had a level piece of ground on which to pour a slab of concrete. Sounded sensible. Even if we had access to a cement mixer, there was no place to plug one in. So we skimped on the concrete recipe of broken clay blocks and river sand. The slab was too thin, too weak, and too close to the ground's surface. We should have filled in the low part or built the shop off the ground on posts.

Instead, what we did was engineer an excavation for a new creek bed that channeled all excess rainwater our way. And it did just that, right under the door. The next day was spent digging— actually broadening and lowering the creek bed to keep water and mud from coming in our front door.

Our only inspector was Orville Floden, whose father was a builder. And he minced no words when it came to pointing out our mistakes. But what a great help he was, especially when it came time to build our permanent homes.

. . .

A few weeks after we moved into the workshop, Blake
Rogers found two hunting hounds for sale in Leticia. Blake and
I each bought one. He named his hound Sarge, and we named
ours Chief. Chief was nearly full grown, tricolored, and friendly.
And could he howl! His bark was one or two blasts, followed by
a prolonged howl that started on a bass note but quickly rose an
octave or two where it held until he ran out of breath.

Chief had been with us for several months when he started
howling around midnight one night.

"Quiet, Chief!" I hollered from under the mosquito net.

He was quiet for a few minutes, then started in again, whim-
pering, yipping, and snarling.

"Chief, will you shut up and get to sleep?" I bellowed.

This time he would not stop. I should have known something was wrong because Chief never barked just to hear his
voice. I got up, closed the mosquito net behind me, grabbed a
flashlight, and slipped into my thongs. From the top of the ladder
I trained my light on the poor dog as he groaned and snapped at
his body while pawing at the door to get out.

"Lemme see what's the matter, Chief," I said, starting down
the ladder. Crunch! Crunch! Something that sounded like Rice
Krispies mashed under my rubber thongs as I stepped onto the
cement floor. I shone the light on the floor and immediately
jumped back onto the ladder.

"Ants!" I yelled.

Nipper ants completely covered the floor from front to back
and side to side. "Man alive, I've got to get Chief out of here," I
cried, leaping two rungs at a time to get back to the attic and don
my rubber boots.

I went back down the ladder, pausing a split second on the
bottom rung before taking three giant steps toward the door
where Chief writhed in pain. As I opened the door, he shot out
like a flash. I slammed the door shut, pivoted, took three giant

crunching steps back to the ladder, and brushed the ants off my boots. I stood for a minute wondering how in the world to get rid of that moving mass of ants. They were at least an inch deep.

"Jessie, sorry to wake you up," I murmured as I bent double to avoid bumping my head on the roof staves.

"At least I'm glad you're sorry," she responded. "How could you imagine I'd be asleep?"

"How are we going to get rid of the Egyptian plague that's happening downstairs?" I asked.

"Did you say 'we'?" Jessie lay back down.

"I figured maybe between two intellectuals, we could come up with a foolproof idea how to annihilate those nippers."

"Remember, I was ready to go back to Bonners Ferry while we were still in Benjamin Constant. Now these ants. How often can we expect this to happen?" was her response. But Jessie came up with an idea after all.

"Are the ants coming up the ladder?" she asked.

I stepped to the head of the ladder and focused the flashlight. "Nope, I don't see one pesky ant on the ladder."

"Well, then, come back to bed and we can take care of it in the morning."

I crawled back into the mosquito net, wondering how on earth we would handle the situation. I awoke at dawn to discover we hadn't been nipped. I peeked over the edge of the bed. There were no ants on the floor. I slipped out of the net, jumped into my boots, and peered downstairs. The ants were still there, a teeming mass crawling all over each other. The light of day made it seem as though there were twice as many as at midnight.

I stepped halfway down the ladder, then sat on a rung to think. Jessie had gotten up and was standing at the head of the ladder, gaping in wonder at the sight of the ants.

We had made double front doors in the event we needed to get a boat through the wide opening.

"Let's try this," I suggested. "I'll catapult myself across to the doors, open them, grab the two brooms in the corner, and fly back to the ladder. While you put on your plastic mud boots, I will sweep the ants away from the ladder until there's room enough for both of us to stand on a bare spot. Then we'll both sweep like mad until we get them or they get us."

Fortunately, nipper ants don't seem to be in a hurry, so we were able to keep ahead of them. In a few seconds I had swept enough space for both of us to stand. Then Jessie stepped down and joined me in sweeping with a burst of adrenalin, elbowing me in the rib cage until we swept ourselves away from each other.

From the back wall and along the side walls into the middle, we swished the nippers. All the while they continued trying to spread out. But we were too much for them and finally got them out the doorway and into a pile.

"Keep them together while I drain gasoline from a barrel," I commanded Jessie. Around and around the pile she went, huffing and puffing, sweeping, sweeping, sweeping until I returned with a small can of gasoline and some matches.

"Stand back, way back!" I shouted. Chief sat on his haunches, watching our activity from a distance. I sprinkled the pyramid of ants with gasoline and threw a lighted match on it. Foomp! It was all over.

The reason the ants covered our floor is that they got in through a two-inch hole I had drilled in the wall to rig a sink drain. I didn't get the project finished before bedtime so the hole had remained open all night. At least one of the ants got off trail and the rest blindly followed, unable to find their way back out. This is a perfect example of what happens to Christians who get in with the wrong crowd and drift along until they get singed or badly burned by the consequences of their behavior.

. . .

During my second trip to the Port of Two Brothers to construct the workshop/house, I preached in Portuguese for the first time one Sunday morning. Services were held outdoors, and the congregation sat on stumps or makeshift benches; some even climbed trees and propped themselves comfortably against a tree trunk.

Fran, with her blond hair and blue eyes, would have drawn a crowd even without a musical instrument. But from childhood she had been adept at playing the accordion, and people were amazed to hear the music burst forth from that pleated squeezebox. For 18 years Fran blessed the people up and down the Amazon with her accordion music.

That Sunday, John cranked the Victrola by hand and played 72-rpm gospel recordings in Portuguese, while helping the villagers learn to sing choruses. He clowned around with the boys after church, and stuck sick people with hypodermic needles, which helped establish lasting friendships. There was always a sick person who needed sympathy and medicine.

As a naturally slow learner, I had to cram for days in preparation to preach. I fairly wore my English-Portuguese dictionary to shreds and pored over the verb conjugations in my language book by the hour. I shuddered at the thought of confusing verb tenses, telling my audience that there is still time "yesterday" to prepare for heaven.

As I approached the podium—a board nailed to a post—to speak, I didn't suffer a cardiac arrest, but I was scared. I felt sure I would be misunderstood. It didn't help to clear my throat and cough, so I jumped right in, mistakes and all. I guess I lasted for three or four minutes before making my way back to my place on a bench.

I spoke on John 11:25–26: "I am the resurrection and the life. He that believeth in me, though he were dead, yet shall he live, and whosoever liveth and believeth in me shall never die.

Believest thou this?" The word for "resurrection" in Portuguese is one of the hardest words for a beginner to pronounce. There were no tears of repentance in the audience, no raised hands, nor did anyone seek spiritual counsel after my profound message. But the listeners were totally respectful, so I considered it a victory. I felt that I had taken my first step toward sharing the Word of God with the people among whom Jessie and I would live for many years.

CHAPTER SIX

I PURCHASED a well-used dugout canoe from our next-door neighbor in Benjamin Constant. With three sheets of corrugated aluminum and some odd-sized pieces of wood, I put a top on the round-bottomed craft. This setup, powered by a little 5-hp outboard, provided tippy transportation to field council meetings and supply replenishment in Leticia or Benjamin Constant.

Since the trip to Leticia took 18 hours, we had to spend the night tied up somewhere along the river. When stopping before dark during high water, there isn't always dry ground to pound a stake in to secure the boat. Plenty of trees line the water's edge, but within minutes the canoe is crawling with ants stranded on the tree by floodwaters. And there is always the possibility of a snake crawling up the mooring lines no matter where the boat is tied.

Our best bet was to carry two poles, sharpened on one end and long enough to reach bottom in a few feet of water. Before mosquito time, I'd slow down and start checking the depth close to shore, sticking one pole as far into the mud as I could and securing the bow line. Then I'd step on toes, knock over cans, bump my head on the roof, and trip on benches all the way to the transom, shoving the second pole into the mud to tie up. Secured at both ends, the lengthy poles could bend with the wind and waves, so we were gently rocked to sleep. No ants, no blowing sand, and less chance for creepy creatures to come aboard. These were more details of missionary life I hadn't learned in missions courses at Biola.

. . .

On October 1, 1952, Orv sent word that our lumber order was complete. It was being tied together with vines at the Colombian sawmill to form a raft. "It should be ready to go by the time you pioneers can get there with equipment and supplies to make the trip," his note said.

I had been helping John build his house full time. Now I couldn't contain my glee at the prospect of beginning to work on mine. Living out of suitcases had ceased to be fun, and Jessie and I had grown claustrophobic from sleeping in the tight space next to the thatched roof.

John and I hugged and kissed our wives and kids, climbed into my little 14-foot homemade cedar boat with a new 10-hp Johnson, and headed for Leticia. When our families saw us out of sight around the curve of the river more than a mile away, we had no more contact with them, nor was there any way they could reach a doctor until our return.

During the seven-hour trip to Leticia, John and I were more than a little anxious about leaving our families behind. We already had suffered with outboard motors: I had blown a cylinder wall; John stripped the gears in a lower unit. Then I smashed into something and broke a lower unit. John's motor slipped off the transom twice.

John and I slowly learned to "read" the river. But all we could study was what we could see. A difference in the surface appearance could mean any number of things. Careful as we were, there was always the possibility of smashing into an underwater snag. Silence is deafening out in the middle of nowhere after the dying shriek of a broken engine.

Arriving in Leticia, John and I trudged up to the Flodens' house, only to find they were not at home. Oh, no! Orville was going to help us float our raft. He was a real Huck Finn since he and Helen had floated the first raft down to the Port of Two Brothers. Orville left a note with his hired man, offering the use of his 21-foot boat, our only protection from the elements. John and I just stood for a minute, leaning against the house.

I asked, "Now what?"

"Now, sailor boy," John said, "you can show your stuff. Or didn't you learn anything but swabbing decks aboard that 'baby flattop'?"

"I'll have you know I learned to load a 40-mm anti-aircraft gun, scrape paint, tie a bowline, a double becket bend, and a clove hitch. My fine-tuned skills might contribute more to our rafting adventure than what you learned squinting into a bomb sight while you pushed buttons and felt for your parachute!" I responded, continuing our combined effort to take disappointment lightly. It didn't always work, but prayer did. How comforting to commit our lives to the Lord and ask for wisdom. Most of His lessons on wisdom came when we fouled up.

"Hey, *gringos*!" Blake hollered from across the street. "Nobody's home over there. Better come over for a stiff cuppa coffee."

There was no way to advise our missionary partners when we were coming. We just showed up, hoping for a positive reception. Blake and Mary were always hospitable. But Mary backed up after greeting John and me, finding it hard to breathe until we showered and ate something to help extinguish the powerful garlic fumes that wafted off our bodies. For lack of green salads and vegetables on the trip, John and I ate garlic cloves as though they were radishes.

"Here, give me your thermos bottle," Mary said. "I'll try to purify it for you before I fill it again." She held it at arm's length on her way to the kitchen to dunk it in strong soap suds.

Jean Ann was the oldest of the Rogers children, smiling, quiet, and sort of a second mother to the other three. Ruthie was next, cute as the dickens, lively and laughing. Mary Lou had celebrated her first birthday the day before we arrived. I think Blake was sure George would become a pitcher for a big league ball club. But poor Georgie got lost in mental thought when he was told to do something. Blake would get hold of the "fish" (a small wooden board the shape of its namesake, used for paddling), which ended George's meditation.

There was still enough daylight to fetch our lumber raft at the Colombian military sawmill before dark. John and I bought gasoline in Leticia, loaded it on the Flodens' boat, put the motor on the transom, and roared off.

The Flodens' boat, the *Mensajero,* was made from heavy cedar boards. It came to a point at the bow, but was flat-bottomed from the transom all the way to the bow, like a barge. Orville constructed it to live in, not for speed. The current was against us so we pulled into the sawmill late, together with the mosquitoes.

John and I couldn't see our raft in the semi-darkness. I idled on to the sawmill proper, skimming close to the shore until a pile of coiled vines caught my eye. They appeared to be floating in the water. Logs and canoes secured by ropes along the shore jerked and plunged as we plowed the water, but the vines were as still as rocks. I eased closer to discover that the leftover vines were piled on top of our huge raft. The raft itself didn't seem to budge an inch in the heavy wake from the *Mensajero.*

The lumber, made from freshly sawed red mahogany (called cedar in Brazil), was so heavy that only about 10 inches showed above the water's surface, while at least 36 inches remained submerged. The raft was 42 feet long by 15 feet wide, and weighed more than 20 tons.

John and I jumped out of our boats and tied up as quickly as we could, slapping at mosquitoes. "This thing must be stuck in the clay. It didn't move an inch when we both jumped onto it," I observed.

"Yup, must be stuck all right. I didn't realize it would be this huge," John answered.

A quick swim relieved us from the mosquito plague. We figured a little piranha nip couldn't be as miserable as being drilled by a thousand mosquitoes. Little did we know about piranhas or we wouldn't have figured that. Still wet, we scrambled under the mosquito net and fixed a gourmet supper of Spam and bread by flashlight.

Before daylight, the one-burner gasoline stove hissed under a kettle of water boiling for coffee and oatmeal while John and I lashed our boats to the raft, one on each side.

As we finished securing our boats, four men from the mill walked along the riverbank up to the raft, smiling.

"I wonder what's so funny," I asked John.

"Maybe it's our looks," he suggested. "A *gringo* sticks out like a sore thumb. And they might have doubts we know what we're doing."

"*Buenos dias, señors,*" the men greeted us in Spanish.

"*Buenos dias,*" we parroted.

Our pronunciation told them there was no use trying to carry on further conversation. So they pantomimed to ask if we needed help shoving off. Neither of us was in any hurry to leave shore. Once we shoved off, there were only two things we were absolutely certain of: that there would be no turning back, and that we wouldn't sink. Our destination was the Port of Two Brothers, about 120 miles downstream.

"*Sim, senhores, vamos e muito obrigado,*" John responded in Portuguese. The men removed their trousers, untied the vines that secured the raft to posts, waded into the water, and started to push. John and I helped push with two-by-two poles.

The four men waded back to shore and watched us as we hit the current. John and I dropped our two-by-twos, hopped into our boats and started the motors, then idled in neutral in case we needed to turn quickly. Quickly? Could anything be done quickly to this tonnage with so little horsepower?

The river at this spot is a *parana* (pah-rah-NAH), a small channel of the main river. It was ideal for the location of the sawmill, but too narrow for any maneuvering we might have to attempt with the raft's unwieldy bulk.

John and I conducted a quick experiment. It was plain as day that no fancy maneuvering was possible with our measly little engines. We stopped the motors and watched the jungle drift by. There was nothing to do but check the lashings a dozen times and wash our oatmeal pan, cereal bowls, and coffee cups. We jumped up and down again on all four corners of this floating lumberyard, amazed that our two 150-pound bags of bones had no effect. Anything looking like danger up ahead would have to be determined at least a quarter-mile before we got there, to give us time to avoid whatever it might be.

Exactly one hour after shoving off, we entered the mainstream of the Amazon River. Leticia, Colombia, was just around the bend, across the shore from Peru. This time of morning river boats and large dugouts would be pulling into port in Leticia, loaded with bananas. The worst thing that could happen, we thought, would be to get caught in back eddies and crash into other boats tied up at the port, tipping smaller ones over, crushing others.

"What do you say we move her out toward the middle so we won't be so close to all the activity?" John suggested.

"Good idea," I agreed. "With plenty of room for other boats to maneuver, it will be their responsibility to avoid hitting us."

We started the little engines, but there was no noticeable progress toward the middle of the river. I jumped out of my boat and ran to see if our two 10-hp motors were pushing any water at all. We were moving—barely—so we held the engines at full throttle until we were far enough from the Leticia shore, but near enough so we could make the left channel where the river forked.

The river was at its lowest level in seven years, we were told. That meant less volume of water and less current. A major obstacle we faced was being stranded on a sandbar until some big riverboat pulled us off or the river rose enough to lift us off.

Water level could easily lower a foot within hours. If this happened while we were hung up on a sandbar, we would be stuck in a big way. It was best to stay in the deepest part of the stream; however, the main current could take us too close to shore.

Throughout the day John and I were thankful we had traveled all over the United States visiting churches and individuals, challenging Christians to pray for us. There was never an ideal place to make landings. Once we started to land we were fortunate to get the monster stopped, let alone maneuver it into a neat, protected cove.

This was wilderness country, but unlike the Israelites during their desert march, there was no pillar of cloud to guide us by day, nor a pillar of fire by night. But the Lord made us to lie down on green lumber to rest. He led us through some rough waters but let us sleep in the quietness of still waters. He prepared our table plentifully and our cups often were filled to running over (Psalm 23, Paul Schlener's version). We rose on the wings of the dawn and we settled on the banks of the Amazon; even there His hand guided us, His right hand held us fast (Psalm 139:9, 10, John Schlener's version). As we traveled we wondered how—if ever—we would reach these people with the gospel of Christ.

After three days of travel, John and I figured we were about six hours from our smiling wives and kids, savory kitchens, and soft, clean beds. Both of us had orders on the tips of our tongues for pancakes for the next day's breakfast.

The current at the Port of Two Brothers was stronger than any of the places where we had tied up. We planned that final landing as best we could, asking God to give us skill to manipulate the rig close enough to throw a rope to someone on shore, just in case we couldn't stop the raft as we headed into the riverbank.

At 10 a.m. we tried to hold to the left side of the channel as we approached the big curve that would lead us to port. If we missed the curve and went straight ahead, we would have to maneuver between and around several islands and come out well below our intended destination. After we agonized our way around the curve, binoculars revealed the palm trees in the front yard at the Port of Two Brothers more than a mile away.

We stopped the motors, bathed, shaved, splashed on bay rum, and put on the clean clothes we had saved for the occasion. We planned to make a grand arrival. "Pride goeth before destruction," Solomon says (Proverbs 16:18). Less than a half-mile from our destination a quick, heavy squall drenched us to the bone. Our bay rum and deodorant washed off, while our clothing stuck to us like we'd been swimming.

A crowd gathered on the riverbank. Gervasio had seen us after we rounded the bend and sounded the alarm to Jessie and Fran. Neighbors from the village came running. Dogs barked and children climbed trees for a better view. Both motors howled, forcing us against the current. We were too close to the clay bank, but not slowing down. Close as we were, the raft wouldn't stop. We sprang from our boats, shouting, "Catch the ropes!" and threw coiled lines to men on the bank.

Gervasio caught the very tip of one; the other fell short. Martins jumped into the water, swam out and grabbed it, barely able to reach land against the current. All hands grabbed the ropes, pulled us in, and secured the lines to heavy posts.

"You hear any band music, John?"

"No, but look at the reception party up there waving at us."

Fran, John Jr., and David stood in one little huddle; Jessie, Tim Jim, and Leanne in another. Hallelujah! No brass band could have thrilled us like the sight of our families waiting on the riverbank for us. How delectable the noon meal was that Columbus Day in 1952, back home at the Port of Two Brothers.

• • •

To see the beautiful lumber carefully stacked, drying in the sun, was better than an Olympic medal draped around our necks. The purchase of the lumber, the trip with the raft, and finding our families in great shape was all God's gracious provision.

Paul and Allene Goodman, good friends from Compton, California, had helped us pack and send out our equipment before we left the United States for Brazil. During the nine months we two Schlener families lived in Benjamin Constant, we wondered how the Lord would scrape up enough money to build our houses. What happened was that the Goodmans wrote a personal note to our supporters and included it with our newsletter of December 1952. They wrote:

> In a personal letter to me, the Schleners made known the immediate need of $1000 for which to build their houses. We could borrow this for them at the regular rate of interest, but wouldn't it be more pleasing in the Lord's eyes if we, their friends and backers, were to give them the money ourselves and not have them go in debt? Five dollars each from 200 hundred of us would give them the necessary amount to build both their homes. Let us make our Christmas gift to them over and above our regular support.
>
> The ABWE mission board in Philadelphia graciously consented to handle the funds and will mail it to them direct. Mark your gift "Schlener Housing Fund" and mail it to the Association of Baptists for World Evangelism. The Lord will bless you for it.
>
> Your brother in Christ,
> Paul R. Goodman

Our sponsors responded to Paul Goodman's letter, so the money was on hand when we were ready to build. John's lumber had arrived at the Port of Two Brothers in March. He had some jungle cleared and had started on the foundation pillars of their house by the time Jessie and I moved downriver in July.

A few months later it was my turn. Once again the Flodens

arrived with nearly every piece of woodworking equipment they owned. I appreciated the way Orville bossed us around; I needed every suggestion and correction he made. We were planning for a long haul in Amazonas, so I didn't argue about how Orville thought things should be done. I figured I should take advantage of his expertise and try to learn; I could change things later if need be. Orville had gone to the expense and inconvenience of having his equipment wheelbarrowed to the port in Leticia and loaded on his boat, to help John and me start building our homes. The way Orville placed a steel square on a board and drew a line with a pencil spoke of his craftsmanship.

Riverboats from 1,000 miles downriver carried staples for sale: gasoline, kerosene, soggy sugar, salt that was never dry, rice, beans, laundry soap, hand soap, some medicines, shotgun shells, and pitifully few items of hardware. Keeping supplies on hand wasn't always possible. Imagine us Americans running out of something and having to go without for a while. It was good for us, although we didn't think so at the time.

· · ·

From the very beginning we were forced to do what we could to help the sick. Local people concluded that anybody with the intelligence to build homes equipped with kerosene refrigerators and ranges and to run motorboats should be able to lance boils, stitch lacerations, set broken bones, and extract teeth. John and I were glad to help when we could, but we had no training or equipment to meet the people's physical needs.

We should have been MD's, dentists, mechanics, journeymen carpenters, electricians, plumbers, naval architects, and theologians. All we could do was dabble in each of these areas while God kept us from killing anyone. When illnesses seemed minor, with no fever and mild symptoms, an intramuscular injection of 5 cc's of distilled water and an aspirin every four hours pulled sufferers through. It was sort of funny, but this was better than sending people away discouraged, or giving them the wrong medicine. The distilled water and aspirin was mostly for hypochondriacs who would come for treatment to get a little attention. Some returned to thank us for the treatment, saying, "Senhor Paulo, that was *santo remedio* [holy medicine]. I'm feeling so much better."

Another miraculous healing balm was a Colombian liniment called Number 9. We bought it by the caseload. Its spicy odor and the burning sensation it caused on a sore spot was also considered *santo remedio*. It had a high content of ammonia, which made it an excellent reviver for those who passed out.

A young Indian family on their way upriver waited at our port while the man of the family came to the house for medicine. "Ah! Hurt shoulders. Tah! Hurt all arms, chest, too." He was ruggedly muscled, the kind to stay on the good side of. I looked him over, admiring his build.

"Where are you coming from, and where are you headed?" I asked.

"Come up from Caruara. Going Black Creek," he answered, fishing for the right words in Portuguese.

"That's a long trip. How long have you been paddling?" I asked.

He held up his hand and started with his little finger, slowly working his way to his thumb, figuring out how many days he had traveled. It took all fingers on one hand to complete his addition.

"Are you telling me you have been paddling upstream for five days?"

He answered, "Mmm, cook in canoe. Stop night, only sleep."

"Anybody along to help paddle?" I further questioned him.

"Only my woman. No paddle much, mostly steer from *popa* [stern], kids too small."

Paddling a dugout canoe for five days upstream gave the man

a good reason for the soreness he felt. I sat him down, reached for a bottle of Number 9 and gave him a brisk rubdown. His nostrils dilated at the pungent smell of the liniment and his overworked muscles relaxed after a few minutes of massage.

"Mmm, *tah quente* [it's hot]. Good," he said, as he stood up and slipped into his shirt.

I turned around to replace the bottle of Number 9 and nearly bumped into an older man standing there with his shirt pulled up to expose his abdomen. I hadn't seen or heard him arrive.

"Hurt stomach, need rub," he said. Without bothering to explain that liniment couldn't fix his insides, I daubed a generous amount of the potion on his stomach and assured him it would heat up without massage when he tucked in his shirt. I also gave him a dose of worm medicine, which he probably needed more than the Number 9.

As John's and my responsibilities increased, we saw a need to establish a schedule for treating the sick. We were interrupted from studies, building, and mealtimes. Special hours worked well for the people who lived nearby, but not for those coming from great distances. Of course nobody can schedule emergencies. We felt fulfilled in helping people get well, but it was even more encouraging to see our friends responding to the gospel message.

While we were still camping in the workshop, I observed the first agonizing death from a snake bite. Two men carried the victim in a hammock up the riverbank after traveling 10 miles by canoe. After the usual greetings and questions about what happened, I knelt down to talk to the patient. His pulse was fast and weak, and he burned with fever. There was no color in his lips or fingernails. Every short breath was a groan. His left leg was swollen to twice normal size.

"Friend, was it a *jararaca* that bit you?" I asked.

He nodded. I looked at the men who carried him and they nodded in agreement. At this point it didn't make much difference which snake bit him; he was dying.

I ran to the workshop, put needles and syringe on to boil, and took an ampule of polyvalent anti-venom serum from the refrigerator. I hurried back to the poor man, hearing the ominous gurgle in his throat: the "death rattle." It lasted less than a minute, then he was still and lifeless.

Oh, God, how can we handle this? We are here to tell people about God. What are these people thinking? As far as I know, this young man hadn't heard the gospel; now it's too late. Lord, maybe we should quit and let intelligent people take over, I preached to myself, at the same time pleading with God as I looked at the young man.

I swallowed until I could speak, apologizing to the people who had brought the young man and expressing my sorrow that he had died and I hadn't had opportunity to help him as soon as he was bitten. I explained as best I could that we all have to die someday, but we will go to heaven if we trust Christ, who died to save us from sin. They nodded without comprehension. They gathered the two ends of the hammock and carried the young man's body down to the port, seemingly unmoved by his death.

John, Fran, Jessie, and I understood our job was to preach the gospel, live exemplary lives before the people, and establish local churches. It was natural to assume there would be a certain amount of medical work to do in a remote area with no doctors. The more we learned about the hazards of the Green Hell, the more concerned we were about our children, and the more precious they became to us.

While the kids were small, we had to insist on immediate obedience, especially to commands like stop; don't move; don't go near the river; stay seated in the canoe. During their nap times and at night, Jessie and I stood by our children's beds, committing them to God's protection and asking Him to help us take proper care of them.

CHAPTER SEVEN

JESSIE'S AND MY NEWSLETTER of January 1953 told of the first three men who made professions of faith in the Lord at the close of our 1952 Christmas program: Virgulindo, Dorva, and Lazaro. The following Sunday, two brothers and a 10-year-old girl came to the house wanting to hear more of what the Bible says about being saved. Then a student evangelist from the city of Manaus held three special meetings during his stay, and five more men became Christians.

It was a privilege to talk with the men who responded to the ministry of our Sunday morning services in the out-of-doors church. Our language ability steadily improved, and attendance was good for the Sunday services and for the kids' classes on Wednesdays. Little by little we gained the people's confidence. A few disliked us, but they were outnumbered by others who seemed glad we were there.

One Sunday morning two middle-aged brothers walked up to the homemade podium saying, "Senhor Paulo, we need to know God and have assurance of salvation." The next Sunday three more men came for the same reason. Right away we started a Thursday night Bible study, which we described in the same January newsletter.

> Now we have a Bible study class on Thursday nights, and they are eager to learn what the Word of God has to say. Never have I had such a privilege as teaching the Scriptures to these new converts. I translated a simple study course on the Gospel of John for the few who could read a little. Some already have the first part filled out.

After a few weeks, this study group developed into a prayer meeting. How great it was to hear people talk with God for the first time in their lives.

In the meantime, construction on our permanent house continued with a handsaw, a square, a level, a plumb bob, a steel tape, and a hammer. The first time I ripped an inch-thick board, 10 inches wide and 13 feet long, with my handsaw, sweat poured off my nose and chin, and my clothing clung to my body. I thought I would never have the strength to do it again. But it became easier as I toughened to the job.

John and I longed to work without shirts, but it was next to impossible, especially in the newly cleared jungle where two tiny, troublesome gnats, *meruim* (meh-roo-eeng) and *pium* (pee-oong), live. I think a microscope would prove they consist of teeth and a pair of wings.

The most painful flies were the *mutuca* (moo-too-cah) and innumerable species of horseflies. The *mutuca* is the size of a regular housefly, but is barely visible in flight. He stabs his victim and makes a fast getaway, leaving a tell-tale spot of blood. Chiggers in the grass are called *mucuim* (moo-coo-eeng). They drill a tiny hole in a person's skin, then crawl inside and stay there until they are scratched out or the skin becomes become infected and they float out.

An explosion from the direction of the Backsman establishment got everybody's attention. Startled dogs emerged from their napping places in the shade, sniffing in the direction of the loud noise. If the blast was from a firearm, it was of a larger calibre than anything John or I had. All was quiet for a few seconds, until a boy sprinted around the corner of John's house toward us. He hollered, "Senhor Paulo, come and see the enormous snake."

"Where is it?"

"Down at Backsman's."

"Is it dead or alive?"

"Not quite dead." And off the boy shot like an arrow back to Backsman's.

I slipped my belt through the slits on the holster that held my revolver, then lowered my double-barreled 12-gauge from the gun rack in my office and dropped a buckshot load into each chamber. I don't like to see snakes, even in zoos. To the young messenger, "enormous" might have meant four or five feet long.

Armed for battle, I started toward the scene of the confusion. Courageous pioneer that I was supposed to be, I walked slower than usual. Suddenly the MK's passed me like I was standing still. Homeschool had taken an abrupt break. John Read won the sprint toward the center of activity at Backsman's. David and Tim were neck-and-neck in second place. Leanne slowed down to stay close to me.

Little Jorge Backsman, stiff-necked and knock-kneed, stared at me as I approached. I was amazed at the size of the beautiful reptile stretched out on the ground.

"Hi, Jorge," I greeted the boy.

"Hi, Senhor Paulo." His large, liquid eyes surveyed my double-barreled 12-gauge. He'd never seen one before. A couple side-steps afforded him a better view of my spotless sidearm in its shiny black holster.

"Where is your dad, Jorge? I'd like to ask him how he went about killing this monster."

"He's in the house." Jorge let me take a few steps toward the house before he added, "But he didn't kill the snake."

Our kids crept closer to the snake for a good look, but when the tip of the tail twitched, the kids took flight and kept their distance.

"Who killed him then?" I asked.

Jorge hesitated before answering, "I killed him."

I dropped down on my haunches to meet his eyes. "What? You killed him? How did you kill him? Where was he? How did you find him?"

Looking at the ground again, Jorge formed a little pyramid of dust with his calloused toes and began to explain. He turned and pointed to the window. "I noticed something move on the ground right below the window. And there it was, all stretched out. I think he was after the new little piglets under our house. I turned around and reached for the old rolling block .44 that was hanging on the wall and brought it down. I had to get a bench so I would be high enough to hold the gun to my shoulder and aim. I finally got a bullet into the rusty old thing and shot him in the head. The kick knocked me off the bench and I wasn't sure I hit him till I got to my feet again."

"Good boy," I said, and patted him on the back. Jorge finally smiled. "Now what will you do with this gigantic sausage?"

"I don't know. Nothing, I guess."

"Would you sell him to me? I'll skin him and stretch the hide out to dry, then take him to the United States when I go."

"Sure, Senhor Paulo. You can have him."

That 21-foot anaconda skin was displayed in churches and schools, and used as an object lesson for many years.

. . .

Living out of suitcases for almost two years taxed Jessie's and my patience. We could hang some things on nails in the wall, but in a few days the nails rusted from salt left by our sweating fingers. We learned to wrap the nails in paper.

It was great to have a partner like Jessie, who bore the brunt of the inconveniences without complaint. She had a knack for making do with what we had. She could see that I worked on our house from daylight to dark, studying before daylight and after dark to prepare messages and Bible lessons. And someone always needed medical attention.

You can guess how happy we were to see the Flodens pull into our port with a small generator, table saw, and jointer to help get our house in a livable condition. John and his family had left for Leticia and Peru, so the Flodens stayed in their house while helping Jessie and me build ours. Jessie's letter to Mom and Dad Schlener in Bonners Ferry after the Flodens left said:

> The very week John and Fran left, the Flodens arrived with their machinery, saw and planer to start work on our house. For two weeks in February and March we were really busy. There were three Flodens and their hired man, so all I seemed to get done was cook and cook some more. Whew! Did the men ever eat! And I had to have something at coffee breaks: 9 a.m. and 3 p.m. I also had lessons and handwork to prepare for the kids' classes on Wednesdays. Well, anyway, things are getting back to normal and we are really thrilled to be living in our new house two weeks after the Flodens left in April [1953]. We just have one room mosquito proofed, but it is really wonderful, after almost two years fighting mosquito nets, to be able to walk into the room through a doorway, standing up straight, and just hop into bed. We surely like our house—big and airy, plenty of room for the kids to run. We thank God. Tim has never lived in a normal size house. During Biola days we lived in John's single garage apartment, then the one in Benjamin Constant, so he is really enjoying this place.

For lack of knowledge about plumbing, our shower setup looked like a WWII classified secret. We were fortunate to buy three used steel barrels from a Peruvian riverboat. Imagine the noise caused in cutting out the tops of the steel drums with a maul and cold chisel.

Four heavy, termite-proof posts from the jungle and smaller poles made up the framework of our bathhouse. The barrels had to be joined together so all four would fill simultaneously, with an outlet for a valve and shower nozzle underneath. I finally figured out what a "union" was for, and it saved me from becoming a first-term missionary casualty. The exterior was boarded up for privacy with cull boards from our lumber supply. I had needlessly used so many tees, elbows, sleeves, nipples, and reducers that the undersides of the barrels, where bathers stood, looked like school playground equipment for kids to climb on.

I wired a piece of corrugated aluminum from the valley of the hip roof just above the back door to the closest barrel. The tops of the barrels were just the right height to take a gravity flow, leaving plenty of head room for the bathers below. What a noteworthy engineering achievement!

Rainwater baths were luxurious right after a rainfall and while the barrels remained quite full. However, a few days without rain lowered the water level to about six inches. The sun warmed it to ideal temperature for raising healthy pollywogs. The slippery creatures slid down the pipe and got trapped in the shower head, which smelled pretty bad after a few hours. After several pollywogs bounced off our toothbrushes and careened down the drain, we moved our dental hygiene station to the kitchen, where we used boiled water.

Surprises taught us lessons along the way. Jessie used diapers for our kids that had a black trademark in one corner. She usually left a large aluminum basin filled with diapers soaking in soapy water in the bathhouse. Even with a hired laundress, Jessie took care of the diapers herself to make sure all soap was rinsed out of them.

One day I heard my name called in such a loud, high pitch that I thought there was no way I could get from my workshop to the other side of the house in time for the emergency. I skidded into the scene, full speed, to learn that one of the black marks on a diaper lifted its tail and walked away as Jessie reached for a diaper; it was a scorpion.

PART THREE

THROUGH SWAMPS IN A DUGOUT TO
THE JACURAPA RIVER

(1953)

CHAPTER EIGHT

"TELEGRAM!" John shouted from his boat, having just arrived from a supply and mail trip. The word "telegram" always sent our imaginations in overdrive. Heart attacks, automobile accidents, and death passed through our minds. But the cable was from Dr. William W. Orr, pastor of Hope Union Church and vice president of Biola, stating his intention to visit us in June with our good friend Paul Goodman.

John met Paul Goodman in 1940 in Seattle, where they both became Christians; I met him a year later. Goodman was a multitalented man, built like a prize fighter at six feet tall. His expertise and success came through courage and hard work. Throughout our missionary career, Paul and his gracious wife, Allene, contributed in many ways. Paul planned to bring with him a 16mm movie camera and a suitcase full of film, plus some goodies.

While John and I attended Biola, our practical work assignment was at Hope Union, and our two families were the first foreign missionaries the church sent out. Our send-off celebration was called "Schleners' Day." After the evening service they gave us a shower of household items and clothing. Forty-five years later Jessie and I still use the heavy duty stainless steel mixing bowls from Hope Union.

We were excited as we worked day and night to get ready for the visitors. The rainwater shower wasn't finished in time for their arrival, and we wondered if they would appreciate bathing on our little thatch-covered raft at the edge of the river.

A newsletter published by Dr. Orr in October 1953 described his experience in the bathhouse.

> Even bathing along the Amazon offers its thrills. The boys [John and Paul] have built a bathhouse on the river which consists of a log raft about four feet square. There is a hole in the center for dipping water with a *cooyah,* a gourd bowl, and pouring it over one's body. The walls and roof of the bathhouse are made of palm leaves that afford housing for many types of insects, not the least of which is a six-inch tarantula that this reporter had for an audience each time he visited the bathhouse. The first time we tried to end his career we didn't know he was jet propelled! From then on we had to satisfy ourselves with washing him into the river and hoping we wouldn't dip him up in one of the cups of water we spilled over ourselves while bathing. This type of bathing, my friends, is decidedly hard on one's nerves.

To come from ultra-modern homes such as Dr. Orr and Paul Goodman enjoyed, and be forced to use our outdoor toilet, was an even bigger adjustment. There was no way we could get the upper hand over cockroaches. And a walk in the grass was an invitation for chiggers to invade all tight places where clothing clings to the body, mostly sock tops and belt lines. They seemed especially hungry for fresh American blood. Insect repellent helped, but to be free of these mites required a tankful of the stuff.

Gervasio, my first hired man, was about 30 years old, slim but strong. A childhood skin infection left his elbows and parts of his forearms covered with large white blotches. Scars from *candiru* fish bites showed when he worked without a shirt. Gervasio had a short temper, but he never exploded in my presence during all the years he worked for me. When he was on the verge of losing it, his face turned stiff and cold. But I think he would have died for us if faced with a situation that required it. He and his son, 12-year-old Adenil, paddled our heavy dugout canoe 115 miles from a Colombian carpenter's shop loaded with the furniture I ordered months before. They pulled into port a few days before the eagerly awaited guests.

Jessie sewed curtains until 2 a.m. the day before John and I arrived in the Flodens' *Mensajero* with our guests. She had the place looking neat and smelling clean. Nothing was painted, but our guests thought the bare red mahogany boards looked elegant. I had the ancient cast-iron sink braced to the kitchen wall. Buckets of river water were positioned nearby for cooking and washing dishes. The guests never once complained about shaving and brushing their teeth in cloudy river water.

We had only been on the field a couple of years, but were excited to receive all the wonderful, useful stuff our visitors brought from the United States. There were baby clothes for John and Fran's infant son, Phillip (which is Filipito in Portuguese, and quickly shortened by the locals into Pito), still in his crib, and the baby Jessie and I were expecting. Candy, toys, and clothes for the other kids made Christmas fall in June that year. Allene Goodman seemed to know exactly what we needed and wanted.

The men were impressed with the open-air Sunday services and with the Wednesday kids' Bible class. They took turns speaking at our regular services, giving their testimonies about how they came to know the Lord Jesus Christ as Savior.

Most of our neighbors had never seen men the size of Dr. Orr and Mr. Goodman. Even more unusual was Dr. Orr's complete baldness. His neat little mustache was another amusing subject. Little groups of kids pointed at him and giggled. He smiled back at them, gently patted their heads, shook their grimy little hands, and took their pictures. From then on, bald men with mustaches enjoyed a good reputation with the local children.

"Are those drums beating in the distance? We've been hearing them since we first got up this morning," Dr. Orr asked several days after his arrival.

"That's the start of an Indian *festa* [festival]," John explained.

"I heard a strange sound from some sort of horn this morning. Maybe that's what woke me up," Goodman said.

"The folks here in the village tell me that the blowing of the horn is the invitation to all the Indians within hearing. It means everything is ready and the festivity is beginning," I explained. The horn sounded again as we talked. We were amazed at how well sound carries through the jungle.

"It sounds close. How far away would this festival be?" Pastor Orr asked.

John cupped his hands around his mouth and hollered to his hired man, busy leveling ant hills with a hoe. "Brother Martins, come here, please."

Martins was a muscled young man of 20 who had worked hard in the jungle since childhood, felling trees with an axe to clear land for planting. He dropped his hoe and approached the shady spot where our big conference was in session.

"Martins, just where is this *festa*?" John asked.

"Senhor John, the festival is on the Jacurapa (Jah-coo-rah-PAH) river," he answered.

After John and I interpreted this conversation to our guests, Dr. Orr asked, "How far away is the Jackerapper river?" doing the best he could pronouncing Jacurapa.

Another exchange of conversation—gibberish to our visitors—informed us that it was about 10 miles away. Martins had been there numerous times during the dry season when jungle trails were dry enough to hike.

"What an opportunity!" Dr. Orr exclaimed. "We must see what's going on. I suppose you fellows have attended a *festa* or two."

John and I looked at each other, then at Goodman who smiled, raised his eyebrows, and shrugged his shoulders. We took turns and interrupted each other with excuses why we had never been to an Indian festival and why we shouldn't go now.

"People tell us it's an orgy that lasts three days or more. A lot of bad stuff takes place. We've patched up Indians badly lacerated during knife fights at these *festas*. We don't know how welcome we would be. If a few dozen short-tempered, inebriated Indians, soused from guzzling their fermented manioc, decided they did-n't like us, even Goodman with his six-foot stack of muscles might not be enough to save our hides." We tried to discourage Dr. Orr's suggestion.

"Even if we were welcome, our presence as missionaries might place a stamp of approval on this type of carousal. On the last day of the merriment, the women pull the hair from the head of the celebrant, a girl who has spent three months in confine-ment and is now available for marriage." John and I persevered, hoping our friends would give up on the idea.

Goodman, miraculously returned alive from piloting DC-4's over "the Hump" during WWII, was now a building contractor. He was ready for anything. John and I looked puny in compari-son to our two robust visitors.

I wondered if Dr. Orr, pastor of a large and growing church and a man of vision, thought that John and I were destined to become first-term dropouts. Maybe he thought, *They have come with their families to this Green Hell to reach people with the message of salvation and don't even have the courage to see how the people live!* If these were his thoughts, he was about right. He continued per-suading us to take the trip, and humbly encouraged us with wise counsel during his entire visit.

John and I called a private meeting with Gervasio and Martins in the shade of the *ing-gah* tree. "Do you guys know any of the folks from the Jacurapa?" we asked.

"Sure. The two main families there are the Macarios and Fideles," Gervasio said.

"Are you acquainted with the men of the families? What kind of people are they?"

"The Macario brothers come to the trading post often. They

seem to be good guys, but you can never tell with Indians; they're all thieves. They cut the trader's wire fence to make fish spears," Gervasio continued. Most Brazilians in the area considered Indians low class. Our two workers judged the whole tribe by the few with whom they had had trouble.

"Well, our two visitors want to go to this Indian *festa* [festivity] we hear going on now. What do you think?" John asked.

The two men hesitated. Then Martins said, "I don't know. It might be okay and maybe not. I've never gone to one."

"I went to one a long time ago," Gervasio said. "I didn't stay long. They don't seem to want outsiders around, especially toward the end when they pull the girl's hair out."

"How would we get there?" I blurted, figuring when our American friends heard about a long trek through Amazon jungle it would bring a halt to their enthusiastic curiosity.

"Good question," Gervasio said. "The river is at flood stage now, but has started to recede. We could get there only by canoe; the overland trails are flooded."

"How long do you think it would take us to make the trip?" John wanted to know.

Again the men looked at each other and made "guesstimations." Gervasio said, "I've made the trip in a canoe a couple of times during high water to hunt and fish, so I know the canal that leads to the Jacurapa."

"Your visitors must weigh around 200 pounds each, so it will take a large canoe to handle us and our baggage," Martins laughed. We agreed. His smile disappeared as he continued, "Another thing to consider is that if we stay too long and the water drops even a few inches, we would be stranded!" I wondered if Martins' concern was really the water or if he feared attending the *festa*.

Gervasio, some 15 years older than Martins and more experienced in jungle travel, said, "It will be all the heavier to drag the canoe over fallen trees and dry land unless we all get out of the canoe and step in the *tijuco* (tee-JOO-coo) [soft, fluffy mud] to help push. Can't tell how long it will take us, but we should be able to make it in one day."

John and I related all these hardships to Orr and Goodman, who simply nodded. Gervasio and Martins consented to be our guides. Each of us would have a canoe paddle, although only the Brazilians knew how to use them. They were experts with canoes and paddles, having used them since they were toddlers.

It wasn't easy for Jessie and Fran to be left alone, but they didn't complain, and hurriedly prepared food and water for our trip. Gervasio and Martins hightailed it into the village to advise their families of the trip to the Jacurapa. They grabbed mosquito nets and machetes, then hurried to locate a large dugout we could borrow.

John and I rolled up our mosquito nets, took anti-venom serum from the refrigerator, mixed gasoline and oil for the little 5-hp outboard motor, prepared a first-aid kit, and grabbed the old single-shot 16 and a box of shells. Goodman was ready with his Bolex 16mm movie camera and enough film to open a Kodak shop. Orr had a 35mm slide camera and his boat captain's cap.

In less than an hour, Gervasio and Martins paddled up in a 20-foot-long dugout. Oops! No transom for the outboard motor. In 30 minutes a makeshift transom was nailed to the stern. We loaded in all our luggage and took off downriver, waving to Fran and Jessie and the kids until they were out of sight.

• • •

We nosed into the narrow channel that would take us to the Jacurapa. Low-hanging branches that knocked our hats off kept us laughing. *"Pare a maquina!"* [Stop the machine!] Gervasio hollered periodically, just before we felt a thud followed by a bump along the bottom of the canoe. Gervasio's warning usually gave just enough time to jerk the motor's tail unit out of the water before it hit a log. Occasionally an underwater snag slipped by unseen and knocked the engine tail out of the water, startling us with a loud "waaahoo" until it dropped back into the water again. Besides keeping the canoe pointed in the right direction, Gervasio had to cut vines and branches that hung in our path.

"Oh, gracious, *stop!*" Dr. Orr howled as he was pulled almost completely off his narrow bench by an innocent looking vine. Every few inches along the stem a thick, exceedingly sharp thorn curved downward like a fish hook. John cut the engine and the guides paddled in reverse until Dr. Orr got unhooked. From then on, realizing he had neophytes on board, Gervasio called out, *"Cuidado, espinhos!"* [Look out for the thorns!]

Gliding silently into the depths of the jungle gave us a feeling of being swallowed by the endless vegetation. Tranquilized by the experience, completely submitted to our two guides, we were brought back to our senses by a sudden eruption of screeching and rustling foliage above our heads. We saw little monkeys leaping back and forth among the branches, scolding us for invading their territory. The full volume of the commotion lasted only a few seconds, then dwindled off as the little creatures disappeared into the limitless expanse of forest.

The monkey racket was replaced by bird calls. A loud call nearby was replicated in the distance. Toucans, with their great colorful beaks, swooped in flight as though their beaks weighed them down. Later we learned that their bills are unbelievably light, thin-walled but exceedingly strong.

We pestered our guides with questions. "What's making that low groaning sound, Gervasio?" I asked. He wasn't thinking so much about insignificant noises as about pythons and anacondas, crocodiles, and which canal fork to follow.

"There it goes again," I said.

"Oh, that's a tree frog," he answered.

"Man, it must be a whopper to make a noise like that!"

"No," Martins said, "those little *pererecas* are small in comparison to others."

From the narrow, shady channel we emerged into a vast open area in the bright sunlight. At least two acres covered in lavender flowers released a heady aroma. Goodman hadn't said much up to now, when he leaned over and picked a blossom. "Has anything ever impressed you more?" he wondered. "To think that only a handful of human beings will ever see this."

Dr. Orr agreed, "We can be reasonably certain there are thousands of other lovely gardens in this Amazon forest where no person will ever walk. Praise God for His wondrous creation!"

What looked like a meadow parted as our canoe plowed into it. We were in a lake completely covered with plants. We learned later that the lavender flowers were water hyacinths. These acres of green plants that looked like a pasture are called *muriru* (moo-ree-ROO), God's non-fat, no-cholesterol diet for turtles. Another feast for our eyes awaited us at the far end of the lake: giant lily pads called *Victoria Regia,* some four feet across and adorned with beautiful white blossoms.

We left the fantastic floating garden, pushing out into the canal again. "How, under the sun, did our guides notice where the canal started again?" Dr. Orr gasped. None of us could answer. What was invisible to our untrained eyes seemed like neon road signs to the two guides.

Our outboard motor ruined the majestic solitude of the jungle. But in a few minutes we scraped into an unavoidable shallow spot. Just as the motor stopped, raucous squawking startled us as brightly colored macaws took flight, honking for all they were worth.

"Sorry, men, but we are reaching higher ground and we'll have to get out and drag the canoe over land," Gervasio told us as he pulled off his trousers and stepped into the water and muck. Although neither he nor Martins owned a pair of shoes, the soles of their feet came close to the toughness of rhinoceros hide.

We Americans followed suit, displaying our lily-white legs. "No matter how wet and muddy you get, don't take off your shoes," John warned. No one argued after feeling and seeing a few of the menacing thorns, briars, and saw-edged plants.

On the other side of this hump of ground, we came upon a small Indian village in a clearing without much dry ground. Two emaciated dogs, plagued with festering sores from live larva, yipped at us, then cringed in fear and retreated under a house. The Indian custom is not to jump out of a canoe and run up to the house. Visitors stay in their canoe until the residents come down to greet them; that is, if they are welcome. So we stayed put, numb as our behinds were, until a suspicious, sober-faced man sauntered down to our canoe. The Indians had heard us coming for hours, thanks to our motor.

The Indian walked slowly toward us. I spoke quietly to Gervasio, "Ask if he has room for us to hang our hammocks overnight. Explain that we are on our way to the Macario *festa,* but got a late start, and will be glad to pay." John and I could have negotiated ourselves, but I thought it best for a Brazilian to do the talking.

"*Muito bem* [Very well]. I've seen this fellow at the trading post. There'll be no problem," Gervasio assured us. And there wasn't. Hospitality, we later learned, is automatic with most Amazonians.

The short, stocky Indian was dwarfed by Goodman and Orr. The first thing Americans do upon meeting is shake hands, which wasn't the custom of Ticuna Indians. They learned slowly, but never gripped firmly. The man's hand was totally engulfed in Goodman's big mitt. Orr and Goodman had one important thing in common: friendly smiles. This always helps put people at ease.

It was getting dark so we set to work rigging our hammocks and mosquito nets, Gervasio and Martins helping the American guests. They made a few wisecracks about our greenhorn guests, to which John and I contributed, of course. But who was greener than we? Our laughter gave our Indian hosts license to smile at our awkwardness in stepping in and out of our canoe and rigging our hammocks. Our clothing, funny-sounding speech, and general appearance kept them snickering until bedtime.

Before slumber overtook us, we reminisced about our families, soft beds with clean sheets, ceramic bathrooms, and bedtime bowls of cereal. Dr. Orr caused the vine-bound framework of the shack to squeak as he shifted around trying to get comfortable, which he said he never accomplished. The distant beating of drums continued, sometimes faint, then louder. Tired as we were, it was hard to relax.

The bathroom was the part of the jungle out of sight of the village. To wash up, we squatted at the water's edge and splashed around a little. Our hosts jumped into a canoe and paddled out to deeper, cleaner water. The people appeared happy with a little remuneration as we loaded up and paddled back into the swamps.

Around 9 a.m., we came to an area of deep water, so the motor propelled us for a stretch. Just as we started the motor, we heard a roaring noise from the jungle, increasing in volume. The sun was quickly hidden by clouds and within minutes we were drenched. The coolness of our wet bodies felt good until the wind hit, chilling us to the bone. The storm passed as quickly as it came, decreasing in volume as it continued on.

The drums were louder now. Gervasio and Martins agreed that the people at the *festa* knew somebody was coming. "Every time we started the motor yesterday, they heard us," Martins said.

"Within the hour we should be there," Gervasio added. He didn't sound too eager. None of us had any idea how we would be received. We weren't interested in becoming the subject of articles describing our massacre while on a peaceful mission to a Ticuna Indian festivity. It would have been better to have made the acquaintance of the some of the Indians first, instead of dropping in, cold turkey, on a big event. *Pastors seem to need exotic stories to report to their congregations,* I thought, trying to blame my wimpiness on someone else. *Why did we let them talk us into a dumb stunt like this?* I'm sure each of us agonized in fervent prayer that this pilgrimage would result in honor and glory to God.

Two boys in a small canoe appeared, like magic, ahead of us, still as statues, blending in perfectly with their background. A glance at us and our equipment told them that we were a strange foursome. Two were pale giants. Dr. Orr looked especially important with his captain's cap and neat mustache. The camera cases hanging from our necks and shotgun must have made them wonder. Goodman's equipment was immaculate: a metal suitcase that carried his big 16mm camera, another container for film, and another one for lenses and a tripod, which looked like a three-legged stick. The boys studied us, unsmiling. We kept coming. Suddenly, as though connected to an electric timer, they dipped their paddles and disappeared into the foliage. I wondered what the two young reporters told to the crowd, because a few minutes later, the din of the *festa* ceased abruptly.

"Too late to turn back now," I whispered, thinking things got too quiet too fast. "We may end up on a skewer in a bigger kitchen than the one we slept in last night," I half-joked, for we were genuinely concerned about what might happen on this little expedition.

. . .

As we paddled through the last bushy swamp and out into the open, there sat the multitude as though they had dropped from the sky. In the eerie silence, every man, woman, and child fixed his eyes on us. Nobody smiled.

John spoke, "No matter how bad our teeth need brushing, gentlemen, we had better plant smiles on our faces and leave them there until our cheek muscles cramp."

The host of the *festa* walked haltingly down to meet us. Gervasio and Martins were first out of the canoe. They stuck their pointed paddles into the sandy shore and tied our bow line to one. I was glad to be in the back seat by the motor as our guides spearheaded the invasion of Indian territory.

Our faithful pilots greeted the men they had known for years. Seeing those friendly exchanges was encouraging. Women stayed in the background with babies tied to their sides in slings. Dr. Orr jabbered away in English as though he stood in front of Hope Union Church on Sunday morning.

"Good morning, folks. My, how nice to see you here. And how are you, sir? Such a lovely place you have! Goodness me, aren't you a fine group of people!" No matter what the language, his audience would have known by his tone of voice and smiling face that the Reverend was not looking for trouble.

Not knowing how much or little time we had, Goodman set up his camera and tripod, loaded film, attached a zoom lens, and focused on the action. He was easy to spot in the throng: not many reached his shoulders. John and I did fine with our Portuguese, for most of the men were bilingual and could say *"Bom dia."* [Good morning.]

Most of the crowd were inebriated from guzzling their homemade liquor, called *paiauaru* (pie-ow-ah-ROO). Some were wobblier than others, tired from celebrating the night before. Others stood at a distance, not wanting anything to do with us. An elderly man slept under the floor of a small house, his face resting in his own vomit. Lines of six to eight men wandered aimlessly, hand-in-hand, laughing, as though they were about to play Ring Around the Rosy. The multitude, little by little, resumed their program, and Paul Goodman started shooting film.

Gervasio and Martins were served homemade brew brought to them in gourds. It was sickening just to watch them drink it. Green strings—like cooked spinach—oozed down their chins. I wondered if the potion was going in or coming out. An elderly

man with a toothless grin tottered up to me with a drink offering. Steadying himself on my shoulder, he stammered, "Wanna
drink *paiauaru*?" I put both hands on my stomach and bent
over slightly, grimacing and saying, *"Dor de barriga, dor de barriga."*
[Stomachache, stomachache.] He staggered away.

The traditional beverage of the Ticuna Indians and many
other South American tribes is made from cassava or manioc,
grown on small plantations. The plants' long roots are peeled,
ground, and boiled until the mixture becomes a paste, which is
poured into long wooden troughs. During this lengthy process,
women put the paste into their mouths, chew it, and and spit it
back into the troughs to start the chemical reaction that turns the
concoction into an alcoholic beverage. What a tiny amount of
yeast does to bread dough, the small amount of masticated paste
does to the trough. But where bread dough swells, manioc paste
becomes alcoholic. Great volumes of this draft are stored in giant
earthen jugs, fermenting more every day, ready when the *festa*
starts.

· · ·

At puberty, Ticuna Indian girls look forward to a ceremonial
festivity that can't be much fun for them. But it is the one and
only celebration in the girl's honor for her entire life. No birthday parties, since no birth dates were recorded; no school graduation, because there were no schools for them; no wedding
ceremony.

When the girl notices her time has come, she removes her
necklace of carved animals or birds, animal teeth, and brightly
colored seeds and hangs it on a crossbeam. She runs immediately to the water's edge and bathes, pulling her simple dress over
her wet body and running into the jungle.

Believing there are demons in the forest that wish to harm

her, the girl hides a short distance from her house. She strikes two sticks together, making a continual clacking noise until her mother sees the necklace. The mother realizes what the necklace means and follows the sound of the sticks to her daughter's hiding place. As they walk back to the house, the mother consoles her daughter, knowing what lies ahead. The mother immediately hides her daughter from the eyes of men. The father warns the mother to watch closely so the evil spirits will have no opportunity to harm their daughter.

These girls are as isolated as possible from men for three months. While the girl is in hiding, any man who approaches the house is supposed to whistle in case the girl is outside her secluded area. The hideaway is prepared in anticipation of the day the girl will need it, and is located at one end of the massive thatch-covered house. In some cases it is a very small shelter outside the large house.

The girl's mother spends time with her, teaching her how to fulfill her responsibilities as a wife and mother. The girl learns to weave various kinds of baskets. Strong, thickly woven baskets for carrying heavy loads of manioc root, bananas, and fish require a special type of vine. Long, narrow compressors, called *tipiti* (tee-pee-TEE), for making *farinha* require a lot of practice to fabricate. When the compressors are full of the rancid smelling, soggy manioc, they are hung on a limb and stretched from top to bottom, squeezing out most of the moisture before it can be toasted *farinha,* ready for eating. The girl learns how to gather material from palm trees covered with thorns called *tucumzeiro* (too-coong-ZAY-roo). From the sprouting new stems of this palm she learns to make string, brooms, hats, fans, sieves, fishnets, rope, and other items.

If the celebrant is the first daughter, an exceedingly large house is built during the three-month seclusion. Friends and relatives help the girl's father build her house. The Ticunas are a sociable people and have good times at these working bees.

"Paul, take a gander at the size of this shack," John exclaimed.

"Man! How long did it take them just to cut the thatch from the jungle, pack it, then cut the palm sticks and weave the stuff?" I wondered.

"How many people could hang hammocks in the place?" John asked. He answered his own question, "Not that many, I'll bet, because the entire middle is open space."

The immense thatch roof extended about five feet off the ground, rendering walls and windows unnecessary. Then we noticed the double row of posts all along the outside edge of the house, with just enough space between the posts to extend hammocks. This was strictly to accommodate guests during these *festas*. Indians sleep on the floor, using mats made from the bark of a *samumeira* (sah-moo-MAY-rah) tree. Here nearly all the spaces were occupied, with two to four hammocks hanging one above the other.

"Hey, Bud [Goodman's nickname]," I spoke into his ear while he doubled over, peering into the camera. "Pull your eye away from the lens and look how this house is built."

"Well, I'll be! The whole thing is held together with vines, from top to bottom," Goodman exclaimed. "It wouldn't be easy to tear this big shack apart," he said, grabbing a stanchion and shaking it. "Notice how cool it is under this thick thatch roof?" He was amazed at the Indians' ingenuity. A small, floored area had been formed with shiny palms laid down without fastenings.

"That's where the family sleeps. The guest room must be between all the posts up and down both sides," I remarked.

A dozen low fires were being loaded with fish, monkeys, and large rodents. Kettles blackened with soot hung over some of the flames, steam puffing under the battered lids. Long, ripe, unpeeled cooking bananas had turned as black as licorice, their seams dripping sweet juices onto the coals. Peeled green bananas

were placed all around the edges of smaller fires that had dwindled to coals, like white petals of a giant daisy. Occasionally, a
smoke-free breeze wafted a delectable aroma.

I felt hungry until I saw monkeys roasting over the coals.
Their hair is singed off before the little fellows are placed over
the embers for roasting. As the monkeys roast, eyelids and lips
burn first, exposing sightless eyeballs and teeth, which make for
a repulsive smile. Smoked tapir meat, venison, and fish had been
prepared by guests and brought to the big event.

Drums six inches thick and 10 inches in diameter, made
from monkey skin, throbbed monotonously. Hollow turtle shells,
hung on string between poles, were beat with sticks in a vain
effort to keep time with the drums. Thousands of hollow seeds
the size of sleigh bells were tied into bunches and fastened to
five-foot-long sticks. The sticks were jabbed onto the hard
ground to make the seeds rattle. This also was meant to keep
time with the drums and turtle shells, but in the Indians' tipsy
condition, accuracy was lacking and the occasional bare foot was
stabbed by the rattle stick. A high-pitched yelp relieved the
drone. Men without instruments shuffled around with their arms
around each other's shoulders: back and forth, back and forth, in
circles, in time with the primitive orchestra.

Two-inch-thick whistles made from bamboo played only
one note, but each whistle had a different key. The crowd, under
the influence of *paiauaru,* was able to endure the terrible din better than we Americans. After an hour I was tempted to halt the
program, line up a half-dozen drummers, and teach them some
paradiddles I learned as a kid with the drum and bugle corps.

The noise subsided and the crowd, apparently in response to
an announcement, formed a circle around an open space. The
drums continued because, according to the Indians' belief, if the
drums stop completely, harm will befall the maid of honor.

Goodman shoved a new roll of film in the Bolex. Dr. Orr
crowded in as close as possible, squinting in the bright sun, now

almost directly overhead. He looked like Admiral Halsey with his captain's cap protruding above the crowd. He was deeply concerned about these people groping in the darkness of ignorance and superstition.

Four masked men entered the center of the arena, arm in arm, and struggled to put on a little dance. Then four more joined the frolic. Their full-body masks, called *tururi* (too-roo-REE), were fringed around the bottom, and made from the same bark as sleeping mats. Grotesque, hideous faces carved from balsa wood represented the man-eating demons from which the initiate is in danger. Two men with more elaborately decorated masks charged out of the big house into the arena. Fastened to each man's back was a perfectly round framework covered by *samumeira* bark.

After the masked dancers finished their contribution, they backed off and sort of stepped in place in cadence with the drums. Then two teenaged girls emerged from the big house, singing in high-pitched, squeaky voices while they shuffled around the edge of the circle. They had attempted to put on makeup. Pure white talcum powder on their cheeks, with red rouge dots in the center, made their faces look like Japanese flags.

Their act ended when one of the masked men began to chase the two young ladies around the arena waving male genitals carved from wood, until both the pursuer and the pursued disappeared into the big house. This was the main event of the morning show, and brought laughter from the multitude. No one was supposed to see who the masked men were until the end of the *festa.* How they could stand the terrible heat, wrapped up as they were in the tree bark costumes for three days and four nights, was more than we could understand.

John and I made our way to Gervasio and Martins, who sat on a large log away from the crowd. "Do you think maybe we should leave soon?" we asked.

Gervasio said, "I don't feel as comfortable as I did when we first arrived. A couple of guys started playfully poking at us a few minutes ago, and it was hard for me not to punch them in the face." We couldn't afford to have Gervasio's short fuse touched off. "I think it would be best to go soon," he continued.

"I agree," Martins quickly responded. "Several men got a little mean because we wouldn't drink any more *paiauaru*. They wanted to know what we wanted here. I'm ready to go," he finished, noticeably ill at ease.

"Okay, you guys saunter over to our canoe. Don't hurry, but get things ready so the rest of us can shove off without wasting any time." Then we walked over to the father of the young girl who was hosting this celebration.

"Senhor Manuel, we'd better be leaving. We have a long way to go, and we want to get home before dark," John explained as the man strained to focus his bleary eyes on us.

"Thank you for entertaining us. We are disappointed in not being privileged to see the daughter for whom you are celebrating," I added.

He looked down at the ground and mumbled, "Mmm, tah." He staggered over to his daughter's hideout inside the big house, where the ladies had just finished decorating her.

While he was gone, I slipped over to Bud and Dr. Orr. "Gather your stuff so we can carry everything to the canoe without lingering. We'll give you the signal. Just keep smiling. I think our host is going to bring out the maid of honor. You'll want some pictures of her," I said.

I had no sooner gotten the words out of my mouth than the elaborately decorated girl appeared with her mother. The jungle symphony continued, but the crowd backed off, forming a semicircle, all eyes focused on the girl. Orr's 35mm camera clicked and Goodman's Bolex whirred as the girl and her mother stood in a stupor. They were fatigued and full of *paiauaru*. Their faces were sad and they were unsteady on their feet.

The girl's entire body was painted with *genipapo* (jenny-

PAH-poo) juice from a hard-shelled fruit the size of a large plum. The juice is clear when applied, but turns black as it dries. She wore a sarong and headdress made of bright red macaw feathers stuffed into a wide headband, much like North American Indians. Garlands of feathers hung around her neck. Hawk feathers, like cotton, were stuck to her skin in numerous spots. A dead toucan hung from her waist, and bracelets of feathers adorned her ankles, calves, and knees.

The final ceremony would take place the next evening, the third day of the celebration. An elderly man with two firebrands leads the way to a tree at the edge of the clearing, followed by the crowd. He hurls the burning sticks against the tree, making sparks fly, to symbolically kill the demons that seek to harm the girl. A triumphant cry echoes through the jungle now that all danger is past.

After dark, the whole crowd enters the great house to finish the ceremony. Her mother spreads a blanket in the center of the area, where the daughter is seated. The girl's paternal uncle approaches and jerks strands of hair from her head, letting out a yelp, which is echoed by the onlookers. With rapid movements, the women pluck out tufts of hair from the girl's head. They are indifferent to the girl's pain and continue jerking out her hair six or eight strands at a time.

An Indian friend responded to my stupid question if the hair pulling hurts, saying, "Yes, it does, but the girls don't always cry. Sometimes they faint."

"What do you do when they faint?" I asked.

"Rub lemon juice on head, loosen the hair," he said. Lemon juice on any sore I ever had burned like sulfuric acid.

Some say the celebrant is sexually abused after the festivity. Since the *festas* vary from one area to another, the level of the group's depravity determines if this cruel rite takes place.

We bade farewell to the host, his wife, and the others near us before stepping into our canoe. Two men who spoke Portuguese held out their hands and demanded money. We just laughed and shook their hands as though we didn't understand.

A few paddle strokes took us out of sight of the orgy. It was good to point the dugout toward home, but we didn't talk much. There was a dismal, depressed feeling among us as the beating drums and turtle shells faded away. Those people were in a sad state of spiritual, moral, and intellectual darkness. They knew nothing of the true and living God. They didn't have a written language, nor could they read or write Portuguese, the language of Brazil. The Indians gave no reason for celebrating these puberty festivities. Officially the Indians were considered minors, a nation within a nation. Knowledge of God was their only hope for the future.

Children from our Bible classes ran along the riverbank shouting, "Dona Jessie, Dona Francisca, here come the men. You can see them on the far side of the river."

This brought everybody within earshot to see what we looked like as we pulled into port. We hadn't shaved, and any exposed skin was as red as a tom turkey's neck.

Our wives looked as though they had tied for first place in the Mrs. America pageant. They smelled like a combination of Easter lilies and lilacs. That they hugged and kissed us was purely a stroke of graciousness on their parts. In a few minutes there was a lineup at the bathhouse.

. . .

The sweltering afternoon before John and I took Dr. Orr and Paul Goodman to Leticia to catch the plane to Bogotá, Dr. Orr sat in the living room holding Leanne on his lap. "Paul, I want to talk to you," he said. "I will never be the same after seeing and hearing all that took place during those few hours with the Indians."

"It was an 'eye-opener' for us, too, Dr. Orr. We had some idea of what happens at these *festas*, but seeing it firsthand was some-thing else," I told him. "I'm beginning to think the Ticuna Indian population is larger than we imagined."

Then Dr. Orr fired straight from the shoulder with a ques-tion that buffaloed me. "What are your plans for reaching these people with the gospel?"

Plans to reach these people? I thought. *Huh!* "Well, Pastor Orr, John wants to do river evangelism, so it looks like Jessie and I will be stuck here in this tumble-down village," was my scholarly response. "I figure I'll try to get this house finished as soon as possible, keep pecking away at the language, and if we can stick it out for 20 years or so and see about that number of conver-sions, we'll be glad." No one could accuse me of being a man of great vision.

"Paul, I want to remind you that we have a big and power-ful God. He can fill us with His all-prevailing, irresistible power and wisdom. You should plan now how to reach the Indians for Christ. Set goals; work hard; pray. When I go home I'm going to get the people at Hope Church to beseech God on your behalf. I'm going to ask my people to pray for *1,000 souls.* I will need to hear from you regularly so I can keep you and the work at the Port of Two Brothers before my people. We want to hear of answered prayer, because this encourages Christians who pray to pray more," Dr. Orr declared.

Jessie called from the kitchen to say supper was ready, saving me from the embarrassment of another response. I thanked Dr. Orr for his challenge. "I won't forget it," I assured him. "Both Schlener families are thankful that you came all the way down here to visit us."

Not many days after the two men returned to the United States, we received an enthusiastic letter, two typed legal-sized pages, single-spaced, from Dr. Orr. Then in a few weeks came another, then another. He kept us on the edges of our chairs as we read these inspiring letters aloud.

The morning after I returned I preached along the theme: 'Whether or not the Schleners ever amount to anything for God as missionaries will be dependent upon the degree of earnestness and the volume of prayer that ascends to heaven from this end of the line.' We wait almost breathlessly for further news of God's moving in your midst. I DO BELIEVE, BELOVED ONES, THAT YOU CAN HAVE ONE OF THE GREATEST WORKS IN MISSIONS IN A CENTURY, AS WE COOPERATE. I want you to be not only missionaries, but some of the greatest missionaries the world has produced. I want you to not only work for God, but I want you to do a work for God that will make the whole world sit up and take notice . . . why not? Is God able? Is not this His will? I am telling our people to pray for 1,000 CONVERTS and 10 CHURCHES AS OUR IMMEDIATE GOAL. We are asking God for a great harvest of souls. We, as a church, are not going to let this thing go until God bares his mighty arm in a super-abundant blessing on you, and your field.

I wondered if he failed to notice how little and miserable this village next door to us was; how backward the people were; and how they were scattered throughout the jungle. Why do pastors have to talk about big numbers? Dr. Orr continued his letter with a short message to each of us:

Paul: Set some goals that you want to accomplish. Make your plans big, remembering that you have a big God and that we at home are pledged to ask God in behalf of your plans. Plan for a big church, plan for the salvation of the entire village, start a school there in Santa Rita, small of course, endeavor to limit your medical work to certain hours. Give special attention to the 'brighter boys' who might act as your assistants. Spread out up the river some.

John: What a field is yours . . . the amazing Amazon. What a joy to look into the future and see scores, perhaps hundreds of points where there are indigenous churches . . . started by you.

Map out your work . . . make your plans big. Ask God for anything you need . . . bigger boats, more helpers, greater ability in
the language. Don't forget that we here at home will back you
in your need. We'll pray to a great heavenly Father to supply
anything you ask that is in line with His plan and glory.

Jessie and Fran: Work together, of course, but you girls have a
purpose of your own too—in the women's work. Endeavor to
teach them to help themselves. Remember that your first duty
is to your husbands, and to your dear children. But God will
help you too—we'll pray for you mightily.

I found it hard to believe that Dr. Orr was so certain we
would achieve his challenges, especially after he lived in the same
house with us for several weeks. In another paragraph, he tried
to make us understand how God could work through us.

I am sure that you know full well, that all of us—you and
I included, are only flesh, and in flesh is no good thing. Don't
misunderstand me, I think you're all great guys . . . but I'm
talking about our relative values in God's sight. It's only as we
come to God as utter nothings that He can fill us with His all-
prevailing and irresistible power and wisdom. That is what I
want to happen to you. We're going to pray that way!

The amazing thing to me was that Dr. Orr not only wrote
eloquent letters of what he thought could be accomplished—and
suggestions of how we might do it—he printed large 10 x 15-inch
prayer cards with our pictures for church members to tack up in
their homes where they would see them often. He duplicated
our prayer letters in full and handed them out with the church
bulletins. He spoke of our work during his two daily radio programs, asking Christians to pray for us. He requested meetings at
other churches in southern California—San Gabriel Union,
Calvary Baptist, Burbank, his Pomona Bible class—to show the

slides he took while visiting us. He wrote three articles about his trip to the Amazon for *Christian Life* magazine, challenging Christians to pray.

Paul Goodman also wrote encouraging letters. He sent funds to supply needs he had seen. Paul took on himself the painstaking, expensive job of making the film called "The Port of Two Brothers." That film was used of God to recruit hundreds of prayer warriors and to challenge young people to go to the mission field.

CHAPTER NINE

IN A NEWSY LETTER to Dad and Mom Schlener, Jessie wrote,

> Well, now brace yourselves. Seems like this disease of having babies is really contagious. First Fran, then Mary Rogers, and guess who has it now? That's right, yours truly! I'm sure glad the first three months are over. A couple of those weeks were when the Flodens were here and I had to cook when I didn't want to even look at food. Paul is hoping for an August William [Dad Schlener's name], but no doubt we'll have another girl. Oh well, Leanne needs a little sister with all these boys around here.

Jessie was unable to get close to the kitchen sink. She said, "My arms are getting shorter and I huff and puff during this hottest time of the year."

Not many days later, on August 31, 1953, about 26 days before the baby was due, our little family stepped into the Flodens' aluminum-covered boat with John's 25-hp outboard motor to make the 100-mile trip upriver.

I didn't realize at the time the great courage my wife had. We faced an extremely rough trip in the boat with no assurance that the once-a-week amphibious plane would fly from Leticia to Iquitos, Peru, where the closest hospital was located. We wondered how Jessie would be treated in the hospital. Was the hospital equipped to handle complications?

Forty-five miles from home, a rainsquall came up from the opposite side of the river. We raced it, keeping far enough ahead to stay dry, but the wind raised whitecaps. How could Jessie stand the bucking and pitching of the boat in her condition?

"We'd better pull over and wait this thing out," I bellowed above the roar of the engine, wind, and pounding waves.

I made a sharp turn into a protected inlet where we waited. I refueled and took a sip of coffee from the thermos. We had to make Leticia before dark, but the rough water wouldn't smooth out.

"Let's go!" Jessie said. "I can stand a little bouncing. I'll hold onto the gunnels and sit on my haunches through the rough stretches. Remember, Bud Goodman said that we should roll with the blows. We've got to get there before dark!"

"Yeah, let's go, Dad. I like the waves," four-year-old Tim Jim said.

With no other options before me, I untied the bow line and grabbed the starting cord. Once, twice, three times I yanked the cord. Figuring I'd forgotten to squeeze the primer bulb, I corrected that oversight and pulled the cord again. Nothing. I pulled it another half-dozen times and squeezed the primer until gasoline dripped from the housing—not even a sputter. Removing the engine cover, I checked the spark plugs. They were wet with gasoline, so fuel was arriving at the right place. Jerking the cord faster this time, I entertained the theory that I could generate more electricity with quicker pulls.

My shirt was plastered to my body with sweat that dripped off my chin and nose. Now I was doing the huffing and puffing.

"Sit down and rest," Jessie ordered. "You're going to have a heart attack! Both you and the motor need a break."

"Jessie, we have more than 50 miles to go. How are we going to get there if this egg beater won't start?" I groaned, discouraged and angry, wondering what the Lord had in store for us. I couldn't help thinking how we did this in the States: call a tow truck and spend the night in an air-conditioned motel.

"That's what's so nice about living downstream," she reasoned. "When you finally give up on starting the donkey, we can shove off into midstream, and we'll get home eventually." I remembered drifting downriver with the lumber raft. It traveled faster than this rig would; we'd drift for two days to get home.

"Funny thing, the engine was running fine when we stopped," I puzzled.

"What a remarkable observation: 'It was running fine when we stopped'!" Jessie chuckled, but failed to get a chuckle from me. "Isn't that true about everything that quits running?"

"I mean it was running smooth as silk, no missing, no funny noises. It's got to be something simple," I explained, trying to sound like a mechanic.

I removed the engine cover again and laid hands on everything I could see. I messed with wires, flexed hoses, felt for leaks and loose parts. It's interesting that prayers don't have to be lengthy when a person is at the end of his rope.

Lo and behold, there was a dangling wire. I don't know where it came from or where it was going, but I could see where it had been, so I put it back. With one yank, the engine started and we sped upstream.

The water was still rough, but we had wasted so much time getting the motor started we had to keep going. Jessie stayed on her haunches, tightly gripping each side of the boat to cushion herself through the roughest areas, until we arrived in Leticia.

From Leticia, the same old rickety Catalina flew us the final 350 miles to Iquitos. Leanne was afraid of the airplane, jeeps, cars, horses, and cows in the city, but Tim enjoyed every minute.

Jessie received wonderful treatment at the hospital. Her prophecy was fulfilled. Cynthia Lou was born at 11:30 p.m. on September 25, six months after her cousin Pito's birth. "She's so pink," the nurses said. Everyone raved about how cute she was. All the nurses huddled around the little tyke to check her coloring.

Jessie tried to enjoy the little tyke, but when I arrived the next day with a bouquet of flowers, she was in pain from infection. A fever of 104°, lasting two days, made her miserably ill. Our heavenly Father used a combination of penicillin, T-bone steak, and ice cream to put Jessie back on her feet.

Before we knew it we were rattling our way to the Iquitos airport, getting our passports stamped, and showing Cynthia Lou's calligraphic birth certificate. Strapped into the wicker seats of the faithful old Catalina, we watched the pontoons tuck themselves into the wing tips as we were lifted free of the river. Somehow the jungle looked a richer emerald green. The mighty river had turned into trillions of cups of coffee with cream. We were headed home with our tiny gift from God cradled in Jessie's arms.

When we eased up to the buoy at Benjamin Constant, we saw John on shore.

"Johnny on the spot again," Jessie cracked, thrilled that we could head home immediately.

John had borrowed Jack Looney's launch to take us home. It was already blowing smoke rings and sending out ripples from the throbbing single-cylinder engine. The trip in Jack's river launch was both a blessing and a curse. We were out of the rain and hot sun, and had plenty of room. But for 10 hours the one-cylinder engine made like a sledgehammer on its mountings. How it didn't loosen the caulking and start serious leaks was more than we knew. The noise from the engine was deafening. Any attempt at conversation strained blood vessels, not to mention the saliva spray on forceful pronunciation of sibilants. I felt sorry for Jack having to do river evangelism in a rig like this, but he thoroughly enjoyed it.

What a beautiful sight: the Port of Two Brothers with a crowd waiting to greet us on the high riverbank. Everyone crowded around to see *Cintia* (seen-tee-ah), and to touch her little hands.

We jumped into the work with renewed enthusiasm: Sunday

Aerial view of the Port of Two Brothers: (far right) Ticuna church and school; (middle) Brazilian school and soccer field; (extreme lower left) village of Santa Rita starts; (middle left) Paul's house with workshop/clinic/Paul's office behind; (upper left) John's house.

Left:
Pictured from left: (front row) Rena Marie, Jessie, Paul, and Cindi Schlener; (back row) Leanne and Tim

Below:
Pictured from left: David, Fran, Allene, John, and Phillip (Pito) Schlener; (standing) John Read.

The *Timoteo* under construction at the Port of Two Brothers.

Left:
Willard and Grace Stull, Iowans, with their children, Billy, Diana, Perry, and Coralie.

Below:
Drunken festivities usually ended in knife fights like the one that caused this man's wounds.

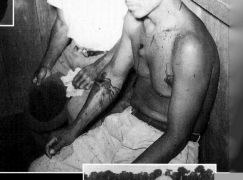

John at the helm of his speedboat.

Pets such as this armadillo, javelinas, capybaras, monkeys, macaws, and parrots came along to church.

Group of hunters showing off their kill. Andy is on the extreme left and I'm kneeling at the rear of the group.

Antelmo, teacher from the Jacurapa, who borrowed my volleyball and invited me to his school's end-of-year program.

Meeting people's physical needs on the *Timoteo* made them more willing to hear of their spiritual need.

Isabel, whose husband had an epileptic seizure while fishing and was consumed by a school

Some of the village guests had never eaten at a table before attending our banquet.

Above:
Port of Two Brothers; John's house at left, Paul's on right.

Left:
Some Brazilians paddled for four hours in a canoe like this to get to church.

services, Bible study and mid-week prayer meeting, and Thursday night doctrinal study. I started an evening literacy class for adults on our front porch by the light of a gas lantern. Medical work continued, although John and I were discouraged that we couldn't help people suffering from agonizing toothaches.

Just a couple of days after I returned from Iquitos, Gervasio called to me from the back door instead of going to the work-shop. He said, "Senhor Paulo, I can't work this morning because my wife, Maria, became sick in the night with high fever, vom-iting, dysentery, and leg cramps."

"That's too bad. Shouldn't you take her some medicine to stop the vomiting?" I asked. "Be sure and force all the liquids she can take. Sugarcane juice would be good for her," I recommended. Brazilians reason that since a person with vomiting and dysen-tery loses fluid, liquid is causing the problem. Consequently, many people die from dehydration. Gervasio took the medicine and I returned to my studies in preparation for Sunday.

At 9 a.m., Gervasio reappeared at the back door, out of breath and fighting tears. "Senhor Paulo, I don't think Maria will escape death. She can't hold the medicine down and everybody warns me not to give her anything to drink. Do you have a hot water bottle I could borrow? Her hands and feet are cold."

Gervasio paced back and forth while I filled the bottle. "Oh, God, what can I do? What can I do?" I prayed.

In silence we hiked briskly to Gervasio's house. The small room was filled with friends and relatives. Gervasio's children were crying, and the rest of the people started wailing and sob-bing as we stepped inside.

Noxious odor from a garlic and lemon liniment halted my respiratory system for a moment as I knelt under the mosquito net beside Maria. Six women inside the net watched over her, emitting fumes of sweat, wood smoke, and fermenting manioc into the already contaminated air.

I convinced Gervasio, against custom, to raise the mosquito

net so Maria could get fresh air. Her pulse was weak, her eyes
dilated. She complained that her legs hurt. Her extremities were
cold and wrinkled as though they had been soaked in water. She
asked for water, but they gave her only a spoonful at a time.
Gervasio cried out and prayed that the Lord wouldn't take
Maria; he needed her help to take care of their seven children.

I returned home to study the *Merck Manual,* and was hurrying back to the village when I met Favorita, Gervasio's oldest
daughter. She wept bitterly while she struggled to speak. "Dad
sent me to tell you that Mother is getting worse, and to ask you
to come."

I massaged Maria's hands and feet and watched her breathing
in readiness to give her artificial respiration.

"Is she gone yet, Senhor Paulo?" Gervasio asked.

"I can't say for sure, Brother Gervasio." I answered.

Maria raised her head slightly and cried, "My Jesus," then
stopped breathing. I tried artificial respiration, but she was gone.
Gervasio knelt beside her and took Maria's lifeless hand in his.
His words shocked me, "My woman, you deceived me, you lied
to me. You told me you were all right yesterday and now you
have left me with all our children. Oh, God, give her a good
place to live up there."

Gervasio was grief-stricken. He said, "Brother Paul, I know
it isn't your custom, nor is it part of our religion, but I want all
my children to come, one by one, to ask a final blessing from
their mother."

Each one, starting with Favorita, knelt down at their mother's side and said, "Bless me, Mother." After the older ones finished, Gervasio took the baby, born the same month as our
Cindi, and held him down to touch his mother's forehead.

"Brother Gervasio, how can I help you now?" I asked when
the wailing subsided.

"Several brothers from our church are here; I would like us

to sing *What A Friend We Have In Jesus,*" he said. So we did. Singing a hymn established Gervasio's testimony as a true Christian in the village.

We heard the pounding of hammers throughout the night while Maria's casket was made. The next afternoon, at the same hour Maria died, a large crowd gathered at Gervasio's house and the casket was taken to the little village cemetery. Gervasio referred to me for the first time as pastor, saying, "Pastor Paul, do you have a few words you can share with us before we lower my wife into the grave?"

I read from John 14:2-6. I assured the family and neighbors that Maria, having trusted Christ as her personal Savior, was now with the Lord and would remain with Him for eternity. Then we sang *When The Roll Is Called Up Yonder.* After prayer, we lowered the casket, and nearly everyone tossed a piece of clay into the grave.

Gervasio was ridiculed by friends and relatives for causing his wife's sudden illness and death. "How many times have we warned you about entering the religion of the foreigners? Now see what has happened! Get out of it as soon as you can, or something else will happen."

The next evening, during prayer meeting, Adenil, Gervasio's 12-year-old son prayed, "Dear Lord in heaven, take care of my little mother who is there with You now. Please give her a good place to stay." Two years later this young boy died of spinal meningitis in Benjamin Constant shortly before we left for our first furlough. Again Gervasio was persecuted.

Not long after Adenil's death, Noemia, Gervasio's six-year-old daughter, became deathly ill with infectious hepatitis and died a few days later. Soon after Noemia died, Favorita, the oldest daughter, vanished. Gervasio learned she had sneaked on a Peruvian riverboat and was living in Iquitos, Peru. She ran away because she feared the whole family would die. Narciso was a toddler when these trials visited Gervasio's family, but at the time of this writing he is the successful pastor of a church in the capital city of Manaus.

. . .

I had just flopped into the wicker rocking chair with a *Readers' Digest* to wait for the supper bell when I heard loud clapping at the front door.

"Senhor Paulo, Senhor Paulo," a man called. He was on an errand for his neighbor whose nine-month-old daughter lay dying.

"What seems to be the matter with her?" I asked. He described her symptoms as best he could, pleading with me to see the child. From his description, I figured the girl was convulsing. I grabbed an ice pack from our kerosene refrigerator, a small medical kit, and a flashlight before heading for the man's canoe. "Lord, help me!" I prayed at times like this, repeating the words over and over again.

The child rolled her eyes, gritted her teeth, and waved her little arms. We plunged her into a basin of cold water, then applied the ice pack. She stopped convulsing and went to sleep.

While I treated the child, another man came to our house, clapping loudly and calling for me in a loud voice. This type of greeting on dark, windy nights sent Jessie into a mild frenzy, especially when she was alone with the kids. The man explained that Gervasio had stiffened from head to toe, unable to speak. His family was frantic.

"Paul hasn't returned yet from seeing a sick baby. As soon as he arrives, I'll send him right over to see Gervasio," she assured the man.

After returning home and finding out the bad news about Gervasio, I ran as fast as I could in the dark to check my faithful hired man. His jaw was so stiff, I couldn't pry it open. He was breathing steadily and had a low fever from what I thought was a common cold. Not many days before, his children had watched their mother die. Now they all cried, fearful of losing their father. I rubbed him with alcohol and put a cold pack on his head. We all stood beside Gervasio's mosquito net and prayed. The children stopped crying, and I was able to console them with verses of Scripture. I feared Gervasio might have tetanus, but never did figure out what ailed him. The next morning he sat up and ate a little, and was soon back to work.

I never refused a request, day or night, to visit the sick. That people called on us was, in itself, a great victory, an indication that they were beginning to trust us. Witch doctors had been the only source of help for as long as anyone could remember.

To relate in detail all the cases of those we treated might lead one to think we offered discounts and weekend rates for guaranteed healing. We saw machete gashes, snake bites, malaria, amoebic dysentery, punctured eyeballs, amputated fingers, pink-eye, lacerations, boils, carbuncles, and open ulcers. John and I often wondered how many we helped and how many we hindered, but we were the only "port in a storm." I never dreamt I would have to make a coffin, and didn't keep track, hoping each one would be the last. Some of those we suffered with most in our attempts to keep them alive never accepted the gospel.

Not all visitors to the Port of Two Brothers came for medicine or to attend church. Our fellow missionaries upriver thoroughly enjoyed getting out of town. Our 175 x 350-yard clearing expanded as time went by. Natural grass quickly covered the grounds, keeping two men busy five days a week mowing it with hand-pushed, non-motorized machines. The place looked like a park after nearly three years, and there was ample space for volleyball, badminton, croquet, and a full-size soccer field.

CHAPTER TEN

BY NOW, BOTH SCHLENER FAMILIES hankered for furlough. The ABWE Board voted in favor of a three-year term for Central Amazon missionaries, with a list of good reasons why. That meant the Schleners' furloughs were due in August. But it was impossible to abandon the work for a whole year. One family would have to remain at the Port of Two Brothers. Which family would be unable to pack up and head for home? We all looked forward to landing amid the sparkling lights of Miami, then speeding away to an air-conditioned motel and phoning our moms and dads. We dreamed about cruising along smooth highways and feasting our eyes on the mountains, lakes, rivers, and "fruited plains."

I wanted to catch my dad by surprise in his leather shop, see him take off his apron, grab his hat, and say, "Paul, let's go to the Fountain Cafe and have a cup of coffee and a piece of pie." Mom would serve chicken and dumplings, pear supreme, and my favorite: her crab apple pickles.

Jessie had 10 brothers and sisters to get reacquainted with. Her mom was the main chef in the Fountain Cafe, where Jessie had worked as a waitress. And Jessie could surprise her by arriving unannounced, as she flipped hamburgers and T-bones in the kitchen. Doris, Jessie's oldest sister and head waitress, would dart from one booth to another, laden with plates.

I think Jessie anticipated invading the department stores. The grandparents had to see their wild Amazonian grandchildren, and we wanted the kids to become acquainted with their grandmas and grandpas.

John and Fran had these same dreams. So which family had

to wait a whole year, sweating it out, and counting the days? The Lord knew exactly the kind of spoiled brats He had muddling around in the Amazonian jungle, so He reached down to a fine Brazilian couple from the city, newly out of seminary: Otacio and Itamar de Figueredo.

We met Otacio for the first time when he came from Manaus to help John and Fran with the Christmas program in 1951. The distinguished couple was totally dedicated to serving the Lord. Otacio was a handsome man whose age we never knew; I guessed he was a little younger than John, and a little older than I. He was a gifted preacher with a strong, clear voice. He always carried a briefcase and a long black umbrella. Handy for frequent rain squalls, it was also a formidable weapon against the snarling mongrels in town.

Otacio dressed in tailored linen suits, and could have passed for a senator from the Federal District. The Figueredos were from the city, not used to jungle life or lack of transportation and communication. Otacio didn't know how to shoot a gun or light a Coleman lantern. He was fortunate to have singed only one of his eyebrows, eyelashes, and a few strands of lacquered hair when he opened the valve on the gas lantern *before* holding a lighted match to it. Later, he accidentally shot a hole in the aluminum roof with the double-barreled 12-gauge we left for him to kill snakes.

Itamar had a pleasing personality and dainty features. Her father was proprietor of a shoe factory in Manaus. She was a happy lady, almost skinny, and stood eye-to-eye with Jessie. Itamar was quick to laugh. I think her favorite entertainment was listening to Americans' accents. We told her to go ahead and laugh, but her reaction challenged us to improve.

One field council edict that didn't sit well was that this lovely couple was not permitted to live in either of our houses while we Schleners furloughed in the United States. "We mustn't spoil our Brazilian fellow workers," was the consensus.

Long ago, one field council member had suggested John and I build a small dwelling like a bachelor's apartment where missionaries from Benjamin Constant and Leticia could rest. It would be equipped with a simple kerosene stove, table and chairs, beds, and a large aluminum basin for washing dishes. The outhouse would be a 30-yard hike, no great distance unless you are stricken with diarrhea. Neither Jessie nor I remember any missionaries staying in the little boatel. When visitors came, it was just for a short time, and they preferred to stay in our homes.

But that small apartment turned out to be providential for Otacio and Itamar. We informed our fellow missionaries that Otacio and Itamar would occupy the place while they assumed responsibility for the work at the Port of Two Brothers.

Oh, that first furlough! How great it was after three years and two months in the jungle; the closest we'd come to a vacation in all that time was the trip to Iquitos, Peru, when Cindi was born. John and Fran made that same trip when Pito was born. But, those weren't relaxing experiences for Jessie and Fran, nor did we gain relief from the oppressive Amazonian heat.

Hard as it was to bid farewell to our little congregation, we were confident that we left the work in good hands. The folks would hear excellent Portuguese from Pastor Otacio and his wife, Itamar, although they would miss Fran's accordion music.

Not long before our departure, Gervasio asked me, "Senhor Paulo, is the Amazon River as wide in your country as it is here? Can you make it all the way home by the same river?" With a stick I quickly drew a map of the Western Hemisphere in the soft clay and gave him a five-minute geography lesson. After I explained about the ocean and big airplanes, Gervasio wondered how we could get along without a big stream of water flowing past our village. Right then I felt the Lord's leading to start a primary school.

Strapped to the wicker seats of the same old Catalina, all of us Schleners flew to Iquitos, wondering what it would be like to see our parents again. What would they say about their grand-children? We looked forward to sitting in church, listening to the choir sing, and hearing the pastor preach where everyone had Bibles and could follow along.

A red-eye flight on a DC-4 took us from Lima, Peru, into Miami. We bumped heads, crowding the small windows as we descended to the Miami airport. We figured on another stone-faced customs officer, but, no, he didn't even look inside our moldy baggage.

The 1953 taxi that whisked us up a ramp and onto the free-way toward our motel was as smooth and quiet as a pocketful of jello. Our motel had an all-night restaurant that we planned to visit. But first we checked out our rooms. The TV was showing a Western in which two men were involved in a knock-down, drag-out fight. The loser was just about to be pushed over a cliff when four-year-old Leanne screamed at the top of her voice, "Daddy, stop him! Stop him!" We immediately turned off the TV and went to the restaurant.

After hot water showers and a breakfast of luscious Florida orange juice, ham, and eggs, we were off to the airport again. Our Delta flight to Los Angeles gave us a two-hour layover at Dallas, so we hit another restaurant. We never tired of frequenting restaurants, church potlucks, and savory meals in hospitable homes. For lack of self-control at these places, we were forced to use the rest of the holes in our belts and buy new clothes.

It was great to see Paul and Allene Goodman and their fam-ily upon arrival in Los Angeles. Goodman had purchased two used 1950 Dodges—one for each Schlener family. Allene didn't want our wives to look like they had dressed out of a missionary barrel, so she took Jessie and Fran shopping.

During our short stay in southern California, we enjoyed the fellowship at Hope Union Church, drinking in Dr. Orr's mes-sages, showing our slides, and renewing acquaintances with the friends who gave us our great send-off in 1951. We watched Paul

Goodman and Virgil Wemer, a victim of the Bataan Peninsula death march, chop up the footage from the Indian *festa* and paste it back together. At the same time, John answered questions from Leo Rosencrans, scriptwriter for "The Port of Two Brothers" film.

On Highway 99, fresh air and lush fields of fruits and vegetables assured us we were in the land of plenty. The awesome sight of Mount Shasta left the kids speechless. More mountain passes, lakes, and streams filled the countryside with continuous demonstrations of the wonders of God's creation.

At the junction where Highway 97 split off 99, the Schleners separated. John's tribe headed for Bremerton, where Fran's parents, Martin and Mary Read, lived. And my tribe zig-zagged our way to Bonners Ferry. Before we knew it, we were pulling into the driveway of the little Schlener home on the corner of Cody and Buchanan in Bonners Ferry, Idaho.

. . .

My boyhood home was still painted white with green shutters. Wrinkled tomatoes clung to dying vines. Flowers hung their heads, lifeless from Jack Frost's fatal bite. Smoke puffed out the chimney, signalling Mom must be home. We piled out of the car as though it were on fire and raced to the front door. Mom opened the door in her soiled apron, a smudge of flour on one cheek.

"Gracious sakes alive, Paulie Lou, how good it is to see you! Oh, Jessie, how lovely you look," she said making the rounds to hug all of us. "Mercy! You've caught me in such a mess! I thought I would be able to tidy up before you arrived," she lamented.

The appetizing aroma of apple pies baking in the old woodburning oven, and freshly baked bread overwhelmed our olfactory systems, which in turn opened our salivary glands. The golden loaves of bread were sitting crosswise on top of the bread pans, cooling. I lopped off a heel, sopped it with butter and apricot jam, and wolfed it down just like I did when I was a boy.

"Mom, this is the kind of mess we like to drop into. We have been waiting to see and smell and taste a mess like this for more than three years," I said, hugging her again. "We'll run down and see Pappy, then peek into the Fountain Cafe to see if Jessie's mom is on duty. And finally over to the north side of town to see Dad MacDonald," I outlined our immediate itinerary.

From the front door of the Fountain Cafe to the kitchen was only 40 feet. Mom MacDonald, visible through the narrow opening, flipped hamburgers, scooped mashed potatoes, and stirred gravy over a hot grill. Food orders steamed on the shelf of the see-through opening, waiting to be snatched by waitresses. Jessie's older sister, Doris, was head waitress. Neither Jessie's mother, Doris, nor Jessie, were soft spoken. So there was a brief, explosive greeting in Bonners Ferry's favorite greasy spoon as Doris continued her flight from kitchen to booths.

Mom Mac was barely five feet tall and getting shorter, so her chin wasn't too high above the grill. She beamed as we made our way back to the kitchen. It was noon, not the ideal time for visiting a restaurant cook.

"Hi, Jess and Paul. Gosh, it's so good to see you. You've been gone such a long time," she said, glancing at each of us as she had opportunity while flipping, stirring, and mashing.

She took one look at Tim and commented, "There's a guy that's got a lot of MacDonald in him. Doris and I helped August move some things from his secondhand store into your rented house. It should be ready for you to move right in. I get off at five and we'll see you over there," Mom Mac said as she slid a couple of steaming plates onto the counter.

Just then, the massive bulk of Harley, proprietor of the Fountain Cafe, stepped out of his office and engulfed Jessie in a hug. Her former boss, more than six feet tall and bountifully padded with several hundred pounds, clutched a quart container of chocolate milkshake, leaving his right hand free to help slam things around in the kitchen. The very sight of him did away with the need for a bouncer.

"Well, how's little Mac? Long time no see," he thundered. "You comin' back to work fer us again? Those Greyhound bus drivers still come in here and wonder what happened to you." Jessie had worked there as a waitress during her high school years.

"It was great working here, Harley, but take a look at my new bosses," she said, pointing to our three kids—and me.

Stepping into Dad Schlener's shop, a combination leather shop and secondhand store, found Dad bent over his finishing machine, smoothing the edges of rubber heels on a pair of shoes. The old familiar odor of the leather shop brought back pleasant memories of when I had helped Dad during high school days and after being discharged from the Navy.

He looked up as we entered the shop, turned off the machine and quickly bowlegged his way toward us saying, "Well, I'll be dad-gummed. Who in tarnation do we have here?" Pappy always thought he had halitosis from smoking an occasional cigar, so he talked out of the side of his mouth and never hugged us close for fear of giving off an offensive odor. "*Pauel,* you're looking good, maybe a little skinny," Dad Schlener greeted me with what I guessed to be the German pronunciation for Paul. "Jessie, just look at you! How did you stay so nice looking? And if these ain't the cutest little whippersnappers I've ever seen!" he exclaimed, sizing up the three kids. Their facial expressions showed that they liked Grandpa.

Dad reached for his hat. "C'mon, let's go have some pie and coffee. I betcha the kids could down some ice cream cones in a hurry. Old Hawk-eye Prell's Ice Cream Bar is still running." Dad liked to show us off to anybody and everybody.

"Dad, we should run over and see Dad Mac first. We'll be back," I promised.

We drove too fast across the Kootenai River bridge to get to the north side of town. It was fall and the river was at its lowest level. The leaves of the aspens and birch, and the needles of the tamaracks, had turned to gold and were falling.

We pulled into the MacDonald driveway. Neatly stacked cordwood promised warmth for the cold winter months. A slow tendril of smoke from the chimney assured us the temperature was comfortable inside. The kids stumbled along, trying to see everything at once, wondering what their other grandpa would be like.

Dad MacDonald was soft spoken, not easily excited. He had been a hard worker whose vigorous health was broken from what was called double pneumonia before the days of antibiotics. It was discouraging to him and to Mom Mac that he never regained complete health after his scrape with death.

We followed Jessie through the short entryway, past the wood box filled with buckskin tamarack, and stopped in the kitchen doorway. There he was, Donald James MacDonald, homesteader, teamster, mechanic, carpenter, cook—Jessie's dad—sitting by the chimney close to the kitchen stove.

He had sprinkled smoking tobacco onto the little paper held between his fingers. The tobacco came in a thin red tin can with a hinged top. He returned the little tobacco can to his private cubbyhole at the base of the chimney as we stepped into the kitchen. He quickly spread the shreds of Velvet the length of the tiny paper, rolled it into a three-eighths-inch-thick stick, twisted the tip to a point with expertise, and laid the hand-rolled cigarette on the edge of the kitchen range.

"Well, ya' decided to come back, did yuz?" he said, a hint of a smile on his face. "C'mon over here and let me take a look at yuz," he said looking at Tim and Leanne. They stood in front of him, eyes fixed on his face. He patted them on the head and took hold of their shoulders, giving them a gentle shake. "You kids ought to turn out all right with that mixture of MacDonald and

Schlener blood," he said.

"You're the last one on our route before we check out the house Aug Schlener rented for us. We might as well have a cup of that coffee that's glugging through the percolator," Jessie said as she sat down at the big oak kitchen table.

"Ya bet your curly head, lass. Yuz came just in time and she's ready, b'golly," he said with a brogue that I assume was a mixture of Scottish, Irish, and Canadian. He stood up and pulled the coffee pot to the cooler side of the old range.

The coffee mugs were those white moonstone glass ones, all clean, upside down on the drainboard of the sink. A dozen teaspoons protruded from a mug on the table alongside the sugar bowl. Coffee never had to be offered, you just helped yourself.

Dad MacDonald set his cup carefully on the iron stove to retrieve his homemade cigarette. He lifted his right knee, dragged a big wooden match along his thigh and it burst into a flame that he touched to the pointed tip of his cigarette, sending up a cloud of smoke. Tim and Leanne watched in wonder at the miraculous match.

. . .

The year went by lickety-split. Dental work, physical exams, round-robin missionary conferences, sleeping in different beds night after night, and meeting with the ABWE Board gobbled up the time in a hurry. My itinerary took me all over the states of California, Nevada, Washington, Idaho, Montana, as well as to Kansas, Pennsylvania, and Boston. Our children were so young it was impossible for Jessie to travel with me on all these trips which totalled more than 49,000 miles.

John and Fran lived in Bremerton and kept a separate schedule from ours, with the exception of John's and my trip from Bonners Ferry to Philadelphia to meet with the ABWE Board. From Idaho to Pennsylvania was quite a jaunt by car. At that time some Christians considered it extravagant for missionaries to fly, so we two flew in a brand new 1955 Custom Ford, loaned to us by a schoolmate from Biola days.

Before leaving for mission headquarters, John and I bought new Stetsons, suits, and ties. "Maybe these Western duds will distract the mission authorities enough so they won't crack down too hard on us for our first-term fizzles," I told John as we dressed for our meeting.

Anxiety to return to the jungle set in. The final letter to our mailing list was in the form of a Western Union Telegram, letting the recipients know how far we had travelled during the year, and that we were making final preparations to return.

Other passengers at LA International Airport might have thought we were celebrities, for a sizable crowd of friends from Hope Union Church gathered to see us off. They loaded us down with so many presents that we were buried in our seats until the stewardesses relieved us of most of them so we could fasten our safety belts.

At the morning farewell service for us at Hope Union Church, Dr. Orr's message, titled "Our Message to Paul and Jessie: Six things I want to say," included these words:

1. Paul and Jessie, you are saved people. You belong to Christ who died for you. Down deep in your hearts you know it. Your life is not to be lived in what you want to do. Your purchase price is the Son of God. You must have said, 'not my will but thine be done.'

2. You have been called of God to a special work. It makes a difference to understand who calls you. John 15:16, 'You have not chosen me, but I have chosen you, and ordained you, that you should go and bring forth fruit, and that your fruit should remain; that whatsoever you shall ask of the Father in my name, he may give it to you.' You have been called by a Great God into a Great Ministry. Christ said, 'You have not chosen me.' He has placed His hand on you.

If you can feel that this morning, you are feeling the great scar on His hand.

3. Paul and Jessie, you are in the greatest work in the world, barring none. Tonight you will pass over the works of man's hands, homes, streets, factories. It takes a lot of brains to do these things. Tomorrow morning men will be going to their places of work, but does anyone doubt today that what Paul and Jessie have entered into is the greatest job in the world? Is it the greatest thing in the world, or not? Leading a soul to Christ is the greatest work—there is no other greater.

4. There are and there will continue to be many adversaries. Beside you stands a super-person. He hates you. I am talking about the devil. He will do everything in his power to entangle you. The devil will come up on your blind side. Bear in mind that the Lord has warned us that 'We wrestle not against flesh and blood, but against principalities, against powers, against the rulers of the darkness of this world, against spiritual wickedness in high places.'

5. But God has a method to overcome his enemy. The Scriptures are our recourse. 'Ask and you shall receive, knock and it shall be opened unto you. If you ask anything in my name, I will do it. Be anxious for nothing, but in everything, by prayer and supplication, with thanksgiving, let your requests be known unto God. And the peace of God, which passes all understanding, shall keep your hearts and minds through Christ Jesus.' The Word is full of encouragement that God is on your side and that we are on God's side. Someone infinitely wonderful, The Lord Jesus Christ is your Captain. His plan is VICTORY. A cloud is resting over your field of service. But you have a God before whom all the forces of evil must flee. God has never lost a battle. Make your plans big. A school shortly, a Bible institute, why not? Is God in this thing or not? Let's have a big work for God at the Port of Two Brothers.

6. We will stand with you. The people of God in this congregation are your friends. We are here today because we
love the Lord. Everyone of us, Paul and Jessie, has a private
line to the God of the universe. We will stand with you in
this work. We will talk to the Lord constantly about you
and we will bring down on your heads the power of God.
As God is our witness, we promise that we will ring in on
that heavenly telephone line and reverently, vigorously
assail heaven on your behalf. Because you are our representatives and we are in this work together, we will be
joined at the throne of Grace to pray down God's blessing
on you and your work. This is what we want to do.

What an encouraging farewell as we headed back to
Amazonas for our second term at the Port of Two Brothers! Dr.
Orr's challenges and promises stayed with us throughout our
entire missionary career.

. . .

October came—too soon. Aspens and tamaracks had spread
a blanket of yellow leaves and needles beneath themselves, as
though to keep the grass warm until spring. Cordwood stood
neatly stacked for winter, just like last year. A tendril of smoke
from the chimney was scattered by a chilly breeze, but promised
warmth and coziness inside the little house. Jessie and I said
nothing; the kids were unusually quiet. This was the first stop on
our good-bye route before heading out of town for another four
years.

Jessie stuck her head in the doorway. "Anybody home?" she
called.

A crackling cough broke the silence and then, "Ya bet yer
boots there is. C'mon in." Dad MacDonald sat in the same old
chair by the chimney, close to the kitchen stove. A meatloaf
baked in the oven. Coffee gurgled in the percolator, and a cloud

of tobacco smoke hung above Grandpa Mac's head. The rich aroma from the combination of these three made us want to stay.

We grabbed mugs and spoons and helped ourselves to the fresh coffee as we had done often during the past year. Our intimacy had been renewed during the year in the States and saying good-bye with little hope of seeing our parents for four years wasn't easy.

We did our best to hide our depression as we hugged Dad and Mom Mac and choked out some last words to my dad in the secondhand store. "August, thanks for all the furniture you loaned us. What would we have done without you and your store?" Jessie said as she hugged him.

"I'm glad I had what you needed. If you could stay, I'd make the stuff a gift to you," he said.

We tried to veil our gloom when we pulled into the Schlener driveway and took a last gander at the little white house with its green shutters. As I walked toward the front door, I glanced at the white railing around the porch above the sun room. When I was a boy, I used to go through the hinged window in my attic bedroom onto that cute roof/porch and fire my single-shot .22 at anything that moved.

"Oh, how I have dreaded this moment," Mom said. "We'll miss you so much."

She did an about-face, went to the kitchen, and returned with a cardboard box. "Here's a lunch to eat along the way."

I said, "Thanks for everything, Mom." Then I couldn't talk any more. Mom took a little hankie from her apron to dry her tears. I was 29 years old, and that was the first time I had seen my mom cry. She stood on the front porch waving at us until we went out of sight down Highway 95.

PART FOUR

GETTING DOWN TO BUSINESS

(1955–1959)

CHAPTER ELEVEN

WHEN THE HATCH of Avianca's old DC-4 lifted at the Leticia airport and we started down the shaky ladder, the heat hit Jessie and me like a ton of bricks. The only coolness was in our reception from federal police and customs officials as they rummaged through our bags.

I'm sure Jessie was more courageous than I in accepting the vast change of leaving the United States and returning to the jungle. Her million-dollar smile made it hard for disgruntled inspectors to maintain their stern visage. I had to keep reminding myself that these people didn't invite us to live in their country; in fact, they might resent our coming.

Looking back and remembering how we felt, Jessie and I understand why the incidents of first-term missionary dropouts occur. Some would rather resign than separate from loved ones and experience another stretch of difficult circumstances. They reason that the world is full of sinners in places where conditions are more agreeable: places with proper housing, good food, medical attention, and schooling for the children. Why subject the children to all the bugs, snakes, and diseases? The struggle to maintain fellowship with sometimes unpleasant colleagues and the lack of communication with the outside world cause some dropouts to wonder if the few positive results for all the work is worthwhile.

But we learn that, no matter where we are, circumstances are never ideal when it comes to serving the Lord, whether in the depths of a steamy jungle or in the hubbub of a big city. The ministry of the gospel never offers fields of service where everything is perfect. But there is great fulfillment and satisfaction from being in the center of God's will, no matter what the situation.

Jessie and the kids and I were glad to pull into the Port of Two Brothers after 13 hours of shimmying and shaking from the engine in Jack Looney's launch. The kids were tired and a little sick from the long trip, sudden change of climate, and different food along the way. But they were tough.

By 5 p.m. the place was covered with Indians. This caused concern among the villagers because of recent Indian attacks upriver. Jessie and I shook hands all around like we were on a political campaign. Pastor Otacio gathered everyone to start the program. A banner stretched between two poles said, "WELLKOME AT YOUR BRAZILIAN HOME." (Mr. Backsman had helped with the spelling.) The kids' Bible class recited poems and Bible verses, and sang hymns. Jessie and I gave a few words of thanks and greeting, then we all drank coffee.

The very next morning Otacio and Itamar left to pastor the church in Benjamin Constant. John and Fran didn't plan to return for three more months. The lack of fellowship for Jessie and me created intense loneliness; we were anxious for a letter from anyone in the States.

A telegram from Willard Stull in December revived us. Our shipment had arrived in Manaus, 1,000 miles closer to us than Belém, at the mouth of the river. He needed power of attorney and keys to the locks on the steel barrels to clear our shipment through customs. Then he would load the stuff on a riverboat, to be dropped off at the Port of Two Brothers.

I flipped old Leaky—our new name for the old boat—over and gave it a quick patch job with jungle tar to make it at least appear seaworthy. I knew the extremely brittle tar wouldn't last long in rough water. But the water was like glass for the whole eight hours to Benjamin Constant. After lunch with Pastor Otacio and Itamar, I secured a power of attorney and mailed it to Willard. I included a note asking him to have a strong dock-worker break the barrel locks and replace them with new ones after inspection, since there was no way a dozen keys would make it through the mail.

I got a late start heading home. I should have spent the night in Benjamin Constant, but Jack was gone and I lacked the courage to inconvenience Pastor Otacio's family. Several rain squalls threatened, but not a drop of rain touched me until about 5:30 p.m.

The first gusts of wind pelted me with giant raindrops for a little taste of what was coming. I headed straight into the squall, but a blast of wind twisted me around so that I headed toward an Indian hut. A second before Leaky touched clay, I flew off the bow and pulled the boat as far up on land as I could, certain my tar repairs were already damaged.

Having left town with no food—a sign of intellectual prowess—I bought a papaya and some bananas from the Indian. I didn't feel like staying, storm or no, because there was a corpse lying on the table, awaiting burial.

Traveling close to shore in my boat, I was drenched to the skin by driving rain within seconds. I pounded the waves, hoping to reach the windward side of the river. But it was at least a mile across the channel, and the tiny 10-hp was no match for the treacherous combination of wind, waves, and rain. I had drifted a good distance before I was forced to the edge of a vast area of floating grass. I grabbed a handful and held on while I bailed water. To release my grip for a quick rest gave the wind and waves free reign to blast me further into the endless tangle of wiry grass.

I was reminded of the three typhoons I survived aboard the baby flattop, U.S.S. *Cape Esperance,* during the Philippine liberation campaign in WWII. The second typhoon, with 135 knots of wind, sent me to my knees, pleading for God's mercy. Three destroyers sank in that violent storm. The *Esperance* trembled and stretched as 80 planes were ripped from their steel cable lashings, tearing loose the catwalks as if they were cardboard, and tumbled into the ocean.

The reality of human weakness is fearfully apparent in a storm, whether in the air, on water, or on land. I thought about the letters John and Fran wrote to me after I enlisted in the Navy at the age of 17. They prayed that I would become a Christian and enjoy the new life in Jesus Christ that the Bible promises. After that memorable typhoon, the *Cape Esperance* pulled into Mare Island for repairs.

John was recuperating from a shrapnel wound he received as a farewell gift from the Germans. We made arrangements to meet in San Francisco and have dinner together on Sunday evening, June 17, 1945. John and Fran asked if I would attend church with them. They had me nailed down at a time when I was really afraid to go out to sea again.

The pastor of the little church we attended that night asked if any sailors wanted to have their sins forgiven and be saved for eternity. That sounded good to me, so when he invited those who were interested to come forward, I was the first one down front. And I didn't just stand there. I dropped to my knees. Later I found out that a person can be saved without going in front of a church or dropping down on his knees. Simple faith and trust in the Lord Jesus Christ and accepting Him as Savior are all it takes to be saved for eternity.

Now, years later in the teeth of a squall on the Amazon, I tired of maintaining a grip on the tall grass and bailing water for an hour. The brittle tar was cracking and darkness was falling. One reason God created areas like this was to provide spawning facilities for animals with big teeth. *Oh well, if I can't keep ahead of everything and sink, I'll hang on to the partly submerged boat and keep afloat,* I thought aloud. *When I can't hang on any longer and drink more water than is healthy, I'll drown. Somebody might see the remains of this tub as it drifts by the Port of Two Brothers and figure out what happened.*

Our new boat was on its way from the United States, but that was no help to me now. Instead of being thankful, I coveted all the fancy boats with lights and automatic bailers, parked in thousands of driveways in the States. And here I was in the most important, rewarding business in God's world, riding in a dilapidated, decomposing 12-foot wooden wreck powered by a 10-hp outboard motor. Daylight faded as I rode out the waves. But that last stretch of river was so familiar I could probably make it blindfolded—except for floating logs.

Storms always pass, and this one finally did after two hours. Frogs and toads were tuning up for the evening concert when I headed for midstream. There was just enough light to see how God had protected me during the storm. Had I traveled another 200 yards, I would have dashed against hard clay. I realized how much better it was to ride out the storm against flexible, cushiony grass, even while being eaten by mosquitoes.

Now it was dark: not one twinkling star in sight. Flashes of lightning, as though apologizing for the storm that hit me, helped me see enough to avoid hitting debris. Giant snags loomed up in those split seconds of light like so many monsters waiting to grab me.

Placing my left hand on the rattletrap top, I stood on my left foot, set my right foot on the engine handle to steer, and bent over to bail with my right hand—hour after hour.

Three hours passed without seeing a light. Fatigue and hunger made me think of Jessie and the kids eating supper, then holding family devotions by the light of a hissing gas lantern or candles. Jessie was always a little skittish about lighting those pesky lanterns. The rule is: always light the match *first* and hold it close to the mantle *before* opening the valve—or else. Jessie and the kids would be praying for me about now. We were never immune from concern when someone failed to show up as planned from these supply and mail trips.

I prayed for a light to shine along the shore to get my bearings. Just then, I bumped into a sandbar. Colliding with a sandbar isn't dangerous in a small, slow boat; in fact, it was nice to know the water wasn't very deep. I jumped into the ankle-deep water and shoved the boat until the water was thigh-high. Back in old Leaky, I bailed water, straining to see the horizon, hoping for at least one star to break through the clouds.

I thought I was close to a long row of houses, called Acaratuba (Ah–cah–rah–TOO–bah). Suddenly I saw a flashlight to my right on the shore and headed straight for it. "Thanks, Lord," I prayed, keeping my eyes glued to the light. About 30 yards from a man in a canoe, I cut my engine.

"Good evening, friend," I called.

He extinguished his flashlight. I could see there were no houses nearby, so I asked him, "How far am I from Acaratuba?"

"Oh, it's downstream a piece," he answered. I had learned that some of the "pieces" turned out to be large-sized. At least I knew I hadn't drifted past the place.

"What are you looking for? Did you lose something?" I asked.

"No," he responded, "I'm looking for crocodiles to harpoon." He snapped his flashlight on again to continue his search for the red eyes of a crocodile, something I wanted nothing to do with at the moment.

I wished him luck, yanked the starting cord and headed back to midstream with my foot on the motor handle, holding on to the top of my boat while I bailed water back into the river.

Two hours went by. It seemed like a week. *Well, Lord, what else do you have in store for me?* I continued to consult the Navigator who planned this excursion "before the foundation of the world." I didn't realize how close I was to shore until I saw a dim light zig-zagging down the slippery bank. A man holding a flashlight shouted, "Pull in right over here."

The man said, "I know who you are, Senhor Paulo. We have heard a lot about you and your brother. Come up to the house." I could have hugged and kissed him. Early in our experience we learned that Brazilians, almost without exception, are the last word in hospitality, no matter what their condition.

Everybody in the house was up and still dressed at 2:30 a.m. A half-dozen men sat on benches, dressed in soiled and ragged clothing, and giving off a potent odor from a combination of tobacco, wood smoke, and perspiration. I was in as uncomely a state as they, with wet shoes, socks, and trousers. A flickering fire danced on the clay kitchen stove.

"How about something to eat, Senhor Paulo?" my host asked. I was so hungry I could have eaten raw dog meat.

"Thank you, Senhor Marino. I appreciate your offer, but I won't eat anything now. If I can just sit here on this bench until it's light enough to travel, I will be grateful." Refusing food made me wonder if I had slipped a mental cog.

"We pulled into port just about an hour before you did," one of the men said. "Five of us have been up the Eetoowee River, extracting and smoking latex. We just finished eating when you pulled in. I wish we could serve you a *cafezinho,* but we are completely out of sugar."

I sat down and gave my audience a blow-by-blow, leak-by-leak, and bail-by-bail account of the past 12 hours. "Senhor Paulo, you must be about done in," Marino said. "Please excuse our soiled bedding—it hasn't been washed since we left home more than a month ago—but you're welcome to crawl into the hammock and get some sleep before you travel on."

"Oh, Senhor Marino, no thank you. I'll be fine stretched out on one of these benches." But they insisted I get into the net to rest. Refusing their generosity would have hurt their feelings. So I pulled off my wet shoes and socks to reveal two pitifully pale, wrinkled feet with sand between the toes. I thought of the verse in Romans about how beautiful are the feet of those who preach the gospel of peace and bring glad tidings of good news. My feet didn't qualify as beautiful, but I crawled into the foul-smelling mosquito net where it was dark enough that my host couldn't see me pull up my shirt collar to lie between my head and the reeking hammock.

I was unconscious for a couple of hours and woke with a start, swinging my feet over the edge of the hammock and nearly stepping on a man who had crept into the mosquito net some time during the night.

"*Bom dia,* Meesteh Paulo," Senhor Marino greeted me as I climbed out of the mosquito net. The poor guy had been lying on a bench, waiting his turn in the hammock. "May we serve you a cup of *cafe-com-leite?*"

I accepted the offer of coffee, pulled on my wet shoes, tucked in my shirt, and combed my hair.

Marino nodded to his wife, who shoved the battered coffee pot into hot coals to reheat. Grabbing a cup, she "cleaned" it with her skirt where the diaperless baby had just been enjoying a kicking good time. Fresh milk is rare along the river, so sweetened condensed milk is used to flavor and sweeten *cafe-com-leite,* seldom served at any time other than breakfast. By the time she opened the can of milk with an 18-inch machete, the coffee was hot. Coffee with condensed milk, to a person on the verge of starvation, is like manna from heaven. She handed me a donut-shaped piece of hard, dried bread called *rosca.* I was as thankful as though I had been served a full-course meal of pancakes, eggs, and bacon.

"Please spend a Sunday in the village and take in the church services," I invited the group.

"We'll do that, Meesteh Paulo. We know several of the folks there who have entered your religion," Marino said.

"How much do I owe for your hospitality?"

"*Nada, nada,* Senhor Paulo. You have done so many favors for our people, we are glad for the opportunity to serve you." Marino's generosity and friendliness were typical of the poor people who lived along the Amazon.

In a little less than an hour, as the warm sun bisected the horizon, I plodded up the riverbank to my house. I tapped on the wall by my bedroom window, immediately wishing I hadn't, thinking of the double-barreled 12-gauge just inside the closet door. Jessie appeared in the window, caught a glimpse of my grotesque figure and flew to unlock the front door. She was quick to release me after a brief hug and kiss; I smelled like the mosquito net, the mat flooring under the net, and the men in Marino's home.

By the time I shaved, took a prolonged rainwater shower with fragrant soap, and donned clean clothes, Jessie had mixed a batch of pancakes. In seconds I had a stack soaked with Australian butter and floating in maple syrup—a little taste of heaven on earth.

Next Sunday morning, I preached on "Christ, the Light of the World." Guess what stories I used as illustrations.

· · ·

"Senhor Paulo, there's a boat coming around the bend of the river," Gervasio hollered to me. He shaded his eyes and pointed with all five fingers in the Brazilian custom. High-rpm outboard motors were scarce, so we all tried to guess who was arriving. From quite a distance we could identify a baseball cap with a bright red face under it. It looked like a masked bandit, for his face was covered by the bandanna. As it came closer we recognized the boat, then the people: Orv, Helen, and Liz Floden. Were they bringing a telegram with bad news from home?

After we had sat around the table drinking coffee and eating fresh cinnamon rolls, Orville handed me a telegram. Since he waited so long to give us the telegram, I was sure it was bad news. Instead, it was good news from Willard Stull: our equipment had arrived in Manaus. We howled with joy before I read the rest, which stated that customs charges were 120,000 cruzeiros (U.S. $2,000). Oh, well, there's almost always a little bitter with the sweet, Jessie and I concluded, but that amount of the bitter we didn't have.

Fran interrupted the chatter to read aloud a portion of a letter from Mary Rogers. Mary wrote, "Wasn't it wonderful the way
the Lord undertook regarding your baggage? It would have been
awful to pay that price."

"I wonder what she meant by that?" I asked, hoping for good
news. Then Orville, a prankster from way back, pulled a second
telegram from his pocket. I nearly tore it to bits getting it out of
the envelope.

The second telegram from Willard said, "Talked customs
down to 60,000. Baggage loaded on river ship *Augusto Montenegro* leaving for upriver soon." This was one of the times it was
easy to forget about the intense heat, mud, and doing without
modern conveniences.

· · ·

"Whaaaw! Whaaaw! Whaaaw!" Three startling blasts from
the ship *Augusto Montenegro* pierced the silence at 5:30 a.m. on
April 17, 1956. The powerful whistle brought the whole village
to the edge of the river to see the largest vessel that had ever
pulled into port. Our spirits soared with ecstasy as she stalled
midstream to unload our 11 steel barrels and boat.

In less than 15 minutes our stuff was stacked on the lawn.
The villagers gathered around to feel the steel barrels and test
their heaviness. They laughed at everything. John and I were poor
examples of sobriety because we joined them in making fun.

The brand new outboard motor lay face-down in water
along with a submerged dinette set. My spirits fell when I saw
water gush over the transom of the brand new boat as it was
hoisted from the ship. I knew what had happened. For five
months our stuff sat out on the dock at Belém. A few rainstorms
filled the boat with water, submerging everything inside. The hull
had stayed full to the top of the transom, where it overflowed
during subsequent rainfalls. Why hadn't the manufacturers pulled

the boat's drain plug before shipment?

The new chrome dinette set had padded seats and backs which never completely dried and began to develop a foul odor; Jessie did an excellent job re-covering them. We cleaned up the rusted bench saw before installing a Briggs & Stratton gasoline engine on it, since we didn't have the electricity needed to run a regular motor. How wonderful it was to be able to rip 13-foot-long 1 x 10's with that noisy rig instead of using a hand ripsaw, which we had done for five years.

The new Johnson outboard had to be disassembled and completely dried out. I whistled while I worked on it, just glad to finally have it. The controls worked fine when dried and greased. The plywood cabin and door had been removed and nested into the hull for shipping, which meant they got soaked and warped. So I installed them while they were still wet and pliable. After a thorough cleaning, drying, and some coats of paint and varnish, she looked like a boat show exhibit.

Four of us climbed into the new boat for a test run. This cabin cruiser was simply constructed with two pieces of molded marine plywood. The only seams were on either side of the keel and around the transom. It was by no means deluxe, but to us it was better than a top-of-the-line Chris Craft. It was ambulance, pleasure craft, rescue boat, and fishing boat all in one.

I glanced at old Leaky tied up to one side, half-full of water, afloat only because it was wood. A second look at it reminded me to thank God for it. The old shell had served us well.

Spectators gathered while I lowered the engine tail and squeezed the priming bulb on the fuel line. With the controls adjusted, I pulled the starting cord three times before the engine released a puff of smoke, then settled into a smooth purr. The sound was music to my ears.

I stepped back to make sure a stream of water poured out of the cooling system before taking my seat at the wheel. I tried the new boat at half-throttle, full throttle, and reverse, and zig-zagged left and right like I would have to do when avoiding snags. She handled beautifully.

"Hey, guys. Want to go for a spin?" I called to the men who helped put the boat into the water and watched my show.

"Thanks, brother Paulo. We'll go another time," they answered.

"Aw, come on. You'll like it," I urged as they sat grinning and exchanging comments. I added, "No sharp turns this trip, and it won't go as fast with all of you on board." Three of the bravest made their way slowly down to the boat. Two sat inside the little cabin, and one stood by me at the wheel. The fastest these fellows had ever been propelled over water was as fast as they could paddle. The man next to me stood with knees slightly bent, ready to leap out if necessary. They hung on for dear life during the unforgettable ride, then walked off to the village, laughing loudly.

CHAPTER TWELVE

DR. ORR'S SUGGESTIONS on how John's and my responsibilities should be divided were accepted during a Schlener summit meeting well into our first term. Jessie and I were responsible for ministry in the village of Santa Rita and small villages and homes in the proximity of the Port of Two Brothers that could be reached with our runabout boat within a few hours. John and Fran accepted responsibility for river evangelism, to reach as far up- and downriver as the field council permitted.

John's hopes to use Jack Looney's diesel launch while he was on furlough were dashed for lack of funds. So for the remainder of that first term and well into the second, John and I continued working together in the village, traveling on the river only in cases of emergency or when collecting supplies.

My new little cruiser made travel to meetings pleasurable. A letter from Jessie said,

> Last Sunday Fran, Paul and I rode the new cruiser about 15 miles downriver [she meant round-trip] for a meeting. A good group seemed very interested in the story of the Philippian jailer. They invited us to come back and we are glad that this is their attitude. Pray that some might be saved through this means of house meetings. Next Sunday we will have another meeting upriver. We are trying to have a meeting every Sunday afternoon.

Those short evangelistic trips were fun and fulfilling. The new engine pushed us along at a nice speed, and the cabin protected us from rain squalls we couldn't dodge or outrun. The poor pilot, positioned outside the cabin, had to crouch behind the low windshield to escape being completely soaked. But the cool rain felt good under the relentless sun.

Villagers met us with hugs and handshakes, lively conversation, and home-roasted coffee. We felt at ease to present our simple programs and we were never hurried off. It was wise to quit while the folks still liked us.

The little crowds in cramped spaces watched every move Fran made with her accordion. She slipped her arms through the leather straps, unsnapped the bellows, and a lively melody—like magic—filled the thatched homes. Curious ones moved closer, staring while the wrinkled box stretched to its limits.

Teaching Bible stories to children was Jessie's specialty. She lived the Bible stories and seemed to become the very characters she described, holding young and old alike spellbound in the few minutes she had. Beautiful hand-painted scenes and paper figures enhanced her enthusiastic presentation. A brisk breeze that sent Moses or an animal flying off the flannel-board brought laughter, while a continual plague of *mutuca* flies and mosquitoes kept the speaker slapping and scratching. Sometimes a setting hen hopped out of its nest and let out a cluck. Pet monkeys distracted listeners in some homes; and pigs oinked their way through other meetings.

· · ·

The village school functioned a few weeks in August in preparation for Independence Day celebrations on September 7, then again for a few weeks in May before the annual festivities in honor of Saint Rita, patron saint of the village. Time was spent memorizing chants and poems for festivities when the Roman Catholic priest attended the week-long celebration which ended in a procession.

We Schleners felt a great need to start a primary school, but not all of the field council members shared that vision. Since my responsibility was to the village and the surrounding area, I realized I would bear the brunt of responsibilities. Unprepared and fearful, I felt I should try with whatever cooperation I was given.

The first hurdle to clear was to get permission from the ABWE Board to do something outside the parameters of accepted mission practice. I was so uptight when it was my turn to speak that my voice rose an octave until it sounded like it belonged to someone else and not me at all. Clearing my throat didn't help. I felt like I had a fever of 104° and at the same time was freezing to death. I was glad for Blake Rogers' moral support. I tripped over his heels going into the conference room and sat next to him; if I could have, I would have sat on his lap.

Dr. Commons said, "Brother Schlener, we commend you and John for the fine work you're doing on the Amazon. The Lord has given you health and courage, and has blessed your efforts. We pray regularly for you here at headquarters." I thought I would pop a shirt button. "However," he continued, "as a mission, our objective is to evangelize the lost and establish indigenous churches. We have never thought that we should establish schools, other than Bible institutes and seminaries."

In this pinch, Blake was my advocate. I think I had put the Board to sleep with my monotone. Although I didn't ask Blake to intercede for me, he had a vibrant personality—whether from the pulpit, around a table, or one on one. He got people's attention, and everyone heard what he had to say.

All eyes focused on him as he made his speech, consisting of four short sentences. "I'm sure the Schleners realize ABWE's objective is to evangelize and establish autonomous, indigenous, New Testament churches. My question is, how will they ever be able to accomplish that objective with people who, for the most part, can't read or write? In Leticia, Colombia, where I work, 100 miles upriver from the Schleners, most of our constituency is literate enough to read the Bible. In Peru, the government successfully completed a literacy program along the river, but in the Port of Two Brothers area, on the Brazil side of the frontier, extremely little is being done in that regard."

I was roused along with the officials, almost forgetting it was I who requested starting a Christian primary school. The men tossed the question back and forth. I thanked the Lord that not one of the men asked if I felt qualified to teach, nor about my academic achievements. I would have had to answer "no" and "none" to those questions; I wasn't qualified for any of the jobs I had to do on the field. But since my request was for a one-year trial run, and because the field council was in favor, the Board granted permission with the provision that it be on an experimental basis for one year, at the end of which we were to send a complete report to headquarters.

Fear took hold. Waves of panic swept over me when I woke up to the reality that I didn't know what was involved in starting a school. John was struggling with back problems, which slowed his progress in getting equipment prepared for river evangelism; therefore, he couldn't promise to take part in a school program. Fran and Jessie were raring to give it a whirl until intruders like childbirth, illness, and furlough threw a kink into the program.

Ironically, massive persecution of evangelicals was taking place in Manaus at the same time we started clearing the jungle for the construction of the primary school at the Port of Two Brothers in June 1956, the beginning of the busiest 20 years of my life.

. . .

"Listen, Senhor Paulo. Sounds like a boat pulling into your port," Dorva puffed, out of breath and sweaty from hewing a log. We all stopped to listen. Not many boats went by in the 1950's. We continued chopping and sawing. More heavy jungle material for the school building dropped from the shoulders of two sturdy men.

A boy ran up to the construction site. "Senhor Paulo, Dona

Jessie wants you to come to the house. The Padre from down-river wants to talk to you." A visit from the Padre at the Cathedral and Seminary of São Paulo de Olivença was rare, indeed.

I jogged over to the house and dried the sweat from my face. I arrived at the front porch door at the same time the priest and another man approached. The priest didn't come to the door, but stopped about 15 feet away, his back to the house. His neatly dressed assistant marched right up to the door.

"Come in. Have a seat. It's a scorcher today; you must be thirsty," I said.

"Thank you," he returned. "I took a drink before I left our boat, so I'm okay." I think he was lying.

"Doesn't the Padre want to come in?" I asked.

"No, he'll wait outside. Our stay is just for a minute," the man said. The priest obviously didn't want to speak to me. I concluded that his prestigious presence on the scene was supposed to be enough to legitimize the request his assistant was about to make.

I could see the man was nervous. "I'm a businessman from São Paulo de Olivença. I'm loaning my boat to the priest to take the Mother Superior of our schools up to the hospital in Benjamin Constant. Our doctor is gone," he explained.

"What seems to be the problem with the Mother Superior?"

"Tetanus, caused by an improperly administered injection. The trip in this vibrating boat is much too hard for her. We've been traveling six hours and have gone only 30 miles," he said. "We heard you would be willing to take her the rest of the way in a faster boat. Or could we rent your boat and motor for the trip? I, personally, will be responsible for the cost," he pleaded.

I looked at my watch and took a deep breath. I would have time, if all went well, to reach the hospital before dark. This was only one of a steady stream of interruptions that made me wonder how we would ever accomplish any of our own goals.

I excused myself to talk with Jessie. She agreed that I should

drop everything, much as she disliked my being away, and take
the poor nun to the doctor. "Remember what you've been
preaching?" she asked.

"Yes, ma'am. I can't forget it," I said, and surprised her by
reciting Romans 12:17. "Recompense *no man* evil for evil. Provide
things honest in the sight of all men. If it is possible, as much as
lieth in you, live peaceably with all men." Since Tim's pal Georgie
Rogers had been staying with us, I could take him home at the
same time.

I returned to the porch and said, "Our policy is to never loan
our equipment, but I'm glad to do what I can for you. I will take
the Mother Superior to the hospital. I'd like to leave in less than
half an hour, so please have the patient loaded into my boat. I'll
send a small mattress down for her comfort. The only thing you
will be responsible for is the gasoline for the round trip. Not
money, gasoline, because money won't pop the pistons."

The man stood in the middle of my speech, mouth open,
waiting to recommend me for sainthood. The priest dropped his
rosary in his pocket and hightailed it to his vibrating boat, never
having spoken to me the whole time.

"Thank you, Senhor Paulo. God will pay you for this," the
assistant assured me. "The gasoline will be here in a few days."

"God will pay you" is a common phrase of appreciation for
a favor, but the words' meaning is usually not taken literally.

"God has already paid me, and I owe everything I have to
Him," I said.

There were two nuns, the Mother Superior and a younger
woman who acted as her nurse. During our tenure in a predom-
inately Roman Catholic country, we made little contact with
priests and nuns, but I was always impressed by the nuns' sacrifi-
cial dedication, which was a challenge to me.

Around 11 a.m. I gently knocked on the cabin door.
Conversation over the motor's noise wasn't easy, so I simply
handed a "Jessie's Special" sandwich to the young Sister. I winked

at Georgie, and together we dove into the rest of the scrumptious lunch. Watching the young Sister devour that sandwich must have been a severe trial for the Mother Superior, who couldn't open her mouth to eat.

John and I were no strangers to the doctors at the new hospital. The building was unfinished and poorly equipped, but fairly well staffed at that time. They were stunned to realize that a Protestant personally brought a Roman Catholic nun 100 miles in his boat to receive medical attention. This gave me opportunity, introverted as I was, to testify to those at hand. And the deed built a little prestige for the evangelicals in the area, which consisted almost exclusively of ABWE missionaries.

On the way home, I noticed a boat headed upstream close to shore, and saw a white flag waving. Either I looked like a pirate and they were already surrendering, or someone needed help badly. I laid my boat nearly on its side in a sharp left turn and headed straight for the other boat. It was my brother, John.

I idled up next to his big dugout and listened to him. "I've got a guy in here who claims he tried to kill himself, but the wound is in his forearm. He failed the course on Anatomy of the Human Body, or he would have held the shotgun under his chin or between his eyes," John bellowed, the veins in his neck protruding.

He continued, "Trouble is, I doubt if I have enough gasoline to make it to the hospital. If you can take him the rest of the way, I could turn around and go back home. Even if I run out of gas, I can drift the rest of the way," John said, realizing the inconvenience to me.

"No problem," I said, as if I could hardly wait to get another glimpse of that miserable hospital. We pulled over and tied to a tree while the man climbed into my boat. Several hours later, I faced the hospital crew again. "I'm trying to keep you folks busy," I wisecracked to Dr. Matsuda.

I learned that the nun hadn't pulled out of the crisis and they didn't hold out hope for her; she should have received treatment sooner. A few days later, she passed away.

Burned from the sun and wind, and tired from traveling, handling outboard motors, cans full of gas, and carrying sick people in stretchers up the high riverbank—ah! how glad I was to be home.

. . .

Most of the building materials for the school were on hand, so I started measuring, marking, and cutting them to size. The trees from the jungle were heavy as lead, and slippery, still dripping sap. They had to be used before they dried or they would have been too hard to pound a nail through. At the same time we helped the Christians build a new church in the village, for they had outgrown their first little chapel.

Constant interruptions delayed progress on the school construction. The crankshaft of the new outboard motor broke; traveling to and from field council meetings took time and money. Study time for the ministry, a continual stream of sick people at all hours, and visiting nearby villages to teach Bible lessons and treat the ill and injured kept us busy. We were on the go literally seven days a week.

Our family was excited about taking a week of vacation in Bogota until we were refused permission to travel in Colombia except in transit. Besides being disappointed to miss out on a few days in a nice hotel, we had a close call in our little cruiser on the way home. My passengers complained when I let Tim steer, so I took over. Within a matter of minutes, I wished I had let Tim keep the wheel. We hit a submerged log so hard that the impact slammed Jessie, the girls, and our baggage into the nose of the boat, and pasted Tim and me against the bulkhead, bumping our faces on the windshield.

Simultaneously, the motor emitted a deafening, high-pitched

howl. The motor jumped off the transom, and landed inside the boat, head-down, between Tim and me. The prop was turning 5,000 revolutions per minute, inches from our faces. The Lord used the controls to keep the whirling propeller from tipping over onto Tim or me, which would have torn us to ribbons. It bent the controls, jerked the wood cap from the transom, and loosened two small corner braces. I checked for a sheared pin while the rig was still upside-down. The pin wasn't sheared, so I replaced the wood transom cap, picked up the motor, dropped it back into place, and we were on our way home.

. . .

By the time I had planed—by hand—all the boards it took to make 27 little tables and chairs, I smelled like a piece of cinnamon toast; brazilian cedar (red mahogany) smells something like cinnamon.

"Good morning, Senhor Paulo," said a woman who appeared at the door of the workshop so quietly that I hadn't noticed her, nor her 16-year-old son. We complained about interruptions while working, but they helped break the monotony.

"My son cut his finger. Can you put some medicine on it?" the woman asked. Sounded simple until I took a look at the finger, bluish-gray clear to the tip.

"When did this happen?" I asked, killing time while I wondered what to do. I took a clean needle and poked the tip of the boy's finger. I had to squeeze hard to get a drop of dark blood to the surface.

"Oh, quite a few days ago," she answered. It didn't make much difference, when or how. The finger had to be removed.

"I'll have to take the boy to a doctor in Benjamin Constant or Leticia. His finger will have to come off or the boy will die; gangrene is setting in," I explained. Of course, she didn't know gangrene from rhubarb, and I wasn't much farther along in knowledge myself. "We will have to leave early in the morning, and we can return the next day if all goes well."

"Senhor Paulo, we won't go to the hospital," was the woman's response.

"You can't let your boy die. Soon his whole arm will rot, if he lives that long," I warned her, trying to scare her into letting me take them to the doctor.

"No, Senhor Paulo, we can't go. Would you please take it off?" she asked. Since there was no way I could persuade her to go to a hospital, after cleaning and bandaging the boy's finger, I gave him a shot of penicillin and anti-tetanus. The pair thanked me and walked away.

It bothered me to see the woman and her son leave. I leaned over my workbench, dropped to my elbows, and agonized for a few seconds. As I stood up again, my eyes fell upon my new two-inch, yellow-handled chisel in its slot on the wall. I grabbed it and tested its edge on the hair of my forearm. It was still razor-sharp.

I ran out the front door, took a deep breath, and blasted a shrill whistle past my teeth. The pair stopped on the spot and did an about-face. I motioned them to come back.

I'll have to sterilize this thing somehow, I whispered to myself as they approached the porch. *Maybe I'll just clean it off with alcohol.* I figured one blow with a rubber mallet should lop off the blue part of that finger, slick and clean. *Then I can bunch up the skin around the end of the bone and tie it off like a sack of potatoes.* This concluded my thinking on easy, logical, cut-and-dried minor surgical procedures.

I brushed the wood shavings and sawdust off my bench and called the boy in from the porch. I excused myself and went into the house to beg a clean towel from Jessie.

I had the boy lay his hand, palm up, on the towel spread out on my germ-free workbench. "Turn your head and look out the window," I instructed him. "This shouldn't take long." The boy never uttered a word.

I laid the chisel on his finger. "Oh, Lord . . ." The Lord knew the rest of my prayer better than I. But I couldn't make myself lift the rubber mallet. I glanced at the boy, the picture of tranquility. I pulled the chisel away and said, " I'll be right back." The mother smiled at me as I walked by, full of joy that I was going to remove her son's finger instead of some doctor who lets people die, which was the rumor witch doctors in the area loved to spread.

"What's eating at you, carpenter?" Jessie asked. "Would you like another nice, new towel from Bethany Baptist's missionary closet so you can punch more holes?"

I didn't answer, waiting until I thought my voice was steady. "I have to cut off a finger. I think it is already gangrenous," I explained just above a whisper. "I figure one blow to the handle of my two inch-chisel will do the job."

"What?" she exclaimed. "How can you even think of something like that?"

"Okay, I'll bring the boy in so you can try some of your fine cutlery on him!" I threatened. "Or would it be easier to place my hand on his head, lift up my voice in fervent prayer beseeching God to give the boy a new finger, then bawl out the mother for not bringing the kid sooner for treatment, before turning them loose?"

Humbler now, Jessie said, "I remember you showing me a little leather case with some funny-looking knives inside. What were they for?"

"Oh, man, I forgot about those! They're in my tackle box." I raced to my office to dig out the little leather case from among my spinners and plugs. Three rusty little scalpel handles that had never been used and some less rusty blades lay folded in wax paper. I sandpapered one of the blades and boiled it for a half hour, then washed my hands. I asked the boy to sit down. I cradled his hand and forearm firmly between my left forearm and body. All the boy could see now was my sweat-soaked backside as I whittled.

I got the finger off. I had to slice it at the joint, for lack of a proper saw. It bothered me more to see the finger separated from the stump than doing the actual cutting. And the boy never let out a peep. "Come back as often as you can for cleaning and a new bandage," I said.

The mother and son disappeared over the edge of the riverbank and never returned. I didn't know if the boy lived or died. More than a year passed before I spotted him in a group of people headed for church. I rushed over to him, gushing, as though he had returned from the dead. I grabbed his hand to look at the stump. The skin had grown nicely over the end.

Later, I was given a well-illustrated book on minor surgery and saw exactly what I should have done.

· · ·

The day before Christmas we butchered a two-year-old bull and a fat pig we purchased from a trading post upriver for a big feed on Christmas Day. It was easier to get help to butcher and cook than it was to get help building the church. From our backyard we could hear the village ladies as they smashed stringy meat into tenderness with short clubs. Those with less ability in culinary arts were kept busy splitting wood to keep the kettles bubbling. Stalks of cooking bananas were peeled and put on the fire to roast.

No one who attended the evening program went hungry; some, in fact were uncomfortably full. More important than all the fun and food that Christmas Day were the people who trusted Christ as their personal Savior after the program.

Shortly after Christmas, a Christmas present appeared in the mail while I worked on the tables, chairs, and doors for the school. A letter from the Secretary of Education and Culture in Rio de Janeiro gave permission for us to open our primary school, using Portuguese as the basic language. This news prompted a family trip to Manaus to buy school supplies.

Cindi, aged three, and Leanne, five, were panic-stricken at the noise of the old amphibious Catalina airplane. To Jessie and me these flights were old hat: water covered the windows and the entire airplane trembled and rocked in preparation for take-off. We went through five take-offs and landings before arriving in Manaus, eight hours later. To this day, flying is not a favorite pastime for either Leanne or Cindi.

Our good friend Willard Stull met us with a big smile, crushing hugs, and the same battered Dodge station wagon. I leaned forward from the back seat and made a request in Willard's ear. "On the way to the hotel, do your best to not leave any wounded and dead in our wake. We aren't in any hurry; we'll be glad just to arrive alive. Besides, we haven't exposed our young'uns to the rigors of city civilization yet."

Willard chuckled, "Now, Paul, how could you bring reproach on my driving?"

"Aw, Willard, just kidding. When we are dropped into traffic like this, we become a little skittish. Paddling canoes and swinging on vines is a hair different."

"Things are picking up in town these days," Willard said as he blasted his horn at a taxi driver. "They have widened the streets and put in a few traffic signals. Your worries are over," he assured us, touching his brakes to spare the lives of several jaywalkers.

We purchased school supplies, guessing at what we'd need. A set of living room furniture captured Jessie's attention while window shopping one cool evening. We also found a dozen heads of cabbage to share with our colleagues upriver. Willard piled our stuff on a freight boat, and before we knew it, our 12 days in the big city were over.

We were met in Benjamin Constant by Pastor Otacio, who told us that John just traveled through on his way to the United States.

"What's wrong?" was our immediate reaction.

"He wanted to check on his back problem. He could hardly get out of bed or out of a chair," the pastor explained.

John had also been experiencing a chronic digestive problem. A quote from his newsletter after his return home says:

> Needless to say, it was a thrill to return to my family after over three months in the States. My experience hitch-hiking by air (free to me on all military planes) would fill a book. I've ridden on most of the conventional aircraft from helicopter to huge KC-97 tankers that refuel smaller planes in the air. But the greatest thrill was returning to the Port of Two Brothers, bringing the Ralph Poulsons with me for a week's visit.

• • •

The next three months were not easy for Fran and the boys, wondering what kind of treatment John was undergoing and how long he would be away. But it didn't stop Fran's ministry of music in church, teaching kids' classes, home-schooling the boys, and going with Jessie and me to Sunday afternoon meetings in the area.

John's absence increased my responsibilities considerably, especially in making supply trips, taking care of the sick, and preaching. But I continued on the school building, finishing the tables, chairs, and blackboards.

Gervasio clapped loudly at the back door one day before starting his daily chores. "Senhor Paulo, I bring bad news," he said without preamble.

"What happened?" Nearly all of Gervasio's family had died, and I almost hated to ask.

"Three men from the village just arrived from a two-day

trek through the jungle where they were cutting rubber to tell us that Dorva died."

Dorva, a member of our village church, had been one of the happiest Christians, faithful in attendance and always ready to help on church work days. But he backslid and was living with another man's wife. Dorva refused to listen to counsel and stopped attending church. While extracting latex in the jungle, he was bitten by a *jararaca* snake.

"Jose said Dorva hemorrhaged from every body orifice the day he died, four days after he was bitten." Gervasio added, "There was no way they could build a coffin. They had no shovels, so they dug a grave as best they could with machetes and wrapped him in a blanket for burial."

The news about Dorva made the church folks and the rest of the villagers question their lives and how suddenly they can end. It was great to have the answers to these questions.

CHAPTER THIRTEEN

FRAN AND KIDS REMAINED IN LETICIA for a few days after the next field council meeting, hoping for word from John. While their house stood empty, I attempted a few projects for Fran. These lighter jobs—tacking screen on kitchen windows, making kitchen cupboards, and nailing slats over spaces between wallboards—were a pleasant change from heavier work on the church and school construction.

Jessie sent our nearest neighbor over to talk to me while I was planing some cupboard parts for Fran's kitchen. "Senhor Paulo, our little baby died this morning," the young father whispered. He cleared his throat and looked down to the ground, unable to continue.

"I'm sorry to hear that, Adelmo," I said, sitting down on the back steps. "What happened?"

"The same old thing, Senhor Paulo. Sickness of the air," he assured me. When no cause of death was evident, the Brazilians diagnosed such cases as "sickness of the air." This popular diagnosis was usually applied to tiny babies and infants, most of whom died from tetanus caused by unsterile scissors or knives used to cut umbilical cords at birth.

It took a few hours to make a small coffin for the tiny baby. I delivered it personally to take advantage of an opportunity to talk to both the mother and father about God and His word.

Infant mortality rate in the area diminished noticeably as time went by. Childbirth was one department of assistance we avoided, but we kept sterilized stainless steel surgical scissors for loan to midwives. A continual supply of medicine against dysentery and malaria helped lengthen the lives of many others, both young and old.

. . .

Blake made a wide approach to our port with Fran and her kids. He was amazed to see the liberty we enjoyed in Brazil. Here we were about to open a Christian primary school with teaching based on biblical principles, while his family and the Flodens were completely shut down and were being threatened, harassed, and persecuted. They were not allowed to hold public church services, let alone start a school.

With Fran and the kids back after a few days' absence, we continued our Monday night prayer meeting. We took turns reading the Bible and messages by great preachers of the past, and prayed. We reviewed the list of registered pupils and considered the list of rules I had concocted, including school hours and the handling of discipline.

The thought of starting a school intimidated us. The easy part was finished: building the simple structure, making furniture, and buying school supplies. But we knew pitifully little about Brazilian history, geography, literature, and all the other subjects a teacher should know. They say a person begins cutting his wisdom teeth the first time he bites off more than he can chew. Staying at least one day ahead of the pupils was going to be a struggle.

A few days before opening, I invited the parents of the registered students to meet with us in the schoolhouse for the first parent-teacher meeting of the Escola Batista do Porto Dois Irmãos. They sat on freshly varnished chairs at smooth new tabletops.

The meeting began with Scripture reading and prayer led by the parents. The stacks of textbooks we would use were something the parents had never seen before. Fran and Jessie each explained what they would teach.

• • •

Three days after the opening of school, we received word that Dr. Paul Jackson, Dr. Bill Kuhnle, Dr. Arthur Woolsey, and Willard Stull planned to visit. Dr. Jackson was national representative of the General Association of Regular Baptist Churches (GARBC); Drs. Kuhnle and Woolsey pastored large churches and were GARBC officials. They wanted to meet with the field council, of which I was chairman.

The news threw me into a tizzy. The very word "doctor" attached to the name of anyone who was neither physician nor dentist gave me chills. How could I officiate at a meeting with these men of God? They could recite *Robert's Rules of Order* as easily as John 3:16. Had I been able to communicate with Leticia or Benjamin Constant, I would have told Orville Floden to take charge.

Instead, I hightailed it in my boat to Leticia to meet the four men. The next morning I left for home at 9:30 a.m. with the whole gang on the Leticia riverbank to see me off and take pictures, as though I was William Carey off to India. Orville and Blake would bring the pastors and Willard down to the Port of Two Brothers to visit on Monday, March 4.

After school Monday morning, I jumped into the boat and took a trip around the islands in search of food while the shower was scrubbed out with stones, fresh paint dried on the toilet seats, and beds were moved around to accommodate our visitors. One old hen and 10 eggs was all I could find. As I started to cross the river to our boathouse, I saw two boats pull into port loaded with our friends. Nobody was there to meet them; both Fran and Jessie happened to be in their respective showers at that instant. I roared in just as our visitors struggled up the riverbank.

The men thought the place looked like a park. The first thing they wanted to do was take a short hike into the famous Amazonian jungle. "Let's have coffee first," I suggested.

"Sounds great," Dr. Kuhnle agreed. This humble man put me at ease immediately, as we sat around the table, downing a batch of Jessie's cookies and drinking hot coffee.

In our backyard we paused for a brief orientation. Before I could even speak, one of the men asked, "I'm wondering if we're wearing the proper clothing for this jungle hike." The Green Hell is so famous for everything unlovely that our little group probably would have felt uncomfortable in anything less protective than an army tank.

"I think you'll be okay with what you have on right now," I said. "Just be sure to tuck your pant legs into your socks; snakes usually strike between the knee and ankle." I got their attention at the mention of snakes. "With your socks tucked in, the snake's fangs have a thicker surface to penetrate," I warned, winking at Orville as they all stooped over in unison—except Dr. Woolsey.

"I'm all set, boys," Dr. Woolsey said. "When I saw all the mud in this country, I borrowed these rubber boots from Orv. I don't know if I would take a chance with just pant legs tucked into socks." They all finished with their pant legs at once and stood up as though doing calisthenics.

"Oh, I almost forgot. Better wear some kind of cap," I told the men. "If you didn't bring one, I can loan you one of my sweat-stained extras. The other day a poisonous snake dropped out of a tree and glanced off my shoulder while I stood talking with some Indians." When I pointed to the tree, their heads turned like puppets on strings.

We started across the open school grounds toward the edge of the clearing. I stopped the parade before stepping onto the jungle trail that led to a creek some 400 yards away. "I'll take the lead," I said, sounding like Dr. Livingston from Africa. "Dr. Jackson, you follow me. Dr. Woolsey, you go third, since you have the boots. The leader usually startles the snake which aims at the second person, but since we'll be moving quickly, it would likely strike at the third hiker," I improvised, liberally stretching the truth. "Dr. Kuhnle, you're fourth, Willard is fifth, and Orville, you don't even have your pant legs tucked in; you'd better bring up the rear," I suggested.

Off we trudged. Only the occasional bird's trill and the muffled sound of our footsteps broke the silence. After a few hundred yards at an easy gait, the breathing of the stouter hikers became audible. But it was shady and cool along the trail, although still muggy, pasting our shirts to our skin with perspiration.

In a few minutes our friends became seasoned hikers, gazing at the scenery instead of keeping their eyes glued to the trail. Entering an especially dark, shady area, the sound of rustling bushes caught our attention. Then three heavy thuds on the ground 15 yards ahead preceded Orville's roar: *"Tiger!"*

Two of the visitors collided head-on in their haste to escape. The other two retreated a few steps to see Orville, doubled over, red as a beet, in his habitual silent laughter. He had picked up a heavy piece of loose stump along the trail and hurled it as far as he could, creating the thumping sound on the ground. Even though we all knew there are no tigers in Brazil, the brave troop leader himself was startled.

Within an hour we were huddled around the refrigerator, waiting our turns for a drink of cold water and *guaraná*. While we men invaded the fridge, Jessie worked at the sink, unusually quiet, her back to us. She was cleaning raw rice to cook for our evening meal, and didn't want our guests to see it . . . yet. But friendly Dr. Jackson, *guaraná* in hand, stepped over to share the exotic adventure with Jessie. She became almost hyper in her animation, hoping to distract him from the dozens of floating, swimming bugs in the rice water. It was no use. He saw them.

She apologized, "I'm sorry, fellows, but this is the way it always is. We've never found rice without bugs."

"What's a few little boiled bugs?" Pastor Kuhnle asked. "Let's just call them added vitamin B complex for our complexions."

The men visited our school the next morning. They thought it was great that the Lord led us to start this school and that God had given us the courage "to be strong and do the work" as King David said when he challenged his son Solomon to build the temple. "We'll pray that God's blessing will be upon your efforts here," Dr. Jackson promised.

After the noon meal, I took our visitors upriver to a large black water creek to visit some Ticuna Indians. When the man of the family climbed down to the riverbank to greet us, Pastor Woolsey's rubber boots made him lose his footing on the slippery mud, and down he went. Somehow he managed to hold one leg up while the other was submerged, filling the boot to the top with cool creek water and gluing his pant leg to his thigh with mud. As soon as we were sure he wasn't hurt, we all roared with laughter.

The three men from the States were interviewed in the evening church service to a standing-room-only crowd with four or five people squeezing in each window. The congregation was impressed to hear how they came to be saved. When Pastor Woolsey mentioned his mishap on the slippery creek bank, it triggered a wave of laughter.

Not much later, Blake requested a transfer from Leticia, Colombia, to Iquitos, Peru, where the Rogers family would work with the already established ABWE field council. Blake was too energetic a person to sit and wait for a change in Colombian government policy that might never happen. The Flodens' river evangelism could continue on both the Colombian and Peruvian sides of the Amazon River from their base in Leticia.

It was a sad day when the Rogerses' equipment was put on a riverboat to Peru. Two weeks later, they boarded the Catalina flying boat and followed their equipment.

Jeannie and Ruthie Rogers cried as they said good-bye to

their Colombian playmates, and to little Elizabeth Floden across the street. Thereafter, when visiting Leticia for mail and supplies, we missed Blake's loud shout, "Hi, guys! C'mon in. What's new?"

. . .

"Senhor Paulo! Senhor Paulo!" I recognized Gervasio's voice through the screened bedroom window even though it was only 4 a.m.

Something must be wrong. "What can I do for you, Gervasio?"

"Senhor Paulo, I'm sorry to bother you so early." He struggled to control his emotions.

"Forget it. It's time for me to rise and shine anyway," I said, yawning.

"It's Adenil. He is screaming with a severe headache and vomiting. With nothing in his stomach, he has the dry heaves. Would you come and look at him? You might have medicine that will help."

"I'll be there in 10 minutes," I promised, my heels thumping to the floor. I headed for the front porch medicine cabinet. "Come around to the verandah and I'll give you some paregoric for Adenil. Put a few drops in a quarter-cup of water. It might relax his stomach."

A crowd of spectators gathered at Gervasio's, their presence eloquently condemning him for entering into this "new religion." After Gervasio became a Christian in January of 1953, his wife died. Then his six-year-old son, Jair, and beautiful little daughter, Noemia, aged 10, died within months of each other. And now Adenil lay deathly ill.

"Gervasio, we'll pray for Adenil and ask that God's will be done. Then I think we should take him to the hospital in Benjamin Constant. There is an excellent doctor in the hospital now, a member of the Methodist church in São Paulo. He'll do his best for us. What do you think? Shall we take Adenil to the doctor or not?" I asked, realizing that this was a hard decision for Gervasio to make in the presence of those who thought he was crazy to let his family die because of his religion.

After a full minute of silence Gervasio said quietly, "We don't know what sickness Adenil has. We don't have much medicine here in the jungle. God has already taken a portion of my family. I'm a widower and don't have a woman to help take care of my kids. I want to do everything I can for my son," he said as Adenil lay motionless.

"Gervasio, you've done the best you could for your family. None of us knows what awaits us from day to day. But God knows, so we commit ourselves to Him and accept what comes our way," I stammered.

"I know the time it takes for a trip like this, Senhor Paulo, but if you feel you can do it, I think we should take Adenil to the doctor," Gervasio said.

"Good," I said. "Let's go as soon as we can."

I sent for two men to help carry the motor, gasoline, and tools to my boat. By the time I ate a bowl of oatmeal and packed a little overnight bag, Jessie had packed a lunch. Adenil was restless, tossing and turning.

Dr. Matsuda diagnosed the case as meningitis. Gervasio stayed with Adenil at the hospital all night. When I arrived the next morning, intending to return home, Adenil was in a coma.

"There is a possibility he could pull out of this crisis and live," Dr. Matsuda said.

I didn't feel right leaving Gervasio until Adenil showed signs of improvement, so I accepted Lindsey Harrell's invitation to stay overnight.

At 10 p.m., an hour after the Harrells and I retired for the night, hands clapped at the front door.

"Senhor Paulo!" a man's voice shouted.

I sat up, wide awake. "I'll be right there."

Gervasio's brother-in-law stood outside. He said, "Gervasio

wants you to come to the hospital."

The calm, moonlit night was an immense blessing. It took five minutes in the boat to reach the hospital. Dr. Matsuda stood by Adenil's bed. He said, "Brother Paulo, I'm afraid Adenil is dying. He never came out of the coma. Gervasio wants to take him home right away and for this reason he called you."

I looked at the handsome boy struggling for breath. Gervasio told his son, "You'll be all right. It's better that you be with your mother up there." Then he couldn't speak anymore. I put my arm around Gervasio's shoulder, unable to say a word.

Dr. Matsuda sent for a stretcher. We gently laid Adenil on it with his little bundle of clothes. Lindsey and I carried the stretcher down the long, steep trail to the boat, praising God that the trail was dry.

"Lindsey, let's rest a minute in this little shack before we get in the boat," I said. We entered the hut used to accommodate those coming by boat or canoe for treatment. It was a relief to set the stretcher down on the dirt floor. I took a New Testament from my satchel as we sat down to rest.

"Brother Gervasio, before we head home, let's read a little from the Word of God."

I read from the Gospel of John: "I am the resurrection and the life. He who believes in me will live, even though he dies; and whoever lives and believes in me will never die. Do you believe this?"

Gervasio assured Lindsey and me he believed it was true and that he would see his loved ones again some day.

As we lowered Adenil into the boat, his eyes were unfocused. And the raspy sound from his throat plunged me into despair.

"Thanks for your help, Lindsey. I owe you one," I said, backing away from shore.

"Glad to help out. Have a good trip!" Lindsey shouted, his voice carrying easily above the outboard motor.

The last thing I said to Lindsey before heading out into the stream with the dead child and his grieving father was, "See you soon." I didn't realize just how soon I would see Lindsey again— in the hospital.

· · ·

On June 26, I was up at 5:30 a.m. feeling fine. I ate breakfast before scooting out to ring the school bell and assign jobs to the workers. I went back in to take another swig of coffee and brush my teeth before going to school at 7:30, when a sudden pain on my right side hit just as I set my coffee cup in the sink. I thought, *Man, that's the last drop of coffee for me,* and grabbed the back of a kitchen chair, clenching it until my knuckles turned white. I broke my arm as a boy, but this pain was more severe than anything I'd ever known.

Jessie was still at the breakfast table with the kids when I gripped the chair. "I have a pain like I've never felt before," I gasped. When Jessie caught sight of me, she ran to tell Fran. John had been in bed for several days to get relief from the pain in his legs, but before I realized what was happening, John was up and dressed, and had the boat ready.

Our good pharmacist friend, Jack Vaughan, from Hope Union Church, had given us thousands of vitamins to bring with us to Brazil. He also handed me a small bottle of pain killers about the size of .22 shells, "For when you're really up against it."

"Jessie, maybe you'd better bring me one of those bullets Jack sent with us," I squeaked. The pain subsided a little after the sedative, so I walked slowly down to the boat. When nine-year-old Tim Jim realized what was happening, he started beating on poor Uncle John for taking me to the hospital to die, as it seemed to him and to most of our national friends. John and I had ferried many sick people to the hospital, but this time I was stretched out on the bench going to the hospital.

Five hours and 45 minutes after we started, John and I pulled up to the hospital's port where, only 15 days before, I prayed with Gervasio. John must have had an adrenalin rush that let him ignore his back and leg aches, for he made it up the high hill to the hospital and back in no time with several strong men bearing a stretcher. In short order, I had a thermometer in my mouth, a blood pressure cuff on my arm, an IV going, and was given a towel and pair of pajamas.

Dr. Matsuda said. "Take a quick shower and we'll see what's the matter with you."

A few minutes after lying down on the hospital bed, the pain increased. I took two fistfuls of sheet and wiggled my toes to keep from hollering.

"My, I declare." I recognized Lindsey Harrell's voice. "I'm sorry to see you suffering like this, Paul."

I groaned. "I didn't think I had enough life in me to hurt this badly."

"Would you like me to pray for you?"

"I can't think of anything I would like more," I said.

Lindsey removed his white pith helmet, bowed his head, and prayed. His clear, resonant voice enunciated every word in a sympathetic tone. For the first time I realized how comforting it is for the sick to be prayed for by a fellow Christian.

From six to nine the next morning, I was in agony until I received a spinal anesthetic. A gloomy aide flopped my rubbery legs onto a cart. Since I was okay from my waist up and feeling so good all of a sudden, I helped get myself all the way onto the narrow gurney.

When Dr. Matsuda returned from scrubbing up, holding his gloved hands chest high, he called for silence and prayed. Immersed in confidence, I was ready to be made into a basket— or casket—case. I am glad I didn't know at the time that Dr. Matsuda was a doctor of internal medicine, not a surgeon. No wonder his prayer seemed so fervent.

Thirty minutes before the surgery was over, I started to feel the activity on the other side of the cloth partition that separated the surgical site from my view. Along with the pressure, I started to hurt. Evidently, I bent my knees and wiggled around too much, so they strapped my legs down. I was glad when the last tiny clamp closed up my incision.

That afternoon Dr. Matsuda showed me my appendix in a tiny vial. "This thing is as normal as Adam's a few minutes after God created him," the doctor said. "It is so small it took me a long time to find the pesky thing, and there is absolutely no inflammation at all." He seemed puzzled as he spoke and apologized for the anesthesia wearing off too soon.

The day after surgery, I developed headaches like never before. Then fever accompanied the headaches at regular intervals. When I complained about the headaches, my blood was tested.

The doctor called me into the laboratory and let me peer into the microscope, where I saw a semicircle with red dots on the tips of the two points. I had vivax malaria, which induces paroxysms at 48-hour intervals. Even if I hadn't been sick when I got to the hospital, I would have been before I left.

Jessie appeared for my release with Tim, Leanne, and Cindi, who were scrubbed, starched, combed, and perfumed. And I looked like Mahatma Gandhi at the end of one of his fasts; I'd lost about 12 pounds.

"Do you think you'll need help getting back home?" Orv asked.

"Thanks, Orv. I think Jessie can help steer, and we refuel only once," I assured him. Jessie's eyebrows raised when she heard about having to steer.

About one-third of the way home, I called Jessie to take the wheel while I collapsed on one of the benches inside the cabin. "Just keep 'er in the main current and we'll make better time," I suggested. "I'll flake out a few minutes, then be right back." Weakness from surgery and malaria made me tremble like a blob of jello. Raising up on one elbow, I watched through the windshield for a few minutes to see how the lady was doing at the helm. *So far, so good,* I thought, and tried to doze.

Every little change in the motor's tune worked on me like an old-fashioned alarm clock. Water hitting the propeller sounds different from every angle. A tough stem of floating grass dragging on the tail; a little stick of hard wood caught crosswise to the engine's tail; a stick down close to the prop—all produce distinct noises. And when prop pins sheared, it set up a frightful scream until the throttle was pulled back.

As I lay looking at the framework of the wood cabin, interpreting every little change and feeling every little correction made by the driver, I could see Jessie's skirts fluttering in the breeze through the doorway. I noticed the treetops seemed too close. I rolled off the low bench onto the deck, crawled out the door, and pulled myself up. "How ya' doin', Mrs. Schlener?" I asked.

"Not bad. This is kinda fun!" she replied confidently.

"Would you say we were headed upstream or downstream?" I gently asked, putting my face close to her ear to avoid shouting above the engine noise.

"Hanged if I know. Why?" she questioned as though it didn't make much difference.

"Remember, we have been living downriver from Benjamin Constant and Leticia for six years now," I reminded her.

"I know that, Smarty. So what?" she snapped. Either she was under more pressure than I realized or my questioning wasn't subtle enough.

"See that big snag sticking out of the water over there?" I asked, making a stab at pure humility as I pointed. "Then you surely see the current hitting up against it. So are we going in the same direction as the current or are we going against the current?"

The change of expression on Jessie's face the second she realized what was happening made her look like a different person.

"I can't believe it!" she exclaimed. "When we passed that island back there I must have come too close to land and didn't realize I was headed back upstream," she confessed.

"It's no big deal," I said. "You saw the mistake soon enough, so we haven't lost more than half an hour."

We lost as many days of school as I did pounds of flesh during my stay in the hospital, but by God's grace I quickly recovered. I moved my study from the hot attic to the vacant one-room "vacation home" where Otacio and Itamar lived during our furlough. It took me 30 paces to get there from our house. The desk I bought from Blake Rogers looked small in the spacious single room. It was easy to install a trapeze and bolt my punching-bag frame to the wall. I figured that when I became discouraged or upset, instead of guzzling too much coffee or pacing back and forth chewing my fingernails, I could do some chin-ups and punch the bag after praying.

To complete the decor, I hung my shield-shaped gun rack, with mule deer horns and hoofs, on the wall.

· · ·

"*Queixada! Queixada!*" pierced the air as Jessie and I wandered down the path from Sunday morning service, shortly after my hospital stay. Two men charged out of Dona Endelinda's house, fumbling with shotgun shells and single-barreled shotguns while running like mad toward our schoolhouse.

"*Queixada,* Senhor Paulo!" the men yelled as they headed for the jungle. Shots were fired, followed by more hollering and more men disappearing into the jungle.

"Tadeu killed six already," one fellow bellowed as he ran by.

A large herd of jungle pigs, called *queixada* (kay-SHAH-da), had drifted to the edge of the school grounds then turned back toward the jungle. As soon as a shot is fired into the herd, they stop to face the noise and just stand there. According to the

Nimrods of the area, one pig with enough courage to advance toward the hunters sets the whole herd loose to attack the men making all the noise. Hunters seek a fallen tree, a stump, or a branch to jump on while killing the motionless pigs. One hunter sometimes kills six or eight animals—reloading his single-shot gun—before the herd turns and runs.

I immediately broke out in goose bumps, and my pulse shot up way above normal.

Here I was with a Bible under one arm, but no musket. I ran as fast as I could to my office to grab my rifle, only to find I had locked the door with my keys inside. I couldn't miss this chance of a lifetime. I laid down my Bible, stepped back a few paces, and flung myself against the door. The door popped open and slammed down on the cement floor with me on top of it. I grabbed my rifle and crammed shells into the magazine as I ran, still in my Sunday best.

I met Erasmo a few paces into the jungle. He stood motionless as a statue, scanning the jungle for any sign of movement. His bronze body shone with perspiration, since he ran full speed from the village.

"Looks like we're too late, Senhor Paulo. You can see where they came to the edge of the clearing and turned back into the jungle." Erasmo sounded disappointed.

"Man, I'm all hyped-up to draw some *queixada* blood, especially after knocking my office door off its hinges to get my weapon. Do you think we might catch a straggler or two, maybe a sick one or a couple of old ones with arthritis?" I panted, trying to catch my breath after sprinting more than 100 yards.

Erasmo smiled. "Let's go straight back to the creek. We can cross it to see if they might have paused to drink," he suggested.

We started through the jungle at a good clip. My nice white trousers were already muddy and wet to the knees, my shirt was pasted to my body, and sweat dripped off both my nose and chin.

The uncanny ability these people have in navigating uncharted jungle is admirable. Although Erasmo was barefoot, the thick skin on the soles of his feet offered as much protection as my leather shoes. He knew when to brush foliage aside, and when not to touch the plants. Nearly sprinting through the tangles, my guide didn't take time to clip off undesirable vegetation with his ever-present machete, but glanced back often to make sure I missed the vicious thorns, fire ants, and hornets' nests.

Erasmo stopped suddenly; I was glad to stop, too. Without moving his eyes, he held up an open hand, signaling me to stay where I was, then inched ahead, his bare feet moving him with the agility of a cat.

I focused on Erasmo, unblinking, until he motioned me toward him. I slid the rifle bolt back as quietly as I could. A round popped up, and I slowly shoved it into the chamber and snapped the safety to "on."

Erasmo motioned me to hurry. He pointed to a low spot barely ten yards away. "There's one, Senhor Paulo," he whispered. I couldn't see anything. "There it is. Shoot!" he pleaded, not believing I couldn't see what—to him—was as big as a barn.

Then I noticed the slightest movement of a big black *queixada,* sitting on his haunches in dark shade under thick foliage. I raised my rifle and caught the unfortunate pig between the shoulders with a 180 grain soft point from above and behind. The recoil fairly rattled my bones, but the pig dropped.

Erasmo was generous, allowing me first shot. We both stood over the kill and gloated for a few minutes. Then I said, "Erasmo, I'm as weak as a kitten. If it's up to me to carry this thing back to the village, it'll have to rot right here where it is."

"No problem, Senhor Paulo. I'll carry the beast," Erasmo offered. He stooped, took the pig's two front feet in one hand, its two hind feet in his other hand, and swung the dead weight up on his muscular shoulders. As Erasmo walked along, blood from the *queixada*'s fatal wound bathed the man's back and legs.

"I'll tell you what, Erasmo. This is your meat. Take it straight to your house and butcher him. Send us a kilo if you like, and keep the rest," I said, trailing along behind. The delicious meat tasted like veal, and nothing at all like domestic pork. Or chicken. So much for having a "typical" Sunday afternoon.

The next Sunday we had good attendance at both services. Eight Christians testified to their acceptance of the Lord Jesus Christ. Tim Jim, age eight, was one of those who testified. And he did it in Portuguese. I could hardly control my emotions for the rest of the service.

The very next day during family devotions, Leanne accepted the Lord Jesus as her personal Savior. Jessie and I couldn't ask for a greater blessing than the salvation of our children.

CHAPTER FOURTEEN

THE SCHOOL'S FIRST INDEPENDENCE DAY program was a memorable occasion for the whole community. We teachers were glad to turn over the marching instructions to John, who had served in the U.S. Marines and in what used to be called the Army Air Corps. I think the kids had to go by the tone of his voice because all the commands were literal translations from English into Portuguese, nowhere close to the official Brazilian military terms.

Fran and Jessie took charge of music and recitations of patriotic poems, discourses about the vast Brazilian wealth and glory, and famous personalities related to Brazil's independence from Portugal on September 7, 1822.

I ordered six snare drums, one bass drum, and a pair of cymbals from southern Brazil. Amazingly, they arrived in plenty of time to polish up eight school boys into a lively drum corps. On the morning of the program, the kids reflected the predominant colors of Brazil's flag in their all-white uniforms with green neckties made by Jessie, and green-and-yellow caps made by a lady from church.

When John barked his first command, a veritable explosion took place. The drums boomed and rolled, cymbals crashed, and the parade officially began. The students marched a short distance to the beat of drums, ending at the flagpole where Fran was positioned with her accordion. John had the parade hold a salute while an official Brazilian song, especially composed for flag-raising, was sung by the student body.

The national anthem, a complicated piece of music, was next, and the watching crowd joined in. Then John gave the

students a "right face" order and led them all around the spacious
school grounds. He had them do to-the-rear-march, single file,
double file, quadruple file, and counter-march. The audience was
impressed.

After the parade, the community joined us in field games.
While I directed races and games, John and several volunteers
slipped away unnoticed. In the midst of the activities while
onlookers jumped up and down, cheering for their favorite contestants, somebody yelled, "Look what's coming," and pointed
toward two men carrying a huge steamer trunk.

"Ladies and gentlemen, may I have your attention, please?"
I shouted from high up on a bench. "Finally, the mayor of our
county seat has made good on some of his campaign promises in
the village. The large trunk you see is the first installment of
many things to come," I fibbed. "It must be something wonderful. See how heavy it is?"

All heads turned to the two men struggling with the steamer
trunk.

"What can it be?" people asked each another.

One man said, "I never believed any of those promises the
guy made, but maybe I was wrong."

The men puffed and sweated as they lowered the weighty
trunk. Everyone moved in close for a better view.

The lid popped open and a scrawny, squawking chicken flew
out, startling the onlookers, before running for its life. Then John,
dressed in a clown suit, emerged. His bulbous red nose was made
from a Ping Pong ball, and his face was liberally daubed with red
lipstick. Pillows padded his tummy and rear. John fired a blank
shell from his shotgun at the fleeing chicken. The black gun-
powder made a large cloud of smoke, and the crowd parted like
the Red Sea, getting out of the chicken's path for fear of taking
double-T lead from the clown's shotgun. John jumped out of the
trunk to chase the chicken, intentionally tripping over his long
floppy clown shoes. He moved through the crowd, stumbling,

chasing, and grabbing some of the people, smearing them with lipstick. The crowd laughed until they cried.

John reached into the depths of his baggy clown suit and pulled out a loaded water pistol he scrounged from the kids' toys. He shot a dozen people, and sent them screaming. Then he walked up to Americo, one of the respected village elders, flung an arm around Americo's shoulder and whispered, "Shhhhh. Watch me shoot old Leodoro in the ear." John aimed his water pistol at the unsuspecting Leodoro. Americo grinned in anticipation of seeing the poor fellow take a cool stream in the ear. But John had turned the water pistol's outlet 90 degrees so that when he pulled the trigger, it was Americo who took a close-range stream in the ear.

. . .

I peeked out the window to see if I knew the people sitting on benches. A man of about 30 was holding a ghostly pale boy, one leg wrapped in rags. I hadn't seen them before. They would have to wait; kids were already gathering for school. I gulped my breakfast and went out to see how serious the problem was. And was it ever serious!

With his leg still wrapped, the boy's vile odor nearly did me in. I tried not to react with grimaces and groaning that might further frighten the five-year-old. The little fellow looked at me, silently, steadily. Perhaps he was afraid I would hurt him.

I slowly unwrapped the crusty rags. When the boy's leg was bared, I turned my head to keep from gagging, and whistled for Jessie.

"Fix me a lunch. I've got to take this kid to the hospital, now," I called. "He can't last much longer."

The rotten flesh had separated at the knee joint, baring the bone and making his left leg three inches longer than the right. It was beyond me how the boy stayed alive. I tried to appear relaxed as I moved around. Looking into his little face, I thought of Tim Jim, Leanne, and Cindi. *Oh, God, this could be one of our kids, but for Your grace,* I said to myself.

The doctor stopped everything to amputate the boy's leg above the knee. Weeks later, Dr. Matsuda told me that the boy lived, regained strength, and left the hospital. We never heard from him again.

• • •

Infanticipating in the Amazon was never much fun. Jessie looked forward to dark clouds on the horizon that stirred up the cool wind and dropped refreshing rain on us while she carried our fourth child. Prenatal exams and special care were out of the question. Ambulances were outboard motors on runabout boats. Local midwives with lots of experience were plentiful, but Jessie and Fran had seen some of the local talent apply their wrestling holds on agonized young mothers during childbirth, and shuddered to think of it. Knowing that hundreds of Christians back home prayed daily for us gave us courage.

We left for Peru on November 20, stopping in Leticia for a field council meeting before catching the Catalina to Iquitos. I stayed with Jessie at the hospital from admission until the baby was born, prepared this time with a thermos of coffee and a few pieces of cinnamon toast.

As soon as Tim found out he had another sister, he wept bitter tears. He wanted a brother for hunting and fishing, and for every other reason. "Tim, listen," Blake Rogers said. "Think of how great it will be to have three beautiful girls cheering for you on the sidelines when you knock homeruns, make touchdowns, or kick goals in soccer."

When I sent a telegram back to the States, I forgot to cross the 7, so it arrived at home reading, "Rena Marie born 16 Dec., 1 lb. 6 oz. Both doing fine." They must have thought we would bring her home in a match box. Jessie's letter to Grandma Rena in Idaho said:

> Our little Rena Marie is certainly a sweet little girl and as bright as a new dollar [silver dollars were in use then]. Paul says she is going to take after her namesake. She looks us over real good—really bright for eight days old. The nurse in the hospital said she was the first baby she had ever helped deliver that didn't cry at first but took time to look around the room. She's nice and fat and white as snow. This surprised Leanne. She thought our baby would be brown, too, like the other newborn babies there. Ha!

· · ·

Brazilian Christian primary school started up again in January 1958, and was well on its way when my brother, John, had a near-fatal accident. His newsletter relates the story.

> Dear Friends,
>
> I had an exciting and almost disastrous experience the other day that I would like to pass on to you while it is still fresh in my mind, although I'm sure I shall never forget it.
>
> Paul and I had been to Benjamin Constant where we had taken some missionary friends (the Stan Bests and Saralie Nelson) to catch the plane to Manaus. We were returning to the Port of Two Brothers in two separate boats, but traveling side by side. It was about 2 p.m. on Saturday, January 18, when I discovered I needed to refill my gas tank from my reserve supply. I slowed to a stop and waved to Paul to continue on. It was a very hot day and he had a quarter of beef in his boat with nearly an hour to travel before reaching home. Ordinarily we would have waited for each other, but as my smaller boat was faster, I filled my tank and hurried to catch up with him.
>
> Exactly what happened, I do not know. One second I was racing to catch up with Paul, and the next I was thrown vio-

lently out of the boat into the middle of the Amazon River. No doubt my boat struck some underwater object or a large fish that was about to surface. The motor was wrenched from my grasp and the boat veered sharply to the right, throwing me out and revolving around in a tight circle.

Immediately I struggled to the surface, gasping for breath and choking. Just then my boat narrowly missed me as it raced by, and I was slapped hard by a wave from its wake as I choked and struggled to stay afloat in my wet clothes. I fumbled for my little emergency life saver (called ResQPak) that I had placed in my shirt pocket, but it was gone! Then I remembered when I dropped it on the floor of the boat, I put it in my pants pocket. I felt for it there but could not find it. I had been feeling with my right hand which was injured in WWII and is very sensitive. My situation was growing worse by the minute. I took off my shoes and tried to remove my pants but had too much trouble keeping afloat in the turbulent water. Paul had disappeared from view, and I knew I couldn't swim well enough to make it to shore. My boat was circling too fast for me to stop it. If I had tried and failed, I would have been swamped in the wake or cut up badly by the propeller.

My strength was going fast and I knew I had only a few moments left, so I did the only thing I could—I prayed. I cried aloud, "Thank you, Lord, for saving my soul!" and committed myself to Him, expecting that in a very few minutes I would surely drown and I would soon be in His very presence.

Like He did to Peter in Matthew 14, His answer came immediately and I began to relax and think more clearly. I tried to float and searched again for my ResQPak. This time I found it, squeezed it, and out popped a little pair of inflated water wings that supported me easily. I praised the Lord because now I knew I was safe. I hollered for help, and I guess you know I can holler! They heard me over a half-mile away.

The wife and daughter of a good friend of mine jumped into a canoe and paddled out to pick me up. I was pretty much done in, but managed to crawl into their canoe. After a moment or two of rest and explanation, I was ready to cope with my next problem: How could I stop my racing boat?

The boat would run for hours with a full tank unless the current carried it to shore and smashed. Seating myself in the bow of my rescuers' canoe, I guided it to where the canoe would intercept the circling boat's course at a tangent. On its next approach I got set and jumped right into the middle, where I was able to regain control and stop the motor.

Praise the Lord! It was good to be alive! I told the whole story to the others who had arrived in canoes to help. I told them how the Lord had surely saved me. I thanked them all and continued on home. This narrow escape, I believe, was of the Lord. It reminded me that I was not my own, that I was bought with a price, and therefore I was to glorify God in my body and in my spirit, which are God's (1 Corinthians 6:19–20). Frankly, I had been discouraged and was about to return to the States because of my inabilities and disabilities. Then came this accident and the Lord spared my life as though to remind me that He could use me in spite of my faults. It also served to remind me that the people in Amazonas are in much the same predicament I was. Most of them are struggling in the waters of sin and death, without hope of rescue. They need someone to tell them that their Life Saver is near and that they need only to reach out and take hold of Him. I believe that "someone" is me, so I'm asking that you friends at home covenant anew to pray for us as we travel this treacherous river, telling the lost of salvation in the Lord Jesus Christ.

John and I were expected to arrive simultaneously that day. Since I showed up alone, I naturally faced an inquisition the minute I stepped out onto the clay bank.

"Why didn't John come with you?" Fran asked.

"He decided to hitchhike to the States to see the Canadian hockey team beat the Russians. He'll be back in a few days," I said, trying to keep a straight face.

"What?" Fran cried. That was the first time I heard her shout.

"I'm just kidding. He stopped to refuel at the Acaratuba and flagged me on because I was carrying meat, and to avoid the wake this thing makes when it stops. It would bounce his little boat around," I explained. "Just keep watching the curve of the river. He should slew around the corner any minute. I thought he might catch me before I arrived, but this mean machine of ours moves along at a good clip."

I took a quick rainwater shower and laid down for a few minutes to relax. But I couldn't. "Jessie," I hollered, "did John show up yet?"

"I don't think so," she answered.

"That's funny. He should be here by now," I reasoned.

I got up and searched with the binoculars, but saw no sign of John. I jogged back to the house. "I'd better jump in the boat and see if he's in trouble. He could have lost the prop or thrown a rod," I told Jessie.

Gervasio had just boosted the engine on his shoulder and headed toward the port when John showed up at the top of the bank. "Put it back on its rack, Gervasio," I said. "Here's John."

His clothes had dried in the wind and sun, but he looked fatigued and bedraggled with tousled hair and clinging trousers. We all gathered around to hear the story of his struggle for life. Together we praised God that John made it back alive.

I celebrated a birthday just days after John's close call. Before going to the house for breakfast that morning, I jotted down the following paragraphs in a notebook.

> Today is my birthday. It staggers me to think I have passed 32 years on this earth and know as little as I do and have accomplished so little. Dad and Mom are in their 70s. I can't believe that soon they will pass on into that other land [our mother lived another 29 years]. I've known Christ as my Savior a little more than 12 years. The assurance of being saved is marvelous, but how many of the 12 years have been failures?

Jessie and I have been married 11 years. We've had good fellowship, but how many of her days were ruined because of my selfishness and lack of ability to lead my family in the paths of righteousness? The Lord has given us four beautiful children. What immense blessings they have been. But how often do I fail in counseling and disciplining? Six years we've been on the Lord's field of service. What a privilege to have the opportunity to take part in the establishment of a mission station in unevangelized territory. But how many of these few years have really counted for Him? And how many have been utter failures?

It is challenging to me to realize that I am the age Christ was during His ministry and shortly before He was crucified. I hope my 33rd year of this life will be totally dedicated to Him that I might be continually filled with the Holy Spirit so that by His power my life will be a fulfillment of His will. May I work hard to that end, namely, to glorify Christ with all that is within me.

John's accident caused us all to take inventory of our lives and realize that our times are, indeed, in God's hands.

. . .

ABWE was pleased with the financial report from the end of the first school year. Jungle cleared, schoolhouse built, tables and chairs made, and school supplies purchased, all at a total expenditure of U.S. $265. They gave us the green light to continue our primary school.

At mid-term during our second school year, we prepared a banquet for the pupils. They had never heard of such a thing. Mid-term fell on May 30, immediately following the town's annual patron saint's day festivity.

Besides broadening the horizons of our pupils' experience, we felt a need to build a bridge of friendliness to the village schoolteacher, Noemia, and her pupils. She prohibited her students from attending our Sunday school and weekly kids' Bible class. The priest had recently visited a few of our church members, threatening them for having left the Catholic Church. Religious differences are understandable, but a spirit of enmity seemed to be growing in the village, and we felt we should make some effort to stop it.

So I invited the schoolteacher and her student body to join us in an early morning track meet, after which they would eat with us at our banquet. The teacher had heard enough about banquets to know it meant food. When food was involved in any of our church or school activities, it was easy to draw a crowd.

Our bell rang long and loud at 7 a.m. to call everyone to the track meet. John and I strapped on our holsters and .22 pistols, to be used to start the various events, and swaggered to the middle of the soccer field like a couple of frontier sheriffs.

Noemia Catique, the schoolteacher, received a flowery welcome. I handed her a clipboard and pencil and said, "Senhora Catique, we would appreciate it if you would officiate at our track meet. Your job will be to call the names of contestants, keep score, take note of the winners, and present the prizes."

"Sounds easy, Senhor Paulo. I have a loud voice, and can get mean when I have to [as well we knew], so there will be no cheating," she said with a big smile.

John and I fired off a few shots into the air to get the children's attention and start the contests. They had never seen high-jumping before, so John and I demonstrated. It looked easy, and the kids were champing at the bit to take a crack. At three feet, everybody cleared the pole easily, although they jumped standing straight up, as if jumping over a log or a ditch. A couple of boys, after a few tries, were able to imitate our demonstrated style perfectly. The broad jump, relay race, sack race, hammer throw, baseball throw, three-legged race, and tug-of-war all proved far more popular than the high jump.

While this hilarious frolic was taking place, everybody could smell the meal being prepared by parents just outside the back door of the schoolhouse. Skewers of meat and fish roasted over the coals, while huge kettles bubbled and steamed with real pork and beans, which never taste better than when prepared with the ears, snout, feet, and tail.

It sounded like a shootout when John and I emptied our revolvers into the sky, gathering everyone around to finalize the program. The sun was hot at 11 a.m., and the kids were tuckered out, sweating, ready to quit. "Thanks for your sportsmanship and cooperation," I shouted. "We especially thank you, Mrs. Catique, for your great help! You kids run home, take baths, change clothes, and be ready to come to our banquet when you hear the bell ring," I instructed.

John and I had bought all the soup plates and spoons we could find in the nearby trading posts, enough to serve 75 kids. Twelve-foot-long boards across the school desks created banquet tables. Single boards across chairs formed benches. A bouquet of whatever happened to be blooming at the time was placed on each table. Our pupils twisted colorful crepe paper streamers and paper chains to drape from the four corners of the room. Little baskets full of candy served as place cards.

Our guests streamed into the schoolroom, amazed at the transformation. They didn't know what to do. Some stopped in the doorway to gaze, and had to be pushed in by those behind them. It was necessary to explain how to find their places.

Four men from church served as waiters, each in a white shirt (loaned by John and me), a green and yellow cap, and a clean white towel draped over a forearm. They were uncomfortably self-conscious, and made fun of each other as they waited for the crowd to come in.

"Look at yourself, Laodelino," Carlindo said. "You look more like a lady than your wife!"

"Don't you worry about me, old sap," Laodelino retorted. "You're the one that does the women's work at home. I saw you chopping wood and washing your pants last week!"

"What's the matter, Valdemar?" Miguel asked. "Afraid your woman is going to make you do all the cooking from now on?"

"Well, at least we keep food on hand. I hear you're starving your family," was Valdemar's rebuttal.

It took several minutes for everyone to find their places and quiet down. After the prayer, and while they waited to be served, the guests tried to figure out what their paper napkins were for. They dug into their food with vigor, as though still in competition for first place. Fran baked 100 fresh rolls and enough cake for the whole crowd. The kids from both schools had never seen or heard of anything like the experiences of that day. It improved relationships with the community members who opposed us and our message, and became an eagerly anticipated annual event, complete with special speakers and music.

During these days, Fran was growing increasingly uncomfortable with her advancing pregnancy. Playing the accordion for church services was difficult, the heat and humidity more oppressive than ever. Toward the end of June, John said, "This is enough! Let's pack up. Fill a suitcase with a month of the kids' homeschooling lessons. We're out of here!" So they went to Iquitos, Peru, where the Inter-American hospital was well staffed. After a few difficult hours in the hospital, all the discomfort was exchanged for a beautiful baby girl they called Allene Louise.

"Praise God!" Fran exclaimed. "Something besides just boys around the house."

Allene was a real live doll, soon nicknamed Enie by the Schlener clan. Within a few years, Enie and Rena were close playmates, swinging their dolls in hammocks like the Brazilians, and playing school or church with their puppies.

For the rest of the school year, I had to run the show alone. Jessie had taught the beginners who needed special attention and didn't know whether they were right- or left-handed, let alone how to hold a pencil. But Rena was still in diapers, and Tim Jim and Leanne needed to be taught correspondence courses. Fran, the arithmetic teacher, now had a tiny baby to take care of, as well as John Read and David to teach.

Ralph and Margie Poulson, with their six-month-old son, Rawlie, arrived at the Port of Two Brothers in June. They had just finished language school and were raring to go. While I taught six subjects to four grades each morning, Ralph helped out with Sunday messages.

John and I hastily transformed a portion of our workshop into barely livable, temporary living quarters for the Poulsons. This must have been extremely hard for them, for they had been raised in lovely homes and had just come from the south of Brazil. The last newsletter from Jessie before furlough, said,

> We hate to leave John and Fran and kids, but they won't be alone. Ralph and Margie Poulson will be there to help. Ralph weighs 240 pounds but looks 180, and has been testing all our wooden steps, chairs, bridges, ladders and floors to the limit. We are so glad to have them, however, that we have issued them a blanket license to break anything within a five-mile radius. Pray for them as they look to the Lord for His guidance regarding their future in this area.

It was little or no chore to get ready for furlough this time. With a minimum of fuss we just walked away from the place, leaving tools, boats, motors, and household stuff where they lay. The Poulsons moved into our house from the workshop hovel, and Ralph finally had room to stand up straight.

The Goodmans met us at LA International Airport and whisked us to their home in Compton, where we were treated like kings. Bud took me out to the driveway.

"Ya think this rig will keep you rollin'?" he asked as we stopped beside a brand new, baby blue 1958 Ranch Wagon.

"What do you mean, 'keep me rollin''?"

"These are your wheels while you're on furlough," he answered.

I looked at Bud to see if he was kidding. I walked all around that dream machine, gazing at it from stem to stern. "You can't be serious," I said. "This is too good to be true!"

"The owner's manual is in the glove compartment. Jump in and whip around the block to see how she moves." He tossed me the keys. "They got the wrong engine in this buggy by mistake," Bud said on a happy note. "It's got a little bigger package under the hood than the run-of-the-mill."

I opened the driver's side door and inhaled the new car aroma. What a fantastic start to our second furlough. Jessie and I never ceased to marvel at God's provision for our needs. He supplied things we needed before we knew we needed them.

Soon the new wagon was filled with empty Cracker Jack boxes, bubble gum wrappers, and comic books. The snow-capped mountains, fruited plains, lakes, and streams thrilled us as though we had never seen them before. We had no idea where we would live, except that we knew it wouldn't be wise for us or them to visit a one-year tribulation period on our parents by moving in.

Pastor and Mrs. Forrest Johnson of Tabernacle Baptist in Seattle, Washington, received us with open arms when we arrived in church. "Where are you folks going to live for the year?" they asked.

"We have no idea, Pastor. We want to be close to our parents here in the Northwest."

It took just one announcement from the pulpit to secure a place to live. Weldon and Pauline Gwinn, a missions-minded couple, gave Jessie and me a vacant duplex they had—both sides. I think Weldon kicked the door down between the two units so we could have full run of the place. Our new address was 8533 Interlake Avenue, Seattle.

Idris and Mary Roberts and others from church scrounged in their attics and garages for enough furniture, utensils, bedding, and lamps to set up housekeeping. Jessie and Idris, both being of Scottish descent, shared a special affinity.

We couldn't wait to sink our teeth into a nice tender chunk of roast beef, and to smell pork chops sizzling in the pan. In the supermarket we handled heads of lettuce as though they were sacred, and gazed at celery, which we hadn't seen for four years. All we could do in the cheese section was stare dumbly, not knowing what to choose, wondering how there could be so many different kinds. The kids went for dry cereal. Other customers surely thought we had been starved the way we darted around grabbing things off the shelves.

Physical exams revealed a set of problems for Jessie. Her blood test results prompted our doctor to recommend exploration of her liver and other vital organs. At the same time he removed her appendix and stripped her varicose veins. Staph infection set in while she was in the hospital; the large incision would not heal.

Idris and Mary had just finished refurbishing a bedroom in their home, and invited Jessie and 13-month-old Rena to stay with them until Jessie got back on her feet. The rest of us learned quickly everything Jessie did around the house. It took me most of the morning to get breakfast, prepare three school lunches, wash dishes, make the beds, and dust. Laundry was not so hard with a washer and dryer, but I lacked dexterity with the iron. It took me hours to do the kids' school clothes and my own shirts.

Idris recommended Dr. Johnny Johnson, an excellent dentist in Seattle. When we all went for checkups, he became interested in our adventurous missionary experiences in the jungle. We shared with him some of the sad dental situations we had seen among the jungle people, and lamented there was nothing to do to alleviate their suffering.

At my next appointment with Dr. Johnson, I stood near the chair while he worked on the kids.

"You know, Paul," he said, "you can extract teeth for those people."

I asked him to repeat himself, not believing I had heard him

correctly. "I don't think so, Dr. Johnson," I answered without hesi-
tation. "I've fixed a lot of wounds, snake bites, and other illnesses,
but I'm not made for getting into other peoples' mouths."

"Listen, Paul, dentists are people just like you, and have to
learn to do these things from scratch. A young buck like you can
catch on," he assured me. Then he handed me a heavy, thick book
called *Oral Surgery.*

The word "surgery" spooked me. I didn't know pulling teeth
was surgery. If it was, I wanted to steer clear of it. I thanked Dr.
Johnson for the book and tried to change the subject while he
poked around in Cindi's mouth. Before we left his office, Dr.
Johnson said, "I'll get on the phone this afternoon and find some
used forceps and other items you'll need."

The next dental appointment was our last before returning
to the Amazon. Dr. Johnson handed me the promised forceps,
which I felt obligated to take out of honor for his personal concern. I thanked him with less enthusiasm than I showed for the
book, and made no promises to try any dentistry. I wondered
which transgression was worse: refusing the instruments and
book, thereby disparaging the dentist's concern and generosity;
or accepting them, knowing I would never try to extract a tooth.
Packed in the bottom of a barrel, those tools didn't see daylight
for nearly a year after we returned to Brazil.

We booked passage on the Moore McCormick Lines. *Moore
McCreed,* on its last voyage before being scrapped, didn't qualify
as a luxury liner. The Christmann family, also members of ABWE
and sailing with us, were headed for Natal on Brazil's east coast.

Rena Marie, not quite two, scared her mother and me into
a panic, the memory of which still causes us to shudder. Leanne
and Cindi had their heads sticking out of the forward porthole
reaching for some fresh air when they suddenly screamed. "Dad,
Rena is about to fall out the other window!" they shrieked. I
took a quick look. Rena was protruding head first up to her

waist, out of the aft porthole, teetering up and down, laughing at how much fun she was having.

"Don't yell at her, whatever you do," I warned the two older girls. I skidded around the corner and grabbed Rena out of the porthole. Had the little tyke teetered too far and lost her balance, she would not have had the strength to keep herself from plummeting into the ocean.

The only part about leaving the States that we really dreaded was saying good-bye to our elderly parents. Each time we wondered if these were our final hugs, and the last time we would hear their voices. Our little Schlener sextet stormed into the Port of Two Brothers on October 26 for a third term of service. Before we reached the house, we were surrounded by our friends from the village, smothering us with friendly greetings.

"Oh, Mister Paulo and Dona Jessie, you both got strong while you were gone," Moon Face said, his face wrinkled in laughter. A fat person is called *forte* [strong], even if he's as weak as a kitten. At 160 pounds, I probably looked healthy to them for the first time. Our house in the jungle was becoming more and more a real home, and Brazil was becoming our homeland.

PART FIVE

MERCY DROPS AND SHOWERS OF BLESSINGS

(1960–1964)

CHAPTER FIFTEEN

I HAD BARELY UNPACKED my medical supplies when a stocky Indian appeared on the front porch. I recognized him but couldn't pinpoint how I knew him. He smiled widely, not ashamed to flash his pointed teeth.

"Come in," I said, reaching out to shake his hand. But it was wrapped in a dirty cloth. I steered him to a bench, in no hurry to see what was under the cloth.

"Where have I seen you before?" I asked.

"Maybe when you came to the *festa* with your brother and those two big guys. Been a long time," he recalled. "And I came to one of the church services in the field in front of your school-house."

"I'm glad to hear you came to a service. Keep coming. We teach what God wants us to know from His own book."

"Everybody likes to come and learn. More are coming next Sunday," he said.

"Do you have a problem with your hand?" I asked. Dumb question.

"I sure do," he said, slowly unwrapping the soiled cloth. There was no sign of a problem until he turned his palm up. All four tendons where the fingers connect to the palm were severed. Only his thumb escaped the gash. The accident had occurred days before.

The four fingers were motionless, bent slightly backward. I guessed what caused the hopeless wound, but asked anyway.

"Got in a fight with my father-in-law. He tried to stab me and I grabbed the knife blade," he explained, flashing his pointed teeth in another big smile. "Better than getting it in the neck!"

I heartily agreed, but suggested next time he might try a sprint into the jungle and hide until his father-in-law cooled off.

It would have taken sophisticated surgery to repair the unfortunate cut. I was humbled to realize there was little I could do for the young man. The new doctor in Benjamin Constant wasn't able to set a fractured leg for the last patient we took, much less repair this fellow's hand. All I could do was clean the cut, suture through his rhinoceros-tough skin as best I could, bandage it, and shoot him with my favorite antibiotics.

In an unprecedented manner, our Indian friends crowded the Brazilian services on Sunday mornings. The friendly Indians were inquisitive and eager to see and hear what went on. Everybody filled in any empty space on church benches. When the church was full, they stood in the doorway and leaned in the open windows.

The interest expressed by the Indians thrilled us missionaries, but most of the Brazilians were not pleased. Indians were officially considered minors, not qualified to sign official documents. Illiteracy at 100% kept them unmercifully indebted to traders. Unable to figure the value of products or to understand prices, the Indians became victims of extortion. By the same token, the Indians were not famous for unadulterated honesty. Some of them coated a heavy clay ball with raw rubber latex to get more money from the traders. Traders learned to cut the rubber balls in half before paying the workers.

The problem of the Indians crowding into the Brazilian church service became greater, making it necessary to hold separate services. The Indian service, held in the field in front of our primary school, started an hour and a half before the Brazilian service. To lead the services, John and I stood on the school's small front porch. Both Brazilians and Indians welcomed the separate services, which actually improved the relationship between the two cultures. That we leaders were foreigners—neither Brazilians nor Indians—was another advantage.

The Indians were glad to stand out in the open, sun or drizzle. When drizzle turned to rain, they simply ran to the edge of the jungle, cut broad leaves for umbrellas, and returned to the service. Some stood under the overhanging thatched roof of the school building until the rain passed.

The Indian services were inaugurated with at least 100 in attendance. Within a few weeks, the congregation increased to almost 500. This was the beginning of God's answer to the continued prayer of many churches and Christian friends asking Him to bare His mighty arm in a superabundant blessing on our field. Dr. Orr's letter of 1953 often came to mind: "We're asking God for a great harvest of souls—*1,000 of them*—why not? Is not our God able? Is this not His will? And if you are faithful, and if we are faithful, what can keep this from being accomplished? God bless you!"

Not all of the Indians loved us. Nearly every afternoon for a few weeks we heard hollering and the sharp crack of rifle fire coming from the edge of the river. Genesio, one of the most influential Indians in the area, hated us. He refused to set foot on our property. Genesio wouldn't even come for medicine, but sent a neighbor or family member when he was in dire need. Traders reveled in getting him drunk on rum while working at the trading post. Intoxication gave him courage to vent his hatred as he paddled by our port on his way home. He teetered unsteadily in his canoe, cursing the Americanos. The side of his 16-inch-wide paddle smacked the water as he screeched in rage.

Years before, according to undocumented history, Genesio and his uncle Nino chopped a man into small pieces, put them into leaf-lined baskets, and tossed them in the creek. They had done this because a witch doctor blamed the hapless victim for placing a curse on one of their relatives.

After Nino became a Christian, Genesio and his wife also accepted Christ as personal Savior. Genesio was one of the first deacons of Immanuel Baptist Church. His son Adercio studied in our primary school and became one of the three pastors of the large church. Diogo, a younger son, was one of the first to establish a private school at the village of Campo Alegre, followed by Miguelzinho, Quintinho, and six others in smaller villages.

Much later Genesio was stricken with cancer and was taken to the hospital in Leticia, where he was carefully treated by Dr. Juan Silva. The doctor always gave us special attention when we brought people from downriver for treatment because of the Flodens' good reputation.

The day Genesio left the hospital, Dr. Silva went to his bedside and said, "My friend, you can go home today. We can't seem to get the big sore to heal. It will be better for you close to your family and your church."

"Do you mean I'm going to die, Doctor?" Genesio asked. "If so, I'm ready; I'm not afraid. I know the Lord Jesus Christ as my personal Savior. He forgave me for the sins I have committed. Thank you for taking such good care of me here in the hospital." Hospital employees heard what he said, and for many days Genesio's courage was often mentioned in the course of conversation among the hospital workers.

It took years for my weak faith to be convinced that what was happening among the Ticuna Indians was real. I lived in fear that they didn't understand the message of salvation, and that they might have ulterior motives for responding favorably to our messages. As far as we could tell, these people lived in total ignorance of God. They were afraid of the powers that caused bad things to happen, which made them susceptible to witchcraft. They didn't give an all-knowing, all-powerful God credit for the benefits they reaped from the jungle, the lakes, and streams. We were convinced that Satan would not let these people go without a fight.

. . .

Seldom a day went by without people arriving groaning, holding their jaws with supposedly medicinal leaves pasted to their faces. Young mothers from 14 years of age on up who never had prenatal care were the most pitiful cases. Some had cavities in all their teeth, surrounded by gums as red as cherries. Others were in such unbearable pain they extracted their own teeth with knives and scissors. Pus sacs were common.

"*Bom dia,* Gaspar. How are you?" I greeted one of the Indians holding a stained cloth under his jaw. A fistula caused by prolonged infection drained pus.

"Everything is just fine." His was the typical answer from patients, even those who had a broken arm or gushed blood from an ax wound.

Travel to the closest town for a tooth extraction was a 200-mile roundtrip by canoe. Most Indians couldn't pay cash for the extraction unless they first sold dried fish or *farinha* in town. I was plagued with guilt for my inability to relieve their problem. I talked myself into thinking that maybe I should attempt to pull teeth, as though our schedule had plenty of room.

"God keep me from ruining our reputation in the process of trying to alleviate their suffering," I prayed. Maybe I should wait until John and his family returned from furlough.

I reached for the oral surgery book a second time. This time I stayed away from the gory photos of faces distorted with great swellings and other disfigurements. I stopped at an illustration of a perfect set of teeth, traced a copy onto tissue paper, and set out to memorize their names and to learn the meanings of terms like buccal, labial, mesial rotation, mandibular, maxillary, and many more. It wasn't easy.

I recalled Dr. Johnson saying, "You don't just yank a tooth out of its socket. A normal extraction, using the proper instrument and proper technique, usually takes a tooth out with minimal or no actual pulling. Never hurry the tough ones. Some are floaters and can be picked out with little resistance."

Overwhelmed with "courajosity" (half courage, half curiosity), I dug my dental tools out of the bottom of the barrel. Some
were stuck shut and some stuck open. Nickel-plating flaked off
most of them.

I soaked the pliers in kerosene to loosen them. Holding them
under water, I worked them until all the black stopped seeping
from the axle pins. Soap and water treatment cleaned them up,
but I boiled them for an hour to make sure. A few drops of veg-
etable oil, so they worked smoothly, finished the job.

A vision of me wrestling a screeching victim with blood
running down his chin made me want to re-wrap the tools and
return them to the bottom of the barrel. Besides, I just didn't
have time for this. My calling wasn't to pull teeth.

I was on the lookout for an individual in the depths of
despair, bellowing in pain, beating the ground, pleading for some
merciful person to tear, jerk, or knock his tooth out of his head.
Someone whom I couldn't hurt any more than he already hurt
might give me courage.

Nobody with those specifications showed up, fortunately,
because I finally tumbled to the fact that I didn't have a dental
chair. The only thing I could find that might work was a well-
worn wicker rocking chair John and Fran didn't use anymore. A
dental chair that rocked was strikingly out of the ordinary. I
propped the rocker back at an angle I guessed was a universal
position, one that wasn't especially comfortable for either uppers
or lowers, but might make both possible. A 1 x 4 clamped to each
rocker gave me the opportunity to adjust the angle before nailing the rockers in place.

Now to persuade someone to climb in to test it. I called to
Gervasio, who was cutting grass in the field and welcomed a
break.

"Gervasio, I'm fixing this rocker into a reclining chair, so I'll
be more comfortable when I take my afternoon naps," I joshed,

thinking if he knew it was for dental patients, he might not agree to the experiment. "Sit down and see how it feels to you," I invited.

After Gervasio settled in the chair, I broke the news about its purpose. His response astonished me. Gervasio said, "Thank God, Senhor Paulo, if you are going to pull teeth. Look here!" He pulled his cheek aside to reveal lots of blank spaces and six or eight cavernous holes in the teeth that remained.

The chair was still wobbly after nailing the 1 x 4's in place. And there was no place for Gervasio to rest his dangling feet. While Gervasio sat in the chair, I clamped a piece of plywood across the two front legs. The arms of the old chair, even with the wicker peeling off, seemed solid enough to withstand spasmodic twitches from sufferers.

The next day I piped water from our rainwater tanks to the little, nicked-up, white enamel sink in my makeshift clinic. A brand-new child's potty, containing a solution of water and cre-osote, would serve as a spit receptacle. I wondered how well my patients would be able to hit the small target with frozen faces, so I hurriedly made a little bench to bring the potty up closer to face level. I later learned that even up that close, a bathtub wouldn't have been big enough.

By now, I thought I knew everything in the first 10 pages of the oral surgery book. Doing a mandibular block looked diffi-cult, but the maxillary block looked easy. I thought I might only take patients with bad uppers for awhile.

"Thursday, starting at one in the afternoon, we will extract teeth free of charge at our first-aid station," I announced one Sunday morning at church. A wave of panic swept over me. I couldn't believe what I had just said!

Thursday arrived too soon. My little enameled sink was spic-and-span by then. Its single faucet brought a generous stream of rainwater that occasionally dropped pollywogs into the sink, wiggling until the current swung them into the whirlpool and down the drain. My forceps and elevators were all sterilized and laid out on clean strips of toilet tissue, out of sight of the seated patients. Germicidal solution was mixed in a war-surplus, stainless-steel pan. I made up a stack of 2 x 2-inch gauze pads and stacked them next to the instruments. An ancient mirror with a hole in the center hung on a rusty nail. A flashlight, small enough to hold in my mouth, was within reach.

I truthfully hoped that no one would come that Thursday, but three ladies showed up, two of them nursing babies. The other was a middle-aged woman named Flora. As they sat down on the porch, I prayed, "Lord, should I send them home and try again next week?" No answer. I opened the "dental bible" and took out the diagram I had made, with arrows pointing from teeth to instruments to pressures to apply for extractions.

The ladies and I chatted for a few minutes while I tried to decide which lady to treat first and they sized me up.

Diapers were unheard of at that time, so I wondered what complications might develop with nursing babies close at hand while trying to extract teeth from the mothers.

I chose Mrs. Flora as my first patient. She was known in the village for her fits of rage. Everybody got out of her way while she brayed and beat the walls of her house. I was relieved to see her smile as she came in. Just the thought of tooth extraction can take the tucker out of the most courageous. I demonstrated how to get into the chair. Flora put a foot onto the plywood cross-piece, pivoted around, and plunked down into the chair. Everything I had studied about tooth extraction evaporated: names of teeth, names of instruments, and pressures. I thought I had suffered a mini stroke.

I had Flora rinse her mouth with rainwater and spit in the potty. She was an accurate shot—so far. The tooth she wanted extracted was a mandibular molar, a good tooth with no decay. It was all by itself; there wasn't another tooth in her mouth. I had

Aldo, my faithful hired man for many years.

Above:
Alberto fell onto a sharp snag while carrying a heavy load.

Sheestoo, a student at our primary school who started one of nine schools in the area for Ticunas.

Left:
Alair and Odete as primary school students. They went on to become camp counselors, Indian school teachers, and Bible institute graduates. They are now married to pastors in Brazil.

Indian *festa*—drummers contribute to percussion section.

Ticuna Indian maid of honor at puberty rites festival.

Indian *festa*—the woodwind section, not at all in tune.

Engine trouble on the 60-hp diesel was almost always my fault—the result of water in the fuel line or hitting a snag.

Indian *festa*—soloist on the turtle shell drum.

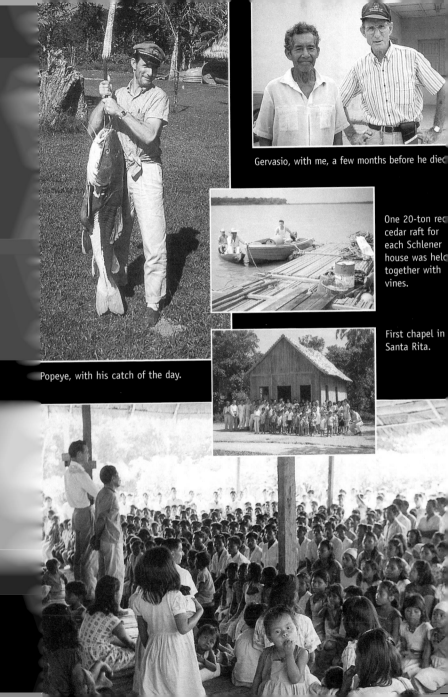

Gervasio, with me, a few months before he died

One 20-ton red cedar raft for each Schlener house was held together with vines.

First chapel in Santa Rita.

Popeye, with his catch of the day.

Ours was the most advanced equipment available for clearing the jungle.

Jessie, First Lady, First Mate, and Galley Chef.

Above:
John's houseboat, the *Casa Branca* (White House).

Left:
Piranhas are easily angered, and devour anything that comes too close.

hoped for a couple of floaters for my first extractions. I had Flora rinse again while I slid behind the partition that separated the workshop from sterile territory. I wiped the perspiration from my brow and confessed to God that I should never have dreamed of extracting teeth.

After getting hold of myself, I returned to face Dona Flora, who was waiting patiently. I tried to force a smile while I had her rinse yet again. Her mouth had never been so clean! I was killing time until I gathered the courage to take hold of the loaded syringe.

I held the syringe behind me, remembering how lethal it looks to a helpless person trapped in a chair. My intention was to hit close to the nerve as it passes from the maxilla to the mandible. Oops! I hit the bone, so backed off a tad and slowly pressed the syringe's plunger. Flora flinched a little and blinked excessively. Any sign of life was better than having her slump over motionless. After Flora admitted to feeling numb on one side, I stepped over to my diagram. I appeared to be studying, but I was making fervent supplication to God for the ability to remove her tooth, and that Dona Flora would be able to get out of the chair and leave on her own power afterward. I wished, even more fervently, that I had never heard of Dr. Johnson.

I tucked the points of the cow-horn forceps between the two legs of the tooth's root and started applying pressure with a straight arm, as far away from Flora as I could get. Her head, as though on a hinge, tipped from shoulder to shoulder; very little pressure reached the tooth. "Lord, by your Grace, get me out of this situation and I'll never touch one of these secondhand tools again. I admit that you didn't call us to this jungle country to pull teeth. I've stepped out of Your will," I confessed to the Omniscient.

I finally got the courage to put a headlock on my patient and was able to remove her tooth. I was wiped out. I dismissed the other two ladies after Dona Flora left. Nearly every Thursday afternoon, and while visiting remote villages by riverboat years later, tooth extraction continued, totaling a few less than 10,000 extractions. But that first extraction still remains freshest in my memory.

CHAPTER SIXTEEN

DURING THE 1960's and beyond, the Port of Two Brothers might have been called a missionary's paradise as 500 Indians, in rapt attention, stood in the schoolyard at 7 a.m. on Sunday singing "Jesus Loves Me, This I Know." Seeing several men walk forward while the message was still being preached, waiting to become Christians, was a sight to behold.

At the Brazilian church in the village, people were receiving Christ as their personal Savior, sometimes entire families at once. Young people led their own meetings, giving personal testimonies, praying, and bringing short messages. They invited unsaved youth to their activities, hoping to win them to Christ. Ten young people from our Brazilian church went to study at the seminary in Manaus, and two at the Bible institute in Iquitos, Peru, but others became pastors, teachers, missionaries, and helpful church members.

Jessie couldn't help in the primary school that year because our arrival on the field was too late to enroll our kids in the ABWE Academy in Iquitos, Peru. She had a full-time job homeschooling our three oldest. Rena, at three, was still too young for school, but she could sing gospel choruses in four languages: English, Spanish, Portuguese, and Ticuna.

Almost three months went by without replenishing our supplies or receiving and sending mail, so we had to travel to Leticia. We missed John and Fran at times like this, and were anxious for their return from furlough.

Our families had lots of fun during our too-few years together. There were all kinds of things to do for enjoyment, but nothing compared to fishing trips. August, September, and

October are the months when the river recedes and wide, clean sandbars appear. That's the time to go fishing in the lakes. John and his boys were as excited about fishing as we were. Jessie still thinks the best fishing is when the Indians come to the back door with fresh catch for sale.

Here, again, ignorance was bliss. The wild country where little lakes are hidden was much wilder than we realized. Danger hid in and around those lakes. Calm, peaceful-looking little lakes are home to giant anacondas and their poisonous associates. They are recreation centers for crocodiles and alligators. Deer, capybara, jaguar, and tapir drink and bathe there. We saw and felt new species of insects on each trip.

Jungle lakes are freshly stocked every year. The Lord does it without the Fish and Game Department. And fish get fat from gorging for six months on the floating fruits and seeds of the flooded swamps. When the water goes down, the fish find themselves crowded in small bodies of water where they get hungry again. This is where we come in.

Before daybreak on one occasion, Tim, my hired man Aldo, and I took a 20-minute boat ride to the trail that leads to Lake Pacu. Like athletes in a triathlon, we jumped out of the boat and tied the bow line to a snag, unloaded our fishing tackle, and hurried up the bank. A loud yell from mid-river brought us to a halt.

"Wait! Wait! Wait!" Two *caboclos* paddled a canoe with such frenzy that the canoe lurched and their paddles threw water with every stroke. We watched them approach, wondering what trouble they were bringing. "Here goes our fishing trip out the window," I said to Tim. "Somebody was probably hurt and they want a trip to the hospital."

"Man, Dad, why does something always have to happen?" Tim lamented.

The racing canoe hit the riverbank full force. Without tying the canoe to a stake, the men sprang from their positions as if catapulted, tossed their paddles to the ground, and sprinted into the jungle.

Those two fellows were hunters. The night before they stretched a string across the trail near a tree where animals eat fruit. The string was attached to the trigger of a shotgun loaded with buckshot. The shotgun was cocked, lashed to a stump, and aimed to bag a tapir or deer when they touched the string. It could have meant a gut shot for Tim, or perforated thighs for Aldo or me.

I thanked the men for stopping us in time. They confessed that they had done a very stupid thing by setting a trap across a trail used by rubber cutters and fishermen nearly every day.

Having escaped the hunters' trap, we hiked along the trail, growing clumsy with excitement as we laid eyes on the placid black water. With our fishing tackle loaded and food hung safely off the ground, we slid our battered canoe into the water and paddled through the narrow channel of thick grass to the main lake. Giant lily pads make a perfect background for their fabulous white blossoms, called *Victoria Regia,* state flower of Amazonas. They also provided shade for our quarry.

Aldo set out to look for another canoe that might be hidden close by, and to cut a fishing pole from the jungle. The canoe he found appeared to have been discarded, but it served him well as long as he kept bailing water. In less than an hour we had more than enough fish for our noon meal. Aldo gathered firewood and cooked them before Tim and I had fished half the length of the lake.

Tim made some spectacular catches, casting toward shore, near snags, and into the shade of overhanging jungle. I was at the prow paddling slowly, ready to charge out to the middle the minute a fish was hooked. Within an hour we had 17 fish of four different species flopping around in the bottom of the canoe.

I tossed a crank bait out to the middle for a try at an *aruana* (ah-roo-wah-NAH). I didn't feel a strike, but suddenly a lunker jumped out of the water with my plug in its mouth. Before it hit the water again, I hauled back full-force to set the hook. But the lure came straight back, barely missing me as it whizzed by my ear.

It takes self-control to avoid carelessness when fishing is as exciting as it is in jungle lakes. Round-bottomed, tippy canoes tax manual dexterity and equilibrium when the angler is pivoting around on a bench to grab a net or gaff hook to help his partner land a fish.

Before moving close to shore, I snapped a large, red and white daredevil spoon with a treble hook to my wire leader, hoping it might "set" better in the mouth of another *aruana*. Reeling the lure in to six inches from the tip of the rod, I flipped to cast. But I snagged something behind me that stopped my cast. At the same instant Tim hollered.

I looked back to see Tim with his hand over his eye, the steel leader protruding between his fingers. "Tim, what did I do?" I swung around and threw myself to the back of the canoe, certain I had punctured Tim's eye and possibly even jerked it out of its socket with the quick power stroke of my cast. It flashed through my mind that from where we were fishing back to the river would take at least 15 minutes of feverish paddling. We couldn't make it over the trail in less than 45 minutes. It would take another 20 minutes in the boat to get home, where we had no communication with the outside world. Once at home, I would have to mix gasoline for the four-plus-hour trip to Benjamin Constant or Leticia, where there might be a doctor and where it would be dark when—and if—we arrived.

"Take your hand away, Timmy. Let me see what happened," I said, dreading the moment of truth. He lowered his hand to reveal the red and white spoon dangling an inch below his right eye. I thanked the Lord that it missed his eye, and that only one of the three hooks in the cluster was embedded under the skin. The trauma lasted less than a minute, but it was the most shaken I had been since my days on the U.S.S. *Cape Esperance*.

We had plenty of cutlery with us. But hunting knives and a

jackknife that had been used to cut pieces of fish and bird for bait weren't choice instruments for the job. Taking a closer look, I noticed that the barb of the hook was under the skin but not deeply buried. It made me think that the point of the hook hit his cheekbone and couldn't go any deeper.

"Hold real still, Timmy. If you feel pain, please don't jerk. You can yell all you want; just don't flinch or grab my hand. I don't want to have to do any cutting." I rinsed off my fishy hands in the lake and dried them on the driest part of my sweaty shirttail. As gently as possible, I took hold of the loose skin where I hoped the point of the hook was located.

"Owwww," Tim complained, holding as still as a statue. Pulling the skin with my left thumb and index finger, I pushed the hook just a tad, hoping and praying that the thing would disengage without snagging. And it did!

I became limp as a rag for a few minutes. I thanked the Lord the accident wasn't more serious, and asked Him to help me keep myself under control during these fishing trips.

. . .

We received word that Dr. Harold T. Commons, our mission's president, was making the rounds to visit all the ABWE missionaries in South America.

"Better tank up your rig, Paul," Orv Floden shouted as he trudged up the high riverbank. "You've got to make a trip to Santo Antonio to pick up the Boss."

Santo Antonio is 130 miles from the Port of Two Brothers, which meant a roundtrip of 260 miles in my little cabin cruiser.

"Orv, you're not only the senior missionary, you are a mechanic. You should go get Dr. Commons. If something happened to the motor, you could fix it. I can barely change spark plugs without crossing the wires. I'm liable to get stranded 75 miles from nowhere," I reasoned.

"I have to go back up to Leticia tomorrow, then turn around and come back for the field council meeting about the time you arrive with Dr. Commons," he explained. We Schleners were located at the halfway mark of the Central Amazon field, and since we had two houses and a good water supply, many field council meetings were held at the Port of Two Brothers.

I went over my almost-new 40-hp outboard with a fine-tooth comb. I put in new spark plugs, checked all wire connections, tightened all nuts and bolts, changed oil in the lower unit, and lubricated everything that moved. I added to my tool supply a new coil, a condenser, shear pins, two extra props, and a pair of spark plugs.

The morning I left for Santo Antonio, I loaded on enough gasoline to carry me to the British Isles, and an extra liter of oil in case I had to mix more gas along the way. Commercial river-boats that could tow us if we got into trouble followed no set schedule in the 1960's. Two might puff by the same day, then nothing for a month or six weeks.

The trip down to Santo Antonio was perfect. The first 30 miles was old hat, but the final 100 miles was new territory. I traveled farther than necessary by not crossing the river at the right places and going around the wrong side of an island or two.

I had never seen Dr. Commons except at mission headquarters in Philadelphia when I was being interviewed by the Executive Committee or giving a work report. I wondered if we could behave ourselves like good Christians here in the wilderness, or if he would discover what we were really like. It might be wise to pass out sedatives to the field council before the meeting at the Port of Two Brothers. I laughed at the thought. I had myself so worried about meeting Dr. Commons that I stammered like a child. But it wasn't long before we were having a great time talking.

For lack of sleeping facilities in Santo Antonio, Dr. Commons and I were assigned to the same bed. He was bushed from the hectic time he'd just spent in Peru and slept soundly, while I stayed so far to the edge of the bed that I had to set my left foot on the floor to keep from falling out.

The next morning we started on the 130-mile return trip to the Port of Two Brothers. A six-hour trip in the wind, rain, and hot sun, bouncing around with the constant whine of the motor made these trips grueling, especially for a person unused to them. But Dr. Commons didn't complain of fatigue or aches and pains; instead, he thanked me for the trip and had no problem negotiating the climb up the riverbank.

Jessie's smile was a healer to most weary travelers. She treated everybody, prince or pauper, alike. Dr. Commons seemed impressed with each of us and what we were doing. The field council meeting was wonderful. I noted, "Dr. Commons encouraged us all to be faithful in the ministry of the gospel and to leave the results with the Lord. He made us all feel like we were God's choice servants."

Dr. Commons left me a personal souvenir. I had taken him on a quick fishing trip to catch a few piranhas. I was careless in removing a hook from the mouth of one of the savages, and had a small chunk taken out of one of my fingers for my pains. "Here, wrap it up with this," he said, handing me his monogrammed handkerchief.

• • •

Fran, David, Phillip, and three-year-old Allene arrived from the States in the first week of October. John Read stayed behind to finish high school at Whittier Christian in La Habra, California, while John gathered the materials he needed to build their houseboat.

The fatherless crew slipped and splashed up the riverbank in the middle of a downpour. The 30 yards of sidewalk between our two houses took a beating for several days after Fran and the kids arrived, as the two groups traipsed back and forth, getting caught up.

John arrived in December with Hank Scheltema, the pilot who brought ABWE's first airplane from Florida, to be stationed in Benjamin Constant. John's newsletter of November 11, 1960, read,

> Hank needed a copilot and navigator to help ferry the plane from the U.S. to Brazil. The plane is an Aeronca sedan on floats. Our route will take us from Philadelphia, down the coast to Orlando, Florida. From there we will begin long inter-island hops across the Caribbean to the island of Trinidad, on the north coast of South America, then down the coast to the mouth of the Amazon River. At this point, Hank will continue to Fortaleza, and I will board the ship that has my baggage, and proceed up the Amazon to the Port of Two Brothers.

The blue and white plane amazed the local population as it circled overhead to land in the river in front of our houses. Many villagers came running, while others ducked behind bushes until things quieted down. Some even grabbed their kids and disappeared into the jungle. Jessie explained in a letter,

> My, it has been something to have this nice airplane in our area. Hank Scheltema has been here nearly four weeks now and has been here three times already—twice with his family. Nice folks, four beautiful children. They can come from Benjamin in less than an hour, about 50 minutes, I believe. He brought us a leg of beef which was enjoyed. He and Paul went to Santo Antonio to hold services for the Paynes while they are gone. This Sunday, Fran and John went. This new way of travel is 'something' for us. We are grateful. The Lord is good.

When the plane was able to keep a regular schedule, we could keep at our work for longer stretches of time without having to travel for mail and supplies. Once, we didn't have to leave town for six months.

. . .

The day our little family had been dreading finally came. None of us fully believed it was going to happen until suitcases were packed. Our happy little family circle was broken when Tim, Leanne, and Cindi went off to school in Iquitos.

Jessie and I often wondered if any family situation is more intimate than that of missionary families in remote areas of the world. There's no one around with whom to speak your native tongue except your own family. You may be cordially accepted by local citizens, but you are forever a foreigner. In our case there were just six of us, with no communication with the outside world other than the eerie reception on our tinny shortwave radio.

We learned to make do with what we had. Family worship was enjoyable. Our fishing trips together were fantastic. We had fun on cookouts, birthdays, and Christmases; playing on the vast sandbars with parakeets, parrots, macaws, monkeys, big dogs, and little yappers. Now we had to separate.

The kids hated it, but they didn't hate Jessie and me. It is hard to look back on those separations without regret. The children wouldn't have believed it at the time, but they now know that family separations are most difficult on the folks left behind.

The return home from Peru was worse than any jail sentence. Jessie and I couldn't stand to see the children's clothes hanging in the closet. Dolls, barrettes, and a few books lay where they had been left; markings on the wall and a burned spot where a candle got too close reminded us of the children's absence. Loud laughter and screeches had come to an abrupt end. We had heard the last doll and puppy dog church service.

When Leanne cried, she said it was because she wanted to repeat fifth grade, where she wouldn't have too much homework. But her parents knew better. Jiggs and Tootsie, the two little dogs, wandered from room to room in search of their playmates.

Tim's fishing rod leaned in its corner near his tackle box. A baseball glove hung on a nail. A soccer ball and dirty tennis shoes stayed where he left them, on the closet floor.

Time and busyness have some healing power. And Rena Marie was still at home. "Just Rena now," Jessie wrote, "and she hangs onto my skirt like a little lost lamb."

At 7 a.m Sunday, I shook hundreds of hands on my way over to the Indian service. Eight hundred beautiful Indians in front of me hung on my every word, watching every move I made. And I thought, as I cast eyes on the multitude, *Our kids are making it possible for me to be here now. This is their ministry and they don't know it—yet.*

· · ·

I had barely stretched out for a half-hour snooze when someone clapped for my attention at the back door. *Don't get upset,* I counseled myself. *You are not here to take naps.*

"Senhor Paulo, Senhor Paulo," a young voice shouted.

"I'll be right there," I answered, hurrying as fast as I could. Teodoro, one of my third-year pupils, stood outside,

"Would you come and kill a snake at the school?" he panted.

"Run back to the place where you saw the snake and keep an eye on him. I'll be right there." I grabbed my .22 semiautomatic, shoving in shells as I walked. The price of a shotgun shell for the local citizens was a half-day's hard labor, so they often used sticks to kill snakes.

"Huh!" Teodoro said, looking around a huge rotten tree trunk lying on the ground. "That's funny, Senhor Paulo. It was all coiled into a small mountain on top of this windfall," the boy said, crouching as though ready to spring.

Uh, oh, I told myself. *If it were a small snake, he wouldn't have used the word mountain.*

I put my finger on the safety switch as I walked around the big log. No snakes. I jumped on top of the log for a better view and noticed an opening about a foot wide at the base where the roots protruded into the air. The crack gradually narrowed until it became a dark hole along the trunk. The decomposed wood in the bottom of the crack was damp and compressed.

By now, curious passersby wondered what the missionary was doing on this fine Sunday afternoon perched on the big log with his rifle, while kids beat on the tree with sticks. "Teodoro, run back to my workshop and bring the ax leaning against the end of my workbench," I instructed.

My hired man, Aldo, returning from bathing in the creek, stopped to offer his services. "Aldo, I think we have a good-sized snake hidden in this rotten log. Do me a favor and chop a hole about ten feet from here. I don't think this trunk is very thick. If it's too thick, we'll forget it."

With four blows, Aldo opened a hole that exposed the skin of an anaconda. "There's a big snake in there, all right," he confirmed.

I aimed my rifle at the entrance of the hole. "Don't anyone stand behind me! If that 'bee-shoo' [universal word for animals in general] comes out in the open and I miss him, I'll run right over the top of you," I warned the children.

All of a sudden, the snake's broad head appeared at the entrance of the hole. Pah! Pah! Pah! my rifle barked. And he pulled his head back in. Now what? Did I hit him or not? Aldo chopped another hole where he thought the tip of the snake's tail might be. Several bystanders got hold of the tail and started pulling. The anaconda measured exactly fifteen feet. Eight school kids dragged it down to the river's edge to skin it for drying.

CHAPTER SEVENTEEN

TWO MEN WERE NEARLY FINISHED working on my new office. Thick thatch with a wide overhang and five big screened windows was the coolest setup available without air-conditioning. In a few days rats and bats moved into the thatch, but the board ceiling caught their droppings. An elevated boardwalk from the doorway to the workshop and first-aid station kept me out of the rain and mud. I could now go from the house to my office without stepping into chigger-infested grass or mud.

John's return from the States with materials to construct their houseboat meant he and I could share preaching duties, supply and hospital trips, and treating the sick. But the fellowship of kindred spirits was what we appreciated most. Our two families took turns inviting each other for Sunday dinner. Jessie and Fran cried on each other's shoulders about how much they missed the kids, and commiserated about the miserable humidity, mud, and insects.

Every Sunday, Indians waited after the second service for medicine, or to learn more about becoming Christians. On one particular Sunday, a group of 40 men hung around.

"Senhor Paulo, we want to talk to you," Miguel, the interpreter, said.

"Good," I answered. "None of you look sick to me, but I have enough needles to stick every one of you."

A ripple of laughter went through the crowd. Miguel spoke again, "Senhor Paulo, we talked together after the morning service while you were in the Brazilian service. We decided we want to build a church so we don't have to stand out in the sun and rain for our church services. What do you think?"

"That's wonderful!" I exclaimed. "Hey, John. These folks want to build a church."

"Which one of them will go to the bank to float the loan?" John replied in English. I had to laugh because these people knew nothing of banks, and there was very little borrowing and loaning of anything in their culture.

That was the extent of the conversation. The crowd broke up and headed for their canoes. We thought they would talk about a building program and have a few arguments over location, plans, and cost.

At seven the next morning while eating breakfast, I heard voices through the window. I stood up to see at least 100 men between John's house and my house.

The men's clothes were ragged, stained, and patched, mostly knee-length. Some wore straw hats. Nearly every man carried a kettle and a little bag of *farinha*. Everyone had a machete, an ax, or both.

"Jessie, take a look. I wonder what on earth is going on," I said to my wife.

I shoved up the bottom half of the screened window to stick my head and neck out. They all smiled.

"*Bom dia,* Rosindo, Plinho, Claudio. How is everybody?" I asked.

Rosindo smiled and responded, "*Nuxmaxe pa chauenexe.*"

"Where are you fellows headed?"

"Right here," Plinho responded.

"Okay," I said. "Sorry I don't have enough benches to accommodate you all."

"No problem; we came to work," someone else piped up. "We came to build the church we talked to you about yesterday."

I couldn't believe it. I pulled my head back inside and dropped the sliding screen. "Jessie, did you hear that? These men are here to start building their church!" I gasped. "They talked about it yesterday after the service, but I thought it might be six months or a year before they actually started."

I forgot about my bowl of oatmeal and went outside to shake hands all around. I spied John and his family through their window and yelled, "Hey John. These guys want to build a church . . . now! All they want from us is to show them where to build it. Better hike with us back into the jungle to choose a place."

"Are you sure you want to build this close to us?" I asked the men, thinking they might want to build in or near an Indian village.

"Here is middle," one of the men said.

Somebody else explained, in broken Portuguese, why "here" would be the best location. "Brothers from Paranapara feel free to come. Brothers from Praia do Meio feel free to come. Brothers from Jacurapa feel free to come. Brothers from Igarape de Rita feel free to come, and from Campo Alegre and Correnteza, and São Domigos and Santa Inez." He seized a finger for every location he mentioned. "This way all village equal. When no church service, you watch place; nobody hurt building."

Building the church in the center of the Indian population, where the Port of Two Brothers "happened" to be, and not in any one of the villages gave meaning to the statement, "This way all village equal."

"Remember, the ground behind the school is high all the way to the creek. Let's show them that spot," John suggested.

The men grabbed their kettles, knives, and axes, and followed us to the edge of the jungle.

"How does this look to you fellows?" John asked.

"This good place, high ground," somebody said. The rest agreed.

Immediately, the men bent and started swinging their big knives. They lopped off smaller bushes and plants. John and I looked at each other in surprise then changed clothes and got our knives. By the time we returned a few minutes later, the 100 men had slashed so much jungle we could see the "lay of the land." It was a perfect building site. The men took a few minutes to drink water and sharpen their machetes. Loud laughter convinced John and me that they enjoyed the project.

"Brother Plinho," I called. "How come there aren't any women with you to make fires and cook your food?"

"Our women folks, and many other men, are in the jungle cutting leaves for thatch and falling trees for framework," he explained.

"Others already make benches," Claudio added, overhearing our conversation. John and I were dumbfounded.

For several weeks while the slashed jungle dried, the Indians' homes turned into veritable factories. Thatch was woven onto slats 12 feet long, each section woven according to the designer's innovation. There were several designs in the finished roof, making it a work of art.

The timing for church construction was perfect: from July through October is the peak dry season, the best time of year to clear the jungle for burning. Even though it rained often during the dry season, it didn't last long enough to hinder the drying process. The men found it hard to believe when John and I told them of the millions of acres of forests destroyed by forest fires in the United States.

No nails were used in the construction of the church, only vines. Great coils of thin but amazingly strong vines were stacked in the shade to stay green and flexible until used to secure the thatch to the rafters. I often wondered how many men it would take to break one of those thin vines. Hardwood trees for stanchions were felled and hewed to shape on the spot. The stanchions served as the foundation to which the rest of the framework was secured. Larger trees, hewed by hand into planks, made heavy, rugged benches.

John and I had trouble controlling our laughter watching the men carry their benches to church on their heads Sunday morning. Each man made enough seats to hold his own family, plus a few more. Some of the benches were only six inches wide and 10 feet long. A few were too tall, leaving space for worshippers to swing their feet during the services. Swaybacked benches needed an extra leg in the center.

The main church floor was clay, packed solid by thousands of bare feet. A raised floor, one-fourth the width of the building and running the entire length of the structure, was built from split palm trees. This served as a nursery area or platform for speakers and special music. It was a clean surface for mothers and infants to sit; just the way they wanted it. And it elevated the speaker several feet above the audience, which helped their voices carry.

This arrangement made interesting background scenery for the congregation. Instead of rows of choir members decked out in luxurious gowns with plenty of space between the pulpit and the choir loft, a hundred or more mothers sat on the floor with their babies. I have stepped on a few pudgy little feet during Sunday services, which caused great laughter from the congregation when the child howled.

· · ·

Violent storms, usually short-lived, are dangerous to Amazon travelers, whatever the size of their vessel. Oceangoing freighters on their way to Peru are forced to drop anchor sometimes for lack of visibility. Runabout speedboats like ours are no good in the big blows. Round-bottomed dugout canoes, not heavily loaded, can bounce, yielding to wind and rolling with waves better than heavier, lower canoes. But with too much freight—like a full load of manioc potatoes or crammed with people—they become helpless in rough water and blasts of wind. Incidents of drowning are common where the only mode of travel is by water.

Travelers headed upstream stay close to the edge of the river to avoid the main current's force. Towering jungle hides the oncoming storm clouds until they are directly overhead. Seasoned travelers, sensing the "calm before the storm," wisely pull over, secure their canoes, and wait. They prefer to be chilled to the bone rather than risk drowning.

We were still waiting for the slashed jungle to dry at the church building site when we were hit with a crackerjack of a storm. Lightning flashed and thunder sizzled, making us cringe. Sheets of rain pounded on the thin siding of our house and roared on the aluminum roof. Tall palm trees in the front yard bent low, their branches outstretched. They looked like umbrellas turned inside-out.

I took a gander at the river from the girls' bedroom, where visibility was better, but the wind still tore at the trees and whipped up whitecaps. Glancing upriver, I spotted a dark object on the far side. It appeared then disappeared, obscured by the waves. When the river level rises, widespread debris—huge trees, submerged logs, sticks, weeds, and bushes of every description—clutters the river making navigation tricky until the river clears.

But the floating object I saw was not debris. It looked like a canoe without a passenger. I hollered out the kitchen window across the lawn to John's house.

"Hey, Joooohn! It looks like there's an empty canoe drifting down the other side of the river." I had to repeat myself several times for John to hear me above the roaring storm.

John went to his front porch to look. By now the object was about three-quarters of a mile from us, close enough to see that it was a canoe.

"We'd better go check it out. Could have broken loose from somebody's port, or it could be somebody in trouble," John shouted back.

As though ordered by a staff sergeant, we flew to the workshop. John grabbed a full tank of gas, a paddle, and the heavy toolbox. I grabbed the 40-hp outboard motor, and we slipped and sloshed down to the port where the boat bounced, slamming repeatedly against the clay riverbank. Muddy feet on the varnished deck, slippery as ice, tested our balance and agility. I yanked the starting cord, and John pointed our boat toward the canoe. I bailed while the waves jerked and twisted us around.

Waves washed over the bow of John's runabout, kicking the stern out of the water and freeing the prop. At midstream we were unable to maneuver the craft enough to avoid some of the debris. Fortunately, enough of the trash fell from the tail of the motor when the prop cleared the water that we were able to keep moving.

In the midst of this predicament, I started to laugh. John gave me a skeptical look. "What's so funny?" he blasted above the din.

"I don't know; must be a pressure valve bursting," I chuckled. Then John, too, shook with laughter as he tooled his boat around a humongous tree.

Sopping wet and buffeted by the wind, John and I were chilled to the bone. But we were glad we inconvenienced ourselves, for we could see a man in the water on the far side of his swamped dugout. Wild-eyed, he clung for dear life to his nearly submerged canoe, his head barely above water. He must have been frightened by our roaring boat as it approached him, towering over his head.

We grabbed the man, hoisted him into John's boat, then pulled his small dugout across our bow. Clothed only in flimsy shorts, the little fellow shivered so violently he could hardly keep his footing until we told him to crouch down on his haunches out of the wind.

We thought he might have said, "Hey, guys, am I ever glad to see you two! I couldn't have held on much longer. Thanks a lot!" But neither a smile nor a word emerged from the Indian.

"Where do you live? We'll take you right to your house," John shouted. This fellow either couldn't speak Portuguese, was mute, or just didn't like us. He slowly stood, clutching the gunnel with one hand and pointing in the direction of his house. We were only a quarter of a mile from the home of our trembling passenger, whom we named Wordless Willie.

As we approached his port, a group of curious neighbors gathered, wondering why a motorboat was stopping. The instant we touched the clay bank, Willie sprang from the boat as though released from a trap. He pulled his canoe from our bow, then turned—still silent—and walked up to his house without turning back.

John and I looked at each other, shrugged, and headed for home. We shook hands and jokingly congratulated each other for bravery, self-sacrifice, and service beyond the call of duty. And did we ever laugh as we bobbed through the choppy water back to our anxious families and the coffeepot.

John and I made fun of Wordless Willie, who failed to express even a hint of gratitude. Later we learned that Indian tribes are not accustomed to outwardly expressing thanks or appreciation.

How often do we Christians fail to express gratitude and appreciation to our Heavenly Father who reached down, pulled us out of sin, brought us to shore, and placed us on the solid Rock, our Savior the Lord Jesus Christ? Wordless Willie, without a word, taught us a valuable lesson.

· · ·

Lambert and Doris Anderson, missionaries with Wycliffe Bible Translators in Peru, were in the process of putting the Ticuna Indian language into writing and translating the Bible into the Ticuna language. The Andersons offered to teach a six-week session on the Ticuna language at the Port of Two Brothers.

Lambert and Doris, along with being gracious and patient, were keen professionals. They had us making noises with our mouths, noses, and throats that we had never uttered before. Indians from the church served as our informants, which gave them prestige and lots of laughs. The Ticuna language is a tonal language, and a difficult one at that. Innocent speakers get into serious trouble by using the wrong tone. We learned enough to carry on conversation about everyday topics with our Indian friends, but never became proficient enough to preach and teach in the Ticuna language.

Shortly after our studies with the Andersons, Indians by the dozens pestered us to start a school for their young people. No Bibles or hymnbooks were opened during church services because nobody could read.

"Senhor Paulo, our church is way bigger than the Brazilian church, but you spend more time with them than you do with us. None of us can read the Word of God. I have four boys who want to learn to read, but nobody to teach them," one father complained.

"We want to be able to read what is printed in the Bible. We believe what you read to us, but we want to see for ourselves." These sincere petitions caused me to lose sleep seeking God's will.

I tried to stall, saying, "If you think God wants you to have a school, you will have to build it yourselves. I simply don't have time. And where will you get teachers?"

It may have seemed that I was being harsh or that I thought they were not worthy of the blessings we bestowed on the Brazilians; namely, building and equipping a school, besides doing the teaching.

While our children were studying in Iquitos, Jessie and Fran were a great help in the Brazilian school. John's progress in building his houseboat for river evangelism was hindered by chronic back trouble. It took from September 1961 to December 1962— 15 months—to build a functional houseboat.

The airplane schedule eased the number of mail and supply trips John and I had to make, but there were emergencies. Medical and dental work continued. I gave up on the idea of starting a school for the Indians, totally stymied as to how we could possibly do it.

The morning after I told the Indian men to pray about a school, 50 men showed up outside the kitchen window. It was just like a few years before when they came to build their church.

"Oh, no," I groaned.

"What?" Jessie asked.

"Take a peek outside."

She stood up from the breakfast table and saw all the men with their axes, machetes, and kettles of food. "How do you think you can start another school? I guess you don't have enough to do in your spare time, right?" she asked.

I admitted, "I simply cannot bring myself to smother their legitimate desire. There is only so much they can do, but they are willing to do anything to learn to read the Bible."

"Paul, something will work out if it is God's will. You keep telling me, 'Where the Lord leads, He provides.' Is it true, or not?" It was great to have a lifetime partner like Jessie who both cautioned and encouraged me.

"What are you fellows up to with all your knives and axes and kettles of food?" I asked, already knowing the answer.

"Build school," one man grunted, followed by 49 "mmmms" of agreement.

I felt I should try to convince them that starting a school for their children was more complicated than throwing up a shack and saying, "Here, brother Paulo, now teach our people to read and write."

I praised them for their desire to learn, but cited a number of obstacles that make schooling difficult. We had permission from the Department of Education and Culture to establish primary schools, but were required to teach in Portuguese, the official language of Brazil. Few Indian children spoke Portuguese. No one knew of a Brazilian who spoke the Ticuna language, nor anyone willing to teach Indians, no matter what language they spoke.

They knew Fran, Jessie, and I taught five mornings a week,

treated sick people in the afternoon, and extracted teeth on Thursdays. They also knew we held three church services every Sunday, that we had to make mail, supply, and emergency trips, and make time for field council meetings.

"Which one of these duties do you think we can quit so we'll have time to teach your people?" I asked.

Subdued mumbling started as they hashed out the problem. Finally one fellow spoke, "Nobody don't know, Pastor Paulo."

"I hope you see the problem starting another school would cause," I said. "This great desire you have to learn to read is an indication that God is working in your lives, and that He has a plan for you. You are willing to do what you can, which is build a schoolhouse and make furniture. But I am only one person and I have a family, too, and only 12 hours between sun-up and sun-set," I continued.

While talking to the men, an interesting idea popped into my head. Four students in our Brazilian primary school who had studied with us for six years might be willing to teach Indians in the afternoons. I explained this to the group and surprised them with the question, "What do you think about our Brazilian students helping teach?"

Another brief, mumbled meeting-of-the-minds took place. One man said, "They don't like us."

I understood. "I will warn the teachers to not make fun of your speech and to have patience with those who are slower to learn. Discipline problems with teachers and students will be handled by me."

Although I was disappointed at having to stop the boys' afternoon woodworking class after only one year, something had to go. The boys had made small wall shelves, simple benches, and, finally (non-existent in the area), collapsible ironing boards. But the Indian school was more important.

The four prospective student-teachers met at my house in the evening, wondering why I singled them out. The gist of my challenge to them was: "You four young people are Christians and have a responsibility to serve the Lord, right?" They nodded in the affirmative. "Teaching the Ticunas to read and write would be a highly fulfilling ministry. Imagine taking an illiterate person who doesn't know the first letter of the alphabet and helping him understand what little groups of letters say."

Trying to make the job sound simple, I told the chosen four that if they could teach the Indians what they had learned in our mission school, it would be a great accomplishment. They were willing to try. I was surprised at how important becoming teachers made them feel.

In less than two weeks, the four-room, thatch-and-palm schoolhouse was finished. A thatched extension with a bench and table provided a place for me to correct notebooks while classes were in session. I could listen to what was going on and make impromptu visits to each class. The effort the Indians displayed in doing whatever was necessary to prepare a place to study was amazing.

Tables and chairs were fashioned from freshly fallen trees using axes, machetes, and adzes. The furniture was a jumble of designs: some tables had 4 x 4 legs and could have supported the front feet of an elephant; others had spindly one-inch legs. Another had crisscross braces between the legs all the way around, with no way a pupil's legs could fit under the table. One of the smallest students had a chair with a back that reached way past his head. Ticunas had never seen much furniture, so they copied simple tables and chairs as best they could.

The teachers taught the national anthem and took charge of raising the Brazilian flag. I handled devotions and warned the teachers never to laugh at their pupils and never to get upset with them for failing. God blessed the efforts of all involved, and the Indians learned. It wasn't long before the brighter students took turns reading Scripture during the devotions.

Soon it became necessary for me to teach a class of older students who whizzed through the syllables and could read well. João, a fine-looking young fellow in my class, fully grown by then, was always clean and well groomed. He raised his hand during class one day to request help with long division using decimals. As I bent over him, I smelled crankcase oil.

"João, what do you use to keep your hair in place?" I asked. It was none of my business, but I had to know where that motor oil smell came from. None of the Indians had machinery to be oiled, with the exception of a few sewing machines.

"Dad bought a liter of crankcase oil to rub on his saw, and we use it for hair oil, too," he answered. Here was one pupil who would never have to worry about head lice.

I was forced to figure out how to limit the student body. Our little group of 60 kids was like a teaspoonful out of the ocean. Parents were disappointed that their children couldn't attend our school. How could we keep the student body to a manageable number?

I brought up the subject during a Sunday morning service. I stated plainly that we couldn't accept more students than we now had. "The only solution I can think of lies with the students who are about to finish the last book in grade school. They should teach their neighbors at home until they can at least read the syllables," I announced. "The only new students we can register are those who can pass a simple reading test after having studied at home, and can show us in a notebook that they have started to learn to write," I continued.

I told the students in school the next day, "After you have taught a few people to read and write as best you can, bring your little group to show me some progress. Then I'll make you a blackboard to take home to help you teach."

In a short time, nine private schools sprang up. Around 300 Ticunas were studying during the morning hours. Some of the teachers built little schoolhouses; the students' parents were glad to help with building and making chairs and desks.

One of the most noteworthy students in our school was Fidelio. He held literacy classes early in the mornings for his youngest pupils, then paddled downriver five miles each day to study two hours at the Port of Two Brothers. He arrived home at dusk, ate supper, then taught his adult class by the light of dim, flickering kerosene lamps made from tin cans.

Fidelio, his father, and mother were waiting for me on the workshop porch when I came home from school one noon. Fidelio's mother had a white cloth wrapped around her jaw and tied at the top of her head. It wasn't Thursday, the day for extractions, and it was only 11:30 a.m.

"Fidelio, I see your mother has a toothache," I said.

"She doesn't have a toothache, pastor Paulo."

"What seems to be her problem?" I asked. Looking closer, I noticed she held her mouth open and saliva streamed down her chin.

"Last night, after retiring to her mosquito net, she yawned and hasn't been able to shut her mouth since," he explained. "She can't eat and she can't talk." Immediately I thought of several women I knew who should be so afflicted.

I went to my office and grabbed a first-aid book to find out how to put her jaw back in place. My thumbs wrapped with gauze, I reached in and relocated the joint. Her mouth slammed shut and she stood up, ready to go home. Normally a jovial lady, this time she was so glad to have her mouth shut after being open for 16 hours that she didn't even thank me. She made a beeline to the port, while Fidelio, his father, and I had a good laugh.

CHAPTER EIGHTEEN

THE GREATEST FUN WE EVER HAD as a family was when the kids were home on vacation. The time of the year was perfect: fishing was at its peak. Great schools of fish were migrating upstream, easy to catch with a net, hook, or spear. John and Fran hadn't returned from the States, so Jessie and I borrowed their unfinished houseboat and took the kids on a three-mile excursion. We spent a week on a clean sandbar, a long way from anyone. There we could go barefoot all day long.

Tim speared a small crocodile. We roasted fish over the coals. Friends from the village came to visit, and Jessie presided over a fish and banana fry.

One of our students, Alair, who later became the wife of a Peruvian evangelist, showed us how to roast fish over the fire without a grill. She sharpened a stick to a point and simply poked it into the mouth of a small fish and all the way out the other side, sticking the pointed end into the sand. The fish was done when it became loose on the stick.

Brazilians taught us to make violent turbulence in the water with poles and paddles to scare away stingrays, whose stab is agonizing. The sting can become an ulcer that leaves a victim crippled for many months. Children have died from stings when no medical treatment was available.

The time always came, too quickly, to pack up and take the kids back to school. Each occasion was a heart-rending experience. The older the kids, the harder it was to send them away. And send them away we did; they never wanted to leave home.

When it came time to take the kids back to school, we all piled into our simple 16-foot fiberglass hull. A hull is all it was:

no top or benches. The kids kept turning around for a last look, watching our house become smaller until finally the Port of Two Brothers disappeared from sight. In Benjamin Constant, Jessie and Rena watched Tim, Leanne, Cindi, and me board the faithful old Catalina flying boat.

Early the next morning I was at the airport in Iquitos to return on the same plane, but there was no seat available. I prayed. I whimpered to the pilots and wrung my hands while agonizing to the Panair agent, but there was no way I could get on the plane; I would have to wait in Iquitos for the next flight.

I could only think of Jessie and Rena expecting me in Benjamin Constant. John and Fran were still in the States because Fran's father had suffered a stroke. Between 500 and 800 Indians would arrive at church Sunday for the early service, and another 150 Brazilians for the second service. On Monday morning, 46 students would listen for the school bell and 60 more would arrive for the afternoon Ticuna school. Independence Day was just a few days away, and our program was rusty. Who would dispense medicine on Thursday? One parrot, two parakeets, an oriole, three dogs, and 55 chickens awaited our return at home.

A Peruvian boat was scheduled to leave Iquitos that afternoon to arrive at the Brazilian border Sunday night. I hailed a taxi and headed for the waterfront to request passage on the boat, whose weather-beaten plaque proclaimed its name, *Triumfo II* [Triumph II], in barely legible print.

"Si, si, si, Meestah. You most certainly may travel with us," the smiling skipper, still in his pajamas, assured me.

When I walked by the bathroom on my way to pick up my baggage, a stench from the doorway almost knocked me over. With my baggage stashed and locked up, I took a taxi to the nearest store for disinfectant, a bucket, and a scrub brush. I was determined to be first on deck next morning to clean the filthy showers, toilets, and sinks before I used any of them. I was afraid of hepatitis, hookworm, and all other tropical diseases.

A glimpse of the galley, the cook, and his flunky didn't lift my spirits in anticipation of healthful meals. I had eaten all kinds of foods in many different places, but had never seen such an unsanitary set-up for food preparation.

"Captain, do I have time to go to the store before we shove off?" I asked.

"Sure. We'll wait for you if you're delayed."

I loaded a cardboard box to the brim with sardines, stale crackers and cookies, a couple of loaves of bread as hard as baseball bats, and rancid canned butter.

Triumfo II sounded like the name of a pirate ship. Three 50-foot, dilapidated, overloaded hulls made up the bulk of the boat. The middle hull, which housed the engine, was in deplorable need of a paint job. Decks jammed with leaking barrels of kerosene, gasoline, and diesel oil made the deck slippery. Mountains of crates and boxes, sacks of imported flour, baskets of *farinha*, stalks of green bananas, herds of domestic and wild animals, and more than 60 passengers left little room to walk. Nervous monkeys chattered and parrots squawked. Several pigs, gorged on bananas and manioc, stretched out on deck, snoozing.

The overload of cargo challenged every inch of caulking, and every handmade nail that held *Triumfo II* intact. The badly distributed weight displaced water past the normal line and covered the rub rails at the stern.

Hammocks, in layers two and three high, dangled everywhere, some with more than one occupant. Passengers occupying the lowest hammocks surely prayed to the saints that the cloth above them absorbed all liquids. Frazzled mothers let their hungry, dirty, sick babies and children play around under the hammocks. I thought longingly of how clean Jessie kept our house.

Engine idling, mooring lines coiled, *Triumfo II* slowly backed out when I heard high-pitched voices from shore. Three boys, as skinny as their bicycles, were silhouetted against the sky, hol-

lering and waving at me from atop the high riverbank. One was
Timmy and the other two were his cousins, David and Pito.
"G'bye, Dad!" "G'bye, Uncle Paul!" they shouted.

"G'bye, guys! See you soon," I yelled back before the lump
in my throat grew too big. I waved my scrub brush at the trio,
incapable of further speech. They had ridden out on their bikes
to see the boat shove off.

"Oh, Meestah. 'Scuse me, I've been so busy," the captain said.
"You'll be up forward in the cabin behind mine." Arriving at the
door, he opened it and acted like he was about to faint, "Oh,
Meestah, I completely forgot. The schoolteacher for Ramon
Castilla is already in the cabin. But you may hang your hammock
topside here where it is a little roomier," he explained.

"Thank you, Captain, but I don't have a hammock," I answered.

"No, problem. I have some for sale," he said. I soon stretched
a brand-new hammock between several hooks and tried to make
myself at home.

At supper time I tried to forget the dirty galley. One table
full of diners was already leaving, while the flunky gathered the
plates and utensils to wash, in readiness for the next group.

Water from the river "washed" the plates without soap. Then
the flunky-turned-waiter pulled a gray towel from his shoulder
to dry them. He blotted beads of sweat from his forehead with
the same towel. Eight plates, cups, and spoons served passengers
and crew. And for three days, there was no indication that the
dish towel had been washed or traded for another. Next morning, after seeing the flunky wipe his nose and mouth on the dish
towel, I went straight to the ship's tiny store and purchased a
plate, cup, and spoon. And I washed my own dishes from that
moment on.

By the light of gray dawn, I committed myself and family to
the Lord before making a beeline to the bathroom with my
bucket, *kiyi* brush, disinfectant, towel, and shaving kit. For 15

minutes I became Sailor Schlener's Sanitary Service, remembering the years aboard ship when a "head" in this condition would have earned me a trial by Captain's Mast. Darting in and out of the *banho,* I threw water onto the bulkheads and everything else. After the plain water treatment, I added disinfectant to a half-dozen buckets and continued dousing the place, scrubbing to beat the band with my long-handled *kiyi* brush.

"The bathroom is closed for a half hour," I announced in dubious Spanish to those standing in line. Then I enjoyed a peaceful shave and shower while others waited their turns in the passageway or used a *banho* located on one of the other hulls.

Three days later the great *Triumfo II* nudged the mud of Leticia's port. I bid farewell to the skipper and gladly contributed my bucket, *kiyi,* and disinfectant to the flunky who had become my friend during the voyage. I was sorry I didn't have a new dish towel to offer him.

The very day after arriving home, I rang the school bell as usual. The pupils were glad to start classes again after a few days off. Just then, Jessie said, "Paul, here comes the mission plane." I heard the engine's whine and saw it coming from a few miles away.

"I wonder why Hank's coming today when his schedule is Fridays," I mused.

John rushed down to the water's edge with Aldo to help tie up the plane. Hank Scheltema trudged up the riverbank. "Looks like you've got plenty going on around here," he commented, observing the crowd of students.

"You were just here Friday, and this is only Tuesday," Jessie said.

Hank reached into his shirt pocket for a telegram he handed to Jessie from Doris, her older sister. The telegram sent by Morse code from the depot in Bonners Ferry said, "Jess, Dad passed away 2 a.m. September 4. Funeral 9th."

Jessie looked at me and whispered, "Paul, my dad died." I

hugged her. Together we walked to the house, leaving John to share the sad news with the gathered crowd.

Jessie longed to be at the funeral with her mother and four sisters, to see her six brothers serve as pallbearers. But it wasn't possible.

. . .

Our village neighbors wondered for 14 months what kind of house John was building on top of four boats. Everyone had seen the outside and all were curious about the interior.

"Come one, come all. See the inside of our houseboat before we take our first trip," John announced from the pulpit one Sunday morning. The next day, villagers streamed down to the port to satisfy their curiosity.

It was a neat little house, 16 by 24 feet, with a walkway on all four sides. The shiny aluminum roof had gutters and downspouts. John's housewarming guests thought the jalousie windows that opened and closed with a crank were an amazing engineering feat. The countertop range, refrigerator, bathroom with a flush toilet, sink and shower, table and chairs, clothes closet, and smooth Formica cupboard tops brought forth ooh's and ah's. Everybody wanted to travel with John and Fran in the *Casa Branca* [White House], so named by the locals because its exterior was white. The name stuck.

John and Fran's maiden voyage took place the next afternoon. The big rig eased away from shore, swung around, and headed upriver. Cheers from bystanders up on the riverbank pierced the air as John shoved the throttle full-speed ahead. She moved nicely for 15 minutes until one engine conked out. Immediately the steering apparatus broke, and before they could gain control, the current forced John and Fran into the riverbank where they tied up for the night. Next morning the spare engine wouldn't start, so they turned around and limped home with one engine. The rest of December 1962 was taken up in finding engine parts, shuttling kids to and from Iquitos, and repairing the *Casa Branca*'s steering system.

"How great it was to snuggle up to Jack Looney's diesel-powered launch for our next trip," John wrote. While Jack was critically ill with hepatitis in Benjamin Constant, he graciously offered John the use of his 36-foot, double-deck launch called *ABEL* for **A**ssociation of **B**aptists for **E**vangelization—**L**ocal.

Not only was Jack's launch offered, but so was his motor boy and helmsman, Jose, whose neck was like an eight-inch tamarack log growing between his wide shoulders. He knew *ABEL* from its keel to its flag mast. Jose could "read" the river, an ability that is acquired only after hours and hours at the helm. He ate like a horse and, from what I hear, never tired.

Jack's ministry was to the Brazilians and Peruvians along the banks of the Javari River, which empties into the Amazon at Benjamin Constant. The Javari is the border between Peru and Brazil where trouble constantly brews among Indians, Brazilians, and Peruvians. John asked, "Jack, while you're sick, what do you think about Fran and me taking the meeting you scheduled at Atalaia?"

"Great!" Jack said. " I could use a couple of days' rest before I hit the river again."

Townspeople were surprised to see a big box with windows pulling up to shore. Kids ran all over the place, like town criers, calling everybody to come and see the strange vessel.

The houseboat crew was well accepted, and in the course of two trips, 16 adults became Christians. Almost everyone issued invitations to return. John and Fran felt good until they arrived back at the Port of Two Brothers, to find a telegram waiting for Fran. Fran's sister, Louise, had written, "Fran, Dad passed away yesterday. Will advise regarding funeral."

Fran answered, "'We sorrow not as others who have no hope, for if we believe that Christ died and rose again, they also who sleep in Jesus will God bring with him.' What a comfort this promise is!"

. . .

Jessie stopped sewing and looked at me, slumped in a chair. "Now what's pecking at your cerebellum, Mr. Nervous?" she asked.

"I don't know. . . . It seems our job is like trying to bail a lake dry with a soup can," I muttered. "We've been plugging away for 12 years with good attendance in the churches, but I wonder if we will ever see witchcraft swallowed up by the truth?"

Jessie reminded me that we have to be patient with those growing in the knowledge of the Lord Jesus Christ.

"I hear you, but I just stitched a four-inch-long ax gash in an Indian's leg. While I was working on him, the friend who brought him told me about a neighbor who died from a poisonous snakebite."

"What's so unusual about that?" she interrupted, still peddling on the sewing machine.

"Nothing, except that the brother of the snakebite victim threw a fit, sharpened his machete and killed the two men whom a witch doctor said caused the snake to kill his brother. Who knows how many other tragedies like this happen without our knowledge?" I persisted glumly.

"Well, Paul, I don't know how much more we can do. We keep our noses to the grindstone so much that vacations for us were the two trips to Iquitos to have two babies and a rare few days to visit the kids in school," Jessie said. "Remember what Dr. Commons told us? 'Be faithful in the ministry of the gospel and leave the results to God.' That is all we can do," Jessie concluded.

"You're right. We should thank the Lord that none of the

murders were committed by Christians," I answered.

What would I have done without this practical, common-sense lady all these years?

Our bliss was short-lived. Two prominent families had been missing from Ticuna church services for about a month. Celso, an elderly man, and Carmelino, his son-in-law, had both become Christians, or so I thought. Carmelino spoke fluent Portuguese and had a smile permanently plastered to his face. I had become better acquainted with him after treating him for anemia and hookworm. Celso seemed like a good old grandpa, not nearly as mean as he looked.

"Brother Claudio, have you seen Celso and Carmelino around the village?" I asked one Sunday. Claudio was a close neighbor to the two men, who lived next door to each other. Claudio didn't answer immediately, but exchanged a couple of sentences with Fausto, who spoke better Portuguese.

Fausto answered for him. "Senhor Paulo, Celso and Carmelino moved away."

"Where did they move to?" I asked.

"Don't know. Downriver near Santo Antonio do Içá I guess."

Santo Antonio is at the far end of the Ticuna Indian territory and distant moves usually occur only when newlyweds go to live with the bride's parents until their first child is born.

"Why do you suppose they moved?" I asked.

Fausto took a deep breath and told the story. "Senhor Paulo, one of Carmelino's sons died with fever. Got medicine from you and *pajeh* (pah-JEH) too, but don't get better. The *pajeh* [witch doctor] blame friend of Carmelino for kill son—lives downriver, in Santa Clara. When Carmelino find out, he go crazy mad. Old father-in-law say, 'Let's go,' and they sharpen machetes and go downriver with mosquito net and food. Get there when sun go down. Ask if can sleep one night." Fausto pointed to the horizon so I would know where the sun rises. "Carmelino's friend say, 'Bring mosquito net to my house.' Three come to house

together: Celso, Carmelino, and friend. Already get dark.
Carmelino's friend put *lamparina* [tiny kerosene lamp] on table,
strike match, bend over to light. When friend bend over, Celso
hit friend with machete on back of neck. Pah! And Carmelino
hit. Pah! Cut head off."

Fausto's story ended my hunger. It bothered me that anybody could behave the way Carmelino and his father-in-law
had. But what made me feel ill was that these two men attended
church regularly and appeared to be fine Christians.

Fausto and Claudio continued to explain why Celso and
Carmelino moved away. "All neighbors around don't want them
live here no more. Can't do that no more. Old life, long ago; we
know God now. Still some believe *pajeh,* not accept God's Son
yet."

During the days when I was concerned that the people
might not understand the salvation message, I challenged a young
man who walked slowly down the center aisle before I had finished my message one Sunday. He was the oldest son in his family, about 18 years old. He just stood with his arms crossed,
watching and listening to the story of the disciples in a storm on
the lake. I let him stand for a few minutes. Then, on a sudden
impulse, I stopped and asked the young man why he came
forward.

Upwards of 800 were present that Sunday, with quite a number standing for lack of benches. The young man unfolded his
arms and began to clean a thumbnail with the index finger of his
other hand. He hesitated, then spoke in a low voice, pausing after
each short sentence. A hush fell over the congregation as the
young man spoke.

"My father was a *pajeh*. No like Christians. Never come
church. Come home drunk; beat my mother; beat us whole family. We run, hide in jungle. We poor. No shoes, ragged clothes. We
hear neighbors across creek singing. They happy, we sad.

"Always neighbors invite Dad go church. Never go. One day

Dad go, but stay in soccer field. Listen singing. Hear you two holler. Next time come closer. Stay outside, just listen. Next time come inside, stand in back." He turned slightly and gestured toward the back of the church. "One time, he accept Christ as Savior. No more get drunk. Not *pajeh* no more. No more beat my mother. Work hard. All family have shoes now. Little brothers learn read and write. Pray before eat. Nighttime recite Bible verses brothers learn in school. If God do that for Dad, can do for me, too. I'm oldest brother, need Christ, too. I accept Him today," which concluded his explanation. By this time, his thumbnail was clean, and his words proved that he understood the gospel message.

CHAPTER NINETEEN

"ALL ABOARD!" JOHN SHOUTED, attempting to shorten the time spent shaking hands and hugging all the folks that came to see Jessie and me as we left for furlough. John and Fran offered to take us in their houseboat to Leticia where we caught the plane for the United States. When the jet engines quieted and we began to lose altitude over Miami, we experienced the familiar thrill of returning to our home country.

The U.S. Customs officials could identify returning missionaries from a block away. "Welcome back. How long were you out this time, folks?" our inspector asked. He merely glanced at our mound of baggage before saying, "Have a pleasant stay."

A big, quiet station wagon whisked us to a motel where we flopped on the beds, drank water from the tap, and shoved quarters in the pop machine. Like the last furlough, the first thing the kids wanted was to hurry downstairs to the restaurant for some dry cereal with real milk from a cow—not powdered stuff from a tin can.

The Goodmans had asked us to phone them when we arrived. They greeted Jessie and me, "Hey, you river rats made it back alive again." Allene and Bud asked, "What are your plans? Where do you go from Miami?"

"All we know is we're headed west to report to Hope Church and visit you guys briefly. We want to get settled first, then report to the mission in Philadelphia."

"Better stay where it's warm. We have an apartment for you while you're on furlough," they told us. The Goodmans' news threw Jessie and me into a state of ecstasy. God had provided for us again.

. . .

"What's that funny smell from up there?" Bud called after
parking in the carport. "Better close the window. It's bad for my
respiratory system."

"Hey, you're just in time. C'mon up and have a cup; the percolator just finished its tap dance," I yelled out the window.

After downing a mug of coffee, Bud said, "I want to show
you something, just to see how it fits." The apartment, built on a
hill, was higher than the other buildings in the residential complex, which included the Goodmans' house and swimming pool.

He stopped next to a white 1963 Impala, a two-door hard-
top with white upholstery. "What do you think about this rig?"
he asked. It all but spoke to me as I gave it the once-over.

"What I think is that this is a fine chariot. I'll bet it can scam-
per like nobody's business," I answered, walking around the car.

"This is Bobby's car. He said you folks could use it while you
are in the States if it fits your need." Bobby was the Goodmans'
teenage son.

"Oh, man, does it ever!" I exclaimed. "I don't even have to
touch the door handle to know it's just our size," I exclaimed.
"Jessie!" I hollered. The screen door slammed before I could take
another breath. "Look at this buggy the Goodmans are letting us
borrow."

"Pretty stylish set of wheels," Jessie commented, casting big
brown eyes at the shiny Chevy. "I'll have to buy a whole new
wardrobe before I can ride in this automobile," she added, poking me in the ribs.

I cringed at the thought of young Bobby dressed in sackcloth
and ashes, despondent over losing full use of the Chevy. But
Bobby, still a teenager, had inherited his parents' graciousness and
generosity.

While basking in God's gracious provision for us, Jessie and
I heard from John and Fran. John wrote:

Our precautions were of little avail. Just after dark, as we were eating supper, the storm struck. At first all went well, then the wind shifted. We were blown away from the bank. Our anchor didn't hold; stakes were yanked loose. The main line securing the houseboat to Jack's launch snapped like a guitar string. The small boat we were towing broke loose and everything was pushed into the main current of the river.

I only had time to pray, 'Lord, help us,' as I rushed around trying to establish order. Jose, our motor boy, was stranded on shore trying to hang onto the lines. He was forced to give up and courageously swam to us in the dark. The wind shifted again and slammed the houseboat back against the launch.

We quickly pulled Umbelinda, our kitchen helper, back into the houseboat from the launch where she slept. The launch nearly capsized and was half full of water. With strength which can only come from above, we were able to tie up to the launch again before the strong current drove us to the shallow water where the keel of the launch stuck in the sand until the fury of the storm abated. We were successful in catching up to the smaller boat and order was restored. We praised God for our deliverance.

Sometimes we wonder 'Why?' But the next morning before breakfast, we knew. A young fellow arrived asking if we would treat his friend's bad machete cut. A half-hour hike across the sandbar and into the jungle brought relief to the injured man and a brief testimony to the saving grace of the Lord Jesus Christ. We hope this will eventually produce fruit.

• • •

"Send Schlener to see me at 8 a.m. on Wednesday. I have a hip nailing to do. I could give him a few pointers on stitching some of those knife and ax wounds," Dr. Masters told Bud Goodman.

Dr. Masters, chief surgeon at a huge hospital in the area, was a good friend of the Goodmans. While lunching with the doctor,

Bud had spoken of his visit to the Amazon and some of the medical problems we encountered.

When I appeared as instructed, I was tossed in with a group
of surgeons studying under Dr. Masters. I was told and shown
everything to do and not do. "Here, put this stuff on and go in
there with the rest of the fellows and scrub like they do for 10
minutes," some fellow said before disappearing.

I thought I'd scrubbed for at least 15 minutes, and I glanced
at the clock to find only three-and-a-half minutes had passed.
Having come close to drawing blood on the backs of my hands,
I finally finished, walking out swinging my hands at my sides like
I was walking down the street.

"Whoa!" this time it was Dr. Masters. "Go back in and scrub
up again—all 10 minutes—and do not drop your hands. Keep
them above your waistline." I wondered why he cared about my
being so clean when I was only going to observe. I didn't dare
scrub quite as vigorously as the first time or I would have needed
skin grafts.

The patient was an elderly lady, wide awake and looking
around although she had been given a spinal block. On the
opposite side of the operating table stood a female doctor and
two male doctors. Dr. Masters and two other doctors huddled
together on my side, with hardly any room for the two nurses.
Masks made it hard to determine who was the dumbest or ugli-
est; we all looked the same.

After drawing lines along the patient's thigh with what I
thought was a cotton swab soaked in merthiolate, Dr. Masters
called for a scalpel. He made a rapid incision a quarter of an inch
deep from the patient's hip along his mark as though he had
unzipped the leg of a pair of insulated coveralls. "This is fat; we
all have fat," Dr. Masters said running his fingers along the incision while nurses clamped off tiny spurts of blood.

Then he "unzipped" the incision some more. This time

about a quarter inch into the tissue, almost to the patient's knee. When I saw the raw red flesh, coupled with regular hospital odors, I started feeling funny. I lowered my head, which greatly improved my health for the moment.

"How, ya doin,' Grandma?" Dr. Masters asked, glancing over the cloth partition that hid the patient's view of her surgery. I didn't hear a response, but she must have been okay. I was reminded of my appendectomy in Benjamin Constant.

Next Dr. Masters made a short incision all the way to the bone near the hip joint, shoved his thumb into the hole, and ripped the muscle to the end of the incision.

"Would you gentlemen please step to one side? I want to get this fellow [referring to me] down here to help me suture," the surgeon said. My heart nearly stopped. The professionals that had to step aside for me didn't know who I was. I might have been an inspector from the Surgeon General's office. The minute I took needle in hand, my lack of sewing skill became apparent. Dr. Mathews skillfully put a stitch in the middle of the great gash. "Did you see that? Now you suture to the right and I'll go to the left," he instructed.

It was a small miracle how quickly and accurately he sutured with no thread going across the top of the incision, but tied on one side. "I'm sorry Dr. Mathews, my thoughts must have been overseas. Would you do that again, slowly?" He did it again and I dove in. He corrected every wrong move I made

Dr. Mathews took me to his office. "You did fine, Paul. I have a gall bladder removal and a thyroid coming up soon. I'll get Goodman on the phone when I'm ready so you can give me another hand," he said, smiling, as though I actually helped rather than hindered.

Driving back to the apartment I thought of the surgeon's great knowledge and ability. My prayer was a question. *Oh, God, will I ever be a missionary that comes even close to the expertise of this*

man? Will I ever know Scripture like he knows scientific terms and intri-
cate procedures? Will I ever be able to teach and preach with the same
dedication, accuracy, and efficiency?

I felt the answer was, "No, but stay on the job and keep trying."

Back home, poor Jessie had to sit through a detailed run-down of what happened at the hospital. "When I'm finished with the gall bladder and the thyroid, I'll be able to keep you patched up should anything happen down in the jungle," I assured her.

"Mr. Pajeh, don't you even try to imagine a situation in which I would let you touch me with a needle and thread!" Jessie was not convinced of my great ability as a surgeon.

· · ·

Furlough was running out. In a few weeks we would return to the Amazon without Tim and Leanne. The day we had to head back to Brazil, we dropped them off in front of their school, according to the house parents' suggestion, hoping the daily school routine would take their minds off the heart-rending separation.

Tim's last words were, "Mom, are you leaving us again?" Leanne was unable to say anything. Jessie, Cindi, Rena, and I pulled away from the curb and headed for Miami. Two city blocks was as far as we got before we had to pull over for every-body to cry.

Cindi was getting a foretaste of what she would suffer in a few days at the ABWE Academy in Iquitos, Peru. We prayed that our family would learn to appropriate God's grace during these trials and not become bitter.

PART SIX

THOSE FRUITFUL YEARS

(1965–1968)

CHAPTER TWENTY

INDIANS WERE NEVER IN A HURRY to approach our house. Someone could languish in a canoe, dying from a severe knife wound or snake bite, or burning up with malaria fever, and the friend seeking help for the victim might lean on a tree in the front yard for 20 minutes before requesting assistance. After greetings, a lengthy time of casual conversation followed before we learned of the serious medical problem. By contrast, those who walked quickly or ran up to the house were usually Brazilians. Poisonous snake bites, lacerations, toothaches, gun shot wounds, violent vomiting and/or dysentery, stingray punctures, high fevers, boils, and burns could be expected at any time.

Late one afternoon, Gervasio clapped his hands at the back door to get my attention. "Senhor Paulo, the neighbors are bringing Luzia for you to remove a fishhook from her leg."

Luzia's father, Laodelino, was considered one of the best fisherman in the village. "Do you suppose Laodelino is teaching his daughter to do the family's fishing?" I jested. Rarely is a Ticuna female responsible to bring home the fish or game for family consumption.

Gervasio chuckled. "No, Luzia wasn't fishing. I didn't get all the details, but it sounded like she was playing around the house when she got hooked," he explained.

At that instant Luzia's aunt Selma trotted up, dabbing at her eyes with a cloth. "Senhor Paulo," she sobbed.

"Dona Selma, slow down. What happened?"

"Oh, Senhor Paulo. It's terrible." Selma panted and cried at once. Her face shone with a mixture of sweat and tears. "Luzia—you know Luzia?"

"Sure. She comes to Wednesday kids' Bible class and Sunday school; she's something of a prankster, but a likeable kid."

Selma jabbered on. "She's so foolish. She's plain crazy. Ave Maria, Senhor Paulo, she couldn't even take care of her younger brothers and sisters while her ma and pa went to the plantation across the river." Selma paused to catch her breath. "Oh, mother of God! The little idiot climbed up on the cross pole near the thatch. She was acting like a monkey is what she was doing, when she slipped and fell onto a set-line hook."

I suddenly realized that Luzia and everybody else expected me to extract the hook. Goose bumps popped out on my arms.

I urged, "Dona Selma, sit down and rest."

She resumed her tale of Luzia's accident. "We heard her scream and ran to find her dangling there. Oh, God in heaven, I couldn't bear to see her hanging there, so I ran here to tell you about it."

Set-line hooks are used to catch the world's largest fresh-water fish called *piraiba,* a giant catfish, and *pirarucu,* which has flesh like cod. Fifteen to 20 hooks are secured to the main line with heavy cord 12 inches long. These same hooks are also used to hang salted fish and meat above the kitchen's wood fire. Heat and smoke help preserve the meat, and discourage the accumu- lation of maggots. The single hook was bare the day it caught the chubby 12-year-old in the thigh. The big hook worked its way deeper into Luzia's thigh as she dangled, struggling. Her screeches brought neighbors running to cut the cord and get her down.

Unlike the average fish hook, the one embedded in Luzia's leg had an irregular bend from four-inch stem to barbed point. Instead of a smooth, gradual curve, it had two 90° curves. Three-sixteenths of an inch thick, with almost two inches between point and shaft, the hook was meant to catch fish larger than a full-grown man. Normally, the stem of a fish hook can be cut and the curve forced through with pliers, but I would have to dig for this one.

Why didn't Luzia's jaw slam shut from an attack of tetanus caused by the contaminated metal? Again, none of my Bible college courses furnished a clue on how to take care of problems like this. Nor did the oral surgery textbook shed light on the removal of fish hooks.

When I laid eyes on the thing, I lost any vestige of self-confidence I had and wilted to the limpness of a noodle. The hook had sunk past the second curve. "Be anxious for nothing," Paul wrote to the Philippian Christians, "but in everything, by prayer and supplication with thanksgiving, let your requests be made known unto God." The prayer and petition part came automatically, but the "be anxious for nothing" part of his admonition was hard to apply.

I had a passing vision of the luxurious hospital back home where Dr. Masters had showed me a few pointers. In less than five minutes the hook would have been removed. Although Luzia didn't seem to be in severe pain, each time she glanced at the piece of steel embedded in her thigh, she buried her face in her hands and groaned.

"Luzia, you are a tad too big to be used for bait, so I'll have to get this hook out of your leg. Or should we just clean it and leave it where it is?" I tried to relieve her anxiety with a little humor, as if I wasn't every bit as anxious as she. My jesting might not have been proper, but Luzia's sobbing changed to giggles, and she seemed to relax.

"Oh, no, Senhor Paulo. Please take it out!"

"Okay, I think I can do it without hurting you as much as it will hurt me, if you will let me give you four tiny injections around the hook."

"Yes, Senhor Paulo, I've had shots before. I know they hurt, but I want you to take that hook out!" I was thankful for Luzia's cooperation. There was no struggle to hold her down during the front porch surgery. And I was glad for the few hours of experience suturing with Dr. Masters. My stainless steel scalpel with

razor-sharp, disposable blades had been used to amputate a couple
of fingers, but never had I dug as deep as I would have to now.

Luzia didn't flinch at the first injection, nor at the second, so
I gave her more than the promised four. Too many spectators,
mostly relatives with somber faces, increased my nervousness.

Because darkness was falling, I had to hurry. Night comes
quickly along the equator, and gas lanterns attract myriad insects.
I politely dismissed those spectators not related to Luzia who had
gathered around to witness her ordeal. I quickly painted around
the hook shaft with merthiolate. My fingers trembled as I slipped
a fresh blade onto the scalpel handle. "Lord, steady my fingers so
I can cut a straight line," I prayed. "And please help me miss the
big artery I read about in grade school."

The Lord answered my requests. When I bent over the hook
and made the incision, I was steady as the Rock of Gibraltar.
Since I couldn't cut the hook at the base of the curve, I laid the
scalpel next to the shaft, using it as a guide. I opened the skin to
a quarter-inch depth, two-and-a-half inches long. More spectators skedaddled at the sight of blood.

I sopped up the blood with gauze and quickly dug a half-
inch deeper. A combination of fat and blood made the incision
difficult to hold open enough to see where I was going. Luzia lay
patiently, apparently not feeling pain.

The sun quickly disappeared into the jungle, so I sent Leanne
back to the house for one of the new missionaries who had con-
siderable experience helping the sick. "Tell him to bring a flashlight," I instructed Leanne.

My colleague proved an able assistant until my scalpel was
about a half-inch from the barb. The beam from the flashlight
moved slowly away from the incision. "Whoa! Keep the light
right on the scene," I pleaded. As I sliced again, the light moved
a second time.

"Hey, pal. You've got to keep the light focused smack-dab on
the hole I'm digging, or this might turn into an amputation," I

exaggerated, glancing at my willing but wobbly partner.

"I'm sorry but I'm going to have to go back inside," he apologized.

All three girls—Leanne, Cindi, and Rena—were home from school. They stood between me and the wide-eyed audience.

"Here, Pa, let me hold the flashlight," Cindi offered when she saw me holding the flashlight in my mouth as saliva ran down my chin. She stayed at my side as I removed the hook and sutured the incision. After applying a clean bandage and administering a shot of penicillin and another against tetanus, Luzia and company thanked me and left. Her mother could be heard scolding as they carried the patient back to her village. But Aunt Selma gave me a broad smile and a big hug of appreciation.

I'm not sure how much cross-beam climbing Luzia did thereafter, but later she became a Christian and studied in our primary school at the Port of Two Brothers.

· · ·

"I never got no education; never sat at a desk in school. But I want my son here to get an education and be somebody besides a jungle animal, and do something for God."

Those were the sentiments expressed by most of the parents in our congregation. During those fruitful years in the 1960's, 12 primary school graduates enrolled in either the seminary in Manaus or the Bible institute in Iquitos, Peru. We were fortunate that the seminary accepted applicants without a high school diploma. And we were thankful for their patience with our young people, some of whom had never been farther from home than two bends of the river.

According to ABWE dictates in those days, all the help we could offer those willing recruits was to encourage and uphold them in prayer. The kids busied themselves to pay their way to school. They made and sold *farinha,* extracted and smoked latex, caught fish and dried fillets to sell on commercial boats. John and I did everything we could to create jobs around the Port of Two Brothers so the kids could earn a little money for travel to seminary.

It was great to see how their parents helped. Several fathers sawed boards for sale. Others shared the family crops, and did without as much so the kids could go to school.

Most of the seminarians were anxious for their parents to be married so they could have birth certificates that declared them legitimate offspring. Little by little, they all came under the bond of matrimony. Fran and Jessie made cakes for the newlyweds, whether they wanted them or not.

One couple, having lived together for 20 years, set a date and hour for their wedding to be performed by the local "justice of the peace," who was appointed by the county mayor. This man just happened to be the groom's uncle and one of the few village adults who could read and write. John and I were invited to perform a religious service after the civil, or legal, ceremony.

Spiffed up in Sunday clothes, camera and extra flashbulbs in hand, off we went to the wedding. Venerando, the J.P., was sitting on the steps of his little house in work clothes, machete in hand to cut weeds.

"Looks like we are a little early for the wedding," the Schleners chimed in unison.

"Martins must have lost courage," I said.

"On the contrary," Venerando chuckled, "you are an hour late."

"What?" I exclaimed. "We thought the ceremony was set for 4 p.m."

"Martins and Lucia came at 3 p.m. with their witnesses, and we wrapped the whole thing up in 20 minutes," Venerando said. "He was too ashamed to have anybody see them get married after already having nine kids."

Martins, who later became lay pastor of Hope Church in

back of the village of Santa Rita, was one of the guides who had taken John and me to the Indian *festa* in 1953.

Many of the students who finished at our primary school went on to higher education. One of the boys became a county commissioner; another is a missionary in Portugal with ABWE. One student became a pastor's wife and teacher of a Christian day school; another is the wife of an evangelist. Two became successful teachers, and two others pastors in the capital city of Manaus. One former pupil even became a practicing lawyer in Manaus, and still another an engineer for Sanyo Electronics.

I happened to meet the young lawyer in the airport on my way through Manaus. He ran up to give Jessie and me good Brazilian bear hugs, and was full of questions. When our flight was called and he said, "Pastor Paulo, if you ever get into trouble, just give me a call. It would be my pleasure to help you," I wondered what kind of trouble he thought I was prone to.

. . .

The first two boys to leave the village for the Bible institute were Evandro and Flavio, who were accepted at the ABWE Bible institute in Iquitos, Peru. When it came time for them to leave for Iquitos, Flavio and Evandro had the needed fare for the old Catalina. They were the only first-year students who knew all the books of the Bible by heart. They did well in their studies, but didn't return to Iquitos after the first year, transferring instead to Amazonas Baptist Seminary in Manaus. They were able to complete their seminary work in their native tongue—without the added complication of being foreigners.

Flavio accepted Jesus as Savior at the age of 11. He ran up to me while I was installing a shutter on our house and blurted out, "Senhor Paulo, I have just accepted the Lord as my Savior during kids' Bible class."

He was the shortest and loudest member of his family. Flavio wasn't a likely candidate for the ministry because of his stutter. He stammered on the first letter of the first word of a sentence. If he got a good start, he could glide through the rest of the sentence uninhibited.

Flavio was probably the hardest worker of all the kids in town. He was unmercifully disciplined with severe beatings at home—which possibly explained why he stuttered.

While Flavio studied in our primary school, we put a stop to mimicking and mocking by disrespectful students. God must have healed Flavio's stuttering during his first year in seminary, because from then on it rarely showed up.

Evandro, slightly younger than Flavio, was the object of envy from peers and his own relatives. As he chalked up achievements in his studies, he became the subject of ridicule. "Who do you think you are? You're just a *caboclo* like the rest of us."

Usually young people who displayed a measure of accomplishment and were maligned by jealous peers, stopped trying, figuring achievement wasn't worth the hassle. Part of our job in primary school was encouraging the kids to try hard and do their best. Commending others who excel in their efforts was another difficult virtue to instill.

Evandro was gifted with athletic dexterity, musical talent, a keen memory, and an insatiable desire to study. He didn't reach more than five feet four in height, but on the soccer field his stocky legs moved so quickly they looked like spokes on a wheel.

Evandro's grandmother became a Christian only a few years before she died. Her conversion was from a background of fanatic superstition. During Evandro's childhood, she did her best to keep him from attending Wednesday kids' classes and church. But he was so enchanted with the music from Fran's accordion that he attended meetings regularly, nearly always sitting on the front bench to study every move her fingers made as she squeezed out music.

Evandro's dad, Carlindo, played guitar for village dances.

Virgulindo [Moon], his grandfather, in earlier years was the life of the local shindigs as he sawed away on a dilapidated fiddle. His maternal grandfather, Venerando, plunked on a ukulele. As a child, Evandro would sneak his dad's old, beat-up guitar from its hiding place and tirelessly strum away, trying to learn a tune until he got caught.

There were no children's rights activists in Amazonas. It was "spare the rod and spoil the child," sometimes without mercy. In Evandro's case it was sometimes a three-foot-long flexible fruit, like a giant string bean, that left a scar on his hide because he lost a piece of laundry soap that was worth a day's wages. Evidently nobody investigated, because it wasn't Evandro who lost the soap in the creek.

When Fran and Jessie took a break from the kids' program practice on the front porch, they returned to hear whines and groans from Fran's accordion. Evandro had been unable to resist the opportunity to try the accordion, so he hurriedly strapped it on while the ladies were gone. But he had it on upside-down, and could barely see over the top of the bulky thing.

Not many months later, after studying under Fran and using Jessie's smaller accordion, Evandro played "Silent Night" at the Christmas program. From then on, there was no stopping him. Soon he could run his stubby fingers so nimbly over the keys that he could deliver the complicated march called "Under the Double Eagle." He eventually learned to play 11 musical instruments.

Natalicio was the next young man from the Port Of Two Brothers to go away to seminary. He had been altar boy for the Catholic church and knew all the chants and prayers. He assisted the priest during the annual patron saint's celebrations, which always ended with a procession. Natalicio led the devotees in echoing the priest's chants as they dragged along, shielding their candles from the wind.

Natalicio came to know Christ as his personal Savior at Camp

Colinas de Zion. He realized he would be persecuted and harassed for his decision. He was always told by the priest that nobody can ever be sure of salvation. Natalicio didn't realize that sinners could be rescued from the dominion of darkness and brought into the kingdom of the Son, in whom we have redemption and the forgiveness of sins, according to Colossians 1:13, 14.

Natalicio was challenged by the priest in the county seat of São Paulo de Olivença, successfully defending his convictions with portions of the Bible before a sizable group of devoted Roman Catholics.

When the three seminarians returned during vacation, they were raring to get out on the river and preach. They also helped teach Vacation Bible School. They seemed to know everything there was to learn about systematic theology and the latest methods of Christian education. It was a temporary relief for John and me to let the boys take over.

. . .

"It feels like there's been a funeral here," I said to Jessie. "Tim and Leanne are back in the States and it will be a long time before we see them again. Cindi is in Iquitos; the seminary kids are gone; only Rena is left."

Mercifully we were so busy in our work that there was not much time to grieve about our kids being gone. School in the morning and afternoon, medical hours from 3:30 to 5:30, sometimes 30 or 40 teeth to extract, three messages a week to prepare, and several pounds of personal letters to answer made us so tired by nighttime that there was no lying awake to worry.

"Why don't you take Rena camping Friday afternoon and come back Saturday?" Jessie suggested.

That Jessie actually suggested we go fishing was a shock to our nervous systems. I grabbed a flashlight and checked her eyes, offering her a chair. "Rena, what do you say? Would you like to go fishing?" I asked.

"Sure," was all she said.

"Do you want to sleep in a mosquito net all night in the jungle?" I probed.

"Sure," she repeated.

We were both excited: tearing around, gathering our equipment and piling it on the front porch. Our gear was kept to whatever fit in a child-size, handwoven basket to be carried on Rena's back.

We skimmed across the smooth water to the closest of our two favorite lakes. When we arrived at the concealed entrance to the trail, Rena put on an old cap and I helped her hoist the basket of equipment onto her back with the strap across her forehead. She struggled up the riverbank and made it down the trail for a few minutes before she was willing to share the burden with me.

The edge of the lake was beautiful with lush vegetation: water lilies and other blossoms that thrive in shade. We set to work making a lean-to. Rena gathered giant leaves I had cut, carrying them to the rough sapling framework. We automatically surveyed the area for fire ants, scorpions, hornets, and snakes. We carefully laid a row of leaves, overlapped across the bottom, in row after row until we arrived at the cross piece.

Our architectural masterpiece was ready. We stood off, admiring what we had accomplished in about one hour. Rena raked chips of wood and pieces of leaves away with a forked stick, and hung our meager equipment above the ground to avoid the invasion of ants and termites.

I tramped through the jungle close to shore in search of our old canoe, hoping it still had enough bottom to keep us from dropping onto a school of piranha. Rena watched me from the lean-to as I made my way through the jungle until I was hidden from sight by the mass of foliage.

"Dad!" she hollered.

"Over here," I answered.

In less than a minute she bellowed again, "Dad?"

"I'm over here." I wasn't more than 30 yards from her, but Rena couldn't see me.

The vast rain forest takes a while to get used to. Even after living for years in a jungle clearing and enjoying many treks through the rainforest, I never tired of it. I get lost in cities where there are road signs and maps. The immense Amazon jungle is quite another story. A keen sense of direction is essential. I have utmost respect for the ability of the Indians, who have been gifted by their Creator with the uncanny ability to find their way—without a trail—in and out of that mass of vegetation.

Rena and I quietly drifted over the glassy, black water, listening to strange jungle noises.

"Cast your bait over next to that snag, Rena," I whispered as I dipped the paddle and turned the canoe broadside. At only nine years of age, Rena had no trouble handling a rod and reel. I was skittish about flipping sharp hooks in every direction in the narrow canoe. I could never forget hooking Tim near his eye. Trolling put me more at ease.

"Dad, look how big those lily pads are! Do you think I could stand on one?" Rena asked.

"Not on your life, little lady!" A fish grabbing her bait took Rena's mind off lily pads. In a few seconds she dropped a pink-bellied, grunting piranha in the bottom of the canoe. I pivoted around, broke the lower jaw of the little savage with needle-nose pliers, then removed the hook. Coasting over to a large plant, I cut a couple of leaves to shade the fish from the hot sun.

Rena took in all the spectacular scenery as we glided along, catching fish. A pair of black ducks nearly as large as wild geese swished by, patrolling the lake. Bright-colored macaws tested the laws of aerodynamics by flying as slowly as possible. Lime-green parrots passed them up as though attempting to reach the fruit tree first. "They sound like they have sore throats," Rena remarked.

"It's getting hot, Rena. What do you say we go back to our fort and roast these fish you caught?"

Rena set down her rod to clean the fish as we paddled back to shore. She had watched our cook at this task many times and was sure she knew how to do it. She made them look just like the ones Umbelinda prepared for frying.

We chose a spot in the shade of a giant tree which made the perfect spot to broil our fish. A little salt, a spoonful of freshly toasted *farinha*, and a squirt of lime juice with each mouthful of fish made for a combination that no gourmet restaurant could equal.

By 7 p.m. we were in the mosquito net. We crushed all the mosquitoes we could find by flashlight. After we read a portion of Scripture and prayed, we tried to sleep. I'm sure Rena slept well that night, but I didn't. Sunburn made me feel like I was suffering an attack of malaria. On a stuffy night, the air doesn't cool off until well after midnight. And the ground is always lumpy. Although mosquito nets offer a degree of security, you can't forget that you are sharing space with deadly vipers, anacondas, and alligators. We stopped feeling sorry for "poor Mom" stretched out on a foam rubber mattress in a screened, wooden house, several feet off the ground.

Next morning after consuming smoky-tasting oatmeal and sweetened condensed milk, Rena and I fished for fresh catch to take home. When we pulled into our campsite, Rena stayed in the canoe to wash clothing as she had seen the village women do. She got the clothes soapy, then rubbed them together between her fists. She slapped them on the canoe bench to make the same noise she heard our neighbors making. After rinsing and repeatedly flailing the clothes, she spread them out over the tops of bushes to dry.

We broke camp, glad to head back to the comfort and protection of home, leaving our leaf-covered shanty to the nipper ants and termites. Burned to a crisp, smelling of fish, smoke, and sweat, we plodded across the lawn. Skippy met us, jumping and yipping, loving the sight and smell of us.

The next day was Sunday. I had to get up at 3:30 to study, so I was already tired before the 7:30 a.m. service. I had all Sunday afternoon to prepare for the evening service, but would have to hide in order to do it.

"If anybody comes to visit, tell them I'll be back at six," I said to Jessie.

"What if somebody comes with an eyeball hanging out on his cheek?" she asked.

"In that case, run out and clang the big bell three times and I will appear like magic," I assured her. "Then my message will be entitled, An Eye for an Eye and a Tooth for a Tooth."

I waited till Jessie retreated into the bedroom before I dog-trotted 30 yards over to John and Fran's kitchen. It was a good hideout while John's family was furloughing in the States. After breaking up the cockroach convention taking place in the kitchen, I was able to study for hours without distraction.

CHAPTER TWENTY-ONE

HOW ENCOURAGED WE WERE to welcome another family from language school to bolster the work force of the Central Amazon pioneers: Ed and Dot Blakeslee and their four children, Eddie Jr., Lory, Dory, and Samuel.

They took survey trips downriver, finally settling in Fonte Boa, a large enough town to qualify for regular Panair stops en route between Benjamin Constant and Manaus. The Blakeslees started a church, and Ed later built a 40-foot riverboat from which he and Dot did extensive evangelism along the Amazon and its tributaries. Dot, a registered nurse who spoke fluent Portuguese, was deeply loved by the people.

The Blakeslees pulled into the Port of Two Brothers for a field council meeting, at which time they visited our Brazilian and Ticuna primary schools. That afternoon a boy came running to our front door.

"Senhor Paulo," he panted, "would you come and kill a big snake?"

I took my rifle from the gun rack. "Where is it?"

"It's on the other side of the creek, right by the path."

"The creek is pretty high right now, isn't it? Can we get across?" I asked.

"Yes, sir. There is a big windfall all the way across. No problem," the boy promised. Brazilians have different definitions of "big." I hoped that the windfall was big, and that the snake wasn't.

"Wait for me," Ed begged. "I'll bring my camera."

The boy was right about the bridge; he side-stepped across with no problem. He was so excited that we sped down the trail, until he stopped abruptly. I slipped a cartridge into the chamber of my .22 and snapped on the safety. I thought we reached the viper quicker than the boy realized. But no, what he realized was that we had marched past it.

"Jonas, don't do a thing like that," I complained. Jonas looked pale. I said, "Ed and I will remain standing right here until you find the snake. Give us a holler but don't come to get us. Once you find him, don't let the snake out of your sight."

Jonas cautiously started back down the trail. Within 50 paces he shouted, "Here it is!"

The big sausage-like constrictor lay partly coiled and perfectly camouflaged by the undergrowth. It was easy to understand how Jonas missed it.

"Ed, take my gun and shoot him. I just shot one a couple of months ago. It'll give you something to write home about in a prayer letter. I'll take a picture of you."

"That's okay, Paul," Ed demurred. "You shoot and I'll take the picture." All this talking made Jonas nervous, so I plunked the snake in the noggin' while Ed shot a commemorative photo. The snake was only 16 feet long, an adolescent anaconda.

· · ·

The young people's choir waited on the riverbank for John's command to board. "Take off your shoes and clean them before you set foot on deck," John shouted from the meticulously clean houseboat, his hands serving as a megaphone.

The Port of Two Brothers' youth choir was headed up to the Benjamin Constant and Leticia churches where there were no choirs of any kind. Fran struggled to teach the children to sing in four-part harmony, making the choir even more unique.

Some of the young people were less than five feet tall, but the volume of food they put away was amazing. First, a pile of rice laid the foundation for a big ladle of pork with red beans.

Strips of fried bananas went on top of the pyramid. A huge mixing bowl of *farinha* [toasted manioc cereal] was consumed with
vigor. A hot, spicy juice, consisting of vinegar, fresh onions and
garlic, lime juice, and a colorful variety of red and yellow hot
peppers, waited at the end of the counter for those searching for
perfect cuisine. It certainly livened the flavor, and we wondered
if the potent mixture might help cure intestinal parasites and
nasal congestion.

The group was well received in both churches. Several choir
members were crack soccer players and gave the Colombians stiff
competition. We were encouraged to see some Colombian soccer
players in church to hear their opponents sing; they also heard
the gospel.

. . .

Another great family just out of language school joined the
Benjamin Constant forces of the Central Amazon field. Terry and
Wilma Bowers and their three boys, Phillip, Jim, and Dan, were
a blessing from the beginning. Terry was a pilot assigned to the
airplane ministry, and would contribute to the local church as
well.

"What an attractive family," Jessie said after we met the
Bowerses for the first time.

I agreed. "And I noticed the kids answered when spoken to."
We had found the opposite to be true with more than a few
MK's.

Terry was short, but a big man in many ways. He had a low,
resonant voice like a radio announcer. He augmented the ministry as an expert pilot and mechanic. His thoroughness inspired
confidence. Neatness in dress without extravagance set him apart
from some of us sloppy Joes. Even when he worked on an aircraft engine, Terry seemed to remain neat and clean. And his
tools looked like surgical instruments in an operating room. One

of his greatest contributions to the work was individual Bible correspondence courses.

"Here, guys, guzzle this before you pass out. You look like two turkeys, you're so sunburnt," Wilma sang as she exited the kitchen to plunk two tumblers of ice-cold *guaraná* in front of us. Not just once, but every time John or I showed up. Four or five hours of sun and wind parched exposed skin and left travelers near dehydration.

John and I tried to time our arrivals as close to mealtimes as possible. But if we didn't make it, there were always cookies or cake, and the coffeepot on the boil. Wilma was an excellent pianist, accordionist, and soloist for the church in Benjamin Constant.

During their last few years on the field, Terry felt himself losing the vigor he had formerly enjoyed as cancer sapped his vitality. But he plugged away, serving the Lord. Before Terry and Wilma left Brazil for the last time, they volunteered to live in Jessie's and my home in Tabatinga, assuming the responsibilities of caring for mail and supplies for downriver missionaries, hospitality for others, and church work while we took a year furlough. They left our home in better shape than they found it. Thereafter, when visitors complimented the interior decor of our house, Jessie always said, " Wilma did it; it surely wasn't I."

Both Terry and Wilma passed through the crucible of suffering until the Lord called Terry home in 1991. We lost an effective missionary, a real friend, and an affectionate brother in Christ.

. . .

"Nope. No more don't drink *cashahssa* [rum]," the tall Indian said to the owner of the trading post. Manduca was a head taller than most men of his tribe, with an artist's flair for carving canoes and paddles. He gently lowered a huge ball of rubber from his powerful shoulders onto the scale to trade for lard, kerosene, and cloth. I first saw Manduca at an Indian *festa* 20 years earlier.

"Why not?" the trader asked, pouring a shot of rum and offering it to Manduca, who had recently become a Christian. "We always have a few drinks when you come."

"Still come sell, but no drink. Get drunk is bad. Americano read in God's Book that Jesus come back. My family, we want live right when He come," Manduca explained.

I happened to meet the proprietor of the Black Creek trading post in town one day at which time he asked me, "Meestah Paulo, what is happening to the Indians? Hardly anybody buys sugar cane rum anymore. It was the thing we sold mostly," he complained. "Old Manduca used to consume a whole bottle, but the other day he refused. He said he was afraid that when Jesus returns He might catch him drunk." The trader was amazed at the Indian's explanation.

There was a stretch of time—a long time—when the Indians could not get out of debt to the traders. Unable to figure weights and measures, and how much they were owed for rubber, *farinha,* or a slab of salted fish, the Indians were easy to cheat. Even if they knew how much their products were worth, the Ticuna didn't know if they were receiving the correct values when they traded. Their plight was to simply accept the traders' word for everything until some of the Indians studying with us at the Port of Two Brothers started to create their own little schools in each village. The traders were worried.

"What do you need today, Carlos?" the trader asked, after his customer stacked six baskets of *farinha* onto the huge pile at the trading post.

"Need one kilo nails, two liters kerosene, and half kilo candy for my kids," Carlos answered.

"Is that all, Carlos? You only owe 2,000 cruzeiros from last month," the trader said, as he looked in his account book. "Better take your wife and daughters some cloth for new dresses. And the boat just dropped off a ton of new shoes," he said convincingly, as though the merchandise were a gift.

After making his purchases, Carlos asked how much a basket of *farinha* was worth. Then he asked the total cost of the nails, kerosene, and candy. The trader was quick to respond. Carlos, one of Fidelio's evening students, took a pencil stub and folded piece of paper from his shirt pocket. While the not-so-gullible Indian scribbled on the paper, there was silence at the trading post. The trader watched him like a cat watches a mouse, wondering what Carlos was trying to write. Carlos multiplied six times the value of *farinha* per basket. He added the amount of his purchases to the 2,000 he already owed and saw that the total was less than the value of his *farinha*. Carlos looked up and said, "You owe me 500 cruzeiros, sir."

Soon the traders, although they continued to charge exorbitant fees, didn't dare miscalculate charges. At the outbreak of this educational awakening, the traders took a disliking to Americans and tried to harm our reputation by spreading false stories like, "The Americanos buy conversions. They receive $3,000 for every Indian who joins their religion." But the Indians knew differently.

Our indigenous friends, after hearing and accepting the gospel, developed an intense desire to learn to read. We were their only hope to becoming literate. Their desire to learn, bathed in showers of God's blessing, gave success to our meager attempts.

Literacy, accompanied with biblical teaching, brought higher moral standards, making life better for everyone in the Port of Two Brothers area, including the traders. The Indians began to produce more, but cheat and steal less. It took years of perseverance, maintaining an acceptable reputation in the area, to gain a good relationship with the business people. Finally, they were glad when our boat pulled into port, and occasionally they invited us to hold meetings in their homes or on the trading post's front porch. It is possible that our welcome was due more to the medical care we provided.

Our own children contributed significantly to our good

relations with Brazilian neighbors, young and old. MK's usually speak the language of the country fluently and take part in all the daily activities. Jungle hunts and fishing trips took them all over the country with hardly a thought of the dangers that lurk. Canoeing, turtle hunting, and fishing along sandbars at night were great adventures.

Now they were high school kids with lofty ideas. Having developed bulging biceps and pectorals, they were tough and impervious to injury. This time Tim, David, and their Brazilian friends brainwashed themselves into believing they had to capture wild horses up at Vendaval.

Tim had gotten word that a dozen wild horses were running loose in the jungle around the village of Vendaval, one of the trading posts suffering from diminished rum sales. Tim's cowboy uncles in Idaho served as his role models for awhile. They had their insides jolted frequently on the rodeo circuit. This admiration may have given Tim a false certainty that he was a natural at taming wild horses. The kids couldn't rest knowing that horse-flesh was going to waste.

Not much prayer went into their plans, I fear. Within minutes they rounded up a half dozen of their daredevil buddies and roared full speed ahead, disappointed that they only had 40-hp instead of 400.

The trader received the group of boys like long-lost friends. When the kids explained what they wanted, the trader said, "If you will catch two of them and train them both, you may keep one and bring one back to me."

Vendaval was the only place within 100 miles that had horses. The horses were small, possibly from inbreeding, but plenty frisky. The kids went after them haphazardly.

"Head 'em off so they won't go into the jungle, or we'll never catch 'em," Enoque screeched at David and Tim, who were swinging lariats, trying to rope one of the frantic animals. These animals had never been challenged before. Unable to rope any of them in the field, the boys chased two of them into the water. Already fatigued and frightened, the horses swam too far from shore.

"Get in the boat, Dave. We'll try to get a rope around one while he's in the water," Tim bellowed. David grabbed a rope and jumped into the boat. Tim brought the motor to life and David got a rope around the smaller horse before the poor animal drowned. The other boys in canoes paddled like mad to bring the other horse back, but he was too far out and too tired. The boys were worn out, too, and were saddened to see the horse drift away and finally sink.

"We're sure sorry about the one that drowned," Tim told the trader, apologizing for their failure to save the second horse.

"Don't worry about it," the trader said. "I could see it was impossible to catch them on land. These animals are useless and a nuisance to us here, and nobody wants to try to do anything with them except you fellows. Come up to the kitchen and have dinner with us. My woman filled the kettles when she saw you coming." This same trader had complained about Manduca and others refusing to buy rum like they used to, and had suffered the consequences of Carlo's correct purchase calculations.

The boys were relieved at the trader's good attitude over the loss of the horse and thrilled at his invitation. The lady of the house evidently knew about teenage boys and their appetites, for she had prepared an abundance of food.

The young horse still didn't have much fight left, so it was easy to get him into the empty 16-foot hull for the ride home. A crowd of people ran to see the boys pull into port. Some of our neighbors had never seen a horse, although this creature was a far cry from any recognized breed. Since the pony rested on his side all the way back home, he gave the spectators a good show when the boys led him to the backyard.

Tim named him Cholo. Living at our place was like going to horse heaven. He deserved it after the struggle he went through to get there. He was fed fresh cornstalks, huge bunches of bananas, papaya, and dried corn. Tim had ridden an old sway-backed hammerhead in Iquitos; therefore, having become an "expert" horseman, he was ready to ride the young steed without any tack, not even a bridle.

Tim tied a rope loosely around Cholo's neck, then attached it to a tree with about 15 yards of play in the rope. After a little petting and "nice horsey" talk, Tim jumped on and proceeded to get bucked off. The first fling didn't seem to hurt him, but the seat of his Levis ripped wide open. The next time Tim shortened the slack. The little fellow was not mean, and in a short time Cholo submitted to his determined master.

Tim had returned to school when a saddle and bridle arrived from Bogota. By then Cholo was a little older and healthier, with a nice sheen to his hide. It was then Jessie took over to fine-tune the little stallion. She made no boasts about her horsemanship, but the way she sat in the saddle and held the reins proved this wasn't her first ride. Her great success training me as a husband might have convinced her she could do something with a real horse. She remembered the names of the horses she had ridden as a girl: Prince, Teddy, and Sparkie, none of which was pedigreed but filled her family's need for recreation and work around the farm.

Jessie had Cholo neck-reining in no time, making figure 8's all over the place, and steering him around fixed objects until the beast might have wondered if his life's work was to chase snakes. I was glad he lived through those strenuous workouts when the kids came home on vacation. Soon Tim's Brazilian friends drummed up enough courage to ride, and liked it so well we had to put limits on how much Cholo was ridden.

Jessie rode him through the village and down jungle trails, visiting people along the way. "Here comes Dona Jessie," was the cry of the first person to spot her. This notice cleared the streets of children who feared being eaten alive.

Jessie loved Cholo. He was gentle and begged for food by coming up to the patio and stomping with one front hoof, keeping it up until he got a fresh papaya, a banana, or a manioc.

As furlough drew near, we couldn't find anyone to take care of Cholo. Since the boys hadn't caught and trained two horses, enabling them to return one to the trader according to their agreement, we felt that Cholo belonged to the trader. We grieved to think of how he might be treated. He was used to gentleness with the currycomb, and a pasture all to himself with water on the spot.

When the fateful day came, we led Cholo to the edge of the river. We talked to him and rubbed him down one last time. Jessie stayed in the house, lacking the courage to watch as we took Cholo away.

Hoping to avoid rope-burning the friendly animal when trying to get him down the steep bank and into a dugout, I decided to give him a tranquilizer. When I applied the injection in his right hindquarter, he dropped. Several hired men and I carried him down to the dugout and headed upriver. His heart was still beating—but with accelerated palpitations.

"Senhor Paulo, I think Cholo is dead," Aldo said after checking his pulse.

"Naw, the injection put him to sleep. He's just out of it," I replied. But when I checked, I couldn't find any sign of a pulse, nor signs of breathing. I knew Cholo was dead but found it hard to accept. Cholo's body began to swell, and all four of us lowered him into the water.

The trader understood my plight. I'm sure he sensed our chagrin as I told the story of our experience with Cholo and our good intentions to return the fine animal. He was impressed at Aldo's comments regarding how all the village would be saddened at the loss.

"I am extremely sorry, sir. This is all that is left." I handed him Cholo's saddle, bridle, currycomb, and brush. "I hate to think how my wife will react when she learns what happened."

"I knew it!" Jessie exclaimed when I told her the story. She whirled around to the bedroom, shutting the door behind her. She stayed in there a long time, grieving the loss of Cholo.

I paced back and forth, gulped a cup of coffee, and glanced mournfully at Cholo's corral. Finally I got up enough courage to peek into the bedroom to make sure Jessie was all right. There was nothing I could say to make things better, although I had given Cholo the tranquilizer only to keep from hurting him. I still have not completely absolved myself of guilt in the mishap, even 30 years later. As far as my family is concerned, I killed Cholo, and my murderous action will never be forgotten.

CHAPTER TWENTY-TWO

HOOFING FROM MY OFFICE to the kitchen for breakfast one Saturday in 1967, I noticed what looked like a husband and wife with a passel of kids on the riverbank. I had given up wondering how many decades it would take for people to get our medical hours straight. But I stopped growling about it because the Indians could be at death's door and hesitate to inconvenience us.

The family was seated on the workshop's front porch when I hurried out to greet them. I sat my body down, but my spirit was in the office, reaching for my Bible and a commentary to study for the next day's sermon. After going down the short list of polite topics, I asked, "Anybody sick or need medicine?" hoping to cut short our conference so I could get back to my office.

"Nobody sick," the father answered. "Just came to visit."

"Good," I said. Then told myself, *Don't ask any questions. Keep your mouth shut and let time go by in silence until they utter the next word.*

After what seemed like a half day, the dad mumbled something under his breath to his wife, then spoke aloud. "Senhor Paulo, our family came, accept Christ as Savior. You too busy Sunday and too busy Monday. Saturday not busy, so we come." I was taken aback. These folks had been attending church for years, seldom missing a Sunday service or even a workday.

It was true. John and I ran from one service to the other on Sunday mornings. But busy as we were, we never refused to help anyone come to a saving knowledge of the Lord.

"Oh, good. Let's go to my office, read some Bible verses, and pray," I said. I explained the way of salvation and prayed with each family member. I quickly shared this blessing with Jessie and returned to the office to resume my studies for the next day.

Lo and behold, another group of eight people sat down on the still-warm workshop benches. I recognized them as being from Paranapara, five or six miles from the first group's territory.

I wondered, *Now who's sick?* I got up from my desk and entered the workshop through the back door, popping out onto the porch and taking the group by surprise.

This group also looked to be in perfect physical condition. So I did my best to remain silent. Oreliano finally spoke up. "Senhor Paulo, we," he paused to take a quick census on his fingers, "eight men want talk about get right with God."

"That's what I'm here for. I'm glad you came. Wait here while I get my Bible. Then we'll read some portions of God's Word and pray," I said, already on my way through the shop.

I thought it was interesting that neither group knew what the other had planned. The whole morning was taken up with these humble people. Others arrived in the afternoon for the same reason. Before the day was over, a total of 22 people had received Christ as Savior.

The next morning during the Indian service I asked, "Would any of you who became Christians yesterday like to stand and give us a sentence or two about what happened?" So many testified that I had to call a halt in order to end the service.

The next Saturday, several other groups came to faith in Christ, totaling 34 new believers. One group was too large to fit in my office, so we walked all the way back to the church for our talk. I knew most of these folks, and thought nearly all of them had made professions of faith before. So I reminded them that if they had already accepted Christ as Savior, they needn't do so again. Whereupon several said, "We are here because we never really accepted the Lord."

"I don't know for sure if I'm a Christian," one fellow stated.

We praised God for the apparent manifestation of His working in the Ticunas' hearts. But the next morning in church, I said nothing about the 34 people who were saved the day before. I suffered from a touch of doubting Thomas's weakness. Although lives were being transformed, which is the best "proof of the pudding," I was afraid the whole congregation would think they needed to be "born again" again.

However, on March 4, my customary 20-minute siesta was terminated when 64 people came for a variety of reasons in their quest to get right with God. These were humbling experiences. John and I number among the least gifted of gospel preachers, with pitifully few enticing words of wisdom. No special revival speakers came to our church; there were no revival preachers.

A newsletter of April 1967 shared the experiences. "After the 64 came, we kind of thought it might be about the end of the 'Saturday gold rush days.' But on March 11, another group of 28 Indians accepted the Lord Jesus Christ as Savior, and seven more by April first."

On Saturday nights we could see fires burning on the church grounds and occasionally got a whiff of food being prepared as a half-dozen families traveled the 10 miles from the Jacurapa River and other distant villages, spending the night in the church so they would be on time for the Sunday morning service. Our bedroom windows were always open, so Jessie and I could hear the Indians singing hymns and choruses as we dozed off to sleep.

God honored the simple preaching of His Word and the prayers of many back home. And God answered the prayers and evangelistic efforts of the Indians themselves, who gathered each Wednesday for cottage prayer meetings.

. . .

Two employees in company coveralls scurried out to the DC-4 as fast as the rattling ladder would take them, banging against the fuselage of the old plane. Jessie and I froze like concrete statues, staring at the hatch that took forever to open, hungry for the sight of our kids. All was quiet while the passengers descended from the cool airplane to the piping-hot tarmac. Each passenger, in turn, suffered shock from the first blast of Amazon humidity. But no Schlener kids appeared.

"Do you suppose they missed the plane?" Jessie fretted.

"Naw, they just want to be last to make us think they did," I said. Sure enough, there was Cindi waving from the hatch, then Leanne and Tim.

Special Brazilian meals were something the kids missed while they were in the United States. Leanne turned our kitchen into a croissant, cinnamon roll, and doughnut bakery. Cindi brought home little pot-bellied, undernourished babies, whom she showered and fed. Tim consumed enormous slices of homemade bread and sorghum between soccer games and fishing trips. He had received a trophy for most valuable player at Hadden Heights High School, so he joined our local church soccer team immediately.

Leanne and Cindi stood beside our laundress at the ironing board, begging her to hurry and finish so she could take them swimming at the creek. Rena followed her two big sisters around, trying to keep up.

Water skiing on the Amazon makes instant top-notch skiers. There is a great incentive not to fall. For lack of faith in our kids' skiing ability, I always followed behind and to one side with a pickup boat. Sharks have gotten up that far, as have several-hundred-pound catfish called *piraiba* (pee-rah-EEBAH). And one never knows where the pesky piranha lurk.

But too soon we were scattered again. Tim was accepted at Los Angeles Baptist College, Leanne and Cindi went to Hampdon DuBose Academy, and Rena left for Iquitos, Peru, with the Blakeslee girls from Fonte Boa.

We praised God that Jessie and I were able to accompany our three older kids to the States. We weren't allowed to see the girls' dorm rooms in the massive house at the academy; we were stopped in the doorway. "Must be some tradition held over from the folks that came over on the Mayflower," I muttered to Jessie. Nor were the girls permitted to phone their parents for six weeks. How quiet it was in the car as we drove away from the academy. I stared at the road while Jessie dabbed at her eyes with a tissue.

We sank to an all-time low in the motel before taking off for Brazil, where, at 39 and 40 years of age, Jessie and I would return to an empty house with only three dogs for company. Jessie and I repeated Romans 8:28, trying hard to accept its solace.

Back to the grind again, our opportunity to live our convictions before the people continued. Through the screened window of my office I watched Cecilio walk across the lawn to the "stitch and bandage" station. The way he held his head was strangely reminiscent of my days at boot camp in Farragut, Idaho. Cecilio planted each foot toe first, trying to keep from jarring his body. His usual smile was missing.

"Good afternoon, Cecilio. How are you?" I greeted him.

"Good afternoon, Senhor Paulo, I'm just fine," he replied, still without smiling.

I asked, "Brother Cecilio, excuse me for asking, but why do you have a shirt wrapped around your neck? It's a hot day." Beads of sweat gleamed on his face.

"Look," he said, and unwrapped the shirt to reveal an opening over one inch long to the left of his adam's apple. It was swollen, with tiny flecks of leaf and black specks of dirt. It looked like a puncture.

I said to myself, *Man, oh man! How will I clean this thing? How far in did whatever it was go? It must have missed his jugular or he would be dead. Hopefully it missed his esophagus, too.*

I stepped over to the kitchen window and called, "Umbelinda, put two liters of water on to boil in a copper-bottomed pan. When it starts to boil, yell."

I asked Cecilio, "What could have made a hole in your neck that big but not kill you?"

"This morning, carry big load poles on shoulder. Old kitchen rotten. Build new kitchen. Slip off little bridge in swamp. Poke branch in neck."

"Can you swallow?" I asked.

"Mm-hm, but hurts."

"Can you turn your head? Look down? Look up?"

"Mm-hm, but hurts." Cecilio slowly demonstrated his capability to look down, then carefully turned his head left and right.

I suppose there are a dozen kinds of broken neck, and I was ignorant of the symptoms of all of them, but I figured if Cecilio's was the worst kind, he wouldn't have walked across the lawn, nor been able to turn his head.

Fallen trees become makeshift bridges across the deepest parts of swamps. If there isn't one already spanning the area where an Indian needs to cross, he simply sets down his load and fells a tree on the spot. The bridge Cecilio tried to cross was an old one. The remaining stubs from broken branches on one end of the tree bridge were rotten on the outside, but the centers were as hard and sharp as knives.

I had him lie down on the floor of the porch, held the wound open with tweezers, and flushed it with a weak mixture of Umbelinda's boiled water and germicidal concentrate. I rolled him over to drain the water and watched the bits of leaves and decayed wood float away. I squirted more forceful streams into the hole and rolled Cecilio over again and again until no more junk came out.

"God, give me wisdom," I prayed. "Shall I close this thing with a few stitches or just one? Or leave it open in case there might be a pollywog trapped in there?" I decided to leave the hole open, figuring there had to be more infectious debris left.

I gave Cecilio the customary dose of penicillin and anti-tetanus, sprinkled the gash with sulfa powder, pulled the wound half-shut, bandaged him well, and gave him a supply of sulfa powder, gauze, and adhesive tape. I warned Cecilio to keep the injury clean and covered because of gnats that are attracted to open sores.

Two weeks later Cecilio appeared carrying two jumbo stalks of bananas under his own power. The puncture had closed nicely with no sign of secretions or gnats. Both the spring in his step and his smile had returned.

From then on Cecilio was an authority on how to cross swamps with a load. "Know now, carry half. Go back, carry other half. Let woman carry, too. Go slow," Cecilio said.

The rest of the year went by "to beat the band" as my mother used to say. And Jessie and I were anxious to be reunited with the kids. Rena Marie would be home May 18 after finishing fourth grade in Iquitos. Leanne, 17, and Cindi, 14, would have to find a place to hang their hats after June 4 when the academy closed for the summer. Tim finished his first year at Los Angeles Baptist College (LABC), and we didn't know where we would catch up to him.

In April 1968, John and Fran pulled up stakes for good from the Port of Two Brothers. Both of them had health problems. John had sought treatment for his back in the States and Panama, to no avail. Fran needed surgery. A newsletter of December 1971 advised their supporters of John and Fran's new assignment as ABWE West Coast representatives.

> In April 1968, we left the Port of Two Brothers because Fran needed immediate surgery in the States. Then we returned to Leticia, Colombia, to take over for the Flodens while they both were hospitalized. In June of 1969 we returned to the States on regular furlough, having disposed of everything but our personal belongings since neither of us was in the best of health and would probably not be able to return. We lived nearly two years in an apartment provided for us by our friends, the Paul Goodmans, meanwhile trying to recuperate and at the same time work in a limited deputation ministry.

The disappointment and shock of John and Fran's decision to leave the Port of Two Brothers didn't hit Jessie and me full force until we returned from furlough in September 1969.

. . .

"Look at the size of that hat coming down the path," I commented to Aldo. He held an outboard motor steady on its rack as I did surgery on the nearly defunct machine.

Aldo glanced in the direction of the village, smiled, and clucked. "Yeah, Raimundo always wears that big hat. Everybody teases him about his hat and makes fun of his father."

The boy crossed the lawn at a good clip. I had seen him in the Saints' Day procession as the forlorn devotees made a U-turn to avoid stepping on our property. His tall, frail mother marched behind him, nudging him along when he lagged. At 11 years old, Raimundo was skinny and sickly. His neck, in contrast to the enormous hat, looked as thin as the candle he held while sauntering along, echoing the priest's mournful chants. His complexion was sallow, possibly from his addiction to smoking home-grown cut tobacco, drinking rum, suffering from malaria, and intestinal parasites. The whites of his eyes were jaundiced. His soiled, ragged clothing was scanty enough to reveal knees twice the size of his calves. He'd never owned a pair of shoes.

Raimundo stopped a few yards from us and watched, stiff as a soldier at attention.

"*Bom dia,* Raimundo. What can I do for you this morning?"

He pulled off his hat and stepped up on the porch. "Senhor Paulo, my father wants to see you. He's sick with fever." Raimundo ran his thumb and forefinger around the brim of his giant hat during this speech.

Raimundo's father, Manuel, had been pinned under a tree while clearing jungle years before. Of course there was no medical attention available, and he was left permanently stooped, which caused him to walk with an excessive arm-waving motion as he hobbled along. He bore endless teasing and mocking from ignorant people, and, consequently, was seldom seen in public. Aldo had also mentioned that Manuel was a spiritist whom sick people consulted for healing.

"You caught me at the right time," I told Raimundo. "I just finished the job on this motor." I got my little medical kit and strapped on my over-and-under pistol. The pistol had a .22 caliber barrel above and a 410 gauge below, which was best for vipers.

Raimundo led the way through the village onto a jungle trail that ended at his house. From 50 yards away, we could see Raimundo's mother, Maria, with a pipe in her mouth, tamping black powder and lead into a muzzle-loader with a wooden ram-rod. When an emaciated dog announced our arrival, Maria snatched the pipe from her mouth, shoved it into the leather pouch hanging from her skinny shoulders, and shooed the dog away with a swift kick to its ribs. Of necessity, Raimundo's mother was the family hunter, and was preparing to hunt down their noon meal. She was unfriendly, with only a nod of greeting before disappearing into the jungle.

Manuel grimaced as he sat up to greet me.

"Sorry to hear you're sick. Where are you hurting?" I asked him.

"Ah, Senhor Paulo, I hurt all over. This fever is what bothers me now. I'm sorry to interrupt you to come here, but I doubt I could make it as far as your place," he lamented. "No problem, Senhor Manuel. Glad to do what I can, although I'm not a doctor."

Manuel's accent proclaimed that he was not native to Amazonas but came from Ceara, a state in northeastern Brazil.

"I hear that you chant prayers for sick people," I said.

"Yes, that's true. I specialize mostly in little babies."

"I'm always interested to know what other people think

about God, Senhor Manuel. What do you think about Him? Who is He to you?" I asked.

"Oh, I have faith in God," Manuel answered quickly. "We all have to trust God for this and that. He's our heavenly Father."

I shared the message of salvation with Manuel. I told him how my brother, John, and I and our wives became Christians. "Think about these things, Senhor Manuel, and feel free to call me any time, day or night."

"Thank you, Senhor Paulo," he said, making an effort to sit up. "God will pay you for this visit."

As I crawled through the palm rail fence onto the jungle trail, an inch-long poisonous *tucandeira* ant bit me between my thumb and index finger. That took my mind off everything but the throbbing pain of the bite, and left me with a low-grade fever for 24 hours.

A week later, seated at my desk in the office, I saw Raimundo with the same giant hat atop his scrawny neck, padding toward the first aid station.

I met him on the porch. "Hi, Raimundo. How's your dad?"

He pulled off his hat and looked at the floor. "My father sent me to ask you the big favor of coming to see him again. He's worse now, but doesn't want any medicine. He just wants to talk with you for a few minutes."

Down the trail again I went, with my sidearm, medical kit, and New Testament. This time I watched where I put my hand when I climbed through the fence.

Senhor Manuel gave me a friendly greeting but didn't sit up.

"How are you?" I asked. *Why did I ask sick people that question when I knew they were in bad shape?*

"Ah, Senhor Paulo, not so good. I'm getting weaker," he answered, tears running down his face.

"Well, I brought more medicine, this time against malaria, but I would rather take you to the doctor in Benjamin Constant," I said. "He would examine you closely, test your blood, and determine what you need."

"No more medicine, thank you, Senhor Paulo," Manuel sighed. "When you were here last week, you talked to me about being saved. I would like you to talk more about that."

"I want you to know that God loves us; you and me and everyone else. You might wonder, 'If God loves me, why would He let me suffer like this?' But think of it, Manuel. If you had been well and strong, you might never have heard the way of salvation I'm sharing with you now."

I sat down beside him and pointed out in my New Testament how we are saved by grace through faith in the Lord Jesus Christ, not by works. I explained that none of us can light enough candles or march in enough processions or pay enough money to earn our way to heaven.

Senhor Manuel believed the words of Scripture and received the Lord Jesus as his personal Savior that day. He died a few days later, and had been buried before I heard the news. I dropped everything and went to see Raimundo.

Dona Maria was neatly arrayed in a clean dress, her hair slicked back and tied in a bun. Little Raimundo was downcast.

"Could we talk for a few minutes?" I asked. Raimundo was quick to agree. His mother went to the kitchen to make us a *cafezinho.*

"So your dad is gone, Raimundo. I just now heard or Dona Jessie and I would have attended the burial. The folks from church would have been pleased to help out in any way," I began. Raimundo just listened, looking at the dirt floor.

"You're the man of the house now, Raimundo. You'll have to help your mother keep food in the kitchen." I continued.

It took a few seconds for him to answer. "*Sim,* Senhor, but I don't know nuthin'. Mother says I'm ignorant. I can't read or write. I carry water and cut firewood for the trader, he gives me rum and tobacco, and sometimes a little rice and bar soap. I can't go into the village because people make fun of me. Bullies try to get me to fight," Raimundo quavered, unloading the burdens of his sad young life.

"How would you like a job that pays real money?" I asked him.

"Senhor Paulo, like I said, I don't know nuthin'. I was learning to extract latex with my brother, but he moved away with his woman."

"If you decide you want a job, come and see me, and I will explain the job to you."

Several days passed before I saw Raimundo sitting on the porch bench as I rushed out to my office. He appeared to be as nervous as though waiting for a tooth extraction, working the brim of his enormous hat in his hands.

"What can I do for you this morning?" I asked.

"Just wondering what the job is, but I don't think I can do it," he answered.

I asked him, "What time do you get up in the morning?"

"Sunup," he said, pointing to the eastern horizon.

"Fine. Come with me." Together we walked over to the chicken coop. For lack of a market in the area, Jessie and I did whatever we could to keep food on hand. Consequently we tried to keep 30 to 50 chickens on hand for eggs and meat when fishing and hunting were poor. The chickens walked a narrow, slatted ramp from the ground to the coop door four feet off the ground. The bottom board of one wall was hinged, to facilitate cleaning the floor with a hoe.

"See the entrance door to the coop?" I asked Raimundo.

"*Sim,* senhor."

"See this long, hinged board at floor level?"

"*Sim,* senhor."

"There is a small hoe leaning against the fence." I pointed and Raimundo nodded. "You come at sunup every morning and open this little door so the chickens can get out. Pick up this basin and go over to the faucet under our water tanks." We walked over to the faucet together. "Clean it out good, and bring it back full of clean water. You'll find a steel drum behind the workshop with either corn or unshelled rice. Give the chickens one measure. Then lift the hinged board and scrape out the floor of the coop with the hoe. You can do all this in less than 10 minutes. Do you think you can handle the job?" I asked.

Raimundo was sure he could.

"At sunset, your job will be easier," I said. "Before the bats start flying, come and close the entrance door. You can start today at sunset."

Raimundo was elated. "See you at sunset," he said, trotting across the lawn. The first time Raimundo tried to draw water, he twisted the faucet handle so hard in the "off" direction, it was hard to turn on again.

I hoped Raimundo would attend Sunday school and the kids' class on Wednesday. But because of pranksters and bullies, he avoided walking through the village except to take care of the chickens. A month rolled by, and Raimundo never missed a day. When I paid him one day, he didn't turn and run, but stood looking at the ground.

I asked, "What's on your mind, Raimundo?"

"Sssenhor Pppaulo," he stuttered as was typical when he was nervous. "Cccould I study in your school?"

I hated to turn him down, but we were full, and he would have to start from the beginning.

"We don't have one empty desk, Raimundo. When school is out, I'll be making more desks, at which time there might be an opening for you." He left, clearly disappointed.

Months went by. My chicken boy was growing. He had a better pair of pants and a new shirt. I had persuaded Raimundo to stop smoking, and he was feeling healthier.

I was in my study before daylight, as usual, reading by candlelight. Not because I was so spiritual, but the coolness, quiet, and lack of interruptions made it a fabulous hour or two. It was light enough to see the silhouette of a broad-brimmed straw hat through the screen door against the gray of dawn.

Without looking up, I said, "*Bom dia,* Raimundo. What, another dead chicken?" Occasionally a puny chicken died during the night. He didn't answer, and I could hear him sniffing. "Come in, Raimundo. Tell me what's wrong."

He made his way around the brim of the hat, as usual, with his thumbs and forefingers, still not looking at me. "Senhor Paulo," he said, "I want to be a Christian. Do you think I can? Can I be saved?"

I sat beside him on the bench, put my hand on his shoulder, and said, "Dry up your tears; this is the happiest day of your life!" I read some Bible verses to him, and we had prayer as Raimundo came to a saving knowledge of the Lord Jesus Christ. He looked up, smiled, and said, *"Obrigado"* [Thanks], then darted out to the chicken yard.

Raimundo started attending Sunday school, and finally entered our primary school. He was growing fast. Now he seldom wore a hat. His neck thickened and his shoulders broadened. He found other ways to make money—extracting and smoking latex, and sawing boards.

The first summer camp Raimundo attended, he was challenged to turn his life over to God. The year he graduated from our primary school, he attended summer camp again. Upon returning from camp that year, Raimundo applied to the Baptist Seminary in Manaus. After the first year, he returned to the Port of Two Brothers, on fire for the Lord.

Several seminary students from the Port of Two Brothers helped us during school vacation. In the beginning they went to neighboring villages by canoe. When we had an extra outboard motor, we let the students borrow it to travel greater distances. They were careful with the equipment, taking tools to help them change a sheer pin if necessary.

One Saturday morning, Raimundo came to the back gate

for information. "Pastor Paulo," he said, "what exactly does the word 'strategy' mean?"

"Why do you ask?" I wondered.

"Well, I think I know what it means," he admitted, "but wonder if it can be used in reference to the church. I'm preparing a message for Sunday evening."

"Do you want the people to understand what you are saying, Raimundo?"

"Certainly."

"Well, if you want them to learn what 'strategy' means, why don't you be a kind of dictionary for them instead of just using the word. Wouldn't it be better to use the words 'careful planning' so as not to distract them?"

Most of the students returning from seminary struggled with feeling too intelligent. But the Lord has ways of grinding us down to size. However, the Lord used one of Raimundo's fiery messages to challenge Enoch, who had been living out of fellowship with the Lord. And it wasn't long before Enoch, too, headed for seminary in Manaus.

Male graduates choose "Ladies of Honor" to go forward with them to receive their diplomas on graduation night. You can imagine how delighted Jessie was to receive a letter from Raimundo, our former chicken boy, saying: "Dear Dona Jessie, would you do me the great favor of being my Lady of Honor on the evening of the formal presentation of diplomas at the Seminario Batista do Amazonas? I realize it would be impossible for my own mother to be here. You have been another Mom to me and many others. Please come."

Quick as scat, Jessie had patterns spread out all over the bed and a variety of material draped over the backs of chairs. She even asked me for suggestions as to which cloth to choose. Soon the old treadle machine rumbled. Jessie was no beginner at sewing, and the dress looked like it came from Saks Fifth Avenue.

It was a rewarding experience for both of us to travel to

Manaus for the occasion. Raimundo and Jessie were the most fabulous looking pair of the evening. Later, the skinny chicken boy-turned-preacher was called to pastor the First Baptist Church of Benjamin Constant, then to a large church near Brazil's capital city of Manaus.

PART SEVEN

NEW ADVENTURES

(1969–1971)

Independence Day celebrations kept sewing machines humming in preparation.

Below:
On a rainy day, you dare not lose traction going down these clay banks.

Raimundo, once my chicken boy, now pastors a church near Manaus.

Above:
Pastor Evandro and Elina Batista assumed leadership of the Tabatinga congregation.

Left:
These lethal reptiles cause agonizing death.

Gervasio's son, Narcisco, doing handwork. Narcisco now pastors a church in Manaus.

Fidelio, standing at left, taught kids in the morning, studied at our primary school in the afternoon, and taught adults by kerosene lantern at night.

First Baptist Church of Tabatinga, near completion.

Cena and Calua, Antelmo's parents and my hosts at Mu Jacurapa school program

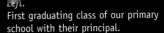

Below:
Shave and a haircut for monkey stew.

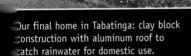

Our final home in Tabatinga: clay block construction with aluminum roof to catch rainwater for domestic use.

Above:
Abraham was nearly decapitated, and lost the use of his left arm.

Left:
I shot this Anaconda just moments before taking this picture.

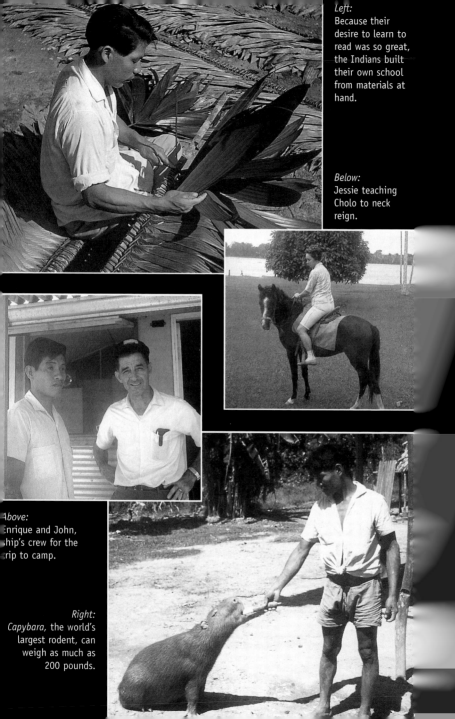

Left:
Because their desire to learn to read was so great, the Indians built their own school from materials at hand.

Below:
Jessie teaching Cholo to neck reign.

Above:
Enrique and John, ship's crew for the trip to camp.

Right:
Capybara, the world's largest rodent, can weigh as much as 200 pounds.

CHAPTER TWENTY-THREE

"PAUL, IS THAT YOU?" I recognized the voice of my sister, Ruth, calling from Omaha. Depression years remained vivid in her memory; she never called long distance just to chat, so I knew she had something important to say. Jessie, Rena, and I were in St. Petersburg, Florida, just about to take off for Brazil; my brother, John, was also in Florida.

"You know Dad has been failing lately," Ruth said.

"Yes, I know. I hope there's some improvement."

"Oh, Pauly Lou. I just got word from Bonners Ferry that Dad passed away last night."

John and I were thankful to be with Mom at the memorial service. I heard almost nothing the preacher said. While I sat holding Mom's hand, my thoughts drifted to boyhood. Dad and I used to hike down the gully behind our house all the way to the railroad tracks. We picked shaggymane mushrooms, and plinked gophers with the .22. I could hear Dad's laugh, and picture him working in his leather shop. Despondency nearly killed Dad in the early 1930's when he worked 12 hours a day for meager profit.

Little things Dad did for us showed his affection. He brought us Eskimo Pies when we suffered with measles. He made sure we got the *un*burnt pieces of toast and the best cuts of meat. It was better to have Dad read us the funnies than to read them ourselves. On cold winter nights, he fixed us hot malted milk at bedtime. Then, hot flatiron in hand, he warmed small areas on our icy sheets before tucking us in. When I was an adult with my own family, Dad told me, "Paul, don't forget: you're always welcome at home, no matter what, as long as I'm kicking."

Dad was nearly 60 when he became a Christian. From then on he was faithful in reading his big Bible every morning by the crackling fire of the kitchen stove. He left the Good Book open with pertinent verses underlined, hoping the rest of us would read it as we straggled down for breakfast, long after he had walked a mile to work.

At 82, Mom was still able to care for herself in her little white house with the green shutters. As Jessie and I boarded the plane for Brazil, I wondered how much longer Mom could survive alone. For a while after Dad's death, when she returned from shopping, as she shut the front door she would say in a loud voice, "August, are you here? You're not here, are you? Oh, how I miss you!"

. . .

The blast of Amazon humidity hit us in Leticia as if for the first time. Orville, Helen, and Liz Floden, smiled and waved to us. Bogged down with hand luggage, we lifted our chins in their direction, trudging across the piping-hot asphalt.

"Dad, couldn't I take a quick a look at our home at the Port of Two Brothers before you take me to the academy?" Rena asked. So we chartered a flight on the mission plane and spent a couple of hours in our old stomping grounds. But it wasn't the same for any of us, especially for an 11-year-old girl trying to figure out why someone else lived in the Schlener homes.

Bob and Rita Wright, living in John's old house, met us as we stepped out of the mission plane at the Port of Two Brothers. And it didn't take long for a crowd of folks from the village to gather. Another family, John and Sylvia Kallin and their kids, were living in our house. They were in the process of deciding where to establish their work in the Central Amazon area.

The Wrights with their four boys, Jonathan, Joel, Tim, and Paul, joined ABWE after accumulating years of experience in central Brazil, working with a different tribe of Indians under another mission agency. They assumed the responsibility of the Ticuna work in the Port of Two Brothers area until they moved to Campo Alegre, the largest of the Indian villages, just minutes from our house.

The Wrights were excellent teachers and counselors. They took the Indian lay leaders into a deeper study of Scripture, and taught them to prepare lessons and messages, giving them opportunity to practice what they learned. Their presence in the Port of Two Brothers area terminated when Bob accepted an invitation to head up the Missions Department of Western Baptist College in Salem, Oregon.

. . .

When Jessie and I took Rena to the academy in Iquitos, the mission residence was full to capacity. But we wanted to be as close to Rena as possible, so we stayed in an outbuilding. Masonry walls and floors were badly cracked in this tropical retreat, but the bedding was clean. The thin cloth ceiling bowed in the center from the weight of animal droppings and abandoned bird nests.

Turning out the single-bar lighbulb was like firing a pistol that started the all-night competition between gnawers and fliers. Rats scurried around frantically, while opossums thumped overhead. Bats swooped above the cheesecloth canopy that separated us from them.

Rena moved immediately into a freshly painted dorm with screened and curtained windows. Lorry and Dorry Blakeslee provided camaraderie for their fellow Central Amazon MK.

Kids who share mutual suffering seem to develop an affinity and become great friends, although the opposite can occur, too. They cry on each other's shoulders and make fun of the quirks they find in their teachers and house parents. Besides being blessed with first-class teachers and curricula, our daughters developed a near-professional ability to mimic.

I have put eye and ear to their door to take in some of our kids' acts. It was easy to tell when Miss Sandra Lyons was being depicted, the way she stood at the blackboard with a hand on a hip, one leg relaxed, playing catch with a piece of chalk, springing gently up and down on the leg supporting her.

By the sound of the voice and the smile, it had to be Miss Fran Weddle they were imitating. If you weren't watching, you would swear Helen Paige had come in the back door. They could imitate her cheerful voice to a T. And Ruth Large's soothing voice helped calm most storms, putting the kids at ease when life wasn't easy. To this day, the kids—now parents with grown children—esteem those faithful teachers and house parents, realizing the influence for good the adults had on their lives.

• • •

In those days, Jessie and I keenly felt the absence of John and Fran and their children. We missed the fellowship, the music, the supply trips, and sharing in the ministry. It was never the same, even though the Wrights were only minutes away. Our concentration was now on the Brazilians, teaching every morning, five days a week, holding four church services a week, maintaining medical hours, and extracting teeth on Thursdays. And soon Jessie and I gathered a little experience in running a riverboat.

"How would you like to take care of the *Mensageiro* while we're on furlough?" Ed Blakeslee asked me at one field council meeting. "We don't know what to do with the thing for a whole year," he said.

Ed designed and built the *Mensageiro,* a 40-foot riverboat, which he used for extensive river evangelism from the base of Fonte Boa, several hundred miles downriver from us. A wooden boat can't be closed up and moored to shore for long. Caulking loosens and the boat begins leaking as it becomes a gourmet meal for termites and a prize for pilferers.

"Whoa!" I gasped. "That's a pretty big request out of the clear blue sky." I looked around for Jessie, wondering if she heard Ed's suggestion.

Ed said, "I don't know of anybody else that could take care of the tub till we get back. Dot and I would appreciate your thinking it over and letting us know what you decide."

I promised that Jessie and I would discuss the proposal, sure it would never come to pass. When I shared Ed's request with Jessie after the noon meal, she didn't answer immediately. "What do you think? You're the one that will have to worry about the thing," she said.

Jessie and I could help the Blakeslees during their furlough and gain a feeling for what it was like to run a big boat. We had done river evangelism close to the Port of Two Brothers for years, but I was pitifully ignorant about the expense and responsibility involved in caring for and using a big rig like Ed's. A little zeal without much knowledge can get a fellow into a corner.

"Well, I happen to know you can't stand it unless your afternoons are as full as your mornings, so do what you think is best," Jessie said, realizing I was already convinced. My wife nearly always went along with what I felt to be God's leading. When I dragged my feet, she encouraged me to get moving. At the same time, she had built-in radar that sent her danger signals which she freely shared. And she rarely erred in reading character. She had all the field council members figured out.

"Look, we have told God we would go where He wants us to go, and do what He wants us to do. We still tell Him that. We left our elderly parents behind to come work in this oven. It nearly kills us to send our kids away to school so we can work full time with the nationals. Individual Christians and churches are investing money in us and our work. Hundreds are praying for us. They believe we are on the job, hitting the ball seven days

a week. If our health fails and we can't cut the mustard, somebody will carry us out feet first, or we'll pack up and hit for the
hills of Idaho." I surprised myself with my eloquence.

A few weeks later we heard the *Mensageiro* plowing its way
upriver at least four hours before we saw it. A top-of-the-line,
three-cylinder GM diesel engine powered the boat. We all kid-
ded Blakeslee when maritime regulations required him to install
a whistle; it was hard to hear above the engine's roar.

The Blakeslees' schedule was to stop at the Port of Two
Brothers on their way to Leticia to catch the plane for furlough.
I boarded the boat as an apprentice seaman, and went with them
to Leticia. I knew every inch of the river from the Port of Two
Brothers to Leticia and Benjamin Constant, so I concentrated on
learning what I could about the big boat. I took notes and
watched every move Ed made, listening to instructions and taking my turn at the helm.

"One mistake I might have made, Paul, was to put the shaft
through the hull too far amidship," Ed confessed at top volume,
to make himself heard above the noisy engine.

"Why should that be a problem?" I blasted.

"Well, she'll turn on a dime; in fact, she'll almost spin in
place. And I get out of tight spots as easy as pie. But on long
drags, you have to fight in crosscurrents and whirlpools to keep
her dead ahead," he roared, spraying my ear. I saw what he meant
when I took my turn at the helm.

Shortly after this, our whole family set out on our first trip
aboard the *Mensageiro*. On the ill-fated voyage, we broke all three
kerosene lanterns, a *kiyi* brush was knocked over the side, and
one whole barrel of diesel fuel seeped into the bilges, leaving us
barely enough fuel to make it home.

Our first night out on the river, Cindi decided to sleep topside in the wheelhouse. She wasn't up there four minutes when
she emitted a bloodcurdling scream. A rat had jumped out and
was running loose. I grabbed a chunk of plastic pipe and flew up

the ladder. One thwack finished the rat.

While we were tied securely to shore in the dead of night, a Peruvian speedboat came by at full throttle. Its wake rocked us so wildly that the water filter crashed to the deck, and a propane bottle fell over the side and sank.

I had helped steer an aircraft carrier from Astoria, Oregon, all the way to Samoa during WWII; later I took my turn in zigzag maneuvers on the China Sea during the Philippine Liberation Campaign. I didn't come close to having as much trouble either of those times as on that first trip in the Blakeslees' homemade yacht.

Villagers seemed happy to see us when we pulled into shore with nothing to sell except Bibles and medicine. Leanne was my professional dental assistant, helping me arrange a small work space and remove 140 teeth. Cindi was the practical nurse, and Rena the coffee-maker and snack-server.

The people along the river enjoyed the accordion music. Jessie's friendliness so disarmed the people that they sang along without restraint. One pleasantly plump little lady got Jessie's attention in the course of conversation, asking, "Are you Senhor Paulo's only woman?" I was surprised that Jessie hesitated so long before answering in the affirmative.

On shorter trips, members of the village church accompanied us. We split into two groups: one group taking the upriver trail and the other heading downriver, to invite local residents to a meeting. The church folk were a great help, and their personal testimonies were probably more effective than anything we foreigners had to say.

· · ·

Hot sun and frequent rainsqualls kept the January days steamy. But we were excited, and so were the church young people, because it was time for camp. Campers scrounged, finagled, borrowed, and worked to pay the registration fee. Some sold dried fish to commercial boats, others made *farinha* to sell. I was glad to buy live chickens for the menu.

Roundtrip to camp was 280 miles, traveling day and night. Failure to cross the river at the right places could add miles to the trip. Aldo and I blessed the GM engine with fresh filter and oil. Grease daubed on pulley pins freed the helm to spin easier. We checked for leaks and filled every available steel drum with fuel. For two days we scampered up and down the riverbank, stuffing the *Mensageiro* with supplies for the trip to Lake Cahrooahrah. Of the 30 on board, 21 of us had mammoth appetites.

With a mixed multitude of boys and girls on board, one adult had to remain on watch throughout the night. One job was to keep coffee brewing for the men at the helm and the motor boy, praying we would miss all submerged logs and snags. An engine failure or a punctured hull would have thrown a kink into the whole program.

The campers enjoyed the trip listening to tinny music from a hand-cranked record player, singing, eating, sleeping, playing dominoes, flying kites, giggling, and scuffling with each other. Four kids from Port of Two Brothers accepted Christ as their personal Savior, and 12 of them surrendered their lives to God while at camp.

During furlough, I was never able to raise sufficient funds for all the field projects I thought necessary. With the balance of funds in our ministry account, plus money from selling a used runabout and outboard motor, Jessie and I finally had enough to order a rough hull from a boat yard in the city of Manaus.

I drew a simple sketch of a riverboat on the back of one of our newsletters with a list of components and their estimated costs. "Don't worry about duplication," I said. "If several keels are spoken for, we Baptists can convert them into ribs or rub rails."

It was amazing how people back home helped us build the

boat. Our next letter related, "Progress on our launch fund is encouraging. We have enough on account for the main keel, upper keel, seven ribs, 18 boards, and a package of gum."

Having no experience in boat building, I was a little leery about constructing a 46-foot boat with money contributed by churches and Christian friends. I told my favorite counselor in the kitchen, "Jessie, now look what I've got myself into. How am I going to build a big boat? There's nobody around to give me advice."

From then on I avidly examined every riverboat I saw. I peeked inside and talked to skippers and motor boys about their equipment. I made a mental note of how they were built, what looked bad, and what looked good.

The use of the Blakeslees' launch served as a revelation from the Lord. The framework for their wheelhouse was made with heavy hardwood 4 x 4's. While the heavy construction made it sturdy, it also enhanced the top-heaviness created by the nearly round-bottomed hull.

Just as canoes do, big boats stay close to shore when cruising upstream to avoid the main current. But when the *Mensageiro* hit crosscurrents, it leaned way over to one side. This reality was frightfully noticeable in the pilothouse. I hung on to the framework the first time it happened, but Ed didn't seem nervous, so I got used to it—sort of. With a too-narrow stern, under full throttle the boat sat on its haunches and passengers had to climb uphill to reach the bow.

With the rugged *Mensageiro,* Ed and Dot did a praiseworthy job of reaching the lost with the gospel for hundreds of miles up- and downriver from Fonte Boa. If Jessie's and my boat was going to be so perfectly constructed, I wondered how praiseworthy our ministry would be.

. . .

Terry Bowers came winging in for a landing with a telegram from the boat yard in Manaus. It said, "Hull completed, MWM diesel engine mounted. Bring remainder of payment."

Brazilians have an innate naval architectural ability for building displacement hulls, a talent they claim to have inherited from the Portuguese who colonized Brazil. I was more concerned about underwater engineering. The bow has to cut the water, not push it. Correct support at the stern is just as important—so the vessel remains level at *all* speeds. With a properly constructed hull, the rest could look like a Chinese junk, if I chose, or a Navy destroyer, and she would travel well.

Leanne, Cindi, and Rena were visiting when I learned of the hull's completion. Already scheduled for an evangelistic trip, the *Mensageiro* was loaded with supplies, ready to sail. Instead, we went to the capital with seven on board. Aldo was the motor boy. Enoch, one of the more mature pupils from school, continued as chief helmsman. He had made the 1,000-mile trip to Manaus before as a passenger, and assured me he could keep us going in the right direction, which was downstream. I was chief prayer warrior and dabbled in everybody's business—from engine to kitchen to helm.

A half-day's travel can be lost by taking the wrong side of an island on a big curve of the river. Realizing the huge stream is 12 times greater in volume than the Mississippi, and that the round-trip was in excess of 2,000 miles, we pored over maps, pinpointing where to cross. Just as I did on the lumber raft years before, I took a lesson from Mark Twain and made a sounding line with one-meter markings to toss into shallow-looking water. Jessie and the girls held court in the kitchen, frying fish and chicken, and baking fresh bread.

Clang! Clang! Clang! Clang! Enoch pulled the bell string four times, the signal for me to go topside immediately. I scampered up the ladder quickly, two rungs at a time. "Looks like a bad storm up ahead," Enoch said.

I agreed. "We'd better look for a place to pull over until she passes. Let's try to guess where windward will be so we don't get slammed against the riverbank."

Before the squall hit us, Enoch stood on tiptoe, pointing to what he thought was an opening in the jungle. A break in the solid canopy of vegetation suggested to Enoch that down below, not yet visible, was some sort of a channel. Sure enough, a little opening appeared.

A blast of wind warned us the squall was about to catch us. Jumbo raindrops tapped on the windshield, cautioning us to hurry. Enoch jerked the bell string above his head five quick times to alert Aldo in the engine room. Aldo acknowledged with a single ring. Already alert to the problem, like Casey Jones, Aldo had his hand on the throttle.

Two more dings from Enoch slowed us. A hard right rudder whirled us upstream against the current. Ed was right, the *Mensagerio* would turn on a dime. Headed upstream, but not holding our own against the current, we drifted past the opening we aimed for. It's tricky leaving strong current and entering still water, especially if the entrance is narrow. The stern can be swept onto the hazardous shore the moment the bow hits dead water. But Enoch did it like the pro he was becoming. Enoch's services didn't come cheap after manipulating us through the narrow entrance to the lake.

. . .

Enoch was a special person. He was quick to learn, and math was his favorite subject in school. I could hardly keep ahead of him. Carpentry came naturally to him. He was slim but muscled, without an ounce of fat, his posture as straight as a general's.

While Raimundo, our former chicken boy, was home from seminary, one of his messages challenged Enoch to turn his life over to the Lord. Not long afterward, Enoch applied to the seminary in Manaus. On his vacations he was willing to go to remote villages on the river with the gospel message.

Unfortunately, Enoch was falsely accused of a transgression and expelled from seminary. Two veteran missionaries testified to the impossibility of his guilt by proving he wasn't in town when the foul deed occurred. This incident was such a blow to Enoch that he never returned to seminary, even after he was permitted to resume his studies. He studied electronics at a state school in Manaus and soon qualified to work for the Sanyo company as an inspector. Enoch eventually was promoted, and traveled to Japan.

· · ·

Aldo started to work for me as a teenager. First he pushed a lawn mower, then he worked himself into a job as chief go-fer. He was only five feet tall, but had he not been so bowlegged he might have grown another few inches. He studied a short time in our primary school but never learned to read fluently, and math was next to impossible. Aldo stammered and experienced more difficulty speaking than many Ticuna Indians.

I taught him to use my simple hand tools to help build our home, school, church, boathouse, and outhouses, and repair all of them as well. I praised him when he excelled and let his mistakes teach him instead of continually finding fault. Aldo soon became good at many jobs, but always struggled with measurements. His only method of measuring was to use his fingers, hand span, arm's length, and paces. Four fingers wide, one finger thick, and six palms long was a piece of wood we would call a four-foot-long 1 x 4. But my palms opened wider than his, and my fingers weren't as stubby, so I had to insist Aldo learn to use a steel tape. I let him take his time at it. He pored over the numbers as if they were classified codes he needed to decipher.

Aldo had never been around machinery. After weeks of being

shown, he could keep the old-fashioned pushed mower lubricated and sharpened.

Years later, when we had a generator, Aldo learned to use an electric table saw. It was such a pleasure he burned out the first motor trying to see how fast he could rip a board. After ripping a dozen boards four meters long and an inch thick with a handsaw, it dawned on him how precious the table saw was. He never burned out another motor.

Aldo could squat down on his haunches, fold a gunny sack to fit his wide shoulder, and heft a 40-hp outboard motor. The big machine hid most of him, making it look like the motor had sprouted legs as he hurried with the unwieldy thing across the lawn, then down the clay bank to fasten it to the transom of a boat.

Long before we traveled on the *Mensageiro* to Manaus, Aldo had become a close personal family friend and my right-hand man. He qualified as a carpenter, painter, motor boy, helmsman, and small equipment repairman. During the 30 years he worked for me, he never uttered an unkind word to me, and as far as I know, he never stole so much as a wooden match.

We spent three weeks in Manaus, a city of 350,000, shoving dead animals and other debris away from the boat, eating restaurant food, buying supplies, and dealing with officials. We missed our quiet little village, the clean water in our rainwater tanks, and all the activities.

PART EIGHT

NEVER A DULL MOMENT

(1972–1976)

CHAPTER TWENTY-FOUR

ENOCH, ALDO AND I SAT AROUND my kitchen table discussing how to fashion the hull we brought back from Manaus into a functioning riverboat.

I said, "Well, guys, we've plowed water together on Blakeslee's tugboat, and it has been a good experience. I'll be forever grateful to Ed and Dot for asking us to take care of the stately *Mensageiro*. We complained a lot about the rig, but how do we do it, if we know so much about how it shouldn't be done? Tell me what you think we should shoot for, and how do we start building onto the hull? How can we avoid mistakes?" I asked. "We're starting from scratch, so we have a perfect opportunity to do what we can with the materials we brought from the city."

This was a strange experience for my two friends. They had never before been asked their opinion about how to do something as big as construct a riverboat. They glanced at each other in disbelief, shrugged their shoulders, and addressed their toast and coffee.

"C'mon guys, tell me what you think," I urged. They had never worked on the construction of a big boat before. Aldo realized that I already knew exactly what he was capable of, as well as some of the things he was unable to do. But he also knew I trusted him.

Enoch had done a good job making simple furniture for a couple of the seminary teachers in Manaus, but naval architecture is plagued with complications that are foreign even to experienced carpenters, let alone three amateurs like us. And there was no one knowledgeable about the subject from whom we could glean information.

Aldo cleared his throat and made the first observation. "I doubt if you will have to worry about tipping over," he said. "Your hull is nearly flat-bottomed with nice round chines [the intersection of the bottom and sides of a boat]. I talked to the man at the boat yard, and he said the hull is designed to draw a minimum of water."

I hadn't paid that much attention to the bottom of the hull, although I've been gun-shy of tippy boats since my days in the Navy. The *Mensageiro* had scared us a few times too, so I was thankful to know capsizing wouldn't be a problem.

"That's true, Senhor Paulo," Enoch said. "We better not make a deep hold under the main deck, or we'll have to make the superstructure high. Then a pilothouse on top of that would make it more top-heavy, not to mention the 500-liter water tank."

Our impromptu conference lasted about an hour. The fellows had some excellent ideas and were pleased to be included in the planning. I had a lot of measuring and figuring ahead of me before we pounded a nail or sawed a board.

During the morning while I was teaching, Aldo and Enoch worked on the jobs I laid out for them. The hull had to be cleaned after our nine-day trip. Materials we brought from Manaus had to be carried up the riverbank and stored in a safe place.

They planed boards, and hewed and squared the extremely hard *acapu* (ah-cah-POO) wood for stanchions. These tough posts became the foundation to which all the superstructure was fastened. I thought, *Boy! With wood like this in the structure, we'd better never spring a big leak.*

The first wracking of brains was over the measurement of the space between the main deck and the hull. All the rest of the structure would be measured from the main deck.

"Let's have another conference," I suggested. "Christians have given money to buy these materials and are praying for us," I continued, "but at the same time, they are trusting me to do the best I can with every penny. Some of the folks who have given money to build this boat are elderly people who have less money than I. So the final decision on how things should be done has to be mine. I feel responsible.

"It's going to have to be like this," I concluded. "I'll lay out the work I want you to do in the morning. You do exactly as I explain, even if you think I'm wrong. Then when I come home in the afternoon and if the work looks like it was planned by the kindergarten class, we'll have a good laugh together, tear it apart, and start over."

The next morning was Saturday, so we three could put in a full day's work. While Enoch and Aldo fitted and nailed joists on the deck, cutting boards into odd shapes to fit the curves and angles, I bolted the long hardwood stanchions in place. I knew the fellows considered me the project's master craftsman, and were watching me like hawks. They probably viewed my admission that I didn't know how to build a boat like this as humility; after all, I had built my big house, workshop, and the schoolhouse.

Aldo beat me back to the job after lunch that Saturday, and had started to work when I arrived. I walked a few yards upriver to take another gander at the side view of the stanchions, and couldn't believe my eyes.

"Aldo, what have you guys done to my stanchions?" I bellowed. "Come up here and take a look!" My companions struggled to control their expressions.

"Feast your eyes on that!" I said to Aldo. "What happened? All the stanchions are slanting forward."

Aldo throbbed with silent laughter until he was able to talk. "Senhor Paulo, the bow was stuck up on ground while you bolted the stanchions in place. Just a few minutes ago I shoved the hull back so it's floating in the water."

I often wonder if the Lord laughs at our silly mistakes? You can believe from then on, before starting work, we made sure the hull was floating and not slanted up on dry ground.

. . .

A few days after beginning construction on the boat, Tiago and Isabel, a young Ticuna couple in their late teens, met with tragedy.

Tiago looked like a weight lifter, with handsome, chiseled good looks. Isabel kept herself well groomed, unlike many of the Indian women. Both had perfect sets of teeth, filed to sharp points, resembling those of a piranha. They had a husky, healthy eight-month-old baby, and rarely missed a church service.

After church one Sunday, Isabel waited to talk with me, her vivacious smile noticeably absent.

"Where's that man, Tiago?" I asked. "I never see you without him."

Isabel made no reply, but bowed her head and looked at the ground, then at her baby. She hesitated, then said in a subdued voice, "He died."

"What?" I looked at her neighbors who stood close, grief etched on their faces. Emotion prevented Isabel from explaining, so the neighbors enlightened me.

"Tiago, he strong man but sometimes fall down, get stiff, foam out of mouth." I knew he had seizures on occasion, but didn't realize they were so severe. His healthy appearance defied any thought of weakness. "Isabel and baby with Tiago, fishing in swamp. He got stiff. Fall out of canoe. Tiago too heavy, Isabel can't lift. Piranhas attacked."

I dropped down on a bench, buried my face in my hands, and quietly agonized while picturing that tragic scene in the swamp. The young mother struggling—in vain—to pull her husband back into the small canoe, the baby clinging to her side. Helplessly watching the churning water turn crimson as piranhas savagely devoured her husband.

I thanked God that Tiago had heard the message of salvation, and received the Lord Jesus Christ as his personal Savior before this tragedy. Once I regained my composure, I took Isabel's hand and reminded her of that truth. She nodded, smiling at me through tear-filled eyes.

. . .

There was no way I could keep my concentration solely on boat building with so many interruptions. Slow as it was, we were encouraged to see the boat take shape. At last the helm was in place. Pulleys, chains, long rods, and turnbuckles were hidden under the gunnels. The boat was drab—bare lumber, far from finished—but with the steering apparatus in place, we could take a short trial spin.

"Aldo, talk to some of the fellows in the village about going with us on a trip around the islands this afternoon at four o'clock," I said. The first island is about three-quarters of a mile from the Port of Two Brothers, with three more between it and the farthest river bank.

Six men from the village appeared for their boat ride. I backed away from shore, grabbing the helm to check the steering. Perfect.

"Okay, Joe, let 'er rip," I cried. Jose rang the bell three times to signal Aldo, who shoved the throttle to full-speed ahead. Our load was so light with only a few gallons of fuel and a few men that we felt like we were flying. The men whooped and hollered as we passed the village. "We'll write to you from Manaus," Laodelino shouted to his wife who was struggling up the steep riverbank with a heavy jug of water on her head. She turned to see what all the commotion was about, and sloshed water down her back.

Women bathing and washing clothes at the river's edge

grabbed towels to cover themselves, rescuing bars of soap and kitchen utensils from the tidal wave our boat created. I noticed that our wake was minimal for a 46-foot-long displacement hull.

Two features I was anxious about were stability in troubled water (like waves, crosscurrents, and whirlpools) and handling at full throttle. Would we have to struggle uphill as we walked from stern to bow, or would the vessel remain reasonably level?

We headed downstream, crossing the river. Jose eased closer to shore. "There's a bad crosscurrent at the point of the island as we head upstream," he hollered.

"Good! We'll see what she'll do." I checked to see Aldo at the throttle.

"Senhor Paulo, shouldn't I signal for half throttle?" Jose asked.

"No. We'll maintain full speed. If she's going to tip over, this would be the best time. Just as the bow yields to the current, give her a hard right rudder. The tail should whip around and put us straight into the current."

Jose didn't blink for the three minutes it took us to hit the current. He was ready to spin the wheel—and he did it just right. We moved a tad to the right without tipping or teetering. And the fantail swung around just like the doctor ordered, as we faced the current head-on.

"Praise God!" I bellowed. Jose smiled.

At full throttle she stayed as level as the water itself. Hallelujah! The men who built our hull knew what they were doing.

I was deep in triumphant meditation on how perfectly things were working when the normally softspoken Jose screeched, "My God, Senhor Paulo! Help!" At the same time he rang the bell a dozen times as fast as he could. He spun the helm so fast it nearly went out of sight. "It won't turn! It won't turn!" he screamed.

Aldo didn't have time to grab the accelerator before we felt ourselves being lifted, as though an underwater monster hoisted us on its shoulder. We were thrown forward, stuck at a 30-degree angle in mud and surrounded by grass that reached up to the second deck.

Jose was as pale as any member of his race could be. "Senhor Paulo, I turned it, and turned it, and turned it, but we kept going into the shore," he quavered, afraid of being blamed for the accident.

"Forget it, Jose. No one could have done any different. And so what? We had a nice, soft landing in the mud and grass," I said. A screw eye slipped off the turnbuckle of the steering linkage on the starboard side, making it impossible to stay away from the riverbank. In less than five minutes the problem was fixed. But we were stranded in the tangle.

Jose dove into the river. "Somebody hand me a knife," he shouted. "I'll cut the junk off the propeller." I hadn't even thought of that. We would have been fortunate to reach half-speed with the grass and roots wrapped around the prop, and I wouldn't have known what was slowing us down.

Construction on the riverboat began to go faster as we learned from our mistakes. Many Christians back in the States provided the necessary funds. My brother, John, and our son, Tim, got jalousie windows from the States, while a friend in San Luis Obispo made monthly financial contributions until the project was finished.

A 500-liter water tank, topside, supplied water for the kitchen sink, the shower, and toilet. John left us the tabletop gas from his houseboat. Jessie crooned, "Oh, wow!" when she checked out the smooth Formica cupboard doors. They would never mold and would always look good.

My insistence in keeping the center of gravity as low as possible didn't leave enough space for an entrance off the bow. All river launches have a forward entrance, but we had just enough room for two jalousie windows. We put a ladder from the bow to the wheelhouse where a door would normally go. When we pulled into a port to minister, people walked up the plank and up the ladder to an area protected from sun and rain by a large tarp. Plenty of benches made this the perfect place to sit and talk or take care of medical and dental needs without crowding into the small living quarters below deck.

Accuracy in post-extraction spitting was hindered many times by the breeze. And most diaperless babies seemed to develop diarrhea shortly after coming aboard. These problems were alleviated with buckets of water and a *kiyi* brush, just as I did on board the great *Triumfo II*.

After hiking down trails, visiting in people's homes, conducting open-air services, and treating the sick, the first thing we did back on board our boat was to clean our shoes at the fantail. Then we drenched all the decks with buckets of water. We ran the bilge pump continually while we scrubbed and mopped. It's a wonder we didn't sink, taking on so much water in our battle against dirt and disease.

· · ·

Although interruptions did their best to delay us, we met our deadline to take 72 young people to camp at Lake Cahrooahrah. A young man with a four-inch-long ax gash to his leg; a baby that fell into a basin of hot water and lost skin from his back, stomach, and legs; and a 12-year-old girl with a knife wound in her back were just a few of the medical emergencies that threatened to hinder completion of the riverboat.

The boat looked like a piece of cake when we finished painting. The hull was light blue with dark blue trim, and all the bulkheads were white. And we finally decided on a name for the boat. Jessie and I thought it should be named for our kids. She said, "Better name it after one of the girls, like they do for ships."

But which girl: Leanne, Cindi, or Rena? First we tried using one syllable from each of the girl's names: CinReLe, LeReCin,

ReLeCin. None of them sounded right, and the Brazilians would wonder about a meaningless, hard-to-pronounce name. We broke tradition by naming our boat *Timoteo*, Portuguese for Timothy. The girls soon recovered from the shock of the boat being named after "spoiled brat" Tim.

Aldo felt like a professional skipper as we entered the narrow Javari River in front of Benjamin Constant. Two dings of the bell brought the pleasant grumble of the engine to a half-throttle while we eased by the town and tied up at the airplane hanger.

"Oh, Jess, she looks bee-yoo-tee-ful," Wilma Bowers squealed as Jessie hopped out onto the floating hangar.

"Thanks, Wilma, but we know it won't stay that way for long. It's like a puppy. If it would only stay a puppy it would be nice, but too soon it grows into a dog," Jessie said, always ready with a little northern Idaho adage.

Young people swarmed over the hangar with their baggage. The "amen" that concluded our prayer asking God's blessing on the 680-mile roundtrip was like a pistol shot at the start of a race. The kids jumped up on the bow and onto the fantail, through the door and up the ladders, taking over the ship like pirates on the high sea.

Enoch had returned to seminary, so that left Aldo, Jessie, and me to handle the *Timoteo*. Aldo manned the helm, checking both sides for traffic. Playing motor boy kept me close to the galley to serve as cupbearer. Here I could jump at Jessie's every beck and call.

Jessie and the counselors immediately struck up their guitars. The kids waved goodbye to the folks on the hangar and burst into singing lively choruses at top volume. As we cruised by the town, they sang even louder and waved the Brazilian flag, a Christian flag, and the two colorful church flags. Within eight hours we would pull into the Port of Two Brothers to load another crowd of lively kids waiting for us on the riverbank, waving flags and singing choruses. Just as in the States, every type of youngster was represented in these groups: prankster, loud-mouth, proud, humble, neat, sloppy, rich, and poor.

We lashed a 50-foot boat called *Silvia* to the port side of *Timoteo*. One of the local traders rented the boat to us. A commercial boat with no built-in comfort, it had carried potent-smelling animal skins, smoked latex balls, and salted fish. The only enclosed areas were the engine space, the little store, and a toilet. The males had the "privilege" of occupying this boat while the females rode first class on *Timoteo,* where there were mirrors, a ceramic floored shower, flush toilet, and bathroom sink.

With the exception of a couple of male counselors playing dominoes by candlelight, everyone dropped off to sleep shortly after we shoved off. What a relief! We who were in charge decided to take turns on watch during the night to keep track of any milling around, less of a problem when the boys and girls rode on separate boats.

Travel was always more dangerous at night. Our spotlights, like yellow sticks, did their best to reveal dangerous snags and shallows, and to keep our distance from shore.

Time spent in preparation for camp and the grueling hours traveling were rewarded by the young people taking revival to their respective churches. Some of the campers sounded like seminary graduates, as they described Bible lessons they learned. They taught new choruses to the congregations and demonstrated useful crafts that impressed their parents. Personal testimonies of how God worked in their lives and the decisions they made at camp challenged the folks at home.

Most of the young people from the Port of Two Brothers area who left home to study in Bible institute and seminary surrendered their lives to God at camp. Not all became full-time Christian workers, but some did and are—to this day—serving the Lord.

Hundreds of Ticuna Christians learned to read and write, but were not qualified to be accepted in any of the established Bible institutes or seminaries in the big cities. Those who spoke Portuguese fairly well kept busy teaching children and adults in their own neighborhoods and villages. It was amazing how so many people became literate, starting with a few of us who could barely read and write ourselves.

CHAPTER TWENTY-FIVE

NEARLY 20 YEARS HAD PASSED since Goodman, Orr, John, and I braved the forbidding jungle swamps in an adventurous voyage to the Jacurapa River. One morning, just as I reached for the coffeepot, hands clapped at the back door. It was Antelmo, a young man from the Jacurapa River. He was the son of Cena, one of the masked participants in the Indian festivity we had witnessed years before Antelmo's birth. Antelmo wanted to borrow a volleyball.

"Where is the game going to be?" I asked.

"I want to take it back to the Jacurapa," he huffed, short of breath from a 10-mile hike followed by a jog across the soccer field. "I'll bring it back day after tomorrow."

He was obviously reluctant to leave as he dribbled the volleyball, and tossed it in the air. "Anything else, Antelmo?" I asked. He hesitated.

About then I had a common-sense spasm that shook my inner man. *You idiot,* I told myself. *This kid has just tramped through 10 miles of jungle and might want a drink of water and a few minutes' rest. Maybe he has a problem and needs to talk. Are you trying to help people, or do you try to get rid of them as quickly as you can so you can go on to the next thing?*

"Sit down and take a load off your feet," I told Antelmo. "How are things going at the Jacurapa?"

"Thank you, but I can't stay long," Antelmo answered. "What I came for mostly was to invite you to attend the closing program of my little school back on the Jacurapa. It's tomorrow morning."

My automatic response was to refuse. "Antelmo, that's a long hike, and I still have to prepare for Sunday. Since tomorrow is Thursday, a bunch of folks will be coming for tooth extractions. Then on Friday, a couple of dentists from my country will arrive for a visit. I'll pray that your program will be successful; I'm sure you have done a great job with your pupils. Is there anything else you need?"

Antelmo tucked the volleyball under his arm and shook my hand politely. "No problem, Pastor Paulo. Thanks for the use of the volleyball. *Adeus*." He ducked under the wire clothesline, accelerating to a lope with the smooth agility of a cat.

As I returned to the kitchen for coffee, I watched Antelmo cross the little bridge, pass the schoolhouse, and settle into the gait he would maintain for most of his trip through the jungle. Like getting hit with a .45 slug, I suddenly felt like the jerk I was. I dove to open the kitchen door, and let out a whistle like Dad's after my mother had called me to supper three times. His whistle always worked, and mine froze Antelmo in his tracks. I motioned him back to the house.

Antelmo skidded to a stop on the cement slab by the back door. "Senhor?" he asked.

"Twenty years ago when my brother, John, and I went to the Jacurapa with our visitors, we traveled by canoe because there was a lot of water in the swamps. Now it's dry and I would have to go by jungle trail. If there were only one trail, I could find my way, but with so many trails made by rubber-cutters and hunters, I would get lost."

"Hmmm," Antelmo responded. "Are you saying you will come?"

"Yes, I'll come, but I'll need a guide," I said.

Without another word Antelmo bounded off to the nearest upriver village.

Jessie was listening, glad for my decision. "How about a couple of sandwiches made with this chunk of Italian salami from

Bogota?" she asked. I grabbed the sandwiches, my mosquito net, Bible, snakebite serum, dysentery medicine, a change of clothes, and a light fishing rod. Before I finished, two young Indian men stood at the back door. "Let's go, sir," they said.

And did we go! I should have conferred with the boys before I turned them loose. Still in my mid-forties, I figured I could hold my own on a trek through the jungle. But these boys made me wonder if they were training for the Olympics. Their solid legs knew no fatigue as they padded along at a rapid pace.

Stepping into cool, ankle-deep puddles along the way was a blessing to my sweaty feet. Side-stepping on submerged, slippery poles to cross deep swamps was another story. This was the backyard of giant anacondas and deadly vipers. I became more appreciative of the Christians who hiked over this trail on Saturdays in order to be in church by 7:30 Sunday morning.

After and an hour and a half, my two guides were as fresh as May flowers, but the great white chief was losing whatever surefootedness he had. I thought they might look back occasionally to see if I was anywhere around. But no, neither "stop" nor "rest" was in their vocabulary. I kept thinking about my sandwiches, wondering if I would live to eat them. I noticed a good-sized windfall lying parallel to our trail ahead. As we appoached it I hollered, "Hey, fellas, how about helping me eat these sandwiches?"

They stopped. I dropped onto the big log like it was magnetized and fumbled for the sandwiches I hadn't planned to share. The two soccer champions clamped their pointed teeth down on their sandwiches only twice before sending them down the hatch. I chewed mine to mush, taking advantage of the rest. Sitting there munching away, I thought, *What a place to have a kidney stone attack.*

The two guides had renewed vigor and set an even faster pace than before. But a jungle trek is unforgettable. Variety of plant life is amazing. Some trees are a tangle of exposed roots. We saw palm trees so plastered with thorns that you wouldn't climb them if the wildest jaguar was nipping at your heels. Manioc plantations on both sides of the trail gave proof that other humans lived somewhere in the area. More than an acre of vegetation lay wilting and drying in the powerful equatorial sun.

Families working in their plantations heard us coming. Heads popped above the plants as we passed by. They were surprised to see me. They dropped what they were doing and swished through the jungle toward the village to sound the alarm before our arrival.

I paused at the edge of the village to feast my eyes on the scene, thanking God for the privilege of being there, the same village where the *festa* had taken place almost 20 years ago. The giant thatched house where the festivity took place was gone, replaced by many smaller houses. The ground had been swept so clean one would think they used vacuum cleaners.

Hundreds of freshly caught fish roasted over green-stick grills. Women darted around splitting wood, cleaning fish, sweeping yards, nursing babies on the run, and gathering clothes draped over bushes to dry. The men relaxed in small groups.

Then I was mobbed. Everybody respectfully waited his turn to shake hands. I felt like a candidate for governor. I knew all these people; most attended church regularly for years, or had come for medicine or snakebite treatment. A good number had toothless smiles as a result of my dentistry.

Greetings tapered off until only Antelmo and his father, Cena, were left. Cena was one of the four Macario brothers who served as masked dancers during the *festa*. He was shorter than Antelmo, only because of his extremely bowed legs. Cena's face was deeply lined from years spent working in the sun. His hands were gnarled, toughened from long hours hanging on to an ax handle and machete.

They led me over to Cena's home, and said, "You sleep here tonight." Cena's wife didn't appear to have just stepped out of a beauty salon, but she was the happiest, most gracious hostess a weary traveler could wish for. Everything was clean, despite the ever-present kitchen smoke. On a little hand-hewed shelf, up high, sat a well-worn Bible, a few notebooks, and school textbooks. I said to myself, *Thank you, Lord.*

Cena offered me a seat made from rolled palm banch string. As if on cue, a chubby girl in a clean dress entered with a nicked enamel cup of coffee. I barely got it down before another girl showed up with the same size cup filled with hot chocolate made from cacau fruit from their plantations.

"Wanna take a bath?" Cena asked politely.

He handed me half of a hollowed, round gourd about 10 inches in diameter. I had my own soap and towel so I went down to the river for a cool bath and a change of clothes.

I was combing my hair in their silver-dollar-sized mirror when Cena said, *"Cunaxwai cuchibu?"* [Do you want to eat?] I had been feasting on the aromas of roasted fish since my arrival. The salami sandwich was long gone, and I was ready for whatever bubbled on the grill.

"Have four kinds fish: matringchaung, curimatah, piranha, and pirapitinga. What kind?" he asked.

I requested piranha. The Jacurapa River produces the large black variety with firm, tasty flesh. In less than a minute, Cena's wife trotted over with a still bubbling fish, which she slid onto my plate. One of Cena's granddaughters brought a generous bowl of *farinha*; a saucer of coarse, wet salt; and a small plate of halved limes.

When Cena bowed his head to pray, everyone within earshot suddenly grew quiet. He thanked God for His provision of food and for brother Paulo's visit. I felt guilty for not having visited more often.

The expertly prepared fish, hot off the coals, were delicious beyond description. It didn't take long for Cena and me to reduce the two juicy fish to skeletons. Cena's wife kept watch from the kitchen for our elbows to stop bending. And when they did, she approached our table with more fish, but I had to refuse. *If only I had it now!*

The chubby granddaughter reappeared with the same cup full of coffee, which was followed by another hot chocolate. I wasn't sure if the coffee and chocolate were boiled according to doctors' recommendation, but the Lord spared us any serious illness from food and drink over the years. We've dipped into the Amazon for many a silty drink with no serious consequences. To have gone thirsty, hour after hour, while perspiring heavily might have been more serious than contaminated water.

Like magic, more and more people arrived. This kept me busy shaking hands. There were very few people I didn't know, and it was a happy time of fellowship.

The sun was slipping down behind the jungle when João and Alexandre Macario let me know they were going to conduct a church service in Alexandre's house. Inside my host's house, I strung up my mosquito net so it would be ready when I returned from the service. I would be sleeping on the floor, for which I was grateful.

Cena walked in while I was tying the knots to hold up my net. He held a bulky cloth bag from which he pulled a brand-spanking-new, factory-made hammock. "Here, for sleep. Bought for you at trader," he said.

I had another of my split-second visions. I could see Cena, rivulets of sweat running down his body, felling an enormous hardwood tree. And then another, and another. There he was in his stained, patched work clothes, his long knife slashing the undergrowth. He slapped mosquitoes, scratched chigger bites, snagged himself on thorns, and was stung by hornets.

As if it were unfolding in front of me, I saw the man and wife silhouetted against high flames, on an intensely hot day, burning logs and brush. I saw them planting and weeding. Later they chopped the high plants and uprooted the fibrous potatoes, peeled and ground them, and squeezed the mush. Again in the heat, steam, and smoke from an open oven, they winnowed the drying mush until 'it was toasted. Mrs. Cena and the girls would go into the jungle to cut reeds and weave baskets lined with leaves to hold the *farinha* they were making. I could see Cena, barefoot, a heavy basket of farinha on his back. Bent forward against the weight, he walked 10 miles down the jungle trail to the trading post. "How much cost big hammock?" he'd ask, dropping the heavy basket of *farinha* on the floor.

I knew the *farinha* wasn't enough to buy a hammock, that Cena was underpaid, and that he still owed the trader several more baskets of *farinha*. Knowing how comfortably I lived in a big painted house at the edge of the river, Cena did his best to make me comfortable during my stay. He made a special trip to buy a hammock, not at all sure I would attend his son's program.

"Thanks a lot, Cena," I said humbly. "I'll sleep like a baby tonight." He smiled his understanding.

I grabbed my Bible and flashlight and walked 50 yards to Alexandre's house. The front had open walls so that when the floor area was filled, folks outside could listen in. Two sections of hand-hewed benches faced a small table that served as a pulpit. It was covered with a simple cloth, which was as valuable to them as the finest lace-trimmed linen. Two kerosene lamps on the table and others fastened to posts gave off a dim glow like a candlelight service.

Neighbors and visitors entered quietly and sat down. There were no announcements, no taking an offering, and no hurrying. When the benches were all occupied, a former student from the Port of Two Brothers school walked up to the little table. Accompanied by a guitar, he led us in songs from two little chorus books, one in the Ticuna language, the other in Portuguese. After a few hymns, he paused for testimonies and Scripture recitation, concluding with prayer.

"Now Pastor Paulo will bring the message," he announced, looking at me with a big smile.

By then, my voice shut down with emotion. I saw again the transforming power of God in the lives of these people. I could never refer to them as uncivilized, for their lives were on a far higher spiritual and moral plane than many people educated and steeped in an industrialized society.

My thoughts went back to the drunken orgy held in this place 20 years ago. No one could read. There were no Bibles, no Christians, no knowledge of God and His plan of salvation; there existed only fear, superstition, witchcraft, knife fights, and drunkenness. I lamented that Jessie wasn't with me to see this; John would have appreciated it as well.

I approached the little table and asked Francisco to lead in another hymn while I gathered my thoughts. I still have the little index card with my few notes on the first sentence of Psalm 23: "The Lord is my shepherd I shall not want." They listened as I made it through the short message without choking up.

Back in my bedroom, I pulled the bottom edges of the mosquito net together to cover all cracks in the floor, and sank into the new hammock.

. . .

The loudest alarm clock I ever heard went off on the other side of the partition in the pit ch dark. It was Antelmo's, an old-fashioned, wind-up alarm with two bells perched on top. No sooner had he turned off the alarm than he touched a match to a firecracker and held it out the window to announce the beginning of the day's activites.

I fumbled for my flashlight and saw that it was only three hours past midnight. A radio blared out a gospel program in Portuguese from the Netherlands Antilles. I just lay there and listened.

At four, I heard axes chopping firewood. By the gray light of dawn, the village was a scene of activity, preparing for hundreds of guests. Neighbors scurried around, talking, laughing, carrying water, and building more fires. Fisherman struggled up the river-bank with their catches of the day.

I made my way to the river to wash up, brush my teeth, and shave. Back at the house, Antelmo's wife served a breakfast of fried ripe and green bananas and tasteless starch cakes called *beiju* (bay-JOO), made from manioc tubers, washed down with more coffee and hot chocolate.

The crowd swelled, some having come from as far away as I had. No horns honked, no doors slammed, no loud-speakers blared. The crowd scattered around the village in clusters. Little kids chased each other, climbed trees, and kicked rubber balls made from raw latex.

Two elderly men hobbled across the soccer field, straining so as not to miss any activity. They grimaced as they lowered themselves onto a chair-high log. I wished for comfortable lawn chairs to offer the old boys.

Tiny, stooped, toothless grandmothers in long dresses were offered hammocks in the shade. These ancients must have thought back on their adolescence, when the only known social activities were the drunken orgies.

A girl's clan was identified by tiny birds or animals carved from wood, strung on fancy necklaces, brightened with seeds and animal teeth in varying colors and sizes. With only two clans in the tribe, finding a mate was simplified. The boys paid attention only to girls from the opposite clan. A young man of the bird clan wouldn't take a second look at a girl who had birds strung on her necklace, cute as she might be.

A referee's whistle blew. After a short announcement, the crowd slowly sauntered over to the area that was indicated for the exercises.

Tum-tum, tum. Tum-tum, tum. Tum-tum, tum sounded from inside the small schoolhouse. Then the students marched out in time with the drum beat, taking short steps, as though their shoes were hobbled. A few were barefoot; others had shoes but no socks, and some wore both shoes and socks. All 26 pupils wore homemade uniforms. They worked to buy cloth at the trading posts, and sewed with needle and thread or waited their turn at one of the two sewing machines in the village.

The boys and men wore dark trousers and white shirts. High-waters seemed to predominate, but some dragged on the ground. All were as serious as military cadets. At a snail's pace they formed a circle around the flagpole. The boy carrying a Brazilian flag broke rank and walked over to fasten the flag to the mast. Antelmo led in singing the national anthem as the flag slowly climbed to the top of the pole.

Antelmo asked us all to bow our heads while one of his elderly uncles prayed, thanking God for the occasion that brought us together and recalling the past when they had no knowledge of God. As I listened to the Indian pray, I thanked the Lord for the time He gave me with the Indian pupils at the Port of Two Brothers, men and women who now taught their own people.

It suddenly dawned on me that, as a "big wheel," I might be asked to make a speech. But my spirits lifted when Antelmo called his Uncle Alexandre forward to speak.

Twenty years earlier when John and I visited the *festa*, we never saw Alexandre, nor his brothers, João and Cena, because they were hidden under hideous, full-length masks.

Alexandre stepped up to the flagpole and raised his voice. *"D'cux, pa chauenegue."* [Listen, brothers.] He testified to the grace of God in his life. Everybody listened intently and nodded in agreement. "The gospel was preached to us by these foreigners, and many of us accepted the Lord as our Savior. We were blind, but our eyes have been opened. We have real life now, and have passed from the power of Satan to the power of God."

When Alexandre finished, João, the younger brother, spoke along the same lines. He was followed by Cena.

When the program was over, I gave Antelmo a big hug. I congratulated him for his faithfulness to the Lord and for his work in educating his people. Then I went over to the student body and shook hands with each one before Antelmo sent me to join his father at the table.

"What will you have?" Cena asked.

"Brother Cena, I noticed a nice rack of *tambaqui* ribs bubbling on the grill. It's my favorite dish. If someone hasn't glommed it, I would really like that piece," I said, my mouth already watering.

"Nobody take. You take first, then me, then others," he chuckled as he struggled with Portuguese.

Three syllables from Cena discharged Mrs. Cena on her familiar trot from the kitchen to our table with the very piece of meat I wanted. Cena chose the hindquarter of the same fish. We wasted no time in demolishing the delectable meal. At least 30 Ticuna gathered to watch me separate the ribs with my hunting knife. They lost interest when they saw me stuffing food in my mouth with my fingers and wolfing it down just like they did.

When my two guides finished playing soccer, I gathered up my baggage and bade farewell to my hosts.

"Wait, Senhor Paulo," Antelmo called. "Here is your volleyball."

"Keep it," I told him. "We have another one at home."

Just reminiscing about all that took place during those few hours at the Jacurapa was energizer enough to put spring in my steps along the same trail that left me breathless the day before.

CHAPTER TWENTY-SIX

AS I LEFT THE JUNGLE AND STEPPED into the vast clearing at the Port of Two Brothers, Dr. Gause, his two daughters, and their friend climbed up the riverbank with another dentist from the United States. These pleasant people were easy to entertain and well satisfied with our limited accommodations. Dr. Gause shared valuable information with me about extracting teeth, demonstrating on dozens of people.

The precaution that stuck with me most was, "Don't get in a hurry. Apply pressure slowly." This took self-control when there were 30 people waiting in line. Dr. Gause probably wondered how many I sent to an untimely grave, but was kind enough not to ask.

Another dentist, Dr. Dick Salter and his wife, Rula, from Whittier, California, visited before Dr. Gause. Dr. Salter used 500 feet of suture during the few days of their visit, and introduced me to a set of basic forceps that greatly improved my little expertise in tooth extraction. But there was always extra pressure "flying blind," not having an X-ray of the roots before extractions.

The village people up and down the river from the Port of Two Brothers seemed always overjoyed to see the *Timoteo* headed for their ports, which may have been a response to our efforts to alleviate pain and suffering. River-dwellers were continually plagued with malaria, pink-eye, infections, lacerations, whooping cough, toothaches, and the common cold. We learned not to extract teeth before evening church services; numbed faces, constant spitting, and post-extraction pain didn't contribute to lively singing and rapt attention. But the people seemed anxious to hear the simple Bible messages. There were many conversions, but follow-up was sadly limited. The harvest was great but the workers few.

Shortly before we returned to the States for furlough, a cult led by an excommunicated Catholic priest started in Peru and invaded our area. Thousands of followers were attracted as cult leaders stopped at every village, claiming to heal people, and appointing a leader for each place. With great excitement and ceremony, these people made wooden crosses 10 feet high at each little settlement, painted them red, and built fences around them. Each follower made a smaller cross to carry on his or her shoulder while marching around the large cross, chanting songs and prayers taught by the priest. Tiny crosses made of the same hardwood as the village's central cross hung from the followers' necks.

The processions around the cross were based on verses found in three of the gospels: "Whosoever will come after me, let him deny himself, and take up his cross and follow me." Twice a day, the followers shouldered their crosses.

The ex-priest refused to talk privately to missionaries, national pastors, or deacons of local evangelical churches. He appeared for the twice-daily processions, then went into seclusion. I was reminded of 2 Corinthians 4:3, 4: "But if our gospel be hidden, it is hidden to them that are lost, in whom the god of this age hath blinded the minds of them who believe not, lest the light of the glorious gospel of Christ, who is the image of God, should shine forth."

We didn't let the Holy Cross cult cramp our style. Nothing but illness made a kink in the ministry at the Port of Two Brothers; even during Jessie's and my absence, the work continued. As far as we knew, none of the Christian Indians paid attention to the cult. I was surprised they weren't more inquisitive.

· · ·

"Salu (Sah-LOO), how about coming with me to the Acara-tuba this afternoon for a service?" I asked one Sunday morning.

Salu, a faithful member of the church in Santa Rita, had been saved from a history of drunken violence. Although considered illiterate, he had experience as a helmsman and was a likable guy. Heavy work clearing the jungle didn't seem to tire him. He was ready to dive into the river and pull a prop or untangle weeds from the underwater gear on the spur of the moment.

We chugged upriver to the house where people were waiting. The river was at flood stage, running fast and carrying lots of debris, which complicated steering. The river was at such a high level we couldn't pull into the house where the meeting was to take place; furthermore, the house was empty, and the neighbors were all gone.

I was depressed as Salu and I headed for home. "Lord, can it be that we've come all this way with no opportunity to preach? Make this trip to be of some advantage to the ministry of the gospel," I prayed.

Four minutes later, I noticed someone way over on the river-bank waving a cloth. I climbed up to the wheelhouse. "Salu, swing us around and head over to the guy waving his shirt. Keep us about 30 yards from shore. I'll jockey the engine to keep us steady against the current until we see what he wants," I said, returning to the engine room.

The "man" turned out to be a boy about 14 years old. *Doesn't that frost you?* I grumbled to myself. *This kid is liable to ask me what time it is, or if we have a soccer ball pump on board. The Lord isn't answering my prayer the way I wanted.*

I leaned out the engine room porthole and, using my hands like a megaphone, shouted, "What do you need?"

"I have a bad toothache," he yelled back. Even from that distance I could see his face was swollen. "Can you pull my tooth?" he asked.

"I don't have my equipment with me today. Come to the house Thursday and we'll take care of it." My response sounded cruel, but by then I had resigned myself to the reality that I couldn't do everything for everybody all the time.

I called up to Salu, "Hey, Salu, let's pull into shore. I'll talk to the kid for a minute."

In an almost miraculous answer to my prayer, people—mostly men—made their way down to our boat. We had never tied up here before, but the people knew who we were. This was near the house where I spent a night years ago, drifting down in old "Leaky" after being caught in a storm. We talked for awhile before stating our purpose. "We need a house to hold about 30 people for about an hour, enough time to sing and hear a simple Bible message."

Jose Marino said, "Mister Paulo, you are welcome to have a meeting in my house. It's a poor man's house, but it is at your disposal."

"Thank you, Senhor Marino. How about next Sunday?" I pressed.

"Fine. The floodwaters didn't chase our neighborhood away. We'll be waiting for you," he said.

Aldo was down with the flu the next Sunday, and Salu hadn't returned from hunting. How was I going to make it to the meeting? Aldo suggested, "Try Laodelino. I think he had some experience on a riverboat a few years ago."

Laodelino was napping in a homemade hammock when I clapped as loudly as I could in front of his house. A good-humored Christian with a nice singing voice, Laodelino helped out often as church song leader. He was the father of Luzia, the young girl who had gotten caught on a giant fish hook above the stove. His oldest daughter, Odete, studied at the Bible Institute in Iquitos, Peru, and helped greatly in the Indian school and youth camp.

"Brother Laodelino, I hear you are one of the greatest navigators on the river," I jested.

"You're right, Brother Paulo. I can paddle a canoe with a paddle in each hand," he responded in like manner.

"Do you suppose you could steer the *Timoteo* as far as the Acaratuba this afternoon? I have a meeting scheduled there. Salu is still in the jungle, and Aldo is burning up with a fever. Aldo mentioned that you have had some experience at the wheel," I added.

"Oh, Senhor Paulo, that was a long time ago. But I can give it a try," he said, swinging his feet to the floor.

Within an hour, Natalicio, the song leader, Laodelino and I were on the *Timoteo* when Pastor Fidelio appeared with his family at the foot of the plank. "Could you tow us as far as São Domingos?" he asked. At that time, Fidelio had been lay pastor in his village for 15 years and taught school, morning and night, on a volunteer basis. São Domingos, some six miles upstream, was where we usually crossed the river. I tossed Fidelio a line, and he tied his dugout to a trailer-hitch on the fantail before taking his family topside.

I hurried up the ladder to the wheelhouse, where Laodelino and Natalicio were standing, laughing. "Do you remember the bell signals, Laodelino?" I asked.

"Brother Paulo, that's what Natalicio and I were laughing about. I'm not sure about the bells," he said. I didn't smile. Bell signals were extremely important; they were second nature to Enoch and Salu.

I gave Laodelino a five-minute course while he stared at the deck in deep concentration. Then I jumped onto the fantail and dove into the engine room. I hit the bell, glued my eyes to the bell's tiny trip-hammer, and waited for Laodelino's response. The bell clanged beautifully.

We pulled away from the clay bank like a chief petty officer was at the helm. I watched the rudder arm, praying the chains would tighten as Laodelino whirled the wheel to head us upstream. Whew!

I sprang up the ladder and scooted across the deck to the wheelhouse where the two apprentice seamen were again laughing. "Great job, Laodelino," I said, slapping him on the back. "There's still lots of current while the water is high, so keep us fairly close to shore. I'll go down and fix us a little snack."

We crossed the channel that leads to Campo Alegre and headed to the east side of the island of Pedrinhas [pebbles]. At the point of the island we were holding to the correct distance from shore. The coffee water was boiling as I arranged cups in a row. I was about to serve the coffee when I noticed a monstrous stump on shore, way ahead. I guessed it had drifted downriver during flood stage, and its tangle of roots caught in the clay and anchored it there until the next flood. No problem, I figured— until I looked again after stirring the coffee.

We were headed straight for the stump. "Lao-de-leeeeno!" I screeched, my head out the port. I rang the bell, and dove for the throttle, cut the engine and leaned against the bulkhead to brace myself for the impending crash. The huge stump shot by the port side, and we stopped five yards up on the clay bank. Tall grass covered the window on both sides of the boat. All was quiet.

Barely enough current to slow us down after cutting the engine saved us from a head-on collision with the stump and plunged us into the tall grass to the side. "Lord, thank you for the nice, soft landing. Help me have the right attitude when I talk to Laodelino," I prayed.

Laodelino wagged his head from side to side when I appeared in the wheelhouse. "Pretty close call, eh, fellows?" I said.

Laodelino's voice was pitched abnormally high. "Senhor Paulo, I do not know what happened. I saw that stump. I was watching it for a long time." He was on the verge of tears. "This wheel would not turn. It just wouldn't turn." And Laodelino was no wimp.

"Let me try it," I said, reaching for the handles. I spun it with ease and we could hear the chains tighten and the long rods slide under the gunnels. "Don't worry about it. I'll get a flashlight and check the whole apparatus. Something must have caught in a pulley. This could happen to any of us."

I checked every pulley where the chain turned on its way to the rudder arm. Both long rods were connected to their respective links, and nothing was in the way of the arm's swing.

"Brother Laodelino, your only punishment for running us aground will be to go under the fantail with this knife and cut the weeds loose from the propeller." We laughed, but he was thrilled at the opportunity to redeem himself. In a flash he let himself over the side, knife clenched in his teeth.

We were glad Pastor Fidelio was on board. Without being requested, he peeled off his clothes and was ready to help push. Laodelino, dripping wet, gave me my knife. I laid a hand on his shoulder and said, "Laodelino, please don't feel insulted, but I'm going to give Natalicio a chance to steer the ship. You keep an eye on him while I finish getting our snack ready."

In a few minutes we arrived at the crossover point. I slowed to idle and adjusted the throttle to hold against the current while Pastor Fidelio loaded his family in their canoe and drifted away.

The wheel moved smoothly in both directions, making it easy to maintain a proper distance from the shore. Natalicio was doing fine, so I went below deck to look at my lesson notes.

Suddenly, the engine room bell rang. I barely got to my feet to jump on the accelerator when we came to a sudden stop. I was jerked backward hard enough that I missed my grab for the engine room doorknob. All was quiet again.

Now it was Natalicio shaking his head, staring at the varnished helm. "I can't believe it, Senhor Paulo. I didn't want to hit the riverbank. Why would I want to hit the riverbank? I'm a small man, but I'm not a weakling. This wheel would not budge. We were pulled right into the shore," Natalicio said.

Another quick inspection revealed nothing whatsoever. This mysterious phenomenon never occurred before or since. To this day when I look back on the experience, Ephesians 6:11, 12 comes to mind: "Put on the full armor of God, that ye may be able to stand against the wiles of the devil. For we wrestle not against flesh and blood, but against principalities, against powers, against the rulers of the darkness of this world, against spiritual wickedness in high places."

We believe the enemy did not want us to have the meeting with the 40 people who had gathered in Marino's house that afternoon. Some heard the gospel for the first time. We left Bibles and simple study courses for the few who could read. James 4:7 says, "Submit yourselves, therefore, to God. Resist the devil, and he will flee from you."

Everything ran factory smooth on our next trip to Jose Marino's house several weeks later. But the one-hour service left us gasping from the stench. Jose's six cows, which established him as one of the more prosperous men in the village, stood knee-deep in water for so long that they developed sores. Jose's only recourse was to bring the beasts inside, out of the water. They had stood belly to belly in the room for a week before the Sunday we held our service on the other side of the partition. The occasional "moo" added off-tune bass to our singing. The odor clung to my clothes so that when I breezed in the doorway at home, Jessie asked, "Tell me honestly: where have you been?"

The apostle Paul told Timothy, "Preach the word; be diligent in season, out of season; reprove, rebuke, exhort with all long-suffering and doctrine" (2 Timothy 4:2). My fellow workers and I agreed that the Sunday service in Jose Marino's house was "out of season."

. . .

In the merry month of May 1973, Cindi wrote a letter saying, "The Lord has given me Larry. Larry Bollback and I met at
Hampden DuBose Academy in Florida. After a few years of
growing in love and a Christ-centered relationship, we became
engaged this Christmas."

Not long after their engagement, they accompanied the
Cedarville choir to Brazil, hitting some of the major cities and
ending in Leticia, Colombia. Dr. and Mrs. Cliff Johnson, acade-
mic dean of Cedarville College, chaperoned the group. Larry and
Cindi interpreted as well as sang, since both had been raised in
Brazil.

The minute we learned that the choir was scheduled to
come our way, Jessie and I groaned and dropped into chairs.
"How in the world will we handle a crowd that size?"

Cramped sleeping facilities and lack of fine foods such as
McDonald's could sour these young tourists. Chaperones might
not want to risk their own lives, let alone the kids' lives, to travel
all that distance into the wilderness where there were no doctors,
nurses, ambulances, or hospitals. But kids that age seem to fear
nothing.

When we took the group on the *Timoteo*, Jessie brought
Candida, our cook, along for the adventure. Aldo was to be a
permanent fixture at the helm. And I was automatically assigned
to the scullery department and engine room. There I would be
handy to slither around at everyone's command. I found protection in the noisy engine room during recreational outbursts such
as tag, water fights, and punching matches.

Jessie's and my qualms vanished, one by one, as we chugged
along. What a gracious batch of young people! They spent most
of the time eating, singing, and sleeping. Some of the fellows
took turns at the wheel under Aldo's watchful eye. Nobody complained about the steady diet of beans, rice, fish, and bananas.

We reached a long stretch of houses called Bananal at pitch dark. I asked the choir to sing one of their special numbers topside. The kids thought I was nuts because there was no one to listen. But as we drifted, people continued to appear from the darkness until we passed the lengthy village.

I think the choir members were trained in the art of body language, for they were great at maintaining eye contact with their audience and their facial expressions that transmitted joy. The Indians were greatly impressed with the singers, and with the truth that we all worshipped the same Savior. But an observer would never know it, for they sat stone-faced.

On the stifling hot trip back upriver, our only relief was from buckets of water with which we drenched ourselves. This activity, bucket by bucket, developed into a water war. Tin cans, soup bowls, buckets, gourds, anything with enough concavity was used to dip water and douse anybody and everybody. Mrs. Johnson got caught in the thick of a battle but proved to be a formidable defense artist, routing several of her attackers. I had to turn on the bilge pumps to keep us afloat.

To Jessie and me, the most impressionable few minutes took place at the Leticia airport while the choir was waiting to board the Colombian plane. I went to the Avianca agent and asked him if he would like to hear some special singers from the United States. "Sure, go ahead and sing. It might calm the nerves of first-time fliers," the man replied.

The agent looked around for a group all dressed up in suits and ties. But the kids were dressed casually in blue jeans and t-shirts. They were laden with backpacks, spears, straw hats, hammocks, bows and arrows, miniature canoes, and carved animals. Dr. Cliff Johnson stationed them to one side to avoid interfering with the activity of boarding passengers.

The director peeped a couple times on his tiny pitch pipe, held his right hand up, and merely dropped his index finger. The dropping of that index finger pulled a trigger that exploded the choir into singing "Jesus Christ is King." It was done with such perfection and great volume that all activity at the airport immediately halted. Ticket agents stopped checking tickets and weighing baggage; passengers stood up to see where the music was coming from. Pilots, engineers, and cabin crew stopped in the middle of the vast room to listen. Before the song was finished, two men from the tower tromped down the steep steps, two at a time, hoping not to miss the show.

After a brief pause, "God Bless America" burst forth with even more effect than the first number, because the music was familiar from radio broadcasts. The audience clapped and whistled, calling for more. And then—all too soon, it seemed to Jessie and me—they were gone.

. . .

A relaxed freedom, boisterous merriment, and adventuresome fun filled our home while Leanne, Cindi, and Rena were still with us. Leanne had recently graduated from dental assistant school and found my equipment rudimentary, but she was a great help with tooth extractions while traveling on the *Timoteo*.

Rena studied high school by correspondence. At the same time, she helped me bandage cuts and sores while enjoying fellowship with the nationals. If a meal was late to be served, it was because Rena was talking with the cook. If the household helper left before her ironing was finished, it was because she and the girls went swimming in the creek behind the village.

We were only a few minutes from home on the *Timoteo* when Cindi swung into the wheelhouse. "Pa, let's see if I can steer this barge," she coaxed.

Having heard our approach for nearly an hour, the neighborhood kids were waiting in their small dugouts to catch hold of our rub rail and mooring rings, to be towed at the break-neck speed of 12 miles per hour. The minute we popped into view, they headed for us from all sides, yelling like Indians on the warpath. They hung on as long as they could, then whooped as they bounced in our wake. A few of the youngsters didn't do it right and swamped their canoes, which was all the more hilarious to their friends.

We were concerned about kids drowning or being ground up in the prop, so we watched both sides of the *Timoteo*, forgetting about anything that might lie in our path. Alas! We were headed right for a farmer, on his way home after a hard day's work on his plantation. It was too late for fancy maneuvering with umpteen tons of hardwood hull.

The farmer, awakened to approaching catastrophe, dipped his paddle deep to thrust himself out of harm's way. Cindi noticed the violent stroke of the paddle. She whirled hard to the left, which would have avoided a collision. But, mysteriously, the frightened man reversed his plan of escape and lunged ahead in perfect timing with Cindi's left rudder. We hit him broadside in the center of his canoe before we could slow down.

The man jumped into the water at the very instant I tossed him a life ring from the bulkhead.

"This is how we'll get our names in the *Rio de Janeiro Daily News,* and get dragged into court by the Indian Protective Service for abuse of indigenous people," I moaned. "We'd better get ready to have our pictures taken, heads shaved, and be shoved into the slammer."

But the farmer swam toward us, pushing the bright orange life ring ahead, thinking it was something we had lost. His canoe was swamped but didn't sink. People on shore watching the episode were laughing, making fun of the poor farmer. I gave him more than enough money to buy a new machete and ax head, then waited until he was "safely" ashore before going home.

Not long after Cindi's disaster, Leanne took a turn at being traumatized on an evangelistic trip weeks before returning to the

States. She stayed alone on board the *Timoteo* one dark night when not a star peeked through the thick layer of clouds. The still air made us think a storm was brewing, as usual, so we were well lashed to stakes at the village 50 miles upriver from the Port of Two Brothers.

A gentle breeze blew hard enough against the water to stir up ripples that slapped gently against the hull. It's an eerie sound when you are alone on a big boat. Leanne could hear the faint sounds of Jessie's accordion accompanying the lively singing in the village.

When the singing finally stopped, all was quiet. In less than a half hour of reading by candlelight, Leanne was startled by strange noises on the fantail. It was as though someone was feeling for the door latch and tapping at the hinges. Leanne tiptoed to the fantail hatch to make sure it was bolted. The scraping and thumping continued.

"Dad, is that you?" she called. "Milton? Enoch?" Silence. Leanne wondered why everything was fine until the singing stopped. My .22 rifle was topside, but there was no way she would set foot outside the hatch. After one more thud on the fantail and a series of tapping sounds, Leanne dove for the forward bunks and slid under one of the heavy mattresses.

Since Enoch was speaking at the meeting, Leanne knew the message would be about eternity, and take almost that long to deliver. The noise stopped, but then she heard a banging on the side of the hull as the wind picked up. "Now someone else is coming," she panicked, while trying to get comfortable under the mattress.

These people knew our boat was scheduled to be here. Why does Dad tell them when we are coming? Fugitives hide out in these remote areas.

Leanne was encouraged to hear the closing song of the service, but knew socializing would follow. And possibly somebody wanted to become a Christian. To Leanne it seemed an eternity before she heard heavy footsteps on the bow. A knock on the rear hatch was followed by the command, "Leanne, open up!"

She sprinted to the hatch and opened it to let in the evangelistic crew, whispering, "Somebody has been on this fantail nearly the whole time you've been gone!"

"How do you know?" I asked. We paid careful attention while Leanne described the disturbance on the fantail, then burst out laughing.

"Come look," Enoch said. He led the way to the fantail, opened the hatch, and showed her two chickens, their legs tied, scratching and pecking at a few scraps. So much for the intruders!

We were talking and eating a snack before bed when we heard a thump bump, thump bump on the side of the boat. "Probably some fisherman returning from all day in the swamps," I said.

Then a masculine voice called, "Oh, Senhor Paulo! Senhor Paulo, may I speak with you please?"

"Speak right up," I answered. I whispered to Jessie, "Go around in back of the partition and sit on the lower bunk."

This side entrance was a blessing. People didn't come barging into our living quarters as is common on commercial boats. It was hard for strangers to find their way inside. I unbolted the door and the man stepped down onto the deck. He was a stocky, handsome man in his early twenties. His smile displayed a perfect set of teeth; for some reason, I always noticed people's teeth.

"Excuse my appearance," he said as we shook hands. "My name is Aristildes." His sleeveless shirt revealed powerfully muscled arms, and a neck to match.

"Don't worry about your appearance, Aristildes. I don't get dressed up in shirt and tie when I go fishing. You wanted to talk to me, Aristildes; did you have something special in mind?"

"Senhor Paulo, was there a gospel service in the village tonight?" he asked.

"Yes, there was. My wife played the accordion, we learned

some new choruses, and Enoch preached. The neighbors loved it."

"I wish I had arrived in time for the service! I've heard about them but have never been to one. I don't know what you tell the folks. I wish I knew because I'm lacking something big in my life. I've been bad."

I listened as Aristildes continued to talk. "Thank you for confiding in me with your personal anxieties. I know how you feel," I said. "Before we continue, let me introduce you to Enoch. He's a good guy, about your age." I tapped the engine room bell to get Enoch's attention, then stuck my head out the hatch and called, "Enoch, come here for a few minutes, please." We had an enjoyable time leading Aristildes to a saving knowledge of Jesus Christ.

Early the next morning, Aristildes jumped up on the bow with a gourd bowl full of fresh tomatoes and pupunhas. His wife, who had attended the evening service, stood on the riverbank holding their baby. On our next visit to Tauaru, Aristildes invited us to hold the service in his home, at which time his wife became a Christian.

CHAPTER TWENTY-SEVEN

DURING OUR FIRST 20 YEARS on the field, Jessie and I sank deep roots in Amazonian soil. It was no longer the Green Hell to us, but a place of great fulfillment and satisfaction. Our love for the people deepened. Back in the 1950's and 1960's, we still talked about "back home" in the States. Visions of strawberry shortcake and apples swam in our heads. But now we didn't look forward to being uprooted, closing the school, storing our things, and saying good-bye to our multitude of friends.

We headquartered in an apartment in Santa Rosa, California, where John and Fran lived. From there we traveled 54,000 miles to visit our supporting churches.

Jessie's mother, Amelia, was still very active. All 11 of her children were still alive, most of them nearby in Bonners Ferry. My mother, Rena, was doing fine at 85, still living in her little white house.

During this furlough we started to lose our children. Cindi promised to love Larry Bollback until death separated them. Theirs was a fabulous wedding at Word of Life headquarters in Schroon Lake, New York, with hundreds in attendance.

Tim met Inaye at Larry and Cindi's wedding. She had come all the way from São Paulo, Brazil, for the occasion. She and Tim were married in a Brethren church in São Paulo, with another multitude present to witness the ceremony.

Leanne married Dr. James K. Pearson in my sister Ruth's home in the mountains north of Bonners Ferry. I talked too long during the ceremony, but a fiddle and a couple of guitars rescued us with tunes that brought two grandchildren to life, jumping around in time with the music.

At the end of this furlough, Jessie and I were hard-hit again when it came time to leave 16-year-old Rena. All four of our kids were tenderhearted, but Rena rarely shed tears. Even when I spanked her as a child she didn't cry, and I thought I was a hard whacker. Our prayer was always, "God, help us to do what is right. Don't let us make wrong decisions regarding our children. If there is something else we should do in your service so that we can stay together as a family, please open the door."

The despondency was lightened by knowing Allene, Rena's cousin, would be at the same school. Allene, six months younger than Rena, was blessed with fine features, intelligence, and a quick laugh. The two shared much in common. Both had been born in Peru, and most of their childhood was spent together at the Port of Two Brothers. They played like little mamas with their dolls. I lost track of all the puppies they raised.

It was fun shopping in malls for the clothing required by the boarding school, but not so much fun to realize we could afford barely half of the school's requirements. Nor was the trip from our apartment enjoyable when the day came to leave the girls at school.

The physical characteristics of the school were fabulous. Neatly trimmed hedges bordered winding paths. Lots of flowers, shrubs, and a formal garden made a picturesque setting for a fabulous mansion. The lawn sloped to the edge of a small lake, where a speedboat was docked.

Cadillacs and Lincolns eased up the driveway with children who had unbelievable volumes of baggage. Some traveled in two cars or towed U-haul trailers. The few people we were close enough to see showed no signs of affection.

Our once-over of the establishment was interrupted by a receptionist with a clipboard and pencil in hand. She had a pasted-on smile and, understandably, was in a hurry. "Allene Seenler, Shelner, or Sleneer. How do you say it?" We interrupted each other, helping the lady with our German name. "Okay, Allene, we have you in the main building. Rena Shhhleener, you'll be in a building down the driveway." We had understood the cousins would room together. "And don't forget: no parents inside the dormitories." She pivoted then stopped, pointing her thick pen at us. "Let me remind you parents and students that there will be no phone calls for six weeks." Quite a reception, we thought.

"But Miss Triddlewitz, that's a whole month and a half." We thought spelling it out would soften her heart. "In a few days we leave for Brazil for four years, and would like to call the girls to say goodbye. . . . "

"Absolutely no phone calls, folks. We treat everyone alike here. It's as simple as that." We stared at each other in disbelief. I started down the hall toward Rena's room with her baggage, thinking I'd sneak a peek into her room, but was stopped by a burly employee who said, "Oops! No parents in the dormitories. Sorry, sir."

I wondered if the administration had any idea of the heart-break involved in leaving a teenager in boarding school and traveling to a foreign country for years. How nice it would have been to at least see the rooms. Future correspondence could have included references like: "Mom and Dad, remember the little table under the window? I put flowers on it when I can. And I got the top bunk closest to the closet." How much easier it would have been for the girls to move in, knowing we would call before we left for Brazil. It seems like it's always easier to figure out what the other guy should do, but we couldn't understand the reasoning for these restrictions when it applied to MK's whose parents would leave the country long before the six-week wait was over. Students whose parents were close by thought the MK's got a raw deal. Others couldn't have cared less about phone calls to or from their parents. And those in charge didn't offer any explanation—or solution—when we complained.

It was a tearful separation as we hugged farewell. Jessie and I were depressed as we drove down the sandy road through the forrest of huge, spooky oaks with moss hanging like black beards from their branches.

Leanne and Cindi had graduated from the same school Rena and Allene were now attending, leaving the institution with few pleasant memories to report. Hats, gloves, and nylons were required for Sunday morning church service. Boys were obligated to invite girls to accompany them to vespers. Any girl without an escort was assigned one from a checklist. And a girl couldn't accompany the same boy two Sundays in a row.

It was Friday afternoon when Rena and Allene were left at school. The following Monday morning, a phone call from the school to the two families in St. Petersburg momentarily traumatized us.

"Hello, John Schlener speaking."

"Are you a parent of Rena or Allene Schlener?" the lady on the other end inquired.

"I'm Allene's father."

"Mr. Schlener, I'm sorry to inform you that both Allene and Rena have disappeared. We searched every closet, and every conceivable hiding place, besides searching the entire grounds with a dog and a fine-tooth comb, and we cannot find them!"

"Thank you, Miss Dropton. I'm on my way," John bellowed, slamming down the phone. Before John made it out the door, the phone rang again. I snatched it up to answer a call from Santa Rosa, California, several thousand miles away.

"Good morning, this is Paul Schlener."

"Mr. Schlener, we just got a call from Allene in St. Petersburg, asking us to let you know that she and Rena are at the bus station near the school."

"Thank you, whoever you are! In case they call again, please tell them I'm on my way." We catapulted off in separate directions, John to the boarding school and Jessie and me to the bus station.

It was a relief to know that the kids ran in our direction. The girls were assured that we loved them, and that we were glad they came to us.

Students were required to write letters home before they could have Sunday evening supper, which was a great idea, we thought. But here are some portions of the letter Rena wrote the night before running away. She handed it to us as soon as we arrived at our apartment.

Dear Mommy and Daddy,

They tell us to write cheerful letters. They tell us that we are rotten to the core and this is the only place that can straighten us out. But I want my own Daddy to teach me. I'm hungry all the time. Please don't laugh at me. I want to be with you, I want to be with people who really love me.

This place is a cemetery. I can't be myself. I can't ever be relaxed. Please take me back. I can't really believe that this is meant for me. You gotta understand. I love you two so much. I guess I can't get over being your baby.

I came here with big hopes, my mind was open for everything, but Daddy this place can't be the place they said it was. Oh, Mommy and Daddy it's easy for you cuz you're at our home, why can't I be? Can't you help me? Thank you so much for all those beautiful clothes. I got too much really. Thank you for being my Mommy and Daddy. I want to call you, but I can't. Please don't leave me. I'm sorry but a happy letter is far from my ability.

Love, Rena Marie.

P.S. Please call me before you leave.

Allene and Rena, now mothers and mature Christians active in their respective churches, still tell the story of their night flight from boarding school, and remain glad they did it. Here's how they managed it. Even though the girls were assigned to separate dorms, they met to plan their escape from the Protestant nunnery. They shared their scheme with a sympathetic student who was acquainted with the lay of the land. He drew them a map of the country roads leading from the dorms to the main highway.

"Try not to fall asleep so we can leave around 2 a.m.," Rena whispered to Allene.

"I'll have to set my alarm and hold it in my hand so I can muffle the sound when it goes off," Allene said.

Rena tried to disguise herself as a boy for the escape. They silently climbed out of their respective windows on schedule. That is, until Rena stepped on a tin garbage can lid, which clattered to the concrete walkway.

The fall night was warm and moonless. Intermittent breeze rustled in the giant oaks that formed a canopy over the narrow road. And there was enough starlight for them to see the hairy moss swing in the breeze. Somewhere close by, dogs barked ferociously. The eeriness increased the farther the girls got from school.

"Let me see that map," Allene said, after the girls had walked briskly for several miles. "My dad was always good at taking shortcuts. It's no use going all that distance. Let's just cut across."

"Okay," Rena agreed. Whereupon they stepped into unchartered territory. But they failed to arrive at the road indicated on their friend's homemade map.

Wet from the knees down, with grass and weed seeds plastered to their legs and shoes, they arrived at the two-lane state highway when it was still dark. They sat down on a curb at a service station. At 8 a.m., an old pickup pulled in and a fifty-something man got out. He glanced at the girls and went about opening up for business. Within minutes the aroma from a percolater tantalized the young escapees. They already had visions of frosted glasses of orange juice and homemade pancakes soaked with butter and maple syrup.

Rena took a small sewing kit from her purse and was nervously stitching a pant leg that had ripped on the shortcut. "I wonder what the old boy is thinking about us. He barely noticed us," Rena whispered to Allene. They felt conspicuous, aware now that they could become subjects of a newspaper article. They had heard about what sometimes happens to hitchhikers.

Allene agreed. "Maybe we should ask the man where the nearest bus station is; he looks kind."

They went into the station. "Hi," Rena said.

"Hi, girls, where ya headed?" I'm sure the man knew exactly what was going on with the two girls. He had watched the traffic in and out of the boarding school for years.

"We wonder where the nearest bus station is," Rena said. The girls had $20 between them that they hoped was enough to get them to St. Pete.

"Well, it's down the road quite a ways in that direction," he said, turning his head to point. "See that wrecker out there? The girls stretched their necks to see. "As soon as the other grease monkey gets here, I'll be going into town with the wrecker to pick up a stalled car. You can ride along if you like, and I can drop you off at the bus station."

"That would be fine," the girls harmonized.

"Have a cup of coffee while you wait." The coffee was another answer to their prayers. But now they wondered if they should get into the car with this man.

I had given Rena a Boy Scout knife with an assortment of blades that would be handy in the dorm for preparing snacks, punching belt holes, or tightening a screw. Rena held the pocket knife in her jacket with the largest blade unfolded, just in case. But it remained, unused, in her coat pocket. The $20 was enough to buy one-way bus tickets to St. Pete, with enough change left to make a collect call to Santa Rosa, asking friends to leave us a message.

Allene accompanied her parents to the mega city of São Paulo, Brazil, where she continued high school studies in an international high school. Rena went to Cedarville, Ohio, to live with her sister Cindi and brother-in-law Larry Bollback, while she studied in high school.

Subsequent to their successful escape scheme, the two young ladies had other ideas that paralleled. The cousins married brothers in the 1970's. Rena married William C. Hopson, a machinist, and Allene wed Stephen W. Hopson, a builder.

• • •

A few days before returning to the Amazon for our sixth term, I qualified myself for the nickname "The Kidney Stone Kid."

After giving birth to three of the pesky pebbles in the past, I was urged to get routine X-rays. As I was trying to concentrate on an article in a *Sports Afield* magazine in a St. Petersburg clinic, the doctor's aide called me into his office. I tried to look pleased as I sprang to my feet.

"Looks like you have a collection of nine small stones here," the doctor said. I instantly disobeyed 1 Thessalonians 5:18: "In *everything* give thanks; for this is the will of God in Christ Jesus concerning you." I found it hard to believe *everything* included nine kidney stones.

"Any one of these could give you trouble some day," the doctor said, "or they could stay there forever. By the looks of their size, they could pass normally, although one looks as if it could be a cluster."

Passing a small stone was agonizing. The word "cluster" made me sweat. "You should check them at least once a year. Drink lots of liquids," was his advice. "And here is a supply of strong pain-killers in case you need them."

A year later I sat in the waiting room again, not wanting whatever bad news was waiting.

"You know, brother Paul," the Christian doctor said, "I can't find even one of those pesky stones that showed up on last year's X-rays."

I was so astounded, the doctor had to repeat himself. "That's right. If you haven't had any painful attacks, the stones must have dissolved to sand and passed with no trouble," he explained.

Now I found it easy to obey Philippians 4:6-7: "Be anxious for nothing, but in everything, by prayer and supplication, with thanksgiving, let your requests be made known unto God. And the peace of God, which passeth all understanding, shall keep your hearts and minds through Christ Jesus." I called everybody I knew to share my good news.

Toward the end of this furlough, I arrived at a church for a scheduled meeting earlier than usual to set up my equipment before anyone arrived for the service. I filled a sizable table with artifacts, photos, and prayer cards, and stretched out the 21-foot anaconda skin that Jorge killed. My 16mm movie projector was loaded with the film "Amazing Grace," detailing our life on the Amazon. The church custodian introduced himself. After exchanging names, the custodian said, "Mr. Schlener, pardon my asking, but are you sure you have a meeting scheduled here tonight? This is the First Methodist Church, you know. The Baptist church is on the opposite corner from us."

"Oh, excuse me," I apologized. In an endeavor to make light of the mistake, I laid a hand on his shoulder and whispered, "I heard this church is a little weak in its foreign missions policy, so I thought I would sneak in and give you a little boost." We had a good laugh while he helped me gather up my paraphernalia and move to the correct church.

Back on the field again for the sixth time, Jessie and I were saddened to learn the Flodens would return to the United States the following April to retire after 39 years of faithful service. Jessie and I felt we should stay in Leticia to help them vacate their home. They had things to sell and give away, keepsakes to be packed and shipped home.

Seeing the Flodens leave the field was a blow to Jessie and me. I guess I took it the hardest, again proving myself to be a weak Christian. I didn't feel any physical pain during those three months, but I dropped from a husky 160 pounds—after furlough feeding—to 130 in just a few days. I couldn't walk more than 100 yards without sitting down to rest.

Drs. Silva and Oldenberg couldn't determine what caused my sudden weight loss and were going to put me on intravenous feedings in the hospital. But I recovered after spending a lengthy time in prayer and poring over Scripture: "Thou wilt keep him in perfect peace, whose mind is stayed on thee, because he trusteth in thee. Trust ye in the Lord forever; for in the Lord God is everlasting strength" (Isaiah 26:3, 4).

Helen was like a modern-day Florence Nightingale in Leticia. She was willing to help out in the hospital or in homes at any time of the day or night, and used their old pickup for an ambulance before the hospital had one. Had there been a Hall of Fame in Leticia, Orville and Helen would have been inducted.

One businessman hired an eight-piece orchestra to play Colombian music outside the Flodens' front porch as a parting gift. And what a crowd at the airport to see them off! But to hear individual Christians express what the Flodens meant to them, and how they helped them come to know and love the Lord Jesus Christ, was surely the greatest of farewell gifts.

· · ·

I had pulled the shaft and prop from the *Timoteo* before leaving for furlough, and left the vessel in the care of an Indian Christian. After returning from furlough, I hired a commercial boat to tow *Timoteo* to Leticia so I could oversee and help with a general overhaul on the hull and superstructure.

Aldo and his family had moved to Leticia, living temporarily with a brother-in-law while they looked for a place to settle. Their older children were ready for high school, something which didn't exist downriver. Three other church families had moved up to Tabatinga for the same reason. What a godsend to have Aldo's help on the *Timoteo*.

Tabatinga is a military zone with an army post of 800 troops and an airport. You can see the Colombian flag in Leticia from Tabatinga, in Brazil, and Peru is just across the river. Officers and enlisted men come to this military post from all parts of Brazil for one-year tours of duty in the Amazonian jungle, drawing extra pay for serving in a hardship area.

During part of the year that we were on furlough, an army captain from a Baptist church in south Brazil came to the rescue of the four Christian families and a few other neighbors living close by. Through the military mayor, he arranged a lot on which he put up some posts with a roof, and a sign out front: *"Igreja Batista de Tabatinga"* [Baptist Church of Tabatinga].

A seminary graduate from Manaus (an employee of the new bank in town) and his wife took over the tiny group, but that ended in a scandal during Carnaval time. At this point, the group came to Jessie and me, begging for help. We were only too mindful of our inabilities, but could see the need for like-minded Christians and, providentially, were on hand to help them "hold the fort."

The brickyard owner, in whose business Hank and Ruth Scheltema held meetings in the past, had been left in charge of the congregation. But Mr. Brickyard couldn't give an accounting of the offerings, and no one knew where they went. The congregation was totally shocked one Sunday morning when the little house next to the tin-roofed church was boarded up. Mr. Brickyard had secretly sold the little, church-owned house, which effectively prevented future expansion. In a few weeks he left his wife and seven children to live with another woman.

So Jessie and I took charge of the services. It was great to be with the four families from the Port of Two Brothers and to meet other fine people in the neighborhood, such as the abandoned wife of the brickyard owner. She had become a Christian years before in Tefé, and was a faithful attendee.

Jessie and I had no personal transportation, but could catch a taxi from Leticia to the Brazilian border, then get out and flag another smoky rattletrap that would take us pretty close to the church. We frequented a few restaurants in town, making it easier for Helen and Jessie on Sundays when the hired help took a day off.

During our stay in Leticia helping the Flodens pull up stake, Jessie and I made contact with the colonel of the military post in Tabatinga. He remembered the presentation that the Port of Two Brothers choir made to the military personnel a few years before. In the course of conversation, he asked if I would be willing to direct the first high school in the military zone. I thanked him and was able to keep a straight face when I refused.

For years the field council had requested that missionary candidates establish a work in the boom town of Tabatinga, but no one felt called to this area. This was Mafia country, and the rush was on for white gold: cocaine.

The Wrights lived in the Port of Two Brothers area. Their burden for Indians was accompanied by plenty of expertise, or Jessie and I would not have considered transfering to another location. The Wrights had moved from John's house to Campo Alegre, a few minutes from the Port of Two Brothers. The large Ticuna church moved from behind John's house and my house, closer to the Wrights' home. The little Brazilian congregation in Santa Rita was now organized into the *Igreja Batista Evangelica*. It had no pastor, but the deacons assumed responsibilities. A number of families wanting their children to have further education were moving up to the larger towns, such as Benjamin Constant and Tabatinga.

The field council unanimously agreed that rather than have two missionary families living close together downriver, the Schleners were the logical ones to move to Tabatinga. Jessie and I could continue a limited ministry on *Timoteo* from Tabatinga.

The bilingual situation among the Indians wasn't conducive

to quick and easy understanding of any particular subject, especially theology and hermeneutics. The Indians had a long way to go before they could be left completely on their own without missionary help for Bible teaching, counsel, and guidance. Not only was Bob Wright making headway teaching Bible courses to a group of 30 promising young men to prepare them to minister to their own people, he also ministered to the Brazilian church. This made it easier for Jessie and me to relocate to Tabatinga.

When the pulling up of stakes started, I walked the 18 paces to my workshop, hands in my pockets, looking at the ground. I took my hammer from its perch on the workshop wall, then picked up the crowbar leaning in the corner. I glanced at each of them and dragged myself over to the front door of John's old house, then went inside. I thought, *Seems like just a few weeks ago I helped John plane the edges of these heavy floor boards.*

I stood in the middle of the living room where I could see the entrances to all three bedrooms. There was John Read's room where he'd worked on his little projects. I remembered putting the lath on the ceiling. They had made a mistake (I thought) on mixing the color when they painted his room. When John Read left, his little sister Allene moved in. What a difference that made in the decor!

The bigger room at the front of the house was where David and Phillip staked their claim. It was abundantly stocked with boys' equipment, and sometimes, to avoid an accident, one had to stop and study the trail before rushing in.

My steps sounded like blows from a sledgehammer as I stepped into the kitchen where our families ate many Sunday dinners. No culinary aromas wafted from the kitchen now; only an acrid, musty odor. Spider webs and cockroaches had multiplied abundantly; a rat galloped across the attic ceiling. I was there to tear the place down, and I didn't know where to begin. I couldn't pry loose so much as a board until a couple of hired men interrupted my train of thought.

People stood at a distance to watch us as we tore boards loose from John's house and stacked them on the ground. Itelvina, a faithful church member since the 1950's, stood watching us before she walked over and asked, "Pastor Paulo, this is the only house you will be taking apart, isn't it? Yours will still be here, won't it?"

I leaned against the wall before I could answer. "Sister Itelvina, I never dreamed this would happen for years to come, but the Lord has a plan for each of us and sometimes He surprises us, and moves us around from one place to another, whether we like it or not."

"I see," she said, nodding her head. But I wondered if she really understood.

PART NINE

A NEW DOOR OPENED ON THE FRONTIER

(1977–1982)

CHAPTER TWENTY-EIGHT

"GO TALK TO LOUIE, THE SPIRITIST, Mister Paulo. If he will sell you that old framework that is falling apart, the lot is yours," the mayor of Tabatinga said when I asked about buying a lot at the river's edge.

The location we found was just right: 100 yards from the river and a mile from the tin-roofed chapel. Jessie and I could keep an eye on the *Timoteo* from where we would build our house.

"No land may be purchased outright in Tabatinga because it is in the military zone. Lots are parceled out to newcomers for residences or businesses, but it has to be used right away or they lose the location," the mayor told me.

"Yes sir, Mayor Vicente. We are glad to pay."

"Let me warn you, Mister Paulo, Louie is as mean as he looks. You really shouldn't have to pay, but it would be a generous gesture and help avoid trouble. Louie's time limit to build expired long ago. If he gives you any trouble, let me know and I'll send some soldiers down there and move his stuff."

"Thank you, Mayor Vicente. I'll try to find Louie, and hope he'll be in a good mood."

When I found Louie, I discovered the mayor's appraisal of the man was generous. His brown, square face under a close-cropped haircut made Louie look like KGB. Wide-set brown eyes, the size of stop signs, promised to deal with whatever trouble I offered. His five feet six inches were stacked on broad shoulders atop a wide midriff without an ounce of fat. Louie wasn't only a spiritist, he was the sect's leader. Feet spread apart, hands on hips, he waited for me to talk.

379

I wished for Jessie's presence and captivating smile. Instead, we two sobersides faced each other. Without revealing the details of my conversation with the mayor, I told Louie I had learned that as occupant of the desired lot, he might be willing to sell the material. My wife and I were in the process of moving up from Santa Rita, and needed a place close to the river for our boat. Louie the necromancer was polite but brief. He said he would have to think about my request because he intended to build a store on the site. The truth was, he knew how badly I wanted the place and delayed his decision in an effort to loosen my wallet.

The Lord had the problem of location all worked out. On my next encounter with Louie, he was willing to sell, and asked a dozen times more than the few sticks were worth: $100.

Once more, Jessie and I lacked money, and we were 6,000 miles away from supporting churches and friends. I never had much success raising funds from the pulpit. I learned that my Source of supply is higher than pulpits, and I had an open line to the Source, 24 hours a day. The same held true as we set out on this new challenge: pitch in, keep going, use what you have on hand, and God will get His people behind you.

It took five trips in the *Timoteo,* towing a barge, to move the used lumber, household goods, school furniture, and aluminum roofing from the two houses, school, and workshop at the Port of Two Brothers to Tabatinga.

I put a man with a peasant-style hoe on the new lot to level a few bumps, kill the nipper ants, and keep an eye on things stacked out in the open until we arrived with our second load. Our plan was to use old lumber to build one good-sized storage unit, garage, workshop, and bunkhouse/office building.

Having failed to sit down and do some figuring before our first trip with the barge, we ran out of fuel after only 75 miles with the second load. Tied up to the riverbank, we waited for a riverboat that might sell us a can of diesel fuel. Situations like this made us glad we had taken time and expense to make the

Timoteo clean and comfortable.

"Jessie, you and Milton grab white towels and start waving and shouting. Here comes a boat." Three of us waved towels and hollered till we were hoarse, but never attracted attention from the disinterested passengers on the other side of the river. Several hours later another boat roared by as far away from us as it could get.

Fish were migrating at the time, and one frisky 15-pound *tambaqui* jumped over the gunnels, landing in the engine room where it set up a fierce clatter on deck until I pounced on it with a hammer to end its struggles.

We had nothing to do but clean the boat. I suddenly remembered the WWII smoke flares in the medicine cabinet. I was tired of pushing them out of the way to make space. I wondered if the lifeless-looking, olive-drab things were still good after all these years.

"I'm going to try one of these ancient flares the next time a boat goes by. Get ready to jump in the drink if this barge catches on fire," I warned Jessie and Milton.

In the middle of the afternoon, a small boat powered by a single-cylinder engine poked its nose around the bend about a half-mile from us. "Here goes," I yelled, setting off a flare. It rose in a cloud of yellow smoke that looked like fire and brimstone falling in judgment upon us. A smoke cloud, the size of a giant oak, hung above us, and the little boat headed straight for us. From a distance they shouted, "We're coming to save you!"

They sold us five gallons of diesel fuel, and within minutes we were on our way again, enjoying fresh fish stew and fried bananas.

It took a day to unload in Tabatinga before we returned to the Port of Two Brothers for another load. This time, the job was one we severely dreaded.

We hoped we had been emotionally conditioned to dismantling our home by tearing apart John's house. But it was harder to tear down our own. *Just get on with the job,* I told myself sternly.

"Go easy on the wall and ceiling boards, fellows, we need them for the next place," I said to Aldo and Arnaldo. The boards came loose easily, but the larger nails in the framework had rusted in place.

I laid aside my tools when I reached Jessie's and my bedroom. As our four kids grew, we marked their heights on one of the louvered closet doors. Every few years we repainted the house, but never did we paint over that closet door. I re-read the measurements and dates.

My fellow workers wondered why all the noise suddenly stopped. They peeked around the corner. "Arnaldo, come here," I called. "See where we measured the kids when they came to visit?"

"Yes, sir. I see."

"I want to keep this door. Take it down to the boat and show it to Dona Jessie, then put it off to one side so heavy stuff won't be piled on it."

He placed the door on his head, shrugging his shoulders and spreading his hands in disbelief as he passed Aldo. The door sat on a high crosspiece in the new workshop in Tabatinga until Jessie and I retired. Being separated from our children was something we never got used to, even after they outgrew their measurements on the closet door.

I jerked cupboards off the walls and stacked them outside to be carried to the barge, thinking they might come in handy in Tabatinga. Indians wandered around on their way to and from the trading posts. It was hard for them to believe we were leaving the place we had called home for 26 years.

"Dona Jessie," someone called from the back door. It was Francisco Taviano, who later became lay pastor of Tabernacle Baptist Church in the village of São Domingos. He was holding the bread board from the kitchen cupboards. "Senhora Jessie, would you please sell me this nice, wide board?" he asked, holding it up.

"I use that for kneading bread dough," she said. "What do you want it for? Are you going to start a bakery?" The group laughed.

"Senhora Jessie, I'm trying to build a pulpit for our little church. and this smooth board would make a perfect top. The pulpit would always remind us of you," he concluded.

Jessie melted. "Francisco, I'm happy to give you my bread board. From that pulpit you are making, the Bread of Life will be preached, which is more important than the kind I make. Besides, Paulo can make me another one."

. . .

After becoming Christians, Jessie and I met many men whom we considered to be great men of God. Two were special in our estimation: Dr. Harold T. Commons and Rev. Wendell W. Kempton. This I can say as a retired missionary, without fear of being ridiculed for trying to make points with the boss.

Wendell Kempton assumed the presidency of ABWE a few years before Jessie and I moved to Tabatinga. Perhaps he'd read one of our tear-stained newsletters that begged for help to build a house in a new location when he contacted us by ham radio to give us the green light on construction. He promised to look for a group of men in the States who would come down and get us started.

This sounded good over Orville's crackling shortwave radio, but the hitch was the few thousand bucks to buy the materials we needed on hand when the volunteer builders arrived. In the very next mail, an advance of $5,000 dollars came from ABWE headquarters. This amount was to be replaced as funds came in from our supporters.

Aldo and I flew to construct the garage, office, and workshop combo, which would serve first as a bunkhouse for the recruited builders. During the whirlwind of construction, Jessie and I made friends with our nearest neighbors, two elderly widows. Laura and Margarida were sisters who looked to be crowding 70, but could have been in their fifties.

Margarida wore a broad-brimmed straw hat and smoked a little black pipe. A pendulous drop of saliva hung on the bottom of the bowl. She pulled the little smokestack from her mouth to ask, "Excuse me, Senhor. Are you going to build here?"

"Yes, ma'am, we are. My name is Paulo, and my wife's name is Jessie. And this is our good friend, Aldo."

"Ave Maria, nice to meet you. Praise our good Father in Heaven that you are moving here, Senhor Paulo. God only knows how dark this street is." Margarida leaned closer, lowering her voice to groan, "These neighbors are bad, bad, bad." She wagged her head and repeated loudly, "Bad, bad, bad."

"Well, thank you for the welcome," I responded, nonplussed.

"This is my sister, Laura," Margarida said as she grabbed Laura by the arm and pulled her closer.

Although slightly crippled from an accident, Laura could move along at a surprisingly good clip. She was the younger of the two sisters. Her lips had streaks of lipstick, probably from yesterday's application, and the corners of her mouth showed remnants of a chew of cut plug. I lack the psychological terms to accurately classify Laura, but she clearly had a mental problem.

With eyes like saucers, and a raspy voice louder than Margarida's, Laura said, "Senhor Paulo, I saw your wife. I saw her when she came up from the port. Or maybe she's your hired girl."

"No, that was my wife. You saw her picking her path through the mud."

Laura lowered her voice, "Oh, Senhor Paulo, she is so cute. Her name is Sergia?"

"No, ma'am, her name is Jessie."

"We are anxious to meet Sergia," Laura repeated. Either she found the name Jessie hard to pronounce or she didn't like it, for Jessie continued to be Sergia for the next 10 years

• • •

The newly appointed military mayor ordered us to build a fence around our property as soon as possible. A fence or wall proves ownership; no fence, no owner. So there's nothing to stop somebody from poking big sticks in the ground, slapping a tin roof on them, and hanging a hammock. It is hard to move squatters once they are rooted down on a lot.

"Get your materials ready, Senhor Paulo," the mayor said. "I'll be over in the morning and establish your property lines."

Working at a feverish pace, Aldo distributed the fence posts, tossing them on the ground, guessing where the property line might be. I made stakes and borrowed posthole diggers, a ball of string, and a sledge hammer. We were ready and waiting when the mayor bounced up on his 70cc Honda.

The second we had one stake on each corner of the property, we stretched a string between them and frantically started digging postholes as though prison guards pointed rifles at us. It was important to get posts in place before the mayor left, so the neighbors could see that the measurements and markings were the mayor's and not ours.

But the rabble-rousers were smart enough to wait until the mayor left. Only a half-dozen posts were tamped into the ground when a portly young woman ran up, calling us American pigs. She wielded a long machete, striking the fence posts with it as she screamed, "This is our land. Go ahead and put these posts in now, but they won't be here in the morning, you _____!" I had lived in Brazil long enough to comprehend her lengthy list of expletives.

"Good afternoon," I replied. Neither of us uttered another word. Aldo was getting red in the face. I told him to keep his mouth shut and just keep digging.

A crowd gathered as Aldo and I dug shallow holes in order to get as many posts as possible in place before a showdown occurred. I kept the crowd in my peripheral vision, ready to do a 100-yard dash if the lady got careless with her big knife. I didn't realize the crowd was on my side. Later we learned the machete-wielder had a bad reputation in the neighborhood. She soon ran out of steam and walked away, mumbling, "I'll be back."

Margarida and Laura took in every detail of the show. They paced back and forth a dozen yards away, cheering for Aldo and me. Both ladies stoked their pipes, spit repeatedly, and released clouds of smoke as though on the warpath. They couldn't wait to approach us after our antagonist left.

Laura jerked her straw hat off and growled, "Good going, Senhor Paulo. I mean really good going. Just keep it up. Stick those posts in the ground. Ave Maria, to hell with that woman. She's a devil." Both women's faces were crimson, and veins stood out on their necks.

Margarida kept up the momentum. "Hah! You should have more land than you are getting. If you want a couple more feet on our side, just move the posts over this way. Didn't we tell you how bad, bad, bad some of these neighbors are?" I backed up a little to avoid the spray of saliva.

"Whoa, ladies," I said, using all the self-control I had to keep from laughing. "We understand how the neighbors must feel. This town is growing so fast that there will be a lot of confusion from now on, especially close to the waterfront. We're glad for this much land. We'll need every inch, though, because the house will be fairly large."

When Aldo and I slipped away for a break, we laughed until our sides ached.

It was a scramble to get the bunkhouse and shower built, and gather material before the volunteers arrived from the States. But we could find no cement. Bags of cement can't be stored for long in intense humidity. The only solution was to load supplies on the *Timoteo* and make the 2,000-mile roundtrip to Manaus to buy enough cement to give us a good start. This would mean up to nine days for the return trip alone.

Our May newsletter explained details of the return trip, loaded with cement and other building materials.

> At this very moment, as I write, we are on board our boat, a little better than half-way to our destination, trusting the Lord to pull us through the storms, sand bars, boiling currents, and snags. Fifty sacks of cement—almost three metric tons—are stashed under our bunks, under the table, on each side of the engine, under the bow and by the fuel tank. Boy, does it look good to us!

> First, a storm flipped waves over our bow and swung our rubber tire bumpers past the window—quite a sight for Jessie from the inside. There was no suitable place to pull over to ride out the storm. But the Lord had our trip all mapped out for us. When things were getting pretty serious, we saw a nice little inlet to a beautiful, calm lake.

> Next we hit a submerged log, resulting in bad vibration. We changed the prop but that made no difference. Further checking revealed a bent shaft and one of the two lug bolts broken off at the bushing. It took seven and a half hours in the water to change the shaft and install new bushings we made from an old tire and a piece of wood.

> Then a weird current shoved us into a big snag in the pitch dark, caving in the bathroom window, breaking the glass and twisting the aluminum frame, just as Jessie was reaching for the latch to step in for a shower. With pliers and a screwdriver we were able to get some spare glass to hold the rest of the trip.

> The next morning our ultra-bright, 17-year-old sailor boy locked the bathroom on his way out. I tore out a section of the louvered door to unlock it.

Then another storm at Codajas came at us from behind the high jungle, just as I took my turn at the wheel. The blast hit from the port side with rain sounding like gravel pelting the wheelhouse glass.

There was no safe place to tie up so we rode it out at half-throttle.

Yesterday we gradually lost r.p.m.'s which caused us to imagine a lot of things until we discovered that our fuel line was full of water. That took a half-hour to clear up. The night was so dark before moonrise that my helmsman, hugging the shore as close as possible, accidentally steered up a wrong tributary for two hours before recognizing his mistake. This used up three hours' travel time but contributed immensely to my helmsman's humility and alertness. If the Lord, in the book of Isaiah, had the Amazon in mind when He said: "He goes before and makes the crooked places straight," He has a lot of work still ahead of Him. Even with good Brazilian Navy charts it's hard to find the trail sometimes.

Eight days passed quickly but uneventfully as we studied navigational charts, scanned the river with binoculars, and watched the water level in the bilges. We had made it with our 50 sacks of cement and a few other building materials.

Then our little crew, as though drawn by a magnet, gathered in the galley and sank into chairs. The strain we had been under gave way to relaxation. We reviewed all the haps and the mishaps, the close calls, the storms, and ended up thanking our Heavenly Father.

Two of Aldo's sons, huddled on shore, waited to meet their father. When we shoved down the plank, they were the first on board. They hugged each other, then said, "Look at your tummy, Dad. You got fat." Aldo lost the weight within a few weeks from carrying cement and mixing concrete by hand for the foundation.

In the nick of time, we were ready for the arrival of the men from New Jersey. Locally baked clay blocks were stacked on the building site. The bunkhouse contained four single beds. A shower on stilts, like the one I rigged 25 years ago, was ready, and the foundation was laid for the house.

· · ·

The four men who came to our rescue as a result of Wendell Kempton's challenge to Bethel Baptist Church in Cherry Hill, New Jersey—Curt Taylor, Dan Pascucci, Bob Grapes, and Steve Harduck—were something like the fabled Four Horsemen of college football fame. I wrote the following letter of appreciation to Dr. Carl Elgena, their pastor.

Dear Pastor Carl,

As we cruise along the Amazon in our boat with a good man at the helm, I felt I should tap out a few lines to you and get them on the next plane headed north.

The four men, Curt, Dan, Bob and Steve, who came to get us started building, are still fresh in our hearts and minds. Some of their footprints are still in the clay around the building project. I feel like taking plaster molds of them to hang on my office wall as a reminder of the testimony for the Lord those fellows left here in this new field of service.

At first I was doubtful that much would be accomplished. We had asked ABWE for at least one bricklayer. The first thing we learned after meeting the men was that not one of them makes his living laying bricks. We wondered what kind of a house would be erected by a soup maker, a train maintainer, an insurance salesman, and a young preacher.

Well, Pastor, they were excellent. Had they built the place lopsided it would have been worthwhile for the fellowship alone. And in the few days they were here, a whale of a lot of building was done. But more important to us is that they left in their wake a wonderful testimony for the Lord Jesus Christ.

Without being able to speak a word of Portuguese, their actions spoke loudly. On the job they worked with national

helpers until nearly over-fatigued. There was fun along with
the work. Attempts at speaking the language brought laughs.
Brazilian helpers jokingly told the men that they were working themselves to death—that vultures hunkering in the
branches of a nearby tree knew it, and were waiting for them
to give up the ghost. The respectful way they treated the
helpers made the Brazilians feel good. The general attitude
of the men proved to many that they were more than just
builders.

Right away the boys made it clear to Mrs. Schlener and
me that they came to get as much of the house built as possible in the few days they had, even though they would liked to
have visited the Indians, and gone fishing and hunting.

Their living accommodations were poor. The weather
was a combination of hot sun, rain, high humidity, and MUD.
Several species of creatures continually feasted on their tender,
foreign hides. There was no entertainment for them at all. But
they laughed off all these pestilences, and seemed to enjoy
their days here, right up to the last dog-tired minute.

In our tin-roofed church, the people were noticeably
challenged by their personal testimonies, special musical numbers, and Rev. Dan's message; attendance increased their second Sunday here.

At the airport, as these four fellows left, Jessie and I were
nearly speechless with emotion. Each in his individual way
had become so close to us we didn't like to see them leave.

There is still much to be done on the building and we
can't move in yet, but the accomplishment of these men
increased the time we could actually work with the people.
Thank you, from the bottom of our hearts, for getting behind
ABWE's LIFT program.

Since Jessie prepared all the meals on board the *Timoteo*,
where she and I lived during construction, the men had to go
down the steep, slippery riverbank for every meal. Snacks were
brought to the job site.

One night, shortly after the men arrived, we had a drizzling rain that lasted all night. Sleep was sweet in the coolness, and it was still drizzling at breakfast time, which meant the riverbank was as slippery as axle grease. After a few steps, traction treads are useless: the treads fill up and become as smooth as marble.

At the very top of the steep riverbank, Curt lost his footing. As though a rug had been jerked from beneath him, both feet went out from under him and he landed hard on his rump. Rrrrip, went the seat of his pants. He was propelled non-stop toward the boat, hands and feet flailing. Severe jolts from deteriorating steps that had been carved in the clay could have injured Curt badly. I thought he would be taking the next plane home— on a stretcher. At mid-slalom, a steeper incline increased his acceleration. His back and shoulders made contact with the goo, and were painted red to match his britches.

At the end of the track, inches short of the boat's hull, he slowly stood to a crouch. He turned and looked up to his more fortunate fellows who cheered him on from the top of the riverbank. No one questioned his record for making it to breakfast in the shortest length of time.

After making sure he wasn't injured, we all roared with laughter. Curt accepted the jesting well, and started to take off his clothes to free himself from the red, sticky clay. In the excitement he forgot anybody else was around. We had to stop him from stripping before Jessie and the hired girl abandoned ship.

Eleven months living on the *Timoteo* was enough. Jessie and I were thrilled to move into the bunkhouse. The kitchen sink from our old home, fastened to the railing of the narrow porch, was supplied with water by a hose from the four-barrel water shower, and drained down a ravine behind the building.

CHAPTER TWENTY-NINE

WHILE I HAD BUILDING MATERIALS, we worked on the house and kept the little church functioning. No more playing doctor and dentist. When building funds were depleted, we cleaned up our equipment, tossed our trowels in a corner, and loaded the *Timoteo* for an evangelistic trip.

One such trip took place a few weeks before we traveled to São Paulo to take part in Tim's wedding to Inaye (Ee-nah-YEH), a beautiful Brazilian girl from a great Christian family.

We shoved off at 7 a.m. with a seven-voice choir from the Tabatinga church, an 8-year-old girl, and an 8-month-old baby as our passengers. Jessie and I brought the total to 11. We hit a gigantic submerged log on our way to Port of Two Brothers territory. We held our breath as it bumped the bow, hoping the snag would clear the stern without hitting the prop. But a violent blow to the stern knocked an ear off the prop and severely bent the shaft. This set up a vibration that shook the teakettle off the range and caused the water filter to dance. With only five miles to our destination, we hobbled along at three knots and made it.

The Holy Cross cult had taken hold in the area, so when Jessie and I visited villages where the ceremonies took place, we simply talked to people without even asking to hold a meeting. There were always sick people to help and bad teeth to extract.

Every Holy Cross follower wore a wooden cross about three inches long with the letters S. T. A. painted on it. The three letters, also painted on the large cross in the center of the village, stood for *Salva Tua Alma* [Save Your Soul].

I asked one of the older devotees who came to me for dental

work, "Did you make that wooden cross around your neck?"

"Yes, I made it myself," he answered.

"What kind of wood is it?" I asked while mixing germicidal solution.

"The wood is special because it's made from a chip of wood from the big cross that we painted red. And we also make holy tea for medicine from the little chips of wood," he explained.

"What does the little cross mean to you?" I asked.

He paused, looked at it for a few seconds, and frowned before he said, "I don't really know. The *Padre Santo* [Holy Father] told us to wear it, so everybody does." It was another case of the blind leading the blind. The apostle Paul ran into this type of spiritual blindness often, and wrote, "But if our Gospel be hidden it is hidden to them that are lost, in whom the god of this age hath blinded the minds of them who believe not, lest the light of the glorious Gospel of Christ, who is the image of God, should shine unto them" (2 Corinthians 4:3, 4).

It amazed us when we were invited to hold children's classes and preach on the grounds of three Holy Cross centers. One leader of the movement who had heard the Cedarville choir sing, sent word for us to stop at his port so he could talk with us. It turned out to be an opportunity to lead his three sons, ages 10, 15, and 16 to a saving knowledge of the Lord Jesus Christ.

Thirty-five miles from the Port of Two Brothers, a sizable group of people on the riverbank yelled and beckoned for us to stop.

"Now what?" I asked Aldo. "We'd better pull in and see what they want."

I knew several of the families from having stopped here before. I was a little dubious, thinking the people wanted to buy sugar, hitch a ride up to Benjamin Constant, or send a sick person to the hospital. Being a Holy Cross center, they obviously didn't want to hear a sermon.

"Senhor Paulo, thank you for stopping. We were wondering if you might have time to hold a service for us. Several of us need teeth pulled, too." The spokesman was Brasilinho, in whose home I held meetings before.

Narciso, Gervasio's son who was now a seminary graduate, Jessie, and the choir struggled up the slippery riverbank to hold a lively children's service while I cleared the *Timoteo*'s propeller of snags.

After I did some dental work, I was invited to hold a service in their new chapel. I couldn't believe it. They had been warned by the cult's founder to prohibit any other religious activity in the chapel—not even Roman Catholic priests were permitted to use it.

Jessie and I were encouraged when people stood up during the service and said, "Senhor Paulo, I would like to receive Christ as my personal Savior." Fourteen people were saved on this trip.

Around this time, Pastor Jim Godwin of Bethany Baptist Church in Seattle wrote a letter to our supporters. The Lord used that letter to touch hearts and open checkbooks. Enough funds came in to finish the house, which was much nicer than sleeping with our feet in the kitchen and our heads in the living room at the bunkhouse.

It wasn't long before 10,000 liters of fresh rainwater above the new bathrooms rendered the outhouse unnecessary. The well-used, rickety furniture we hauled from our old home didn't take up much space. But the four champions who helped us start building also sent personal funds earmarked for buying furniture. Was that ever fun! Jessie quickly put her sewing machine in gear and decorated the place with drapes. Now we were ready to entertain.

We enjoyed fresh eggs from four big hens brought from Bogota. I built a portable chicken-wire pen with a roost, under the watchful eyes of our neighbors Margarida and Laura. When

I turned the four fat hens loose in their pen, Maragarida said, "Senhor Paulo, what a nice place to keep your chickens until you eat them."

"We don't plan on eating these," I said. "We enjoy fresh eggs. The ones we buy at the market sometimes have been under a setting hen too long."

"I see. Then the rooster will come later, right?" Laura asked.

"No, we're not buying a rooster. We don't plan on raising chickens. The eggs are all we want," I explained.

The sisters called me over to the fence. Margarida removed the pipe from her mouth, dried her lips on her forearm, looked me in the eye, and spoke in a whisper. "Senhor Paulo, you will never get those hens to lay without a rooster. You can borrow our big speckled rooster until you find a good one."

I would liked to have put their big rooster in a kettle. He sat 25 feet from our bedroom window and sounded off at 3 a.m. every single morning.

"Thank you, Dona Margarida, but I'll let the hens get used to their pen for awhile."

The neighbor ladies didn't know that I had bought laying hens. The next day when I left the pen with three eggs, I held them up to show Laura, who was hoeing weeds in her back yard. She dropped her hoe and summoned Margarida. They leaned on our fence, staring at our widowed hens. When the two ladies walked away, mumbling, I understood only one sentence: "Unbelievable how these Americanos can have a different system."

· · ·

Not long after Jessie and I moved into our new house, Evandro Batista reappeared on the scene. Evandro graduated from seminary in Manaus with the highest grade-point average. After his one-year mandatory hitch with the Brazilian Army in Tabatinga, he was employed by Varig Airlines in Manaus. Here his intelligence and integrity won him a free trip to Miami. Our son, Tim, was working at Westmont College in Santa Barbara at the time, and helped convince Evandro to continue his education in the States. Cindi and her husband, Larry Bollback, were studying at Cedarville College in Ohio. Through their recommendation to the director of athletics, Evandro was offered a scholarship there. Thus, he graduated from Cedarville College before returning to Brazil.

Evandro's credentials from Cedarville College were validated by Brazil's Department of Education and Culture, and he immediately landed a teaching job in the local high school. Time after time, Evandro expressed his appreciation and thankfulness that missionaries had come to his village when he was a little boy, and that he accepted Christ as his personal Savior. Now he was prepared and eager to help those missionaries establish a church in Tabatinga.

Evandro secured a nice lot from the mayor and started to build a small house. "Looks like you'll become an old man all by yourself in this little house you are building. Besides I don't think you know how to cook a hard-boiled egg," I teased.

"Don't worry folks," Evandro said, taking us by surprise. "I have a new pair of glasses now, and have already seen a fantastic lady in Manaus. She's a member of Faith Baptist Church where Willard Stull preached. Her name is Elina (Eh-LEE-nah). The only problem is that her folks won't let her out of their sight unless she is walking to or from work, or mingling with a church crowd."

Jessie and I traveled to Manaus for school supplies around that time, and met Elina and her dedicated Christian parents. Her father, Ankeazy, was a deacon, and as strict as a 16th-century Puritan. At first he impressed us as being a hard-boiled stone-face—a no-nonsense guy. But Jessie soon melted his hard exterior.

Elina's mother, Mary, was the last word in gracious hospitality. The second we sat down, she placed *cafezinhos* in our hands.

She caught two city buses at 4 a.m. to get to early morning prayer meeting on the other side of town. Mary could do wonders in the kitchen. And while most women were, of necessity, seamstresses in those days, she was better than average.

Elina tried to persuade her parents to allow her to visit Tabatinga and stay in our home for a few days, but they wouldn't hear of it.

"Senhor Paulo, why do you suppose this fellow Evandro is zeroing in on our daughter?" Ankeazy asked. "He's famous in all the churches in this city as a preacher and musician. Why doesn't he pick some other giggling girl?"

"Brother Ankeazy, not even Solomon in all his wisdom understood the way of a man with a maid. I suppose you and I will have to look back and try to remember what brought us to pursue and woo somebody's daughter."

Several days before leaving town Jessie and I went to Elina's home to say goodbye. Ankeazy drew me aside, "Brother Paulo, I've never let that girl out of town. I know too much about these young bucks; I was one myself, you know." His jaw was set, and his eyes looked straight into mine as he continued. "But somehow you folks have disarmed us. Mary and I have confidence in you two."

"Brother Ankeazy, if you want to send Elina to visit one of these days, it would be our pleasure to take care of her. You say the word, and when she touches ground exiting the plane, we'll hobble and handcuff her. Jessie and I will stand guard at her bedroom door in four-hour shifts with our Doberman throughout the night." Her parents laughed.

Elina got time off from her job, purchased tickets, and boarded the plane with Jessie and me when we left Manaus. It was such a big deal to her mother that Mary insisted Elina wear a full-length, formal yellow gown for the 90-minute flight. Although it was the hippie era when blue jeans were the standard dress for young people, out of respect for her parents, Elina didn't breathe a word of complaint about the out-of-place dress.

In perpetual pursuit of turning over responsibility of the Tabatinga work to a Brazilian, I wrote to Evandro on behalf of the congregation, asking him to lead the still-unorganized church. It was signed by every person who could write, and he was welcomed with great gusto. At the same time, Evandro was promoted to director of the largest school in the area. Jessie and I were now free to take evangelistic trips on the *Timoteo*.

We chugged straight to the Port of Two Brothers since the Evangelical Baptist Church had invited us to attend the inauguration of their recently completed clay-block church.

We took a group of young people to help with music as we visited other churches in the area. The most gratifying part was sitting in on the annual meetings. To elect officers, a table was placed near the pulpit. Each member, in turn, walked up to the table and whispered his choice for the office in the secretary's ear. Some were so timid or uptight they forgot to return to their seats after voting.

After the votes were counted and announced, the head deacon called each elected man to the front and asked if he accepted the position. The elected officers' impromptu acceptance speeches gave Jessie and me lumps in our throats as we listened from the back bench. Both the secretary and head deacon had been pupils in our Christian day school at the Port of Two Brothers. It was gratifying to see positive results from the long grind of teaching school.

A year later, on New Year's Day, a great feast was prepared to celebrate the anniversary of the organization of the church.

Little Jorge Backsman, the stiff little arthritic boy of seven who guided Jack Looney, John, and me at the time we purchased the Port of Two Brothers property, bought it back from us when Jessie and I moved to Tabatinga. He built a new home on the spot, taking advantage of our concrete water tanks, bathroom, and laundry space. Jorge was now quite prosperous and fighting middle-age spread.

I think of Nicodemus' story in John 3 when I think of Jorge, because of a visit to my office one night more than 30 years ago. I saw a flashlight coming from the direction of the river and thought, *Oh, man, if somebody's coming by boat or canoe at this time of night, they must be in bad shape.* Jorge was a trader with a good business in the same old shabby house where we three Americans slept in 1951. And he owned a lucrative commercial riverboat. He married a lovely young lady named Francisca, a schoolteacher trained by Roman Catholic nuns.

That dark night in my office, Jorge received Jesus Christ as his personal Savior. Later Francisca accepted Christ, and she and our daughter, Rena Marie, were baptized the same day in the creek behind the village.

Not many days after the church anniversary, hosted by Dona Francisca, Tim and Inaye came from the States to check on us. After graduating from Los Angeles Baptist College, they were raring to take a trip on the *Timoteo*, named after Tim.

Miles of clean, abandoned sandbars were at our disposal, with no empty cans or fast-food wrappers in sight . . . until the Schlener crowd arrived. We plinked with the .22's, ate gull and turtle eggs, and got sunburned. At the Port of Two Brothers, I baptized 18 Christians from an Indian congregation and three from the Brazilian church. Inaye gave a challenging testimony and sang in the services, and Tim preached to the congregations.

The trip was extremely rewarding but left me with a heavy heart regarding the Indians' situation. Jessie and I hadn't finished building our house in Tabatinga, and were just establishing the church there, when the Wrights felt led to teach missions in the States. This left the Indians without spiritual counsel and regular Bible studies, just at the time religious sects started to flood the country. The *Timoteo* had to go into dry dock for repairs, which left Jessie and me without river transportation.

A pastor from Manaus visited us to see the work in the Port of Two Brothers area and as far downriver as Santo Antonio, Jutai, and Fonte Boa. Because time was limited, we used the mission plane. The pastor was interested in forming an association of Baptist Churches of Amazonas.

Of all riverbanks on our route, the one at Fonte Boa was the highest, and a drizzle had made it slippery. The pastor was a congenial, spirited man in his twenties, and hefty. He wore a pair of leather-soled dress shoes. Tired from all the stops and starts, and trudging up and down riverbanks, we dripped sweat, anxious for the non-stop flight to Tabatinga. The pilot and I had coiled the mooring lines to the Cessna, ready for take off.

The pastor's bulk blocked out the sun as he worked up the courage to take a first step.

"See those soft bushes off to the left?" he hollered.

"Yes," the pilot shouted back.

"Well, if I lose my footing, I'll throw myself into the bushes." The pastor gripped his briefcase, crouched, and shoved his tongue out the corner of his mouth for balance. He looked as though he was ready to push off onto a slalom course.

He didn't even complete his first step. The minute he lifted one foot, he was airborne, landing in the mass of foliage. We heard the crunch of crushed plant life. Then silence.

Pilot Hank Scheltema and I looked at each other, wondering if this was now a non-stop flight to the hospital in Benjamin Constant.

Unintelligible speech boomed from the pastor's hiding place. Then he appeared, decorated with leaves and mussed, but unscathed, still gripping his briefcase.

My interest in taking the pastor on this trip wasn't as much motivated by a desire to organize an association of churches as it was to personally invite laymen of the Indian congregations to attend our first short-term Bible institute in Tabatinga. It seemed to me the only way I could help maintain some degree of doctrinal purity and unity among the Christians while working in Tabatinga. With Evandro in charge of the congregation there, I should have time to prepare and teach lessons.

Depending on others for a living was foreign to the Indians' philosophy. The laymen went fishing and hunting prior to their week of studies. They came loaded with dried fish and meat, bananas, manioc, squash, and *farinha*. When the stove was too crowded, they built fires out in the open with the wood I had stacked for their use.

Andy, in whose honor we Schleners had nicknamed our favorite fishing lake, had been a witch doctor before becoming a Christian. It was a blessing to hear his testimony. "Since Gospel come, all good here at Paranapara. Nobody fight now. Nobody don't get drunk. Don't go *festas*. Everybody sing, have good time."

The men enjoyed studying the life of Daniel and the dispensations. Jessie woke them up with lively lessons for children, which they understood far more than what I taught. She encouraged them to teach their children with the set of visual aids they were given.

Later studies were taught by various people: missionary Terry Bowers and pastors Aldeney, Raimundo, and Narciso from Benjamin Constant helped out when they could. Evandro was always ready to help, especially at night for lively song services, and challenging messages. It was amazing how willing the Indians were to travel long distances at their own expense to learn more of God's Word.

CHAPTER THIRTY

I DIDN'T LOOK FORWARD to traveling alone to the Port of Two Brothers. Jessie saw me off on the afternoon ferry from Tabatinga to Benjamin Constant, where I climbed on a big passenger freighter headed for Manaus. I needed two extra arms and hands to handle my baggage. It took numerous trips up and down the gangplank to load all my stuff: a 6-hp outboard motor and tank, a suitcase, a briefcase, a bag containing six liters of mineral water, a quart of oil, a hammock, and two chicken sandwiches.

I swung my hammock in a narrow space with the rest of the passengers, as close to my pile of freight as I could get. Once under way, I couldn't get to sleep. All I could think of was the chicken sandwiches. So I hoisted myself onto the railing and made short work of them.

I catnapped all night, waking frequently, fearful I might miss my stop. It was still dark at 4:30 a.m. when I walked down the plank about a kilometer from the Port of Two Brothers. The water level was too low to pull into shore. Boat crew boys helped with my baggage, and then I was alone, watching the lights of the boat disappear around the bend.

When there was just enough light to see, a barefoot boy of about eight came down the riverbank and squatted at the water's edge. He scooped water with his cupped hands, like a Gideonite, washing his face and brushing his teeth with an index finger. I waited until he stood up to dry his face with his shirttail before greeting him.

"Good morning. How ya doin'?"

His was a quiet, suspicious, "Good morning."

"You live close by?"

"Yes, sir. This is our port."

"Is that your dad's canoe there?"

"Yes, sir." The boy kept looking at his feet, wiggling his toes uncomfortably.

"Would you run and ask your dad if you can give me a ride up to my boat? It's tied up at Backsman's. Your dad and I are acquainted. I've got a few cruzeiros in my pocket to pay you." The mention of money propelled the boy up the bank, and in less than three minutes he returned with a paddle bigger than he was.

My taxi driver was happy to receive a little money as I stepped out of his canoe. I walked up to the clearing of the old Port of Two Brothers. Cattle kept the grass mowed now, and pedestrians had to be careful where they stepped, as I learned—too late.

Within minutes Francisca Backsman appeared in the doorway. She recognized me right away and started talking a mile a minute. In those days, the only way you knew visitors were coming was when they showed up. She seated me at the head of the table in our old laundry room for an enormous breakfast.

Just as I excused myself from the table, groaning from a surfeit of fresh fruit, fried bananas, and a liter of coffee, two men from church appeared at the front door. They provided me with a borrowed canoe, just the right size for my little 6-hp engine for the ride to the big church at Campo Alegre, a few minutes upstream.

The water was so low I had to pull over and walk a kilometer to reach the church. I arranged to meet with the eight deacons the next morning to encourage them in their ministry, and to help them with information and documents required to join the fellowship of churches.

Every morning I went to Immanuel Baptist Church at Campo Alegre and every afternoon to the Nova Vila congregation across the creek. In the evenings I held classes for the leaders of the little Brazilian church in the village of Santa Rita, which borders the Port of Two Brothers.

On Saturday morning I nosed the aged dugout toward São Domingos, more than an hour upstream, accompanied by Brother Luiz from Nova Vila. It took less than 10 minutes to fill the chapel to standing-room-only capacity. Neco led the song service, and I talked about the qualifications for pastors and deacons as found in 1 Timothy.

The brisk walk to Nova Vila on Sunday provided keen enjoyment, for this congregation was ready to organize itself into a local church. I tottered across the windfall bridge onto the immaculately clean terrain where 25 Christians in their Sunday best waited for the service to start. Another 50 or 60, some non-Christians and others who were new converts waiting to be baptized, crowded in.

After the opening songs, I appointed an acting secretary to take notes. Martins, one of my guides to the Indian *festa* nearly 30 years before, was unanimously chosen as pastor even though he wasn't a full-blooded Indian. I asked Pastor Martins to remain with me at the secretary's table to assist in the election of the deacons.

When the main service concluded, the 25 charter members remained to celebrate communion for the first time. This was a mountaintop experience that had taken many years to become a reality.

It was 3 p.m. when I packed up, buzzed downriver, and tied up on the banks of an island. Then I walked on a neglected trail through the jungle—over logs, and through swamps and tall, thick grass—all the way across the island. This trail was used only when the water level was so low a canoe couldn't enter the channel to the village.

My tongue was hanging out by the time I arrived at the little chapel, which would soon bear a sign proclaiming: Grace Baptist

Church. Within a few minutes the whole village met in the chapel. I would liked to have stayed for a week, but had to retrace my tracks before dark.

It was 5:15 when I started toward my final meeting place. Only minutes of daylight remained when I pulled into Andy's port. I trudged up the riverbank with my pack, and Andy led me to his daughter's new split-palm, thatch-covered house. "You sleep here. New house. Smell good," Andy said.

"You eat yet?" Andy asked.

"No, I haven't."

"Mmm, tah." Andy said, heading for his kitchen next door. Inside 10 minutes his wife showed up with a hot roasted fish. I needed both hands to do it justice.

"Senhor Paulo, people waiting, new church. Waiting you speak," said Lito, the fattest of all our Indian friends, who carried his bulk with surprising grace. Lito and his wife were the only ones who came to church arm in arm. Since it isn't an Indian custom, it seemed strange to me until I learned that she was totally blind. She could distinguish only between day and night. Lito impressed everyone with his gentle, tender care for her.

Oddly enough, at the end of the service in the new, unfinished chapel, instead of an altar call, Andy asked for four volunteers to help drag a canoe into the lake so Pastor Paulo could go fishing.

"Sounds great," I said. "But if we leave before 5 a.m., how will I know when to get up?"

"Got two roosters," Andy said, and held up two fingers. "One crow three. Other crow four," he said. "When rooster crow four, I call you."

The first crow I heard was at five minutes to four. By my watch, the chanticleer was only five minutes fast. But strangely enough, when I got back to Tabatinga I found my watch was five minutes slow according to Greenwich Mean Time, broadcast on the radio.

Two hours later the mission plane landed in front of the old Port of Two Brothers. We heard it take off again as we were on the trail coming back from the lake. Before we hiked another quarter-mile, the Cessna circled and landed in front of Andy's house.

The church folks in Tabatinga soaked up every detail of my report on the following Sunday, especially those who had moved from the Port of Two Brothers country. They were full of questions. "How is old Bernaldo? Did he die from the snakebite? Is it true that Guilherme will be moving? Did the bank cave in more in front of the village? How is the church doing?"

. . .

"Here, Grandpa Paul," Jessie said, taking me by the arm. "Let me help you up these steps."

"What do you mean 'Grandpa'? And since when do I need help to take two steps?"

"I mean Grandpa because Rena had her baby yesterday. Read the telegram."

This entrance into grandparenthood gave me a funny feeling, like I had suddenly aged 75 years.

"What this means," I said to Jessie after reading the telegram, "is that now I have to live with a grandmother!"

. . .

For two years the Tabatinga congregation had prayed and looked for the right piece of land on which to build a church, with room for expansion. We needed space for Sunday school, kindergarten, primary school, youth retreats, AWANA, a Bible institute, and whatever else God might have planned. Pastor Evandro had been promised first choice of terrain as soon as the military started to distribute lots. But it wasn't until after the distribution took place and all the choice lots were gone that he was notified. The only lots left were way back in the jungle, inaccessible even by a motorcycle.

Elmo, Aldo, Evandro, and I tramped and slashed our way through jungle and waded through muck on the outskirts of town, wondering if one of the remote lots might serve. On the edge of a clearing we ran into Louie, from whom Jessie and I purchased the lot next to Laura and Margarida.

Louie and his family lived next door to Jessie and me for more than a year. His wife was a perfect lady, while Louie was a sullen man who never smiled. Their children were attracted to the youth activities that took place on our lawn, and they started attending church services. As a result, Louie moved to another part of town as soon as he could, but the kids and Mrs. Louie remained friendly to us for years.

"What are you guys doing back here?" Louie demanded.

"Looking for a place to build a church. The colonel gave all the good stuff to business people."

Several kids splashed in the small creek that ran through this partially cleared area, winding its way to the Amazon River.

"I'll sell you my place here at the edge of the creek," Louie said.

Silence reigned for 30 seconds. Evandro and I couldn't believe our ears. Everybody knew about Louie's place: a full-size soccer field, a dredged area for swimming, a large banana plantation, a house, and a spiritist chapel where he held seances. As we followed Louie on a tour of his layout, I nudged Evandro and whispered, "Don't act too interested. He'll gouge us for a huge price."

Although the church only paid a few thousand dollars for Louie's property, we were seriously gypped in the purchase. When the military surveyor made sure of the property boundaries according to the official map, the only correct line was the frontage. When the lateral limits were squared with the frontage, we lost most of the banana plantation and the swimming hole, probably Louie's reason for selling in the first place.

In three trips with the pickup, the Tabatinga congregation moved from our neat little church to Louie's spooky chapel. We put up our sign that read *Igreja Batista de Tabatinga,* and started proclaiming the Word of God. We were on our way to a building project that lasted until Jessie and I retired.

Jessie and I loaded the *Timoteo* for another trip downriver to visit the churches and to bring back a load of thatch woven by the Indians to build a *chapeu-de-palha* [straw hat], a 26 by 26-foot square with chest-high walls.

• • •

On the return trip from gathering the thatch, it rained. The thatch roofing, six to eight feet long, was stacked topside on the fantail, across the bow, and even atop the wheelhouse. From a half-mile away we must have looked like a shaggy prehistoric monster.

With eight more hours to plow against the current, I opened the insulated door to the engine room and was nearly overcome by fumes. I shut the rig down to idle, closed the door again, and rang the bell four times to get Aldo's attention at the helm.

"Pull into the first place you can find, Aldo. Something's busted," I bellowed out the side port.

The two-inch galvanized pipe, just past the water inlet to the exhaust, was cracked and about to drop off. My mind drifted longingly to the Columbia Basin Machine Shop where our son-in-law, Bill, works. My workbench on the boat was a thick hardwood board, only three feet long, attached to the bulkhead next to the engine. A manually cranked grindstone and a vise were bolted to it. Aldo and I finished twisting and breaking the two-inch pipe loose, sawed off the ragged part, cleaned out the rusty threads that were stuck in the elbow, and screwed it back in with the inch of threading that was still good.

Two days later was the first morning of another week of Bible study for the Indian laymen. João Macario, one of the masked dancers in the 1952 *festa*, attended with a group of men who walked 10 miles to the edge of the Amazon, then paddled 100 miles upstream to get to the classes. They made it in three days.

The men shared that 47 new Christians were baptized in one church, and 17 would soon be baptized at another. These laymen were helping fan spiritual flames, winning others to a saving knowledge of the Lord Jesus Christ.

A cable from the States brought the sad news that Jessie's mother passed away on January 22, 1978. Jessie felt helpless at being so far away. We tried to imagine the activities taking place in Bonners Ferry. Jessie's brothers and sisters would arrive from afar. Mom Mac's six sons would serve as pallbearers, as they had done for Dad MacDonald. Dinner prepared by church friends would be served in the social hall of the Methodist Church. Hours would be spent reminiscing.

The truth that helped heal the sadness of losing Mom MacDonald was that she wouldn't want to return to this world from the presence of her Lord.

. . .

The public address system hissed while a cheerful flight attendant recited her speech about our approach to Los Angeles International Airport. I think more praise and thanksgiving prayers are offered to Almighty God in airplanes than in many churches.

Jessie and I plodded on the quarter-mile uphill corridor with our hand baggage. Waving to us from the end of the corridor were Allene Goodman and her son, Bobby. It's a long freeway drive from La Habra to LAX, but the Goodmans always extended themselves for others, especially their missionary friends.

Jessie and I must have looked done-in to young Robert, for he took over as though Jessie and I were helpless. "Uncle Paul, you and Aunt Jessie don't even touch this luggage." We had to stand clear of Bobby's nearly 200-pound bulk or be boosted up along with the baggage.

While we stood by the curb, a black limousine stopped right smack in front of us and our stack of baggage. This meant we would have to move all of our stuff if Bobby showed up before the limo left. I wanted to see the celebrities inside that stretched-out car, but the windows were too heavily tinted. "These big-timers have crust, don't they?" I whispered to Jessie. "Get out of my way, small fry, here I come, is what they're thinking."

A stocky chauffeur jumped out and walked to the rear of the limousine where he popped the trunk. It was Bobby. I didn't recognize him in the visored chauffeur's cap. The Goodmans were taking us to their home in a limousine. Jessie and I were dumbfounded. We stood with mouths agape, speechless.

Jessie and I planned to stay in our unfinished cabin on the Moyie River in northern Idaho, but our first stop was Santa Rosa, California, where Leanne and her husband, Dr. James K. Pearson II, lived with our grandson, James K. Pearson III. Paul Louis Pearson was born later that year, and Jessie and I got to be there for the exciting occasion.

. . .

I quickly learned how to survive sleeping in an ice-cold bedroom the first time I had the experience. Gracious church folks, brave enough to entertain missionaries in their homes, were a source of inspiration and, sometimes, laughter.

On one occasion, the head of the house shared a bedroom with me. The twin beds looked inviting, but the bedroom doors were kept shut all during the winter, to avoid heating rooms not in use during the day. When we walked into the bedroom to retire, I suffered a split-second body quake. The temperature couldn't have been much above freezing. Our breath turned to steam as we chatted about snakes and vampire bats, which made me think longingly of my 70° bedroom on the Amazon. *Now I know why electric blankets were invented,* I thought. But, alas, there were no electric blankets.

I fumbled around in my suitcase, watching my host in my peripheral vision. I wanted to see how he was preparing himself to meet the challenge.

"We like to sleep in cold bedrooms," my roommate said. "Seems like a fellow sleeps sounder."

"I see; a privilege we don't have along the Equator," I responded. I didn't have any long underwear, but at that moment would have paid a half-month's salary for a pair of thermals. My host pulled flannel pajamas over long johns, tucked the bottoms into a heavy pair of socks, crawled under the covers, and heaved a sigh of total relaxation.

The best I could do was pull my shorty pajamas over my skimpy t-shirt, briefs, and dress socks with the speed of lightning. I laid my head gently onto the frosted pillow. The rest of me remained arched under the covers until, inch by inch, I could straighten my legs. The next morning the tantalizing smell of perking coffee and frying bacon gave me impetus to fly out of bed, dress, and shave in record time.

While Jessie and I were on furlough, the Bowerses lived in our home in Tabatinga, conducting correspondence courses and continuing the short-term Bible studies for both Indian and Brazilian lay-leaders. Pastor Evandro sent word that church attendance was encouraging and that many people had become Christians.

Our year in the States went by like a 100-yard dash, and then Jessie and I were on our way back to Tabatinga for our last full term.

PART TEN

COMING DOWN THE HOME STRETCH

(1983–1991)

CHAPTER THIRTY-ONE

SEEING ALL THE WAVING HANDS at the Leticia airport as Jessie and I approached the terminal made us forget the intense humidity and the scorching asphalt underfoot. A reception helped us feel welcomed back and, for a few minutes, took our minds off leaving the kids behind yet again. After a luscious fish fry prepared by Elina, we were back in gear for another four years in The Green Hell that we had grown to love.

Our job for the next—and last—few years on the field seemed obvious. Our time would be divided among church construction as funds were available, laymen's short-term Bible institute, and river evangelism. This was agreeable to Pastor Evandro. More than ever, Jessie and I wanted to stay in the background, in order to encourage national leadership in the local church.

Fritz and Maggie, our Dobermans, remembered us. The local cocaine market, controlled by Mafia underlings, had escalated, so the presence of these animals inside our walled property gave us a sense of security. Dull moments were short-lived. The Mafia crossed into Tabatinga from Leticia, gunning down five of their debtors with automatic weapons. Three more were killed with pistols. Knifings were so numerous they became commonplace.

Fritz and Maggie weren't trained to attack; simple obedience was enough, we hoped. Visitors were always welcome, especially friends from church, but when strangers appeared at the front gate, they saw red and black: Maggie was red and Fritz was black. Any stranger with excited speech or drunken hollering drew a grumble from the depths of Fritz's lungs which changed attitudes like magic.

Only once did the friendly dogs give anyone trouble. It was sprinkling when deacon Guilherme arrived late for an evening class. For protection from the rain, he wore a large sheet of bright orange plastic over his head, held firmly under his chin with one hand. This framed his face, but the rest of the sheet hung loose down over his back. To Fritz and Maggie, Guilherme presented a strange sight.

Bible and notebook between his knees, Guilherme hurried to open the gate. As he stepped inside with quick, jerky movements, a gust of wind blew the bright plastic straight out behind him. The Dobermans already had their eyes on the gate, so when the orange-winged batman entered, they headed straight for him. Although middle-aged, Guilherme mustered enough spunk to spring to the top of the wall before I could whistle to the dogs. The poor Indian stood there, illuminated by the garage light, while his classmates roared with laughter.

Maggie had proved her mettle before Fritz came to live with us. Something like a Wild West shoot-out took place in the street in front of our house at 1:45 a.m., complete with screaming and shouting, men running, and dogs barking. We should have dived under the bed instead of running to the front window, which was only covered in screen.

At the height of the din, a man climbed over the wall at the left side of our front yard. Jessie and I saw him race across the yard in a crouch to avoid being silhouetted against the streetlight. I reached for the doorknob when my wife hissed in a piercing whisper, "Don't go out there, dummy. They might shoot you!" I let go of the doorknob like I had taken an electric shock, thinking that, aside from calling me a dummy, Jessie had made an intelligent observation.

I tiptoed down the corridor, opened the back gate and said in a low voice, "Git 'em, Maggie!" She shot out silently until she was a few feet from the intruder. Then she roared. The poor fellow did a standing high jump over the wall. He didn't have time to shoot Maggie, she came at him with such silence and speed. But a few days after the shoot-out, we found a .38 slug lodged in a board by the front porch light.

Our June 1985 newsletter said:

> A couple of weeks ago, a woman was found stabbed to death on a trash pile at the edge of town. Just a block and a half down the street a young couple were riddled with bullets as they left a tavern. Last week a man was clubbed then stabbed for his gold chain. On the next corner a young man answered the clapping at his door, and received a fatal knife stab just below his wishbone.
>
> Arriving home from church last Sunday we learned that a man was stabbed to death in the market just on the other side of our wall. In the Leticia port, a few mornings ago, a human head was placed on a five-foot stake as a warning to all those going to the market.
>
> Better news is that few Sundays go by without someone receiving Christ as personal Savior. And Monday nights find us teaching a young Christians' Bible class.

• • •

Alonso and Rosilda and their seven children were possibly the poorest family in the Tabatinga church. But their excellent attitudes, faithful attendance, and natural musical talent made them among the greatest contributors to the ministry. Rosilda had become a Christian 20 years earlier at the age of 16, when John and Fran were doing river evangelism. Alonso, saved much later, struggled deeply in his Christian life.

Alonso was totally illiterate, but had an amazing ear for music. "Give me the note, Dona Jessie," Alonso usually whispered to Jessie before each chorus or hymn. She touched a key on the accordion, he plunked a few times on his banjo, and his two teenage sons scraped across their guitar strings, tuning up. And off they would go with "Bringing in the Sheaves" or "Stand Up, Stand Up For Jesus."

The two older boys inherited their father's musical talent and had excellent singing voices. Cecilio, the oldest son, memorized Scripture by the chapter. Both he and his next oldest brother were sickly, and the only daughter died at the age of eight from pneumonia. I'll never forget carrying Cecilio piggyback into the plane when I took him to Manaus for cancer treatment. The Lord took the suffering boy home a few months later.

In an effort to get the congregation involved in the building project, we challenged each family to furnish one window for the church.

"Brother Paulo," Rosilda said as she approached me at the close of an evening service, "our family vowed to go without rice this week so we could contribute toward one of the church windows." And she handed me a small roll of cruzeiros. I looked at the little roll of money and the calloused hand that held it. I couldn't move for a few seconds. I thought of how hard Rosilda and Alonso worked in their manioc plantation. I had seen her often at the edge of the creek with a mountain of washing. I realized that here was a Christian whose heart belonged to the Lord. And when the Lord has our hearts, He has our all. Solomon said, "My son, give me thine heart, and let your eyes keep to my ways" (Proverbs 23:26).

. . .

It's too much to ask me to build a birdhouse and do it right. I can make one look half-way decent, and birds might even live in it. But there will always be something wrong. I wondered if I should be trusted with the necessary funds to build a church and educational building of the dimensions we planned. Lots of folks were praying for us, however, which gave me courage. And I pecked at the brains of anyone who knew how to grab a trowel or hold a hammer for all the information I could get about construction. With Evandro at the pulpit, I could spend more hours on the job site myself.

Soon it was time for plumbing and wiring, and I had no expertise at either; replacing dead flashlight batteries requires my utmost attention. In the nick of time, David and Betty Roberts from Bethany Baptist Church of Seattle dropped in.

David is a Goliath, nearly seven feet tall and strong as an ox. A second-generation journeyman plumber with expertise in carpentry, mechanics, and electronics, David has to be careful not to strip pipe threads.

Betty is the daughter of a carpenter and knowledgeable about every phase of construction. She is well suited to her multi-gifted husband. Even though she wasn't used to walking in mud on the way to the job, Betty never missed helping her husband every day they were with us in Tabatinga.

She taught me how to run wires through conduits to outlets, switches, and ceiling lights. My Brazilian helpers were amazed. "Senhor Paulo, what a woman! She knows how to hook up the lights," one fellow remarked. They thought women were suited only to bearing children, washing clothes, carrying water, splitting wood, and cooking.

I ducked to keep out of harm's way as David grabbed pipes, sawed, and glued. He sawed a pipe on his thigh while looking elsewhere to determine his next move. The first time I noticed him sawing a pipe, I thought he would cut his leg off. I was about to tap him on the shoulder when he lunged to grab something else.

I made drawings about wiring under Betty's patient tutelage. She studied my face in disbelief that I could be so slow to get such simple matters through my head. After the Robertses left, I finished the first circuit, double-checking every connection. I waited for my hired men to leave, then walked over to the breaker box in the hall. I stared at the maze of connections.

I stood back far enough so I could barely reach the handle of the menacing main switch. After a few seconds, I held my left forearm in front of my eyes, ready to dodge a shower of sparks and flame, and slammed the switch to on. Behold! Every fluorescent bulb lit up as miraculously as the Star of Bethlehem.

I danced a little jig, and thanked the Lord for this unprecedented success. In my euphoria, I tinkered unnecessarily with wire ends that I thought needed tucking in—and gave myself a 110-volt shock. I realized that I should have disengaged the main switch before messing around with bare wires. Back to square one.

. . .

Jessie and I were long overdue for a visit to the churches in the Port of Two Brothers country. Our boat was laid up, so I arranged for missionary Tom Peace to fly me in the mission plane for a Sunday service in an Indian church.

At 4 a.m. I made a pot of coffee and a batch of oatmeal for my breakfast, then fried an egg sandwich for the trip. I tried to avoid disturbing Jessie, but knocked the metal thermos lid onto the tile floor, where it bounced a couple of times before I could catch it. Within a few seconds a loud crack of thunder followed by a rainsquall that dumped 100 barrels of water on our aluminum roof broke the silence.

Ten minutes later, the boy contracted to ferry me to the plane hangar in Benjamin Constant banged on the steel gate. In just over a half hour, I climbed from the rickety little boat onto the hangar. Tom gave the float plane a thorough once-over. The sky cleared, and off we went. The trip to the Indian church took about the same time as traveling in the little boat from Tabatinga to the hangar.

The river was too low in front of Immanuel Church, so Tom swooped down in front of São Domingos where Hope Baptist Church is located. I love nice, soft landings, but the violent whirlpools and back eddies gave us trouble as we approached shore and tied up to port.

Closer to the village we heard singing: "Standing on the Promises." The church service was in progress. The sound was rich and meaningful, the voices of sinners who had passed from the power of Satan to God through faith in the Lord Jesus Christ.

Pastor Fidelio met us at the door of the chapel. I remembered Fidelio as a boy, paddling eight miles each way to study at the Port of Two Brothers. Guilherme, one of Fidelio's evening pupils who learned to read and write as an adult with a family, led the singing.

Fidelio introduced me to preach the morning message. I stood behind the hand-hewed pulpit and looked into those clean, shining faces with their sparkling eyes. I had seen their fathers, uncles, aunts, and grandparents in the drunken orgy at the Jacurapa. I had stitched dozens of lacerations from knife fights and removed buckshot from failed murder attempts. And now some of those same people enjoyed a completely new life, worshiping God.

Retirement closed in on Jessie and me too quickly, which made experiences like these fulfilling to the utmost degree.

• • •

Jessie and I learned of Damivan (Dah-me-VAHN), a young seminary graduate from Bahia who expressed a desire to work with us in Tabatinga teaching Indians. We welcomed him with open arms.

Damivan was taller than most men in our area. He had a perfect preaching voice and was highly intelligent. Our congrega-

tion liked him right away, especially the senhoritas. But his calling wasn't to the pastorate. Riverboat ministry sounded good to
him, so I wanted to get the *Timoteo* in top shape.

Both shaft and prop had been removed for straightening, and
the hull openings plugged. I repaired what I could on the superstructure, although waterline boards needed to be replaced, the
fantail rebuilt, and the whole thing recaulked. The steel rudder
was in bad shape. Once you start digging into old equipment,
other problems always develop.

Damivan and I tested all lines for tightness. We dropped
down to peer through various openings, checking if our plugs
held. Everything looked okay.

The local ferryboat agreed to tow us; its owners were old
friends from the Port of Two Brothers area.

The 12-mile trip downstream usually takes a little more than
an hour. After living so close to the butcher shack in Tabatinga,
with vultures perched on our wall and an open sewer on the
other side of our gate, the fresh breeze was heavenly.

Those moments of relaxation were short-lived. I noticed the
Timoteo wallowing as though overloaded with cargo. It was causing the ferryboat to list.

"Head for shore; the *Timoteo* is sinking!" Damivan shouted.
His warning startled the helmsman who wildly spun the ferryboat's wheel toward the nearest shore.

The cry of alarm brought all of the passengers to the scene
of the disaster, which caused the ferry to list even more. Our
prayer was that we would touch ground before we had to cut the
Timoteo's lines, for they were too tight to untie.

I grabbed my briefcase just before it slipped into the water,
and jumped into the ferry; adrenalin helps even the elderly.
Damivan forgot his satchel, grabbed a line, flew off the bow, and
plopped thigh-deep into the sloppy mud. A ferryboat flunky
tossed Damivan two 2 x 2's, which he tamped into the mud and
secured the line. What a man!

"Come back, Damivan. There's nothing we can do until we get help," I yelled.

"Brother Paulo, these stakes won't hold very long in this *tijuco* [fluffy mud]. I'd better stay to keep the boat from slipping down deeper," Damivan hollered in his resonant voice, while forcing another post into the mud.

I stayed on the ferryboat. The owner promised to take me directly to the dry dock for help. We hadn't traveled more than 300 yards from the *Timoteo,* when a monstrous freight boat plowed by at full speed. The behemoth raised a series of waves that rocked the *Timoteo* so violently that it bent the two posts over like toothpicks. And our boat slipped deeper until only the tip of the bow was exposed.

Damivan's prowess was unbelievable. He was far from stupid, but I wondered if he had taken courage too far: when the boat began to slip further, he wrapped the line around his waist and was dragged down the riverbank toward the water.

Later I said, "I'm grateful to you, but that was too big a risk to take for an old boat."

"It was kind of fun, Senhor Paulo. I figured on releasing myself just before being pulled under the water," Damivan said. "My biggest problem was getting the *tijuco* out of my mustache."

It took 11 men and three boats almost 12 hours to raise the *Timoteo* far enough up off the river bottom to be towed six miles to dry dock. In the process, railings were torn loose, the wheelhouse bulkheads caved in, the nicely rounded forward bulkhead was crushed out of shape, mattresses were ruined, and the engine would have to be completely disassembled.

Damivan's courage reminded me of the fearlessness of one of my best friends back at the Port of Two Brothers.

An overloaded, double-hulled Peruvian commercial boat caught fire while tied up at the trading post a quarter-mile upstream from the Port of Two Brothers. It was something like the *Triumfo II* on which I traveled after dropping the kids off at boarding school in Iquitos. A storage battery exploded in the engine room of the Peruvian craft, causing flames to spread over the greasy decks.

The boat's owner, his flunkies, and passengers, were interrupted during their evening drinking party at the trading post. They stood on shore watching billowing flames shoot into the sky as petroleum barrels exploded. They listened to cows bellowing, pigs squealing, and chickens squawking while being cooked alive. Loud cursing burst from the watching Peruvians.

The proprietor of the boat paced back and forth, and stomped in rage. But nobody did anything. A short, husky man with a long machete leaped up onto the top edge of the large hull that hadn't caught fire. In seconds, the fire would pass to the hull where barrels of gasoline, diesel oil, and kerosene were stored.

The little man quickly chopped the stern lines free. Barrels of gasoline and kerosene continued to explode, but he ducked into the hull, and seemed to disappear. Suddenly, like magic, he popped up at the bow. There he frantically chopped lines loose, shielding his eyes from the flames with his forearm.

Grabbing the top edge of the hull, he turned his back on the fire and gave a powerful shove of his feet to the burning boat— just enough force for the point of the bow to catch the current, and drift away before fire caught the other hull.

The little champion was left dangling over the side after pushing the big boat the length of his body. Violently burning from stem to stern, the boat lit up the entire area. Canned goods in the holds popped like irregular machine gun fire. Jessie and I finally realized the danger posed by the possibility of the inferno passing too close to the *Timoteo*. Underwater currents and back eddies could swing the drifting conflagration right into our port.

I ran down to start the *Timoteo*, in case we had to escape the threatening ball of fire. Aldo was already there, out of breath, with all lines loosened but one. How like Aldo to think of this. I said, "Thanks, Aldo. Man, what a blaze, eh? Do you think we'll have to shove off to avoid that torch when it comes by?"

"I'm guessing that we won't need to, but it's good to be ready," he said.

Standing closer to Aldo, I remarked, "Aldo, you smell like smoke." That didn't sound complimentary, so I apologized. "Excuse me, Aldo. I don't care what you smell like if you don't care what I smell like."

He chuckled, which he seldom did. "Senhor Paulo, I was there when the fire started. I was waiting to buy some of that cheap Peruvian laundry soap when the boat exploded. I couldn't figure why nobody would do anything. I don't know why, but I grabbed my wife's machete and chopped the lines so the barge wouldn't catch fire, too. I got singed a little, which is what you smell."

What a great man to ride the river with. For more than 30 years Aldo was my faithful partner, but he didn't catch that kind of courage from his boss.

• • •

Jessie and I were invited to speak at the annual missions conference of Cariri Baptist Seminary in the state of Ceara, northeast Brazil. We had been on the field more than 35 years, so the seminarians were convinced we knew everything about missions. The students bubbled over with questions about our work from beginning to end. Doctor Silvia, a young female doctor, challenged the students to help us in the ministry.

From the enthusiastic response during the conference, Jessie and I thought we would have so many candidates for the work we wouldn't know how to handle them all. Instead, we received one letter. Thoughts of the 21-foot snake killed just yards from our house may have led them to prefer getting run over by a city bus.

Six years of slopping around in the rain and mud and skinning my knuckles finally paid off; the church was built. And, although the congregation was ready, we delayed organization until it could be done under the leadership of a Brazilian.

The Manaus seminary recommended a young couple as candidates for the pastorate: Rev. Reinaldo and his wife, Dona Ramona, and their three children. The pastor looked like the city boy he had become, but had been born and raised on a tributary of the Amazon. The congregation voted unanimously to accept Pastor Reinaldo. More than 400 people attended his installation service.

A few local businessmen and their wives, and almost the entire congregation from the Leticia church and a group from Benjamin Constant were present for the official organization. Evandro and his family arrived from Portugal in time for him to challenge the crowd from the life of Gideon.

Pastor Reinaldo was not tall, but he was well built and well groomed. He walked so quickly it was dangerous to tailgate him lest he turn abruptly and injure his follower. Even if what he laughed at wasn't funny, you had to laugh just hearing his peculiar high-pitched, tremulous squeak.

Reinaldo had a head for business, and developed a five-year plan for the work. Sympathetic with my desire for a Brazilian pastor to organize the congregation into an official local church, he started preparing for it right away. At the same time he improved the organization of the primary school and charged high enough tuition to pay fair wages to several teachers, plus what the church lacked to complete his salary as pastor and director of the school.

Dona Ramona was comical, a blessing to the ladies of the church, and worked well with Edina in teaching the children.

Miss Lois Wantoch who worked first in Santo Antonio, then with the Kallins in the town of Jutai, a few hundred miles down-river from Tabatinga, accepted Jessie's and my request that she live in our house in Tabatinga and help in the church while we took our regular furlough. Her transfer was approved by the field council. Lois was a Jill-of-all-trades: nurse, musician, teacher, counselor, and midwife. She would work with Edina, showing her some new methods of teaching in the continual effort to keep nationals in leadership positions.

CHAPTER THIRTY-TWO

SOMETHING DIFFERENT was in the wind during the next Sunday's evening service. The congregation usually dallied after services, but this time it dragged on too long. I was ready for my bedtime popcorn and *guaraná*.

One of the ladies secretly beckoned Jessie to the corridor doorway. When I turned to follow, one of the two sentinels said, "Not you, Pastor Paulo," then spun me around with such force I was nearly pitched between the iron gates.

Then I got a whiff of what was going on in the kitchen. And within three minutes I was called into the social *sala*. At one end of the long table was a birthday cake bearing two big numbers standing on end—a six and a three. Not so long ago the numbers were reversed.

Edina handed me a note, which guided me around the building to find presents, the first of which was a child's pink potty. I was reminded of the early months in Benjamin Constant, when we had no bathroom.

When I finished my treasure hunt, a half-dozen ladies glided out of the kitchen carrying trays laden with food. They were followed by girls with *guaraná*. After most of the plates were emptied, Edina pounded on wood to get everyone's attention. When the chatter tapered off, she said, "This occasion is not only to celebrate Pastor Paulo's 63rd birthday, but also to bid the Schleners farewell as they will soon depart for the United States."

Having spent more than half of our lives among these people, and realizing retirement was close at hand, it bothered Jessie and me to think that our sojourn in Brazil was coming to a close and we might never see these brothers and sisters again in this life.

But this departure was only for a furlough, our ninth and last one.

. . .

Age 64 is a little late to start preparing for retirement, but a $2,000 award from ABWE was a great help toward pouring the foundation for a small home on a lot that my nephew, Bryce, and Hope Union Church of Rosemead, California, helped Jessie and me purchase.

By the end of furlough, with the help of some generous Christian men, the exterior of our house was finished enough to meet the subdivision homeowner's agreement before Jessie and I returned to Tabatinga. Rena and her husband lived just across the lawn and could keep an eye on our place.

Within a few days after returning to Tabatinga, Jessie and I could see the time was ripening for our retirement. Church attendance was good, the pastor had the school functioning like a clock and had called a youth pastor, and Lois was well received by the congregation.

Pastor Reinaldo and I continued planning for church. This is what we hoped, prayed, and worked for, for 15 years. "Brother Reinaldo, you set the date," I said, giving him free rein to take the initiative.

The first thing on the agenda was a baptismal service at a creek out of town. The local police chief and his wife were among the sizable group to be baptized. He had never witnessed a baptismal ceremony and was a little hesitant on his way down to the water. When he stood beside the pastor, he said, "Just a minute, Pastor." And, as if he had never been submerged before, he splashed water on his arms and face. Then he said, "Okay."

Dr. Israel Lima, pastor of the largest Baptist church in Manaus, flew up with several officers from his church: a lawyer, a lumber mill owner, and a state collector. Missionaries from Benjamin Constant and the pastor of the Leticia church also attended the big event.

It was great to see a good representation from the 12 Indian congregations in the Port of Two Brothers area, including Martins, pastor of Faith Baptist Church. Seeing Martins, one of the guides who had taken me to an Indian *festa* 38 years earlier, and the two rows of Indians in the congregation, gave me goose bumps as I praised God for making His light shine in their hearts.

Jessie polished up the choir for the last time with two great numbers. Businessmen from local establishments were impressed with the four-part choir and with the out-of-town representatives witnessing the official organization of the church. One of the businessmen had furnished every grain of sand for the construction of the buildings—at no charge.

Never a gifted leader, it wasn't hard for me to cut loose from the leadership, even while still close at hand. But the people were a little slow to wholeheartedly accept a new young pastor.

"Pastor Paulo, what do you think we should do about what the Sunday school superintendent said about . . . ?"

"Excuse me, Brother Benedito. You and I have enjoyed great fellowship for a long time, and you have cooperated as a member of our congregation for years. All these matters concerning the church should be addressed by the other deacons and the new pastor. Maybe it will help if you call me Brother Paulo rather than Pastor Paulo."

"Ahhhh, Pastor Paulo, this won't be easy. We don't even know the new pastor very well," Benedito said. "You and Dona Jessie are like parents to us."

"We realize this, and it isn't easy for us either. But remember what I have told the congregation many times: 'Missionaries and pastors come and go, but you church members are the ones who keep the church going.'"

. . .

"Would you and Dona Jessie come to our house for dinner after church?" Edina asked. Invitations to private dinners usually celebrated holidays, weddings, or birthdays.

"Oh, Edina, what a blessing," Jessie said. "You know I don't have help in the kitchen on Sundays. Thank you."

Morning services finish by 10 a.m., so Jessie and I puttered around at home, killing time until noon, when we were to go to Edina's house. I dreaded the thought of missing my 30-minute nap.

At about 11 a.m., there was a knock at the iron gate. Fritz trotted over to check on the visitor; Maggie had gone where all good dogs go a week before, and Fritz still hung his head in mourning. Since he and Edina were old acquaintances, she had already entered the gate.

I said, "Edina, you aren't canceling the noon meal, are you? My mouth has been watering ever since the invitation."

"*Nada, nada,* Pastor Paulo," she said, smiling and waving her index finger in emphasis. "My mother complained about lack of space in our little house and we wondered if it would be all right to bring our food here to eat. We don't need to come inside. Your workshop is fine. Here we can get away from all the grandchildren and have a quiet, peaceful meal together on the Ping-Pong table."

"Whatever is easiest," I agreed. "We'll wait here."

Edina slid open the gate bolt, and a flood of people poured in—everybody carrying something to contribute to the noon meal. Most of these greatly loved visitors were Christians who, years ago, moved upriver from the Port of Two Brothers territory.

Two whole *tambaqui* fish (25 pounds each) were furnished by the *Timoteo*'s new owner. A barbecue pit made from half of a steel drum was carried by Aldo's two grown sons. Several neatly tied bundles of firewood were tossed to the dirt floor near the barbecue, and smoke was soon rising. A full stalk of ripe cooking bananas was roasted with the fish.

These invaders snatched my hatchet and machete from their perches on the wall, and in less than 60 seconds they lopped over one of our thick bamboo trees and whittled it into skewers. Four sawhorses became two spacious tables, on top of which was placed the largest potato salad we had ever seen; it filled a basin three feet in diameter.

Some of these folks—former pupils in our first primary school—were now grandparents. The giant potato salad was furnished by the granddaughter of one of the original trading post owners from downriver. Her uncle, who once hated the very tracks we made in the clay, sent a half-dozen chickens for barbecuing.

Then came the frosting on the cake. Virgulino [Moon], armed with a staff to make up for his crippled leg from the snakebite 20 years ago, wheezed out a happy greeting.

Jessie and I drifted from one person or group to another, reliving the past until a word from one of the red-faced, perspiring cooks announced that dinner was ready.

Good old white-haired Americo, Edina's father, gave thanks for the food. He reminded the Lord of many things that had taken place over the years. He became so emotional that tears made their way down his wrinkled cheeks and he was forced to pause.

During his prayer I remembered what a good neighbor he and his wife were for many years. His wife, Naynay, used to send us fresh fish, cleaned and ready to cook, and a little bag of freshly roasted *farinha*.

Americo held forth so long that some of the elderly had to sit down. Finally, Edina whispered to Americo, "Dad, the food is getting cold," whereupon he promptly finished.

I noted the way folks enjoyed their food. Those eating with their fingers consumed the most. The rest of us ate with spoons off tin plates, setting up a vigorous clatter. A few nibbled daintily, as though they had eaten before they came, and were there merely to help celebrate.

As departure day approached, more celebrations took place. Several business people surprised Jessie and me with their presence at a "This Is Your Life" program Edina organized. It was no surprise because she had been picking our brains for weeks. Four young ladies recited poems that spoke of the sadness of separations of loved ones, and the preciousness of good memories.

Al and Kim Yoder, ABWE missionaries who had recently transferred to Benjamin Constant from another area of Brazil, came to Tabatinga to help celebrate.

Kim imitated Jessie teaching a visual-aid lesson, then passed out candy to the kids. Al put on some unforgettable mimicry of my person. I didn't realize I scratched so much. With a hammer and saw he made like he was doing some building. Then he grabbed a stove-top popcorn popper and turned the crank, uttering "Mmmm, ahhhh," all the while continuing to scratch.

Early the next morning, during devotions, it finally sank in that we were leaving Brazil for good, not just a year of furlough or a couple weeks' vacation. We'd have to call it quits, and return to our homeland. The joy of ministering to and with Brazilians—laughing, crying, playing—had come to a close. When new little ones came into the world, we wouldn't be there the first time they were brought to church. No more comforting the sick and elderly. From now on, memories and photos would have to suffice.

It wasn't with hilarity or merriment that we prepared to leave, packing and building crates to ship things we considered keepsakes. Some of the folks didn't really believe we would leave. "But Dona Jessie, do you really mean that you won't be coming back?"

"That's right, Helena. It has always been our goal to work ourselves out of a job and put Brazilians in charge of church activities."

"But you are more Brazilian than some of us. You were here

10 years before I was born," a few reminded us, not really understanding.

"Most of us can't remember when you weren't here. You have always been here. We don't think you should leave," was the attitude of most of our friends. But we realized that their adjustment to our absence with the coming of other leaders would be quicker than ours back to the United States.

Several mornings later, Martins stopped by, as he often did when visiting relatives in Tabatinga.

"Pastor Paulo, I'm sorry but I don't have time to come in for a visit. I'd miss the ferry to Benjamin Constant, where I'll catch a ride back home."

"No problem. Give our regards to the family and have a peaceful trip," I answered.

"I also want to remind you about the anniversary celebration of our church in Nova Vila in a few weeks," he called, heading toward the ferry.

I was without transportation, having sold both the *Timoteo* and the outboard runabout. The mission plane wasn't making flights, and we were all pressed for time.

I told Pastor Reinaldo, "If you can arrange a boat for a one-day roundtrip to Faith Baptist Church in Nova Vila, I'll pay the bill." My last four words were the catalyst to motivate the good pastor, and he was off like a shot. I hollered, "Make sure the driver isn't a cocaine peddler, or we might get some free nights in the hoosegow," which triggered one of the pastor's high-pitched, squeaky laughs.

. . .

We needed our flashlights when we stepped into the dilapidated 14-foot boat, equipped with a 40-hp outboard engine.

The owner of the boat was both pilot and navigator. He untied the bowline, hopped into the wobbly rig, squeegeed the

rainwater from the two seats with the palm of a hand, and tossed
a sopping-wet life jacket to each of us.

We could see where wooden reinforcements had been
screwed to the top edges of the hull but now were completely
gone.

"*Cuidado!*" [Be careful!] the boat owner instructed. "I'm
going to start this beast." Those were the only words he uttered
during the whole trip. We all cringed to avoid the knotted tip of
his starting cord that snapped loudly over our heads. The pilot,
standing upright, slammed the engine into gear with a clunk and
immediately twisted the accelerator to full speed. Either he knew
the engine would die at slow speed or he thought he owned the
whole river. He laid the flimsy hull nearly on its side to avoid
smashing into another early riser, and flew into the darkness of
the vast river.

Pastor Reinaldo, song leader Evaldo, and I were extremely
grateful when the gray of daybreak finally revealed floating logs,
plants, and canoes, heavy with produce on their way to market.
Within four hours we pulled into the old Port of Two Brothers.

Since we couldn't promise we'd be able to attend the special
occasion, our arrival was a complete surprise. The little church
couldn't seat one-fourth of the delegates from other churches,
who crowded around to greet us. Pastor Martins thanked us for
coming. The congregation stood while we shook hands with as
many as we could reach. This reception greatly impressed Pastor
Reinaldo and Evaldo.

Of course, my feelings and thoughts were vastly different
from those of my two companions; I remembered numerous
experiences with these people.

By the time Pastor Martins presented me as speaker for the
occasion, I was so emotionally affected that I had turned to stone.
It took a full minute, standing at the pulpit, before I could speak.
I stammered away at first. It was too quiet. I hoped a bench
would topple and spill a row of worshipers, or a couple of babies

would screech—anything to break the silence. But the Lord gave me a few minutes of self-control and I was able to speak on the love and faithfulness that should be demonstrated in the life of each believer.

João Macario, one of the masked dancers at the *festa* in 1952, was seriously ill, his hair now snow-white.

"Senhor Paulo, come here for a minute," he called to me.

Together we walked over to a house near the church where a middle-aged lady leaned against the wall. "Pastor Paulo, do you know this lady?" João asked. I studied her face. I had seen her before and had spoken to her along with the multitude of others. She looked familiar, but I couldn't guess why Macario singled her out.

Then came the jolt. "Pastor Paulo, her name is Rosinda. She was the maid of honor at the *festa* you and your brother attended many years ago with two visitors."

I was speechless. The Lord kept me from picking her up off the ground and hugging her; you don't do that kind of thing with Indians.

"She married Benicio Fideles. Remember him?"

"Sure. I've known Benicio since he was a boy. He used to sell *paca* [large jungle rodent] to me." Benicio was plagued with the memory of accidentally killing his father by tripping on a loaded shotgun while climbing into a canoe. I knew Benicio served as a deacon in the church located at the very spot the *festa* took place. He attended the organization service in Tabatinga. But I had no idea he married the girl being honored at that Indian *festa* so long ago.

"*Ola*, Pastor Paulo," Benicio blurted out. "We have nine children and a batch of grandchildren. The biggest ones are all Christians. Our oldest son is treasurer of Faith Church."

They wouldn't have appreciated a loud whoop-dee-doo demonstration of emotional shock. Neither Rosinda nor her husband could possibly realize what this meant to me. All I could say was, "It's a great blessing to meet this lady, and to know that she and her family are brothers and sisters in Christ, and that you are all following the Lord. Praise God for all this!"

Our Colombian boatman patted his bulging stomach as he waited for us at the river's edge. When he backed away from shore and turned the bow upstream, we waved good-bye to the crowd high up on the riverbank. I was sure I would never attend another church anniversary at Nova Vila.

Thirty-five minutes under way, a fierce storm hit. "Head over to the other side before it gets so rough we can't cross," I roared to the boatman.

The windward side is the smoothest, but Sinbad the Sailor had his face set like a flint, and didn't even acknowledge my authoritative command. Threatening clouds brought early darkness. So we took the beating of our lives in the flimsy, open boat. We didn't care about the driving rain and pounding waves, if we could only make it home. There was nothing but thick jungle on both riverbanks. We missed all the giant-size debris and submerged snags while being tossed, tipped, and pounded in the darkness until eight that night for two reasons: Sinbad knew the river better than we thought he did and God's hand of protection was upon us.

Looking back on all the special occasions we experienced during our sojourn in the Amazonas, it is impossible to say which was the greatest blessing to me personally. But the few hours we mingled with Christians from all the area churches, and seeing the results of God's Word in their midst certainly makes a bid for that honor.

The truth that always hit Jessie and me deep in our hearts as we plugged away in the work was that we played such a small part. Hundreds of Christians held us up in prayer every day. Missions-minded local churches and individuals kept us fed, clothed, and equipped. Ours was the privilege of seeing God work, firsthand, in spite of our serious lack of ability.

• • •

A driveway sale helped me get rid of most of my tools, and I was fortunate to sell the rattletrap pickup. A hole in the floorboard on the driver's side was big enough to shove my foot through in case the brakes failed. Lois Wantoch relieved us of most of our furniture, and we were down to suitcases, resigned to the fact that we wouldn't return to this great country or these great people.

I walked up to old Fritz and scratched him under his powerful neck. "Fritz, old man, you can't come with us. What do you want us to do with you?" He had seen us come and go dozens of times and he seemed to know we were leaving. He sulked during the days we were getting ready to travel, as he did now.

A fine young couple in the wholesale/retail business in town, animal lovers with a Doberman of their own, were glad to give Fritz a home. When the moment came, Jessie stayed in the bedroom. She remembered the pony, Cholo. She couldn't watch me as I slipped the chain over Fritz's head.

From our house to our friends' place of business was about a half mile. We had never taken this route through town on the leash before, so Fritz and I were a rare spectacle. Not many had seen a deep-chested, black-and-tan Doberman.

While he was checking out his new terrain, Fritz spotted a young female Dobie, red like Maggie, lying on the opposite side of the pool. He must have been reminded of Maggie, and headed straight for Miss Red. It was such a beeline that he didn't even think about circumventing the pool, which he had never seen before, and flew headlong into the water. Frankly, I needed a good laugh, as did Jessie when I related the story to her. While Fritz shook himself dry and the red lady was put in her kennel, I slipped away.

Then came Jessie's and my turn to step through the gate and shut it behind us. It was raining on the drive to Leticia's airport. We checked in and chose our seats, talking with the Avianca agent, whose mother we knew as a young lady working in the Flodens' home before her marriage. Other airport personnel bade us farewell and wished us luck, telling us to hurry back, but no church folks came to see us off.

The 727 swished in between squalls, scattering puddles with its big tires, and using up the last half-inch of the runway. People crowded the large windows to watch the big bird park. It would be nearly an hour before it left for Bogota. And the drizzle started again—dreary, gloomy.

Then Marcio and Rannie, Fritz's new masters, scurried in, stamping the rainwater and mud from their feet. They had their own transportation. These great friends helped to cheer us up. And then another downpour roared on the roof like the Lord was emptying all the rainwater barrels at once.

"Sure seems funny that not one of the church folks came to see us off," I told Jessie out of the corner of my mouth.

"Five miles from Tabatinga is quite a hike in rain like this. And how many of them own an umbrella or can afford the roundtrip taxi fare?" Jessie was right. Besides, who were we that we deserved special attention?

The rain was still pouring down when Tabatinga's new Coca-Cola truck pulled up to the doorway. It was overloaded with shivering people, all soaked to the skin. All the smiling men, women, and children were from our church and Tabatinga.

They streamed in like a river, and hugged us until we were as wet as they. Our crowd took up a whole section of the terminal. What amazed Jessie and me—and a good number of spectators—was that every person from the church wore a green t-shirt with enlarged pictures of Jessie and me, and the English words: "Paulo and Jessie—1951 to 1991—We thank you both."

After one of the songs, Aldo's youngest son, Delmacio, handed me the Amazonas state flag. While all was quiet, he said, "This is for you and Dona Jessie, so you will never forget us." The flag bore the signatures of all his brothers, sisters, aunts, and uncles.

Departing passengers lined up for baggage inspection by the Federal Police. A tall young female officer sifting through the bags of nervous passengers looked at Jessie and returned her smile. "You go right through, ma'am. We're not worried about folks like you. My mother was an evangelical, too," she confided.

. . .

Those years in Amazonas were extremely fulfilling and rewarding. Jessie and I thank God and our loving children who sacrificed so that we, and John and Fran, could stay on the job. The Association of Baptists for World Evangelism took care of us like little children, giving us a constant sense of security. And without the dedicated Christians who were our faithful partners in the King's business from the very beginning, we would never have made it to and from the Port of Two Brothers in Amazonas, Brazil.